IMAGE PHOTOGRAPH

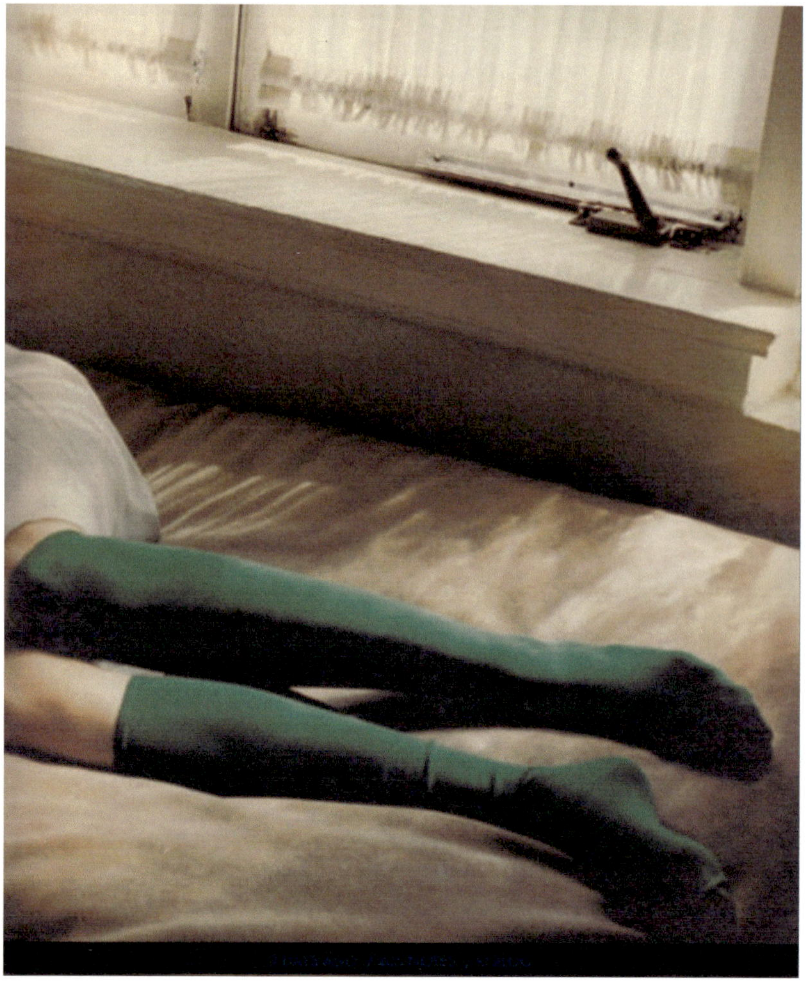

Recto Verso

Marc Lafia

IMAGE
PHOTOGRAPH

Foreword by
Daniel Coffeen

TABLE OF CONTENTS

FOREWORD
Daniel Coffeen

The opening line of Marc Lafia's book is fantastic: "Photography as an image." It's not a sentence. It doesn't have the familiar grammar of subject, verb, object. What I love about it is that it's not the didactic declaration that "Photography is an image." Something much stranger, and more beautiful, is happening here—something more generous.

This is how I imagine the scene just before the book opens. The photographer peers through his lens onto the world to find Lafia standing there—*looking back*! Only Lafia's not looking *over the head* of the camera, bypassing the technology to engage the eyes of the photographer. No, Lafia is looking *through* the looking glass itself. Like the photographer, Lafia sees with the camera, but in reverse. And through the looking glass we go.

When Lafia looks back through the looking glass he doesn't just swap places with the photographer, the seer becoming the seen (even if that's a dramatic scene unto itself!). He creates a living circuit as they both become seer and seen, photographer and image, the technology now within the frame, snapping away. It is a relentlessly creative circuit, forever forging more images.

The great French phenomenologist Maurice Merleau-Ponty argues that the very condition of seeing is being seen. We can only see the world—touch the world, know the world—because we are part of that world, continuous with its fabric. Merleau-Ponty calls this *flesh*. He claims flesh to be an element akin to earth, air, wind, and fire. All things are enmeshed in the flesh of the world. The very conditions of the seer seeing is that he is something that can be seen, that he is part of this flesh.

And that perception, including vision, happens within this flesh. It is not a magical event, a pristine event that bypasses the stuff of the world. Vision is an event that is of the world, that links things together in complex calculi. Vision is what Merleau-Ponty calls a *chiasmus*, an intertwining, of seer and seen, subject and object. Seeing happens within the world, as part of the world, *with* the world.

Isn't this the explicit condition of the digital network? We inscribe and are inscribed in the same breath, our seeing always, in turn, a seen.

It is not a wild hypothesis to claim that we enjoy a different relationship to the image today. The camera is no longer a specialized tool we use to record special moments. The camera is now always on, simultaneously reading, writing, archiving: the Web, the smart phone, Instagram, surveillance, telemedicine, MRIs, Skype, Chatroulette, ATM cameras, credit card imprints. If before the digital, the camera kept a distance between photographer and world, in the digital network, technology entwines us—and entwines with us. The relationship between body, self, technology, and world has shifted. *Il n'y a pas de hors-image*. There is no outside the image.

One way of reading Lafia's book is that he asks the obvious, pressing question: In this world of relentless imaging, what becomes of photography?

Now, Lafia does not give us a ready answer. He can't. To give a ready answer is to be outside the fray, outside the circuit of seeing, this entwining of bodies and things and perceptions. But Lafia's book is situated *within* this fecund, living circuit. And from within, seeks to map a new territory, to articulate the strange and beautiful new relationships between world, technology, image, and us.

Photography is no longer the capturing of a moment, the photographer secure behind his camera and the world framed just so. It has become a relentless event of seeing and being seen. Which is to say, the photograph does not present us solely with *what* it sees: *Look! An antelope! A poor rural American girl! Yosemite!* In this age of the always-on camera—through the looking glass—the photograph presents more than its subject: it presents the very act of seeing these things. The image is at once object and event.

Look at Instagram. We open the app and there, as an image, are the different filters that create the image that we have already taken. We don't just see the image; we see the tools of the image making along with the archiving and indexing of the image—the views, likes, shares, and comments that follow images around. These are not external to the image; they are constitutive of it. The seeing of the image has become part of the image, folded into the frame. (Movies, too, now come with a making of: to create the film is part of the film.)

This has always been the case. Every photograph has always given us the seeing of the photographer. We don't just see Yosemite on the postcard: we see Ansel Adams seeing Yosemite. We call this style.

But there's another seeing we see, as well: the seeing of the image-event. It's an anonymous, networked seeing, a piece of the world forged then and there, in that moment. The photographic image is not a *capturing* of a moment—as if it were removed from the world and silently saving this moment for posterity. No, a photograph has always been something *created* by the very act of imaging, something that wasn't there before. It's not a replica. It's a new thing, quite literally an object, something that inflects light, that takes up the world, that *is* part of the world.

There's a *New Yorker* cartoon that has a woman showing her husband her smart phone: "Look at this image of the thing we're looking at," she says. The implication is that this is absurd, that looking at the Golden Gate Bridge is more profound than looking at an image of the Golden Gate Bridge.

But that ancient, Platonic architecture no longer applies. The fact is that image of the Golden Gate Bridge on the smart phone may very well be more beautiful, more profound, than looking directly at the bridge. In any case, the issue of more or less profundity is irrelevant. What's important is that this image on the smart phone is something—*something* different, something new, something related to that bridge we're looking at, but nonetheless different.

The camera never captured what's there. The camera has always *created* the image—an image that includes what's there but is not exhausted by it. The photographic image is not simply a static image of what's in our minds. I want to say that the photographer is a cut-up artist who takes a mountain, light, sun and gives us this impossibly odd object: a Yosemite image.

To see—to exist—in the new age of the image is always to be participating within this event, always making images, always becoming an image, always seeing seeing, and, in turn, having one's own seeing seen.

Marc Lafia's book is situated within this relentless imaging. This is not a book *about* photography. This is a book *of* photography, *of* the image, *of* the imaging event. It is itself a series of trajectories within the always-on event of imaging that is the seeing-computational network.

As constitutive and constituent of this teemingness, Lafia remaps the space of photography by coming at image making first this way, then that. He doesn't just talk about images—not that there's anything wrong with that. But in this book, he images. And he writes. What we get are all these different permutations of imaging from within the always-on imaging network. The book is, in every sense, a network effect. And Lafia is an explorer of this strange new landscape.

In his brilliant book *The Practice of Everyday Life*, Michel de Certeau juxtaposes the map and the tour. With a map, you are outside the space looking down from an impossible vantage point. Maps are amazing at giving us the lay of the land. A tour, meanwhile, is a navigation of the territory from within the territory: Go straight for a bit, and when you see the big red house on your left, turn right.

Well, Lafia's book simultaneously maps and tours this new landscape of the imaging event. This is not a traditional photography book, precisely because it's redefining the very territory of photography. I think this is, in fact, the new mode of the photography book: a book that simultaneously creates and questions, proffers and performs.

Lafia takes up the prescribed space of the photography and, by touring the new conditions of imaging, remaps the very space of photography. This is not a condemnation of photography. On the contrary, it's an opening up, a yawning of possibilities. The photograph is no longer something that is only over there; it now abounds.

This book operates within the space of photography, within the space of the image event. It asks to be read differently than books about photography and differently than photography art books.

Lafia's images are not illustrations of his argument. And the text is not explanations of the images. Both text and images are images. Both text and images are arguments. They work in conjunction, mapping and touring, creating a performative cartography of image making today: Photography as an image.

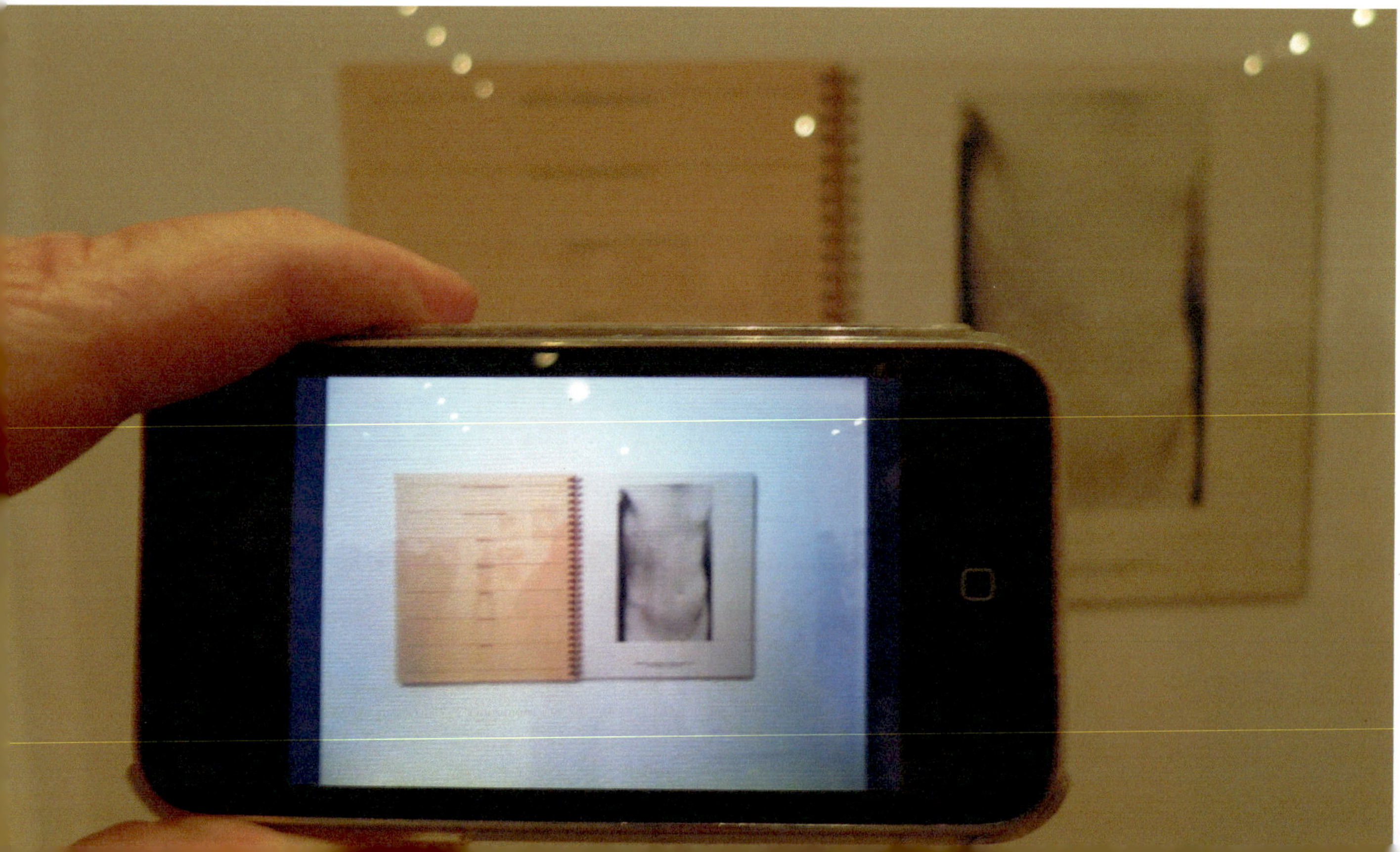

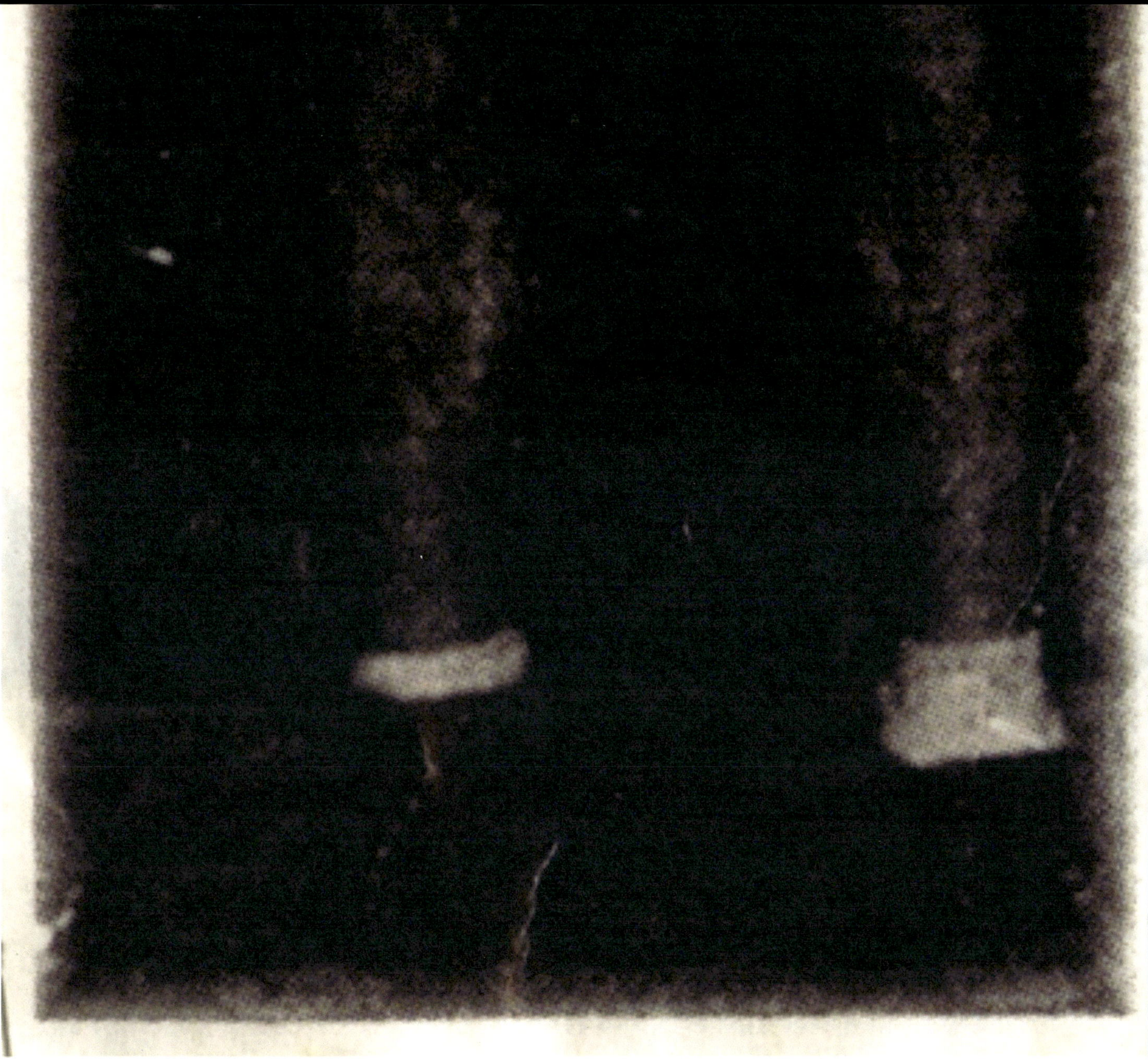

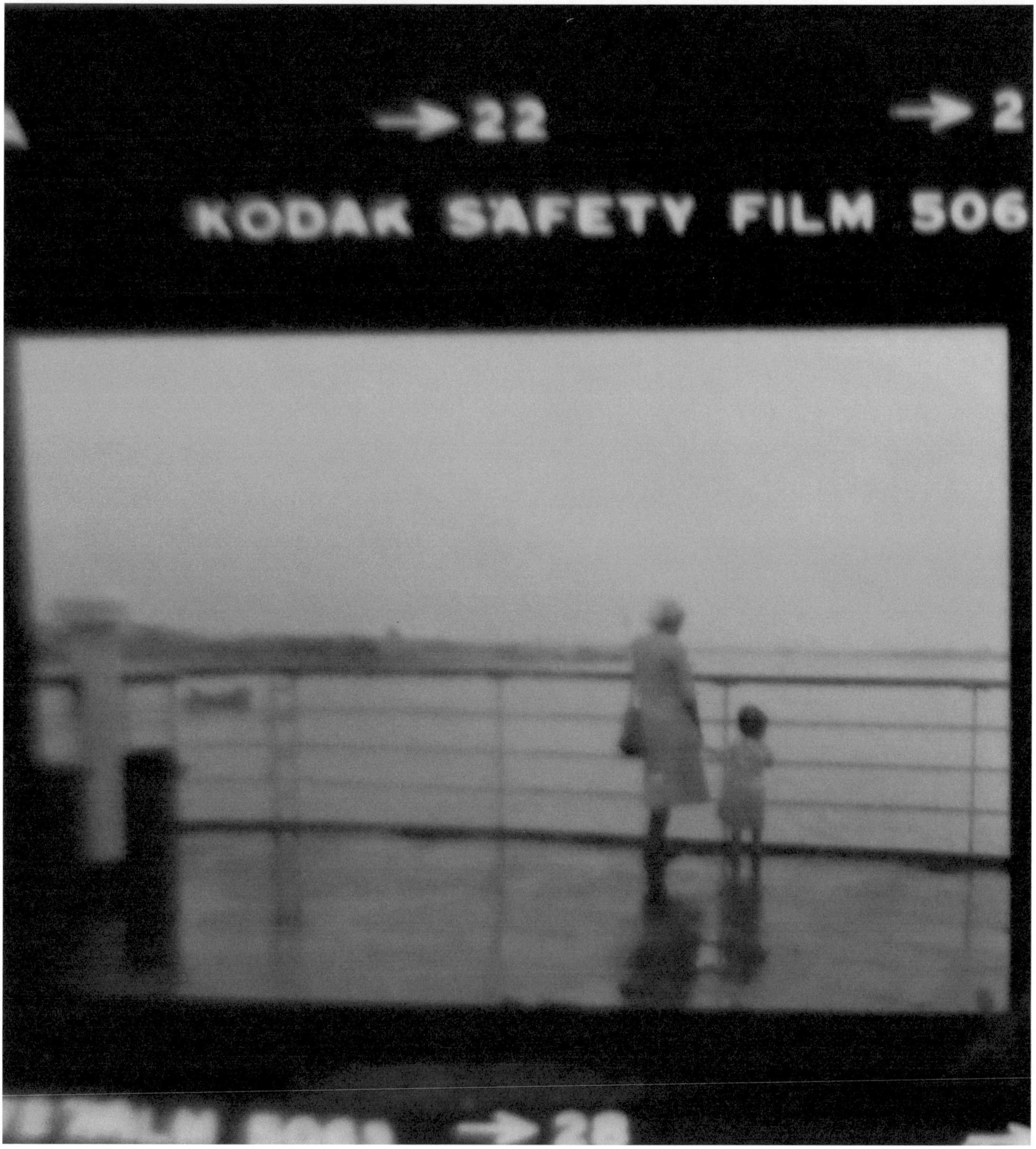
→22
KODAK SAFETY FILM 506

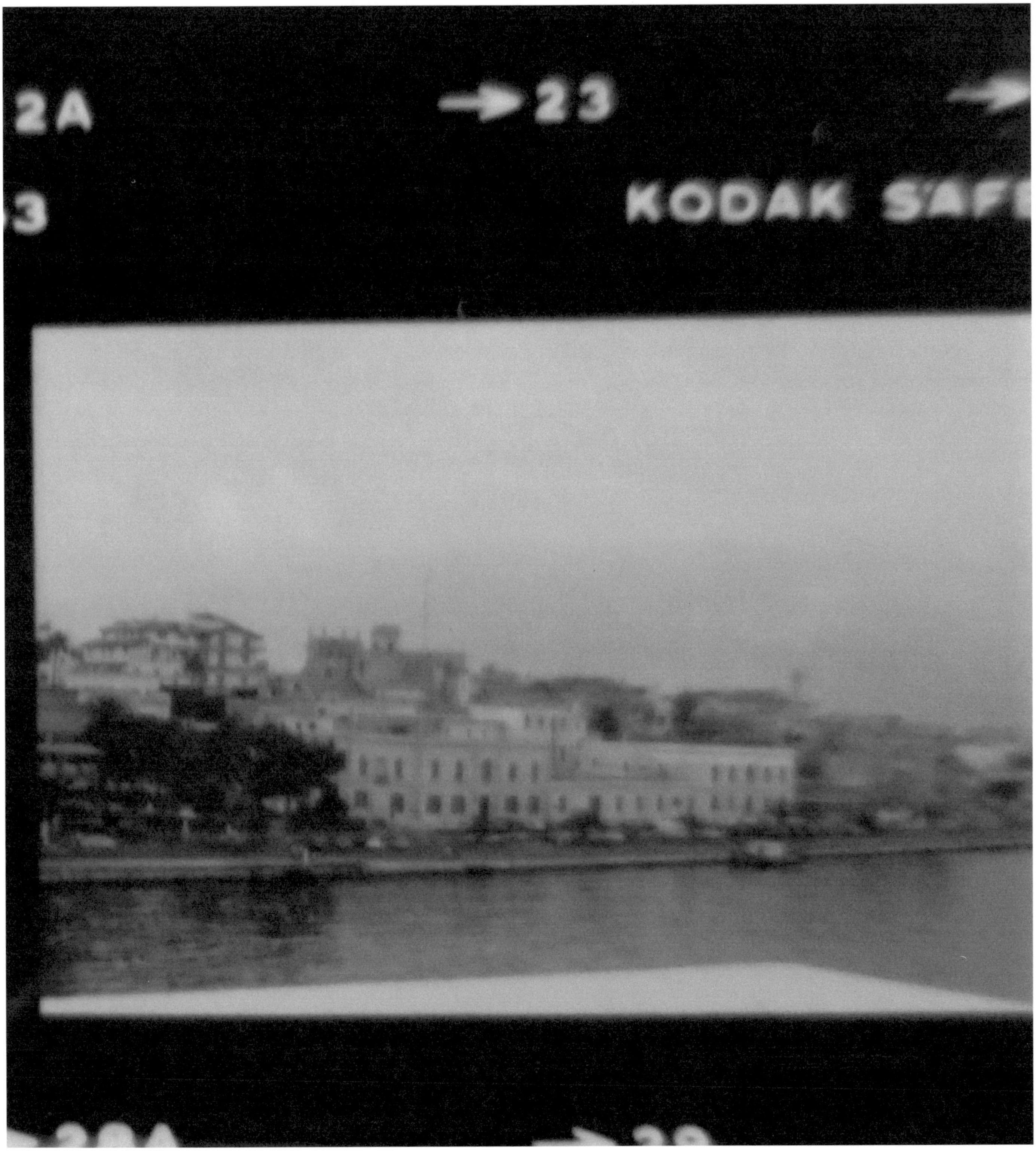

Kodak Safety Film 5063, Contact Sheet,
1977

IMAGE
PHOTOGRAPH

An Essay

Photography as an image, photography as the recording of an encounter, a recording of an apparatus — the aesthetic of the image is the image that reads and performs imaging.

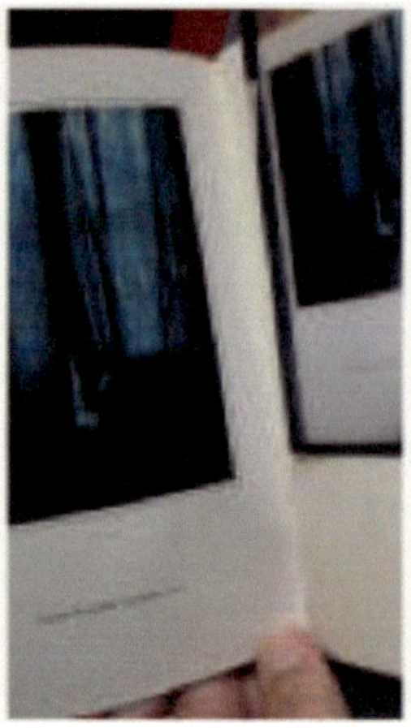

01
Camera Lucida, Daniel Boudinet
Polaroid, 1989

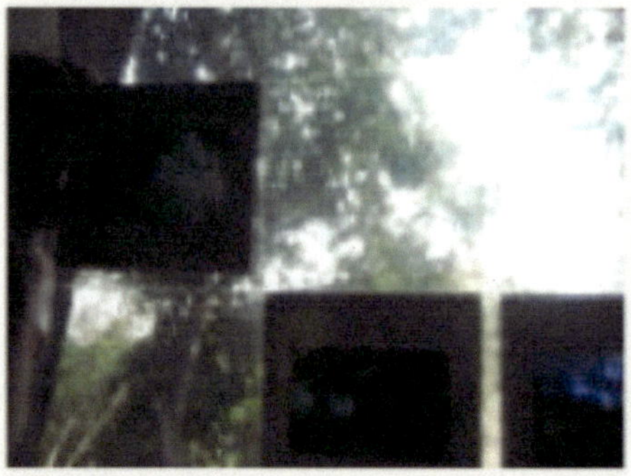

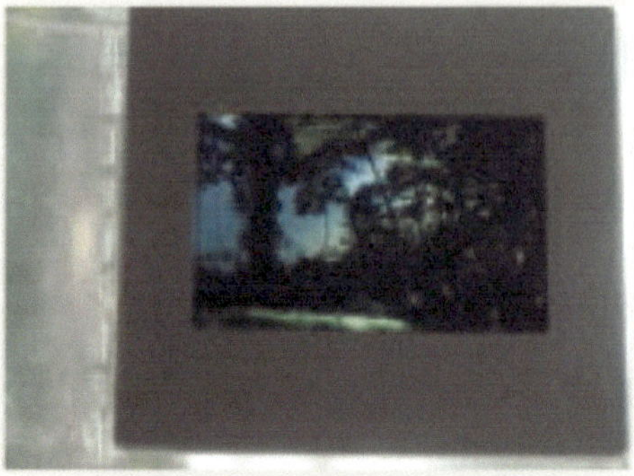

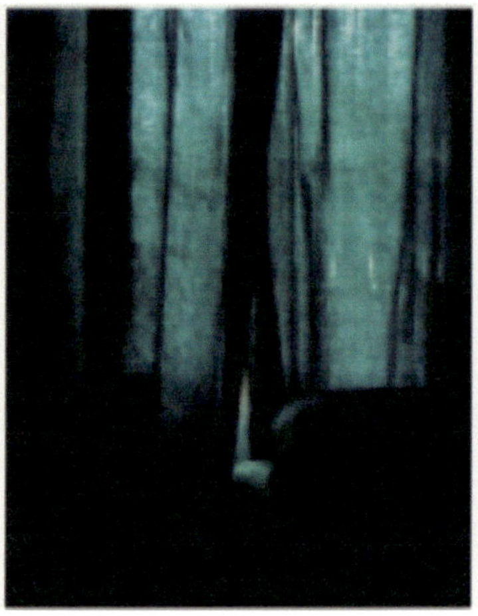

What is recorded is not simply, nor principally, that which is in front of the lens, in the picture, in the photograph—but the event of its recording. The photograph is a seeing, a kind of seeing, camera seeing. In seeing-reading photography, it is the event of the seeing that I see.

This is not solely with my photographs but with all photography.

When I was nineteen, I started taking pictures. I then went to Harvard for a summer and studied photography with Ben Lifson. Over the next ten years I photographed in over thirty-five countries and took some very good pictures. But what is a good picture? Is it photography?

Pondering this, I stopped taking pictures. After about ten years, I encountered the Daniel Boudinet Polaroid in *Camera Lucida* by Roland Barthes. Something about its monochromic quality; that it was a Polaroid (which meant instant, like the digital cameras of today); something about the light in the room, through the curtain, and the pillow in front—it was formal, too neat, so much an "artful" photograph that I could finally really see photography. The appearance of photography proper, that is, the fixing of an image to the substrate of glass or film (something lenses allowed painters to do long before), the pursuit of this transcription, what would be the eventual writing on paper of the image, would become the encoding of a file, and this would become any possible seeing of photography. The Polaroid was then a concept of seeing. Not alone to itself, not yet, anyway. In order to start again, I would have to do so in a way that directly interacted with photography as a seeing of photography. This would have to be an image of photography, and what it could be. To start, I would photograph photography.

01 This was the first photograph I photographed. It was as if I were seeing through the reading of the book, the photographs, and photography.

I can only really see photography when photographing.

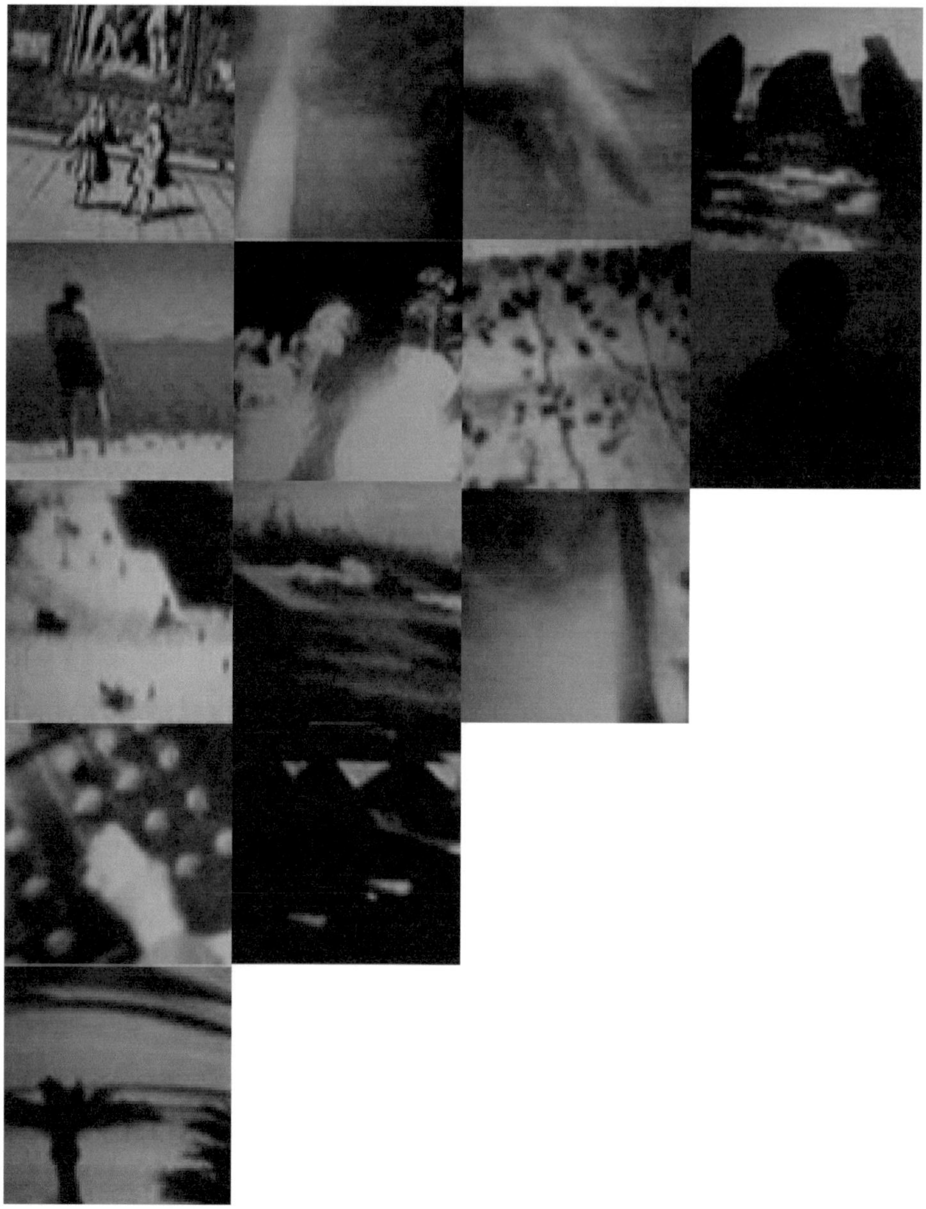

02
Memories of Photography, 1998

02 Photography is often spoken of as memory. Not photographs, not pictures, but the entirety of photography.

I found a wristwatch camera, made by Casio. With my timepiece and a lens, I would go down Telegraph Hill to Stout Architectural Books and open up books of photography and photograph them. I very much liked this small watch-camera, my first digital camera, for its low fidelity and for its timekeeping quality.

A watch and a camera, the camera watching time, the camera reading photography and time.

The quality of the images reminded me of early photography. It is as if the images are already fading, receding away like a distant memory.

In a similar way that video allowed cineast Jean-Luc Godard to look at and read cinema, digital photography became a way for me to examine photography. The digital both imitates photography, while never quite being photography, and carries something of the uncanniness of photography.

For me digital photography is a beginning; it is the image of photography's disappearance. It is the recording of recording. All photography made now is in a sense conceptual and about materialization, the materialization of something in the event of a kind of appearance.

With the digital watch-camera, time, memory, photography, all collapsed in this instrument. What is a camera but a watch seeing time, seeing seeing. With and through it, I could see the memory of photography.

Digital photography, with its filters and settings, confers back to the image a memory of photography. It is a nostalgia for a photography that never actually was. The digital makes the image appear photographic. It makes images "photographs."

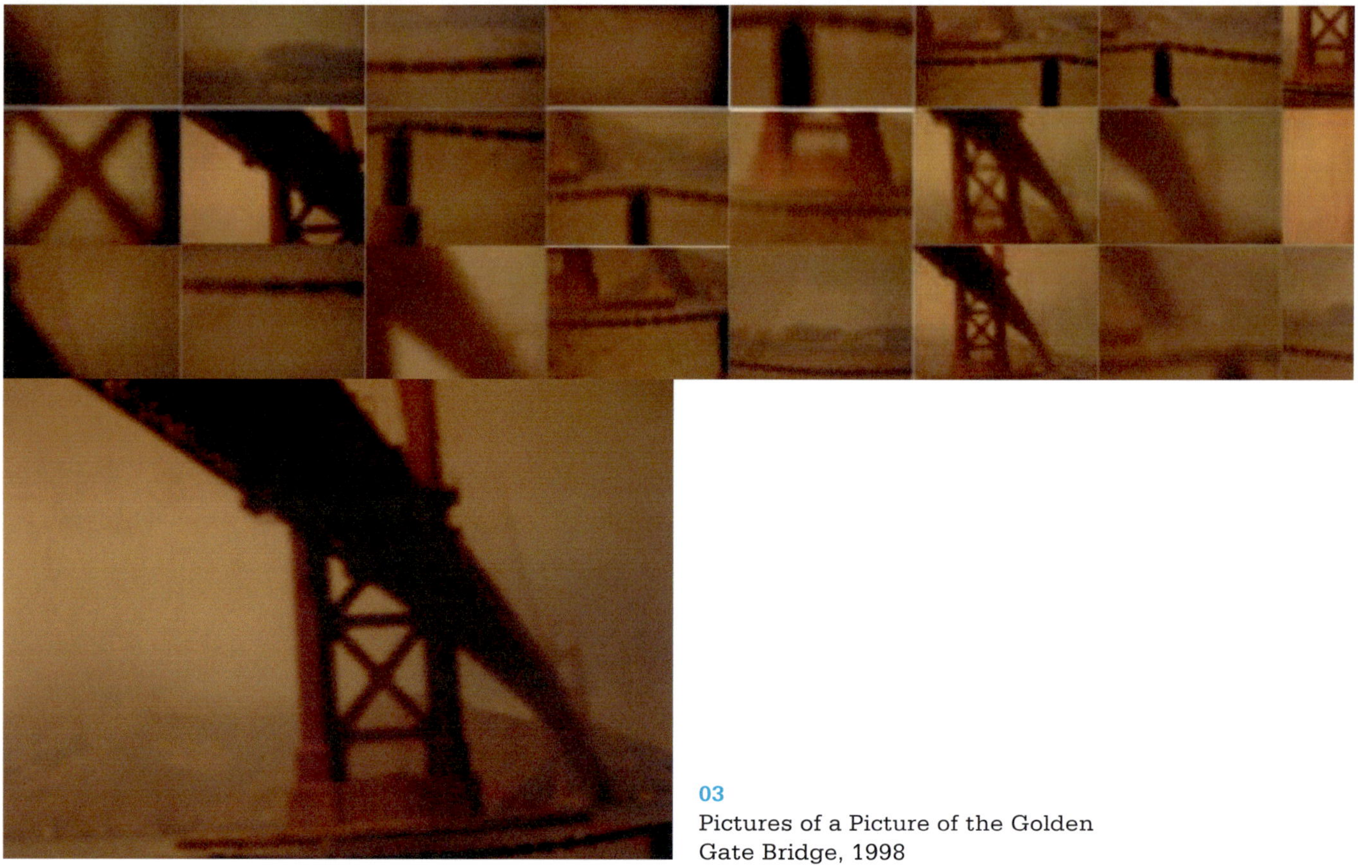

03
Pictures of a Picture of the Golden Gate Bridge, 1998

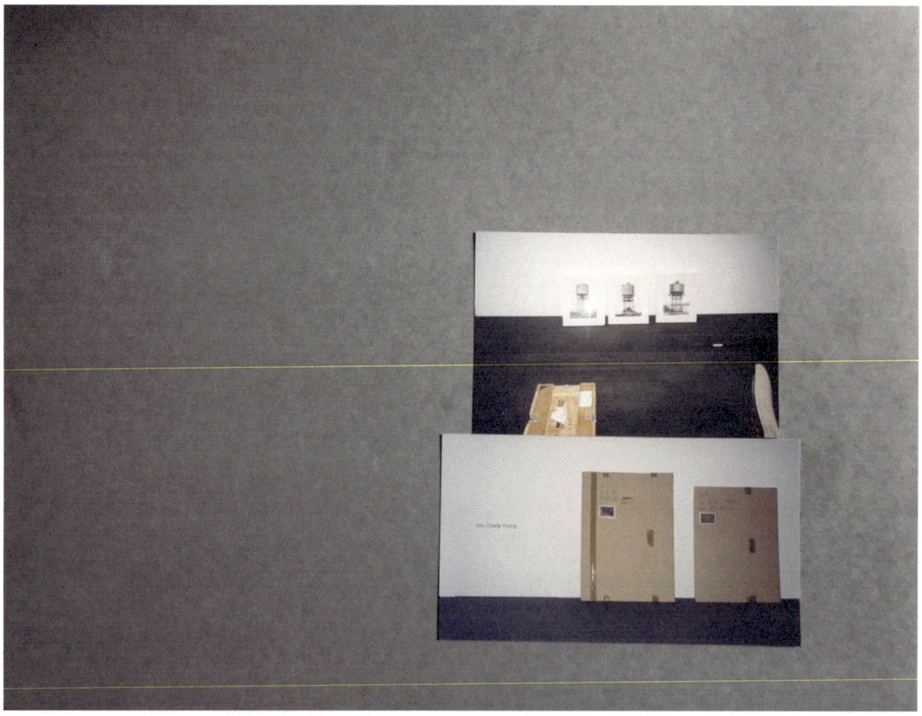

04
A Photograph of Two Photographs Including Three Water Tower Photographs by The Bechers on Top of a Photo Archive Box, 2002

03 From my place on Telegraph Hill in San Francisco I could see out to the bay and the Golden Gate Bridge. It continually took on new appearances, given the varying atmospheric conditions of fog, mist, cloud cover, evaporation, tides, sun, and moonlight. Though given all these conditions make for beautiful pictures, the bridge is almost impossible to photograph and in a sense to see.

Architectural photography often requires large-format cameras and patient study of conditions of light, of time of day and year. This is a kind of photography, a kind of work that I can appreciate but don't practice. I found one photograph of the bridge completely compelling, giving a true sense of its great structure, giving view to the two towers letting the spanning cables suspend and drape like a long elegant necklace, all of it glowing in its international orange vermilion. The photograph allowed itself to be seen seemingly from varied vantage points.

I set out to photograph this photograph as a site in of itself. As I photographed the image I would move the camera while the shutter was open, and the image would blur and image the solidity of this monumental architecture as elastic and fluid.

Digital photography frequently suggests an alteration of the image once it is photographed. I was interested in the event of recording. I didn't want to privilege the single image so set out to record the instruments seeing, to see what kinds of images this produced.

I became interested in the responsiveness of the digital instrument—its capacity to exhaustively catalog or record, no longer constrained by the roll of film and its set number of exposures. And with this the artifacts of the digital: distortion, blur, noise, grain, color shifts, seeing the very electronics of the recording instrument immediately, all of this amplifying sight, giving image to the project of the photographic.

04 Here two photographs rest on top of a photo archive box. Seen in the photograph at the top are three photographs from the Bechers, a series that documents in black and white water towers as types. In the foreground we see a wood packing crate from which the three photographs were removed. Below this photograph, another, where we see two brown paper packages with labeling and tape. Both the water towers and the packing materials are containers, highly utilitarian, and variable as types. If photography was once described as a mirror or window, perhaps today it is a black box.

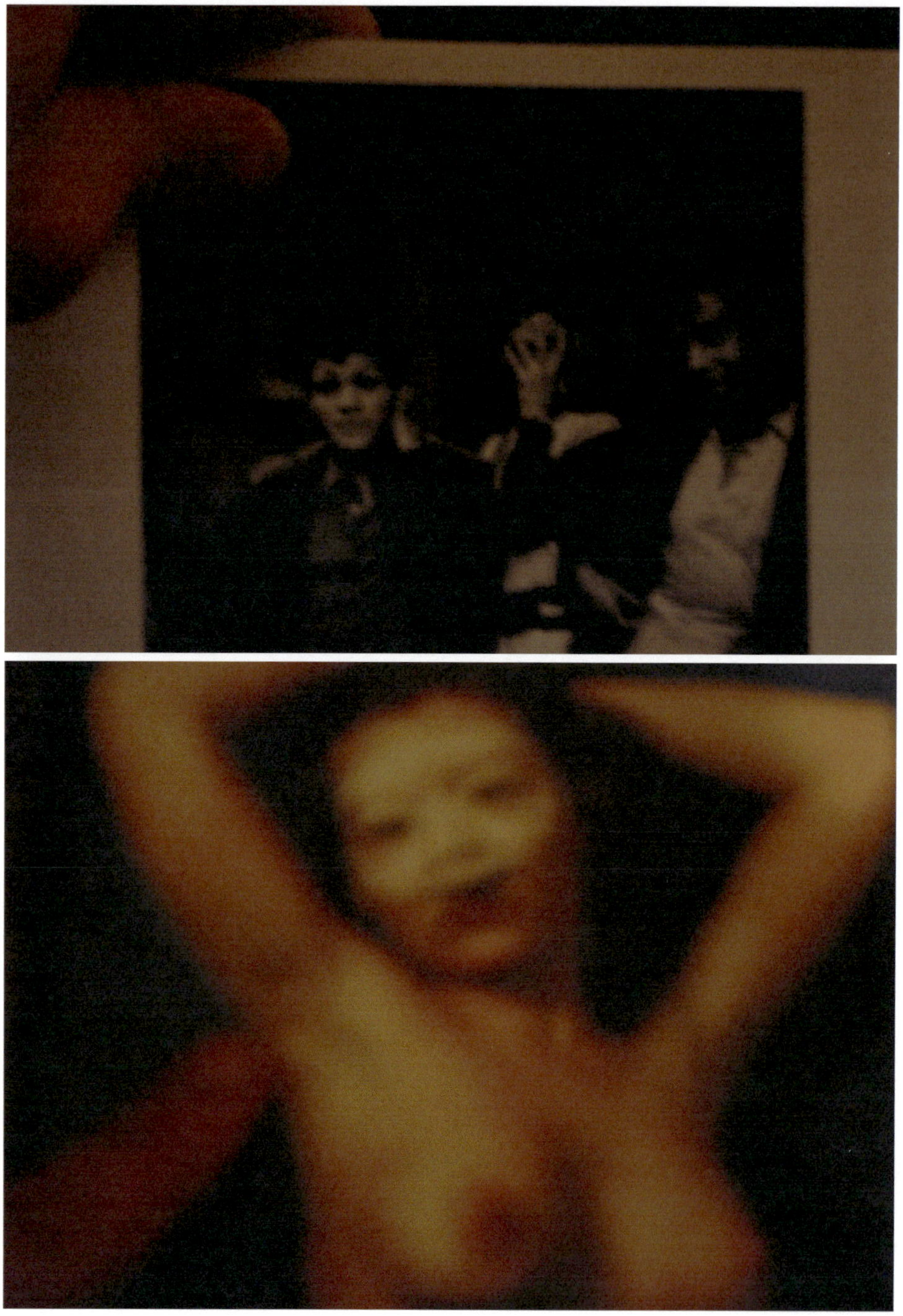

05
Touching Robert Frank, Touching
Paul Outerbridge Photograph, 1998

05 Left, two pictures held by my hand.

The hand, or more precisely a thumb and index finger, point to or hold in place an image, giving us a sense of the scale of these images and a sense that the image is in hand. The image in hand is an object, a material fact, not a file on a screen, but something held.

What is it to have the photograph in hand? We do this when we read the newspaper. We touch the image. Yet the image, a physical reality as a print or reproduction, represents something at a remove, that was seen, representing all that can be seen and not touched. The image is the proof, the fact of a world. But what if images are not facts, not proofs?

But rather something unto themselves?

If photography from early on took two paths, one of objectivity and the other of experimentation, was one a fact and the other a fiction?

Aperture put out a wonderful series of monographs on photographers. I loved collecting these books. They were paperback, maybe four by six inches, affordable collector's editions of great photographers. Each photographer had a distinct style and very often a select subject matter, the style and the subject matter inseparable. The two images here are from Robert Frank and Paul Outerbridge. Frank brought an extraordinary seeing to America, brought us close to something forbidden or hidden that was right there in the open. All the tensions of race, class, social mobility are seething at the surface, the open road and the closed society of America shot from the hip. The objective and the experimental come together with an impending sense of violence ready to break open—which it did in the civil rights movements of the sixties in America. Frank was Swiss, and he showed us what was out there, in the same way that David Lynch did in *Blue Velvet*, a menacing violence, but in Lynch's case not on the surface in black and white like Frank, but beneath the saturated Kodachrome and through the moving image. I am certain Lynch was well aware

06

Touching the Sleep of Reason, 1998

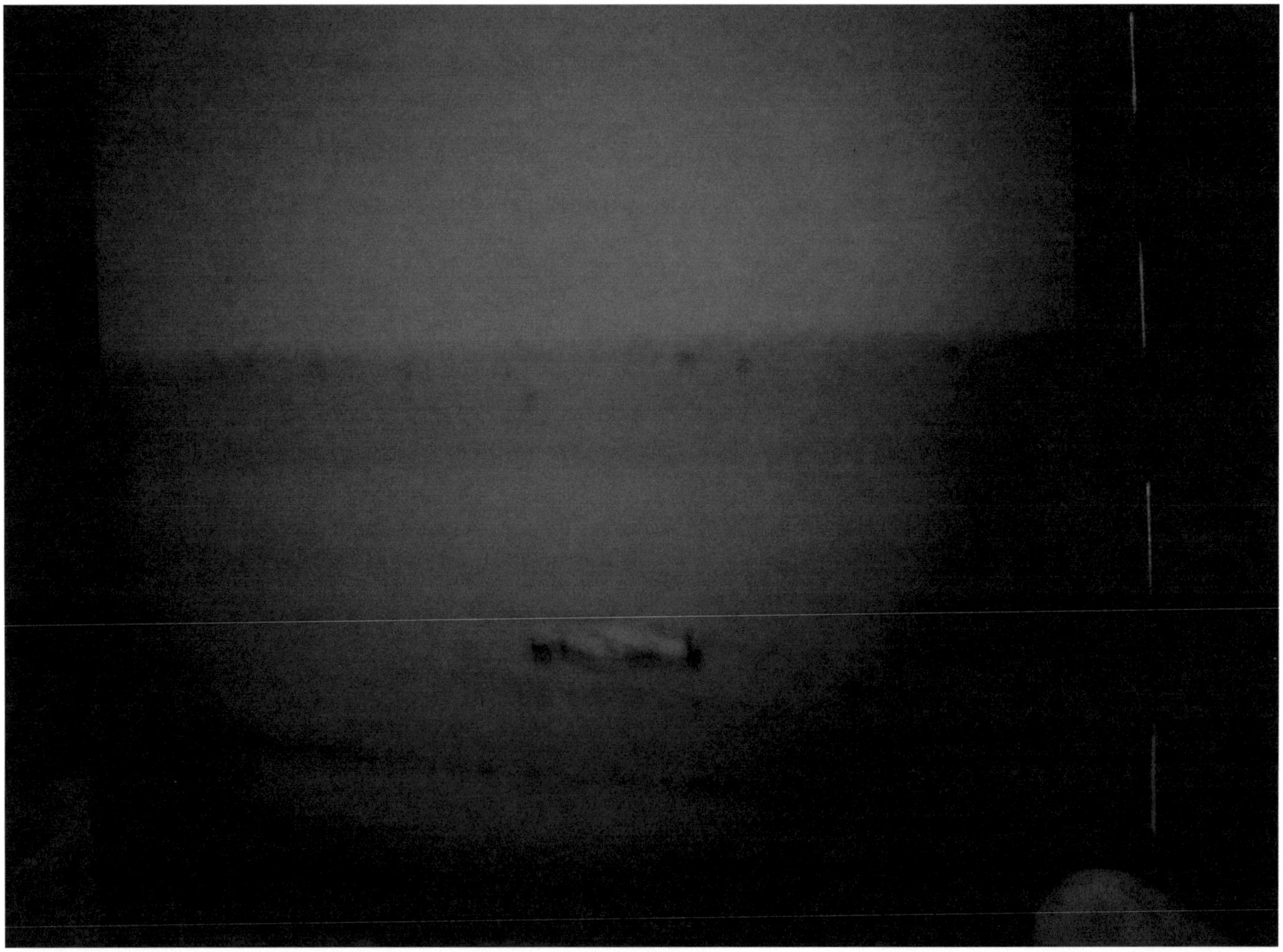

of Outerbridge and the nudes and fetish photographs he shot, which could not be shown in his lifetime.

I can't imagine finding that same feel of the Robert Frank pictures in the color stock used by Stephen Shore. You might say Lynch, like Douglas Sirk, brings us the black-and-white world in color. The movement from black-and-white film to color is not unlike when cinema began to use sound. It goes from seeing to telling.

When we say that something performs, we say that it does not point to an elsewhere, but inherent to itself, within itself, it is alive on terms of its own, it does not point to a fact. It is a fact, an event itself.

Robert Frank does not take pictures of the world out there. His pictures are a world. His is not the decisive moment of Cartier-Bresson, but in a sense the moment in which a relation is seen, an event of seeing not within the frame, not framing the shot, but a seeing of the world, in this case America. Here America does not pose for the camera as in the Civil War photographs of Mathew Brady but is revealed and unveiled through the very unique seeing of the 35-mm Leica, a very fast and sharp lens of a very mobile camera. Here the artist and the apparatus discover each other and become seamlessly one, instinctive and intimate to each other. It is a beautiful love affair, where each player is at its limit.

In 1966 the Beatles discovered that the recording studio was an instrument. Robert Frank, Diane Arbus, Gary Winogrand take us to the limit of that moment, when the camera, its lens, and film stock was a one-to-one recording. That is the moment before the camera became conceptual, became down-the-line software and the 35 Leica and high-speed black-and-white film, another filter in a programmable apparatus or downloadable app. Until then we believed in pictures, we believed in photographs, yet we didn't quite see our instruments.

06 Here I touch the photograph with my hands. I have to touch it to believe it is real. What is real to me is my hand in the picture of the photograph I touch.

07
Staged Photograph of Constructed
Photograph of Thomas Demand, 2008

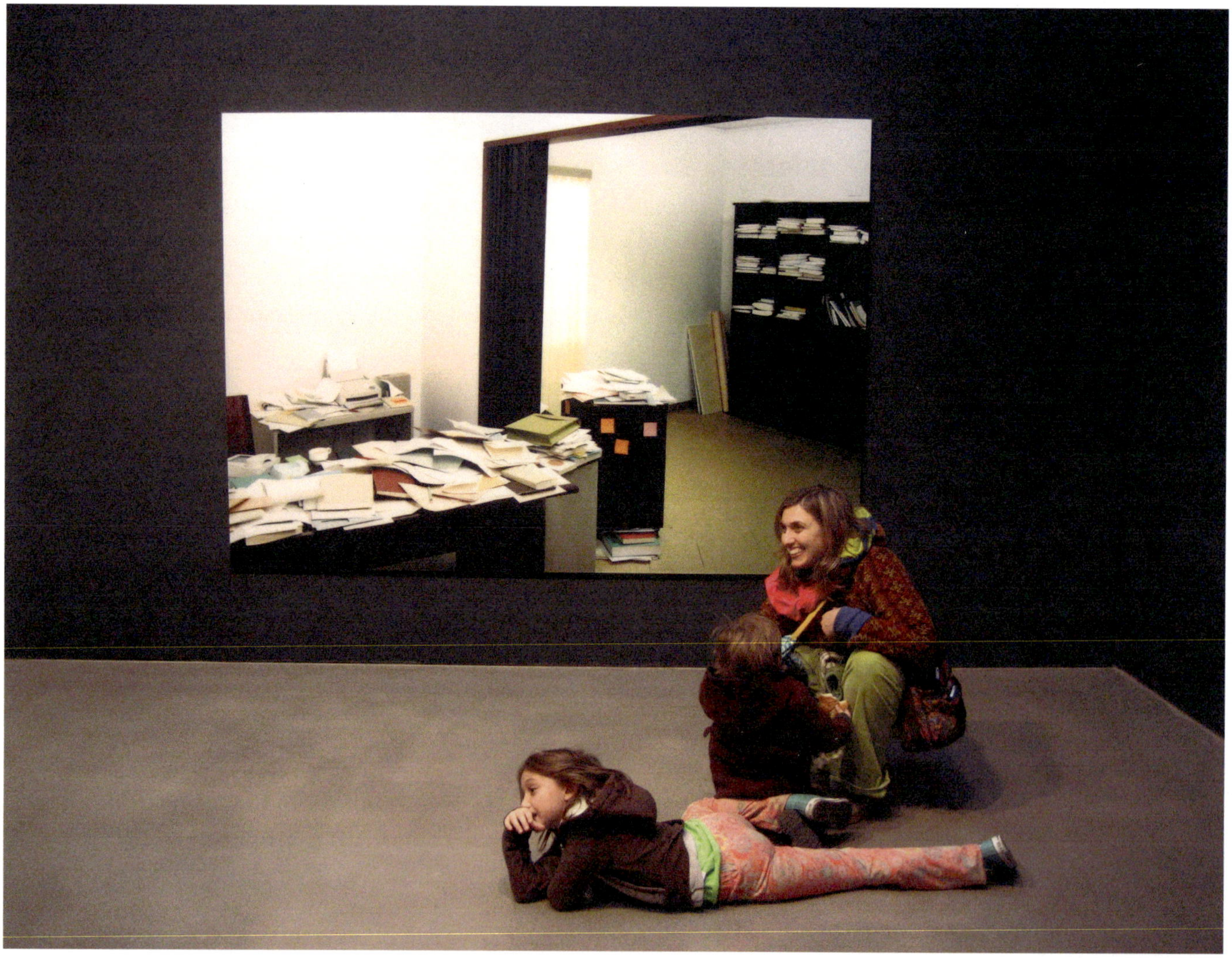

What is it to take a picture? To find an image? To see the world? To see your world? To look upon it and read it, and to see it in that particularity we call imaging or photography. For sight, seeing is the faculty; and for recording, simply reading light. Seeing is always particular, both for human and mechanical vision. We bring our memories, our cultural conditioning, as well, of course, as our physiology to seeing. Machine or digital seeing brings its instrumentation.

For Robert Frank and Diane Arbus, pictures are in the world. The photographer enters the world through the image—that is, she or he sees in the world an image, but much more than an image, he or she sees the relations between men, between things, and we see this relation and them seeing it in their images, in their relation to photography.

07 Jeff Wall, Andreas Gursky, Thomas Demand construct an image, sculpting, staging, and inventing it. Distinct from seeing the image out there, they construct an image.

They do not take pictures, they stage them. Photography is not a relation to their world but an interior vision, an imaging, a putting forward not of something already to be seen but rather not seen until it is constructed. Yet isn't it fair to say that all images are constructions of a particular seeing and a particular instrumentation?

Their work and all photography today is informed by conceptual art. I begin now to photograph and document actions. As in early conceptual photography, it is actions and their recording that interest me. Not the image, but the event of the image encounter.

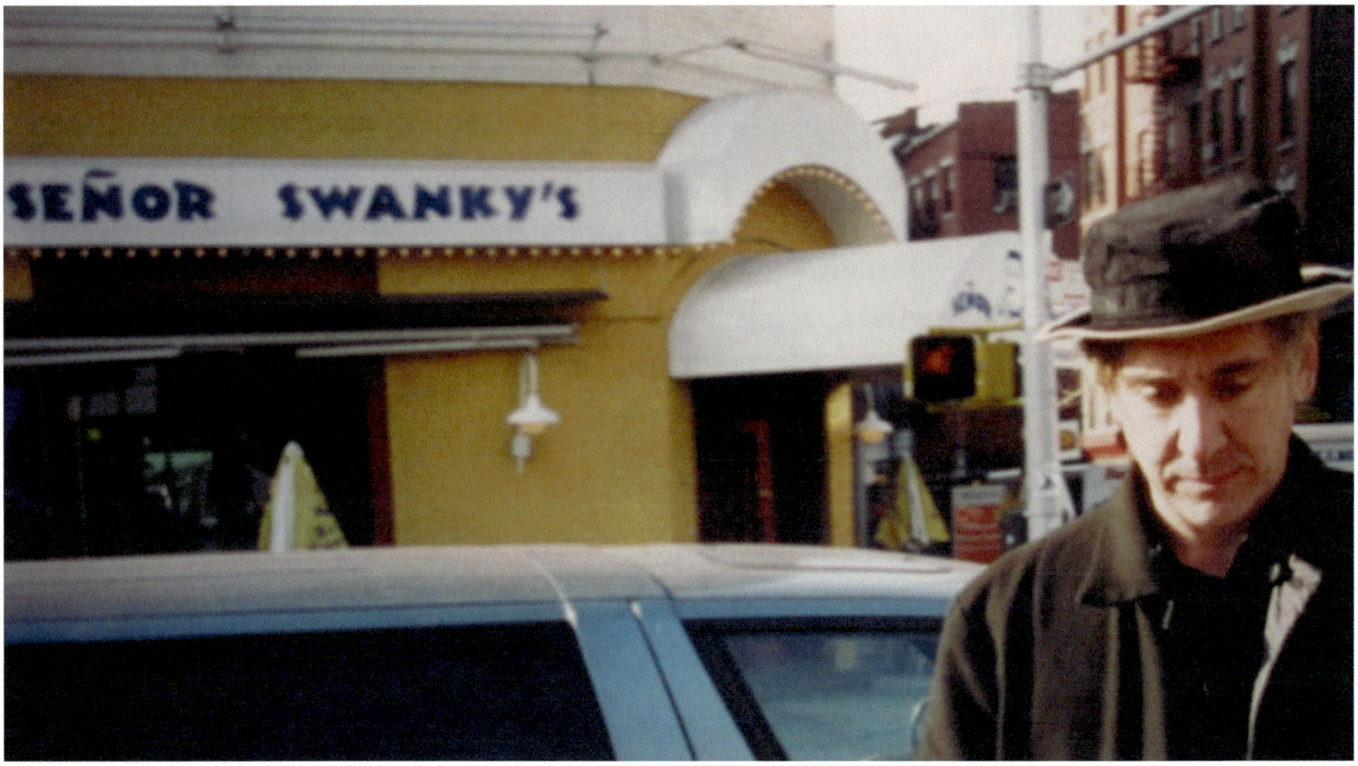

08
One of hundreds of photographs of me in front of Senor Swañky's, Mexican Café and Celebrity Hangout, NYC, 1999

09
American Flags, 1999

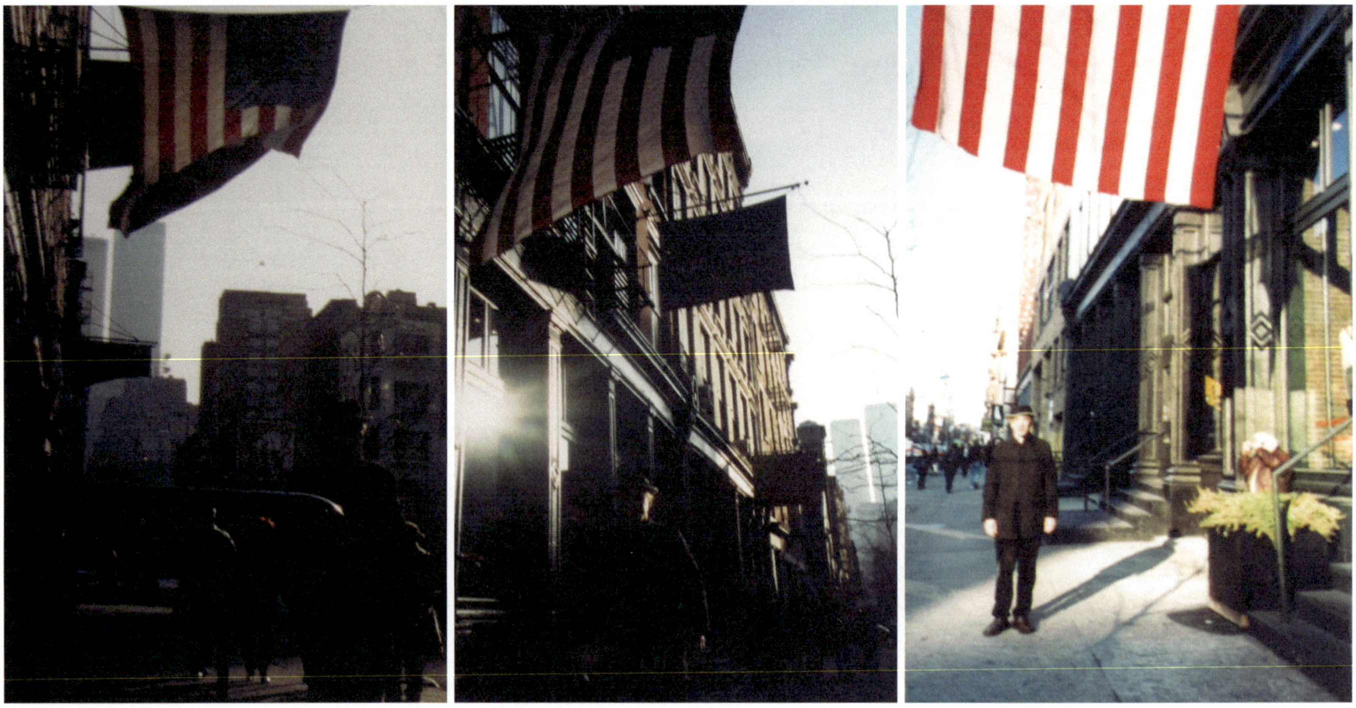

In these works I do not stage nor look for one single perfect moment, but one singular encounter. The photograph is a document of that instruction, that encounter which puts forward the snapshot as a hazard, as obligatory, as a memory.

Take my picture in front of this monument.

08 / 09 In one staged encounter there is a draping American flag, me thinking of Frank and Jasper Johns, and the hard winter light of New York. In another is Señor Swanky's, Mexican Café and Celebrity Hangout. It seems right in both to instruct others to photograph me. I am not really photographing me per se, but that encounter on the street in making the photographic moment, the photographic event—the people I might have in the past wanted to photograph, I now stop and ask to photograph me.

I have moved from taking photographs of photographs to having others take pictures of me.

It is often the interchange with others while producing work that is most interesting. It's a moment where roles are suspended, a certain authority is yielded, and a kind of conspiracy takes place in the production of an event.

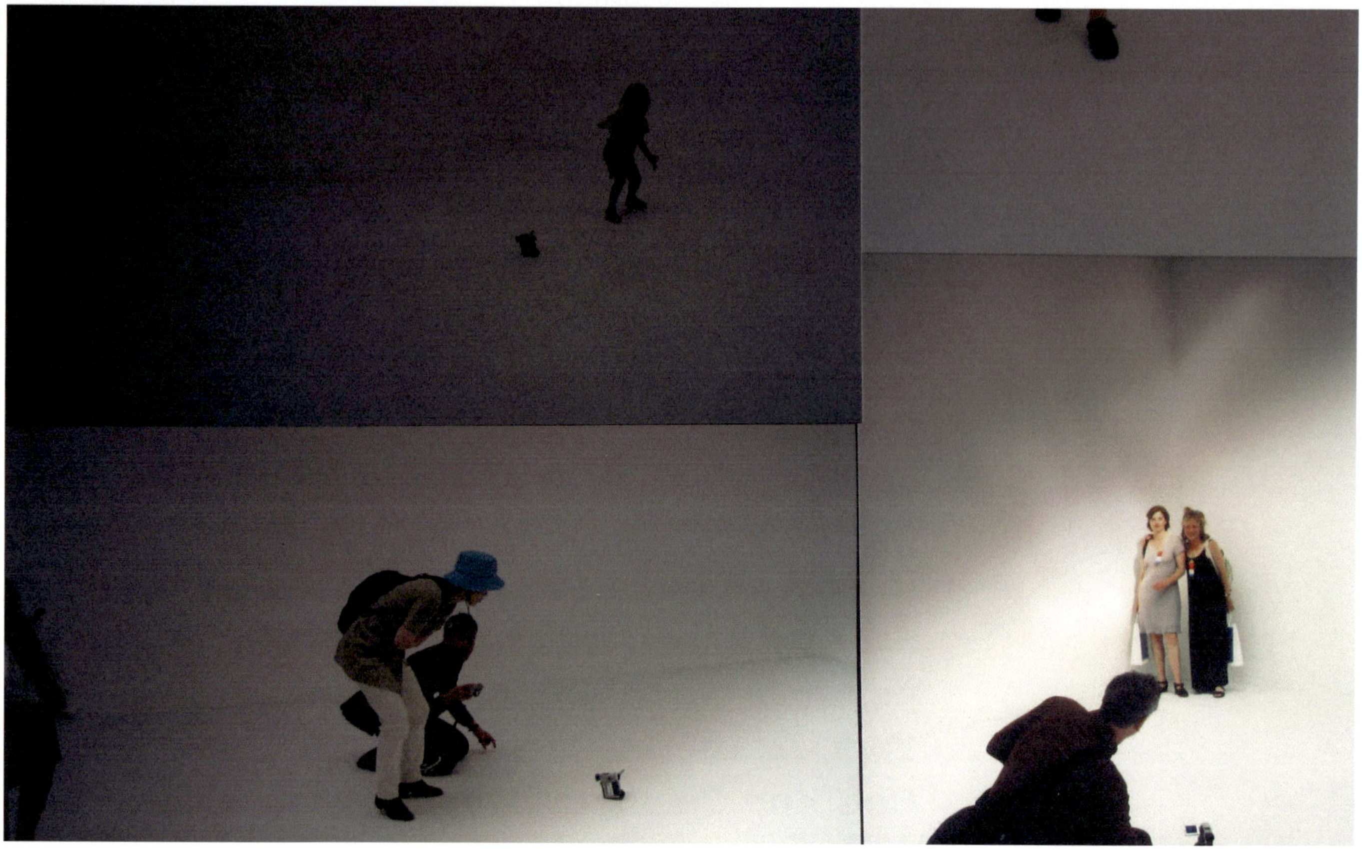

10
Venice, French Pavilion, 1998

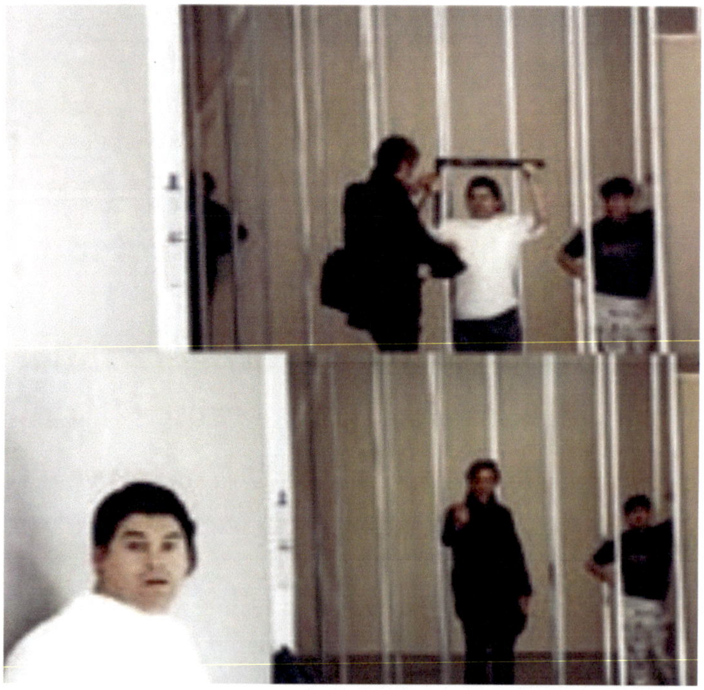

11
Framing the Event, 2000

10 In an empty room in the French Pavilion at the Venice Biennale, I place a camera on the floor in the middle of the room. It activates the space. The camera then demands a performance. It demands to be seen. That we show ourselves to it.

11 I ask waiters in a restaurant, construction worker to do certain things out of the ordinary, quite harmless and banal, though nevertheless these actions give us, if only for a moment, a shared disobligation of the everyday.

From Heisenberg to Derrida, we know that the frame of the event and the observer become the event.

In time I become interested in photographing myself, seeing myself through a twenty-four-hour day. Photography tells me I am alive, will be me again, in time, in image, so I riff with pictures, as they remind me that I have been someone else, somewhere else. An elsewhere that does not exist except in images. An elsewhere that complicates that which existed but points to the absence of the event it depicts, becoming an event unto itself.

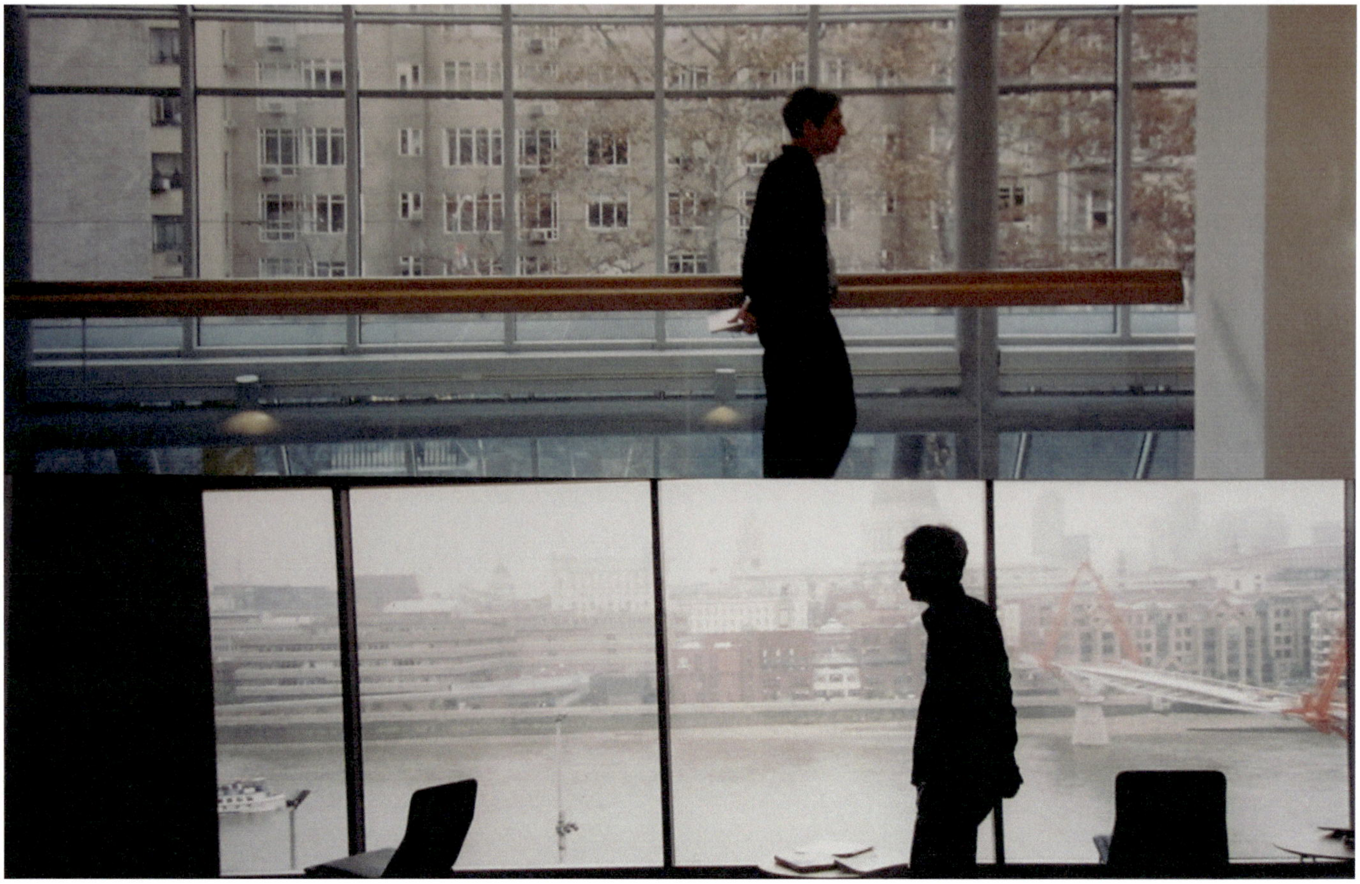

12
MoMA Tate Peregrination, 2001

13
A Fall of the Orange Does not Eliminate
Chance, or, Calamity Physics, 2002

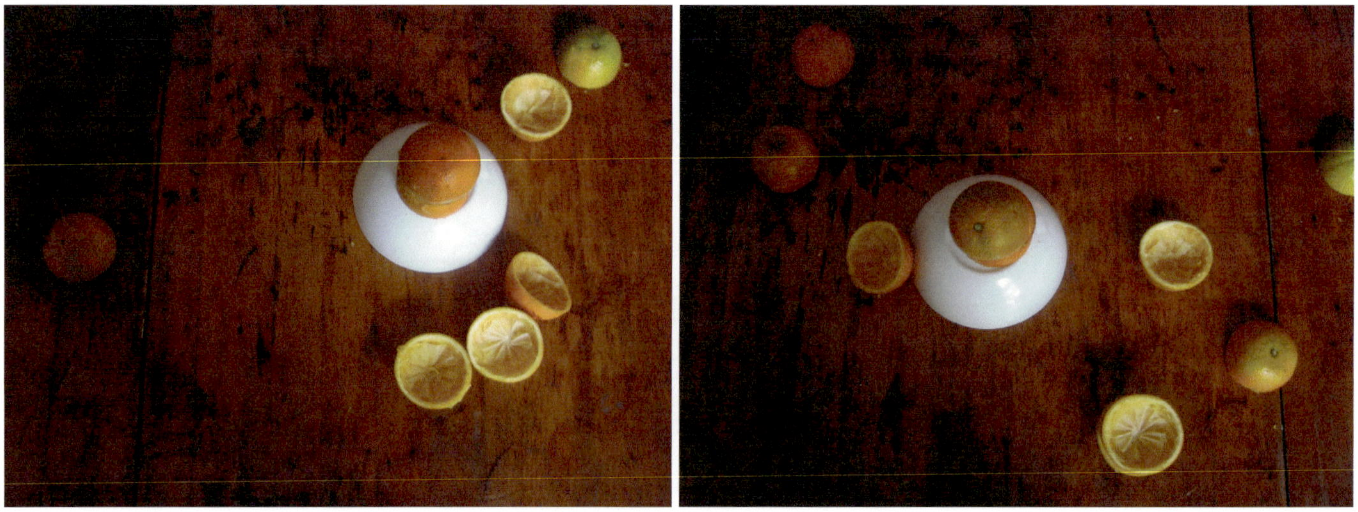

12 I perambulate, walking back and forth in front of the view windows of very similar physical spaces, the Tate Modern and the MoMA in New York. These distinct physical spaces are traversed at different times, but in the representation of these actions, time collapses, and I sense I am walking in a continuous loop between London and New York. Photography collapses the world, compresses it, puts it in our hands, and as Paul Virilio would say, replaces its actuality. Of course we know that's not the case. It is a map, not a territory. There is no actuality to a photograph in the sense of an elsewhere. So in fact, perhaps it is a territory and not a map, but a territory no longer there.

13 In a series of pictures where I let fall juiced oranges, titled *A Fall of the Orange Does Not Eliminate Chance, or, Calamity Physics*, photography records an experiment, me simply placing squeezed orange halves on top of each other on a table and letting them fall. What will fall and how will it fall. The instrument of photography lets me see something I would not see, nor precisely remember. Photography sees things we don't ordinarily see. Photography witnesses things we are not there to see. Photography, an agent of the world. Mechanical seeing has enabled us to amplify our knowing of the world exponentially.

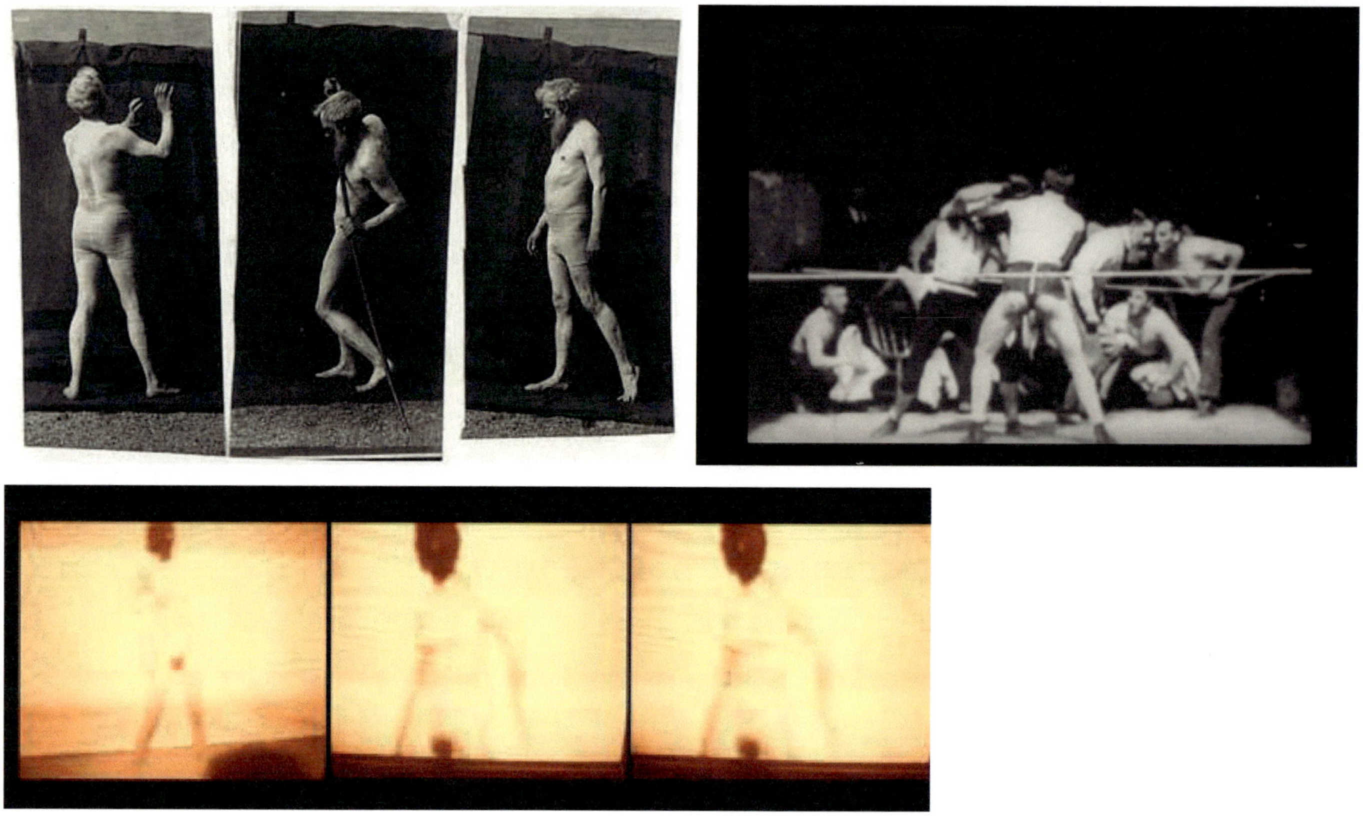

14
Moving Bodies, 2005

15
Time Stands Still, 2001

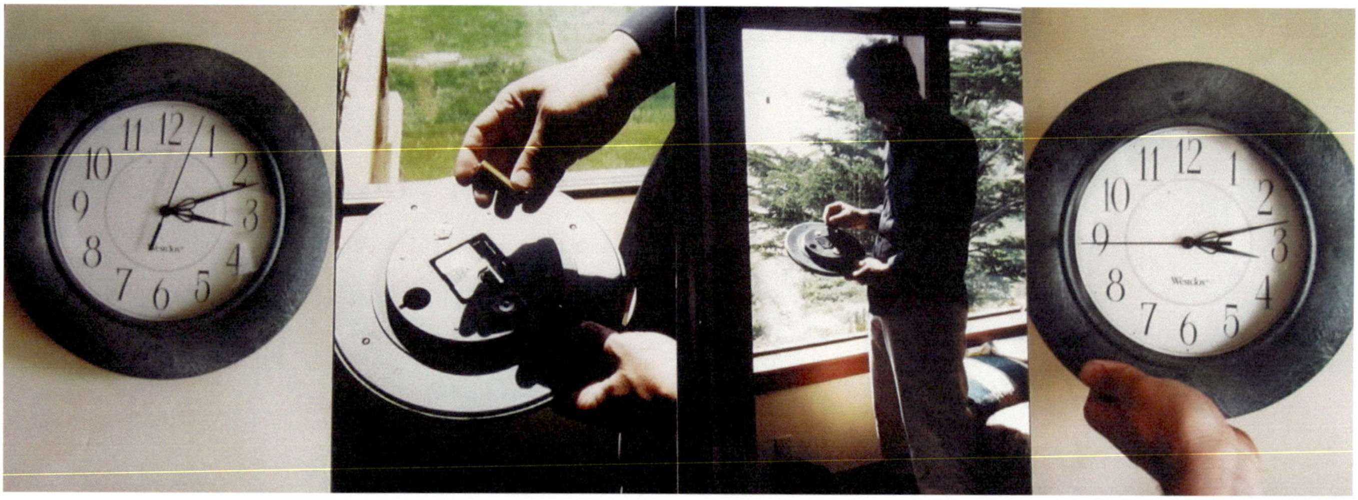

14 We don't think of photography as capturing movement or events at the micro and macro level so much anymore. Yet the science of photography, photography as an instrument to see what exceeds our biologic capacity for sight, is what must be considered to understand the magnitude of mechanical seeing. Photography used in observation, in scientific imaging, the imaging of our anatomy, imaging at the subatomic or satellite scale, or as instruments of surveillance, or war, or software visualization—all these kinds of imaging tend to exceed the photographic, becoming invisible in the conversation around photography.

Yet our pervasive condition of being imaged, tracked, and recorded is an invitation to continually rethink what is photography.

15 I photograph time, literally, as in these pictures, these casual pictures of me taking a battery out of the back of a wall clock and hence, stopping time. Here time literally stands still. But what is time?

A measure, a perspective tied to human biology, human rhythm; mechanical seeing far exceeds the human register of sight.

Photography is a material form that puts ideas about itself into question. Photography is conceptual actions, processes, a seeing and recording.

More and more I stage myself in the photograph. I stage an action. It often has to do with arresting time, framing as an event.

Photography is a recoding of that action, not a perfect moment, not a decisive moment, not action as an image of movement, but an action of the recording apparatus and the photographer. Recording is recoding.

The frame of the event and the observer become the event.

16
Green Dot, 1997

17
John Cage meets Marcel Broodthaers,
film still, 2001

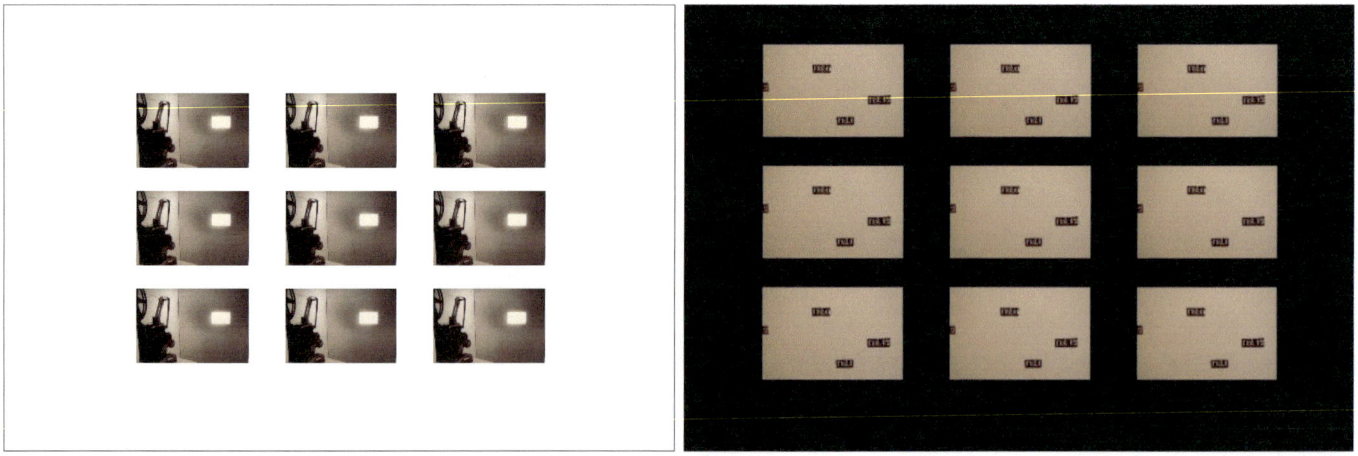

16 The dot as inflection. Do we see the dot or the blackness? How can we not see both? Is photography the green dots of this world?

How can we see photography? What is it that photography gives site to? Is the image sight, a seeing, and photography a place, a thing, a site, an object? Is an image a photograph? Does imaging exceed photography? Is photography a circumscribed parochial form inside imaging? And would that matter?

17 Marcel Broodthaers put forward the idea of the film screen as an indexical zone by projecting films onto a screen marked *fig 1–15*. Such designations are dispersed throughout the screen. The projected image on his screen would not be a composite image but one made of figures, of distinct parts, of distinct particulars. For example, a vase on a table is figure 2; fruit, figure 12; the table, figure 5; across from the vase, two quarreling lovers are figure 7. But saying it this way is not quite right, because in his system the figures precede the image, so that blended blue patch on the left we'd never notice might be figure 21, and the floor under the quarreling lovers that you just didn't see before, figure 13.

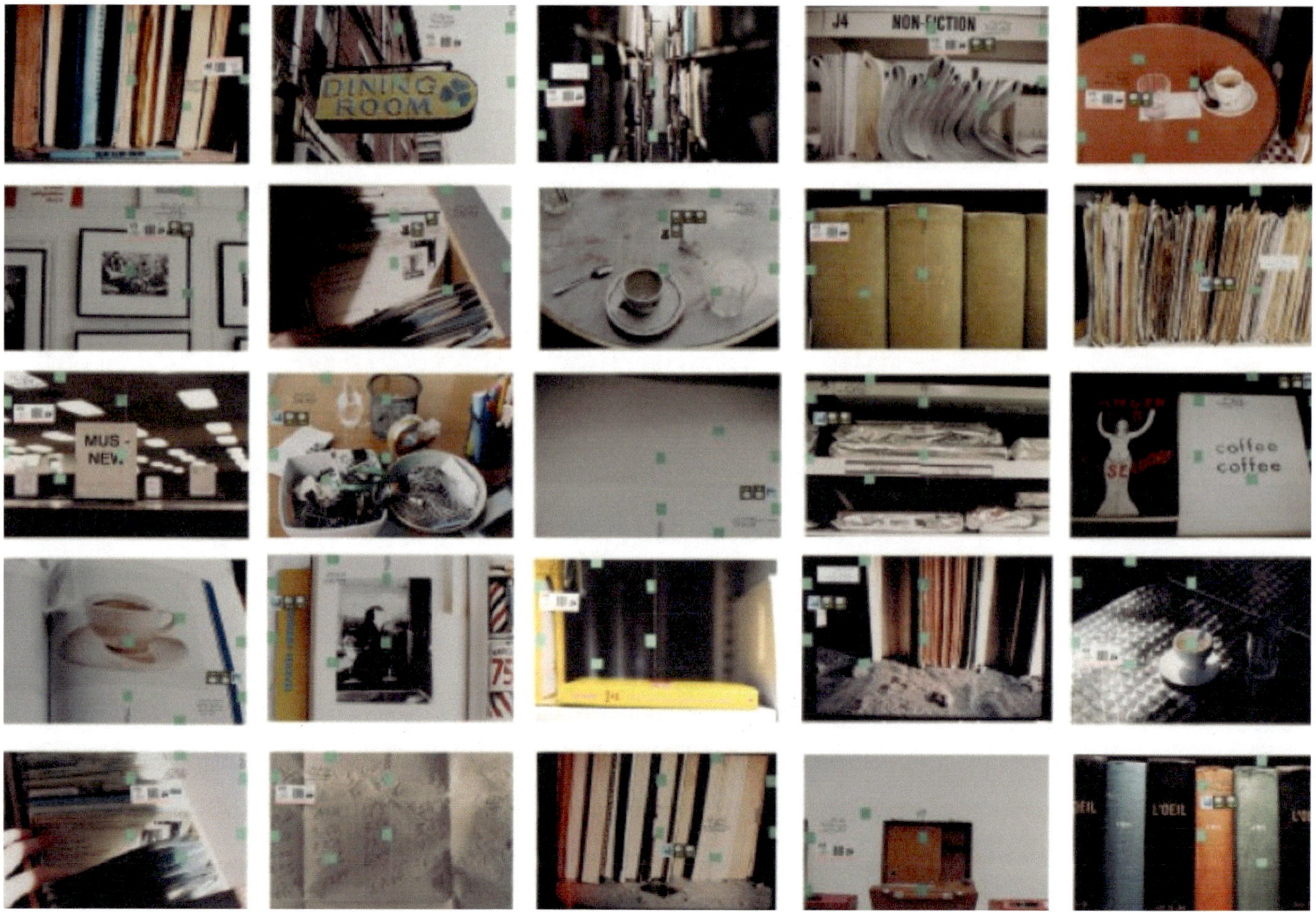

18
Photo from MoMA Show, 2010

18 When we see images, we put the picture together. We don't see the figures, we see the gestalt of a thing. The world becomes all too familiar to us, and only in photography do we see again. Or no... only with those green dots, and figures, do we see again.

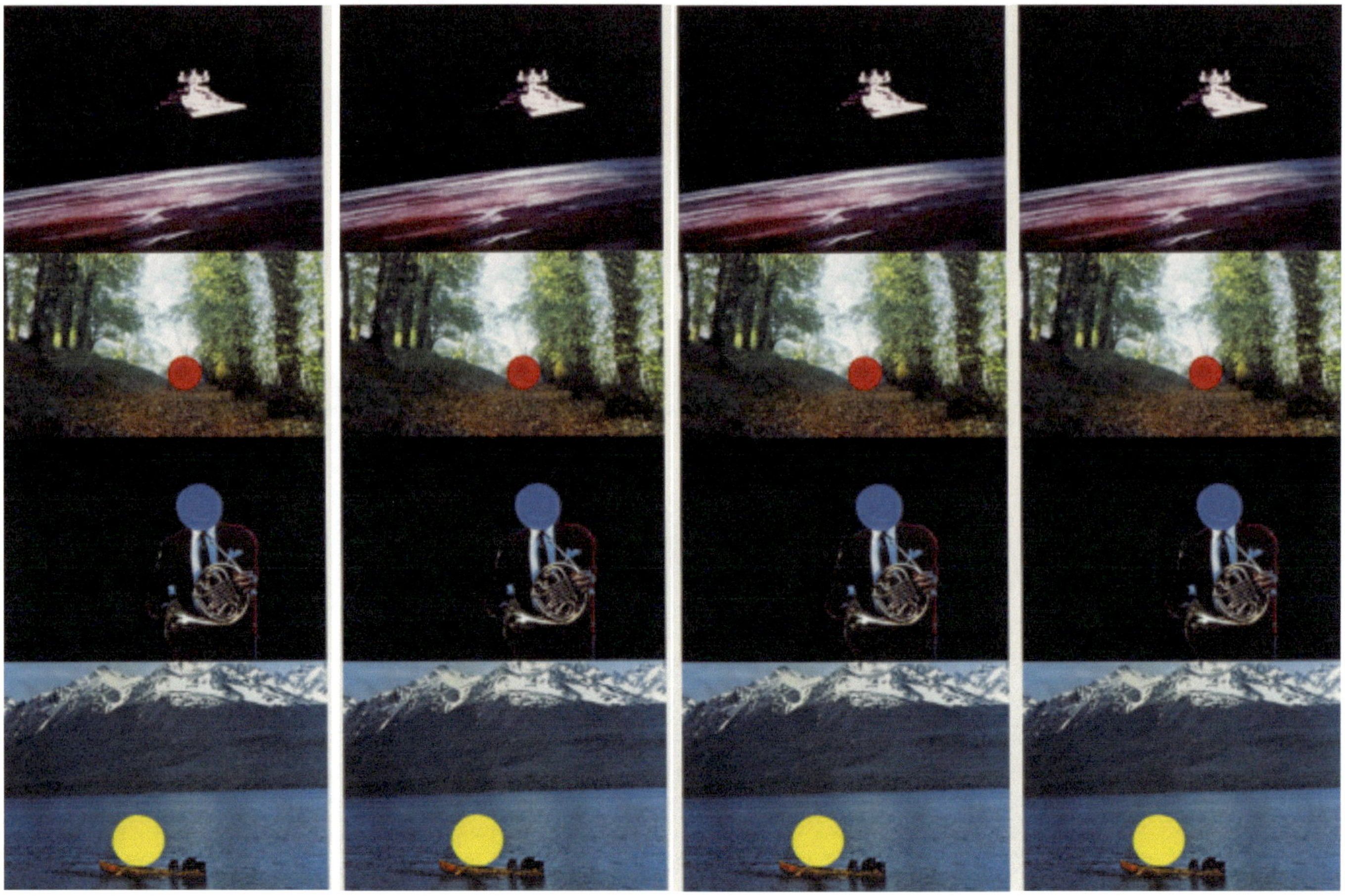

19

Four Times Four, or, Repeating Baldessari, 2012

19 Along these lines John Baldessari uses found photographs, many of them b-film stills, and places on them circles and color-field voids. This voiding out gives the image a new visual dimension, a new direction. They are the figures that give sight to our seeing that has become habitual and routine.

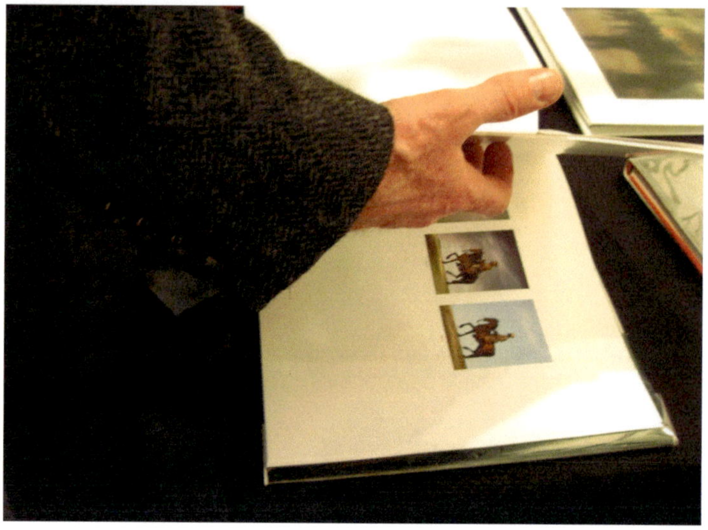

20
Cowboy Pictures, 2009

21
The *New York Times* (Words Removed), 2007

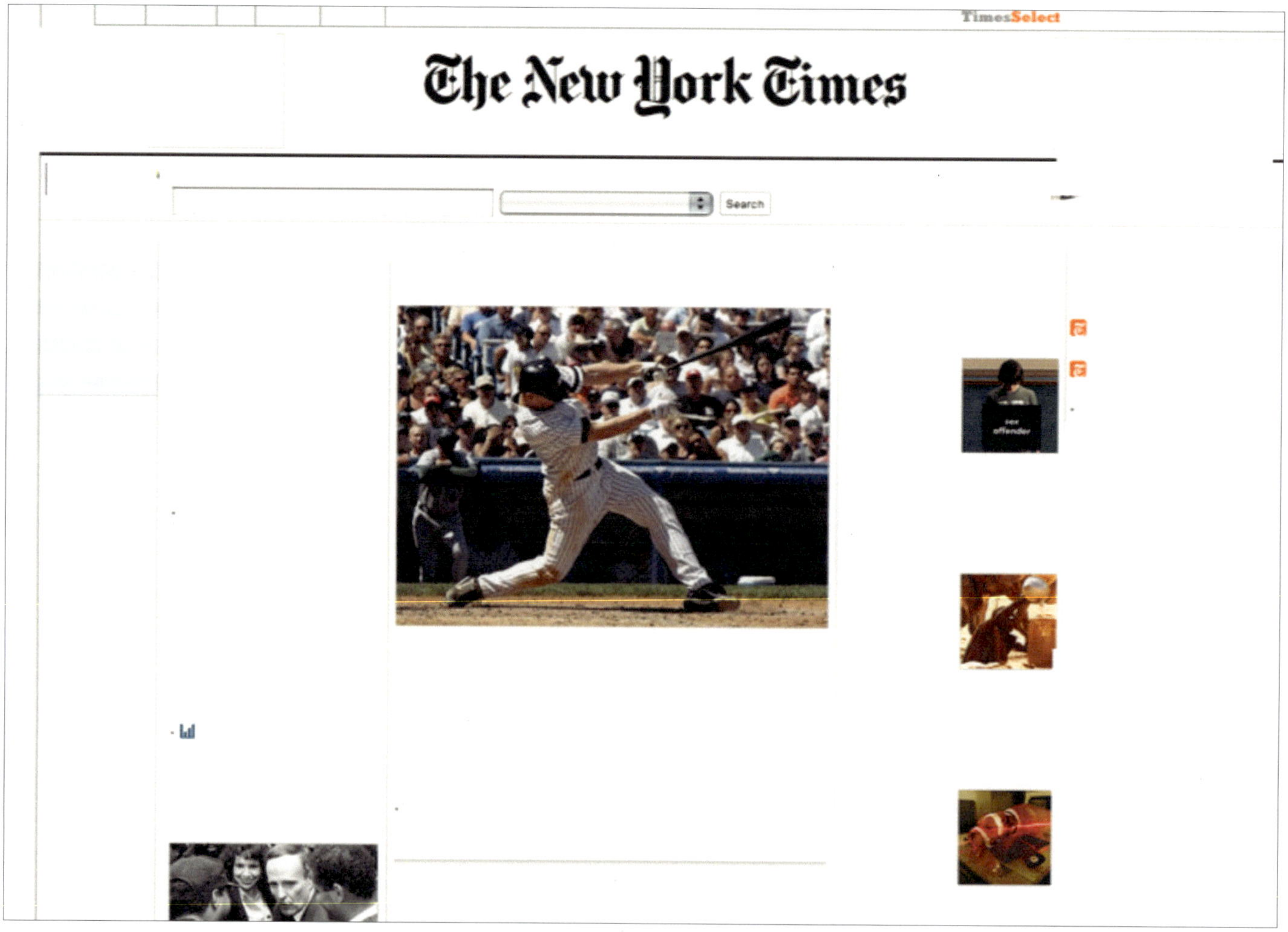

20 Artist Richard Prince presented the once-famous Marlboro cigarette cowboy ads without the body copy, returning the image to an open state.

21 I want to do the same with the *New York Times*, so I write a program with graduate students at ITP at New York University that strips away the text of the *Times*. Do we really live in an image culture? Or is it instead what the caption tells us that directs our sight?

The image is a site, a space, to create a rhetoric about and around the photograph.

The use of photography then becomes a way to read photography.

Tactility is a way we learn to see, and then our sight has us forget our touch.

I had come across André Malraux's book *Voices of Silence*, which contains numerous reproductions of extraordinary works of art, and, as he writes, it is almost impossible to "see," "read," "sense" them bound within a book and far, far away from the context of their initial manifestation.

The reproductions are in black and white. So to see them, I had to touch them. But how do you touch a photograph? How does touch become sight? I brought to the image the stuff of the image, in this case, a variety of local mushrooms, plants, berries, flowers, leaves, and nuts, even a dragonfly. Thinking this is where these colors come from, this is the flora and fauna, the geology of this place. It was in arranging these elements on the surface of the reproduction that I was able to see them, to feel the sense of the objects in these photographs.

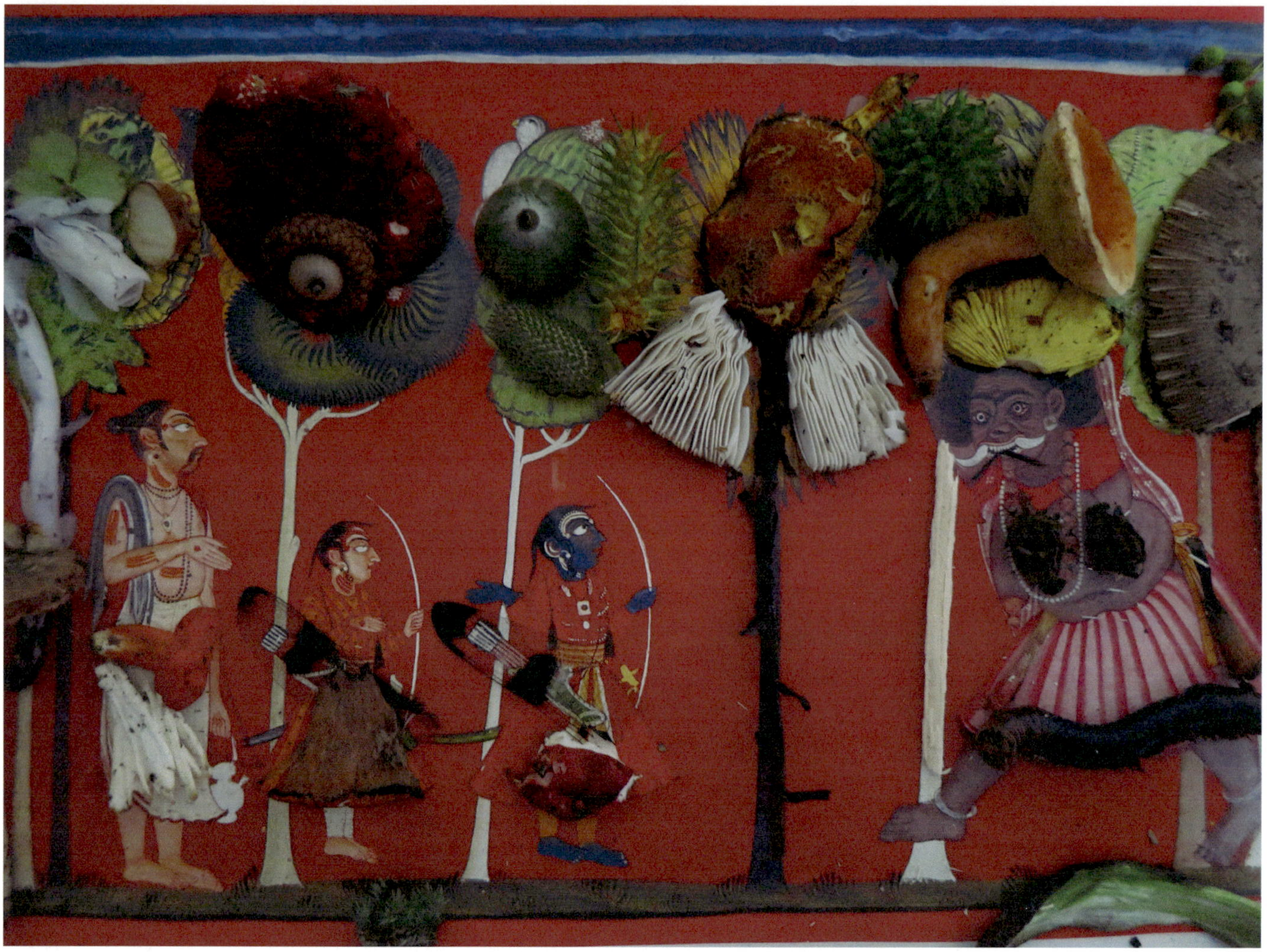

22
India, Mughal dynasty, Uncovering Miniature Painting
Three Archers and Devi, Seventeenth Century, 2012

22 I titled the series *Anatomy of Pictures*. I use would use photography as an instrument to record what I had seen again, the relation between nature and artifice, between sight and touch.

Works of art have genealogies and material form. And like living forms, they continually change over time. The processes that produce artworks, the materials and techniques, their raison d'être in a culture—as these things change, artworks and the activity of art and what we see as the artwork also change and adapt. Just as the movements of the earth—its plates, rocks, flora, fauna—shift together with the magnetic fields, so does art, so does the photographic.

Photography is a material form, especially digital photography. The *Anatomy of Pictures* was the desire to bring materiality back to the photograph. We do a similar thing with our digital cameras and processes, realizing our images this way and that with our filters—tonal, noir, process, chrome, Mayfair, Valencia, X Pro II, lo-fi, earlybird, Nashville, Lord Kelvin, and many more.

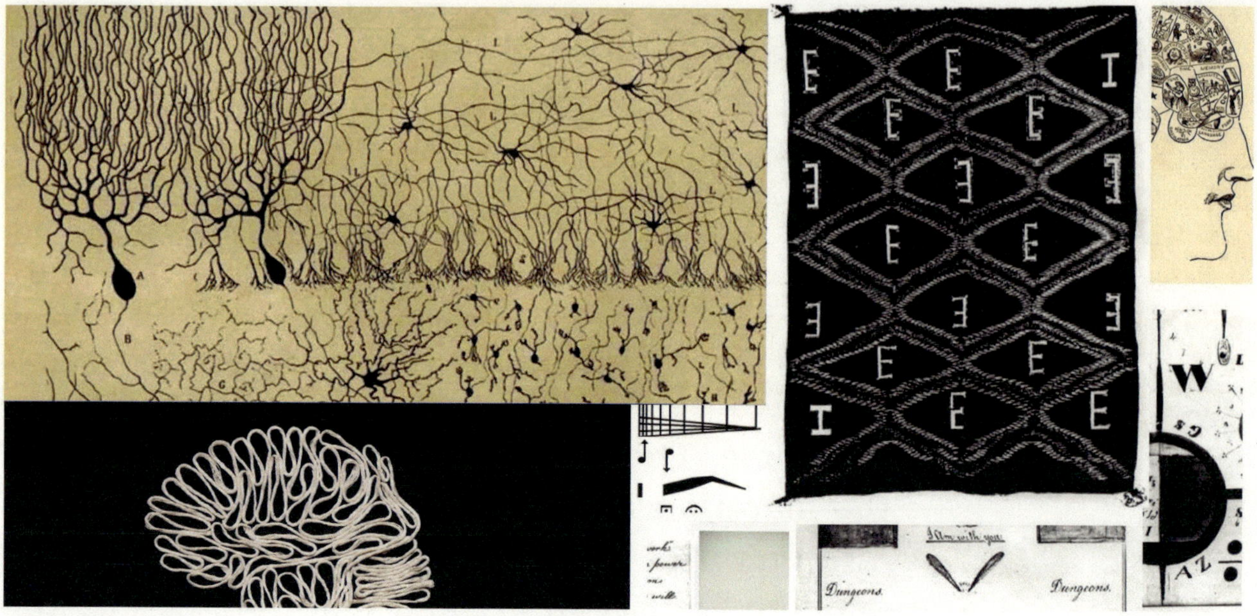

23
Cartography 24, 2007

23 In this assembled photograph from *Cartographies*, I construct a map of seeing, a series of signs, glyphs, to direct sight to the neurons and patterning of our sensorium.

What else is a photograph but this direction of sight, this construction of site, a pattern for seeing.

The pleasure of photography then is not simply the image, but the image construct, the image constructed, the object photograph.

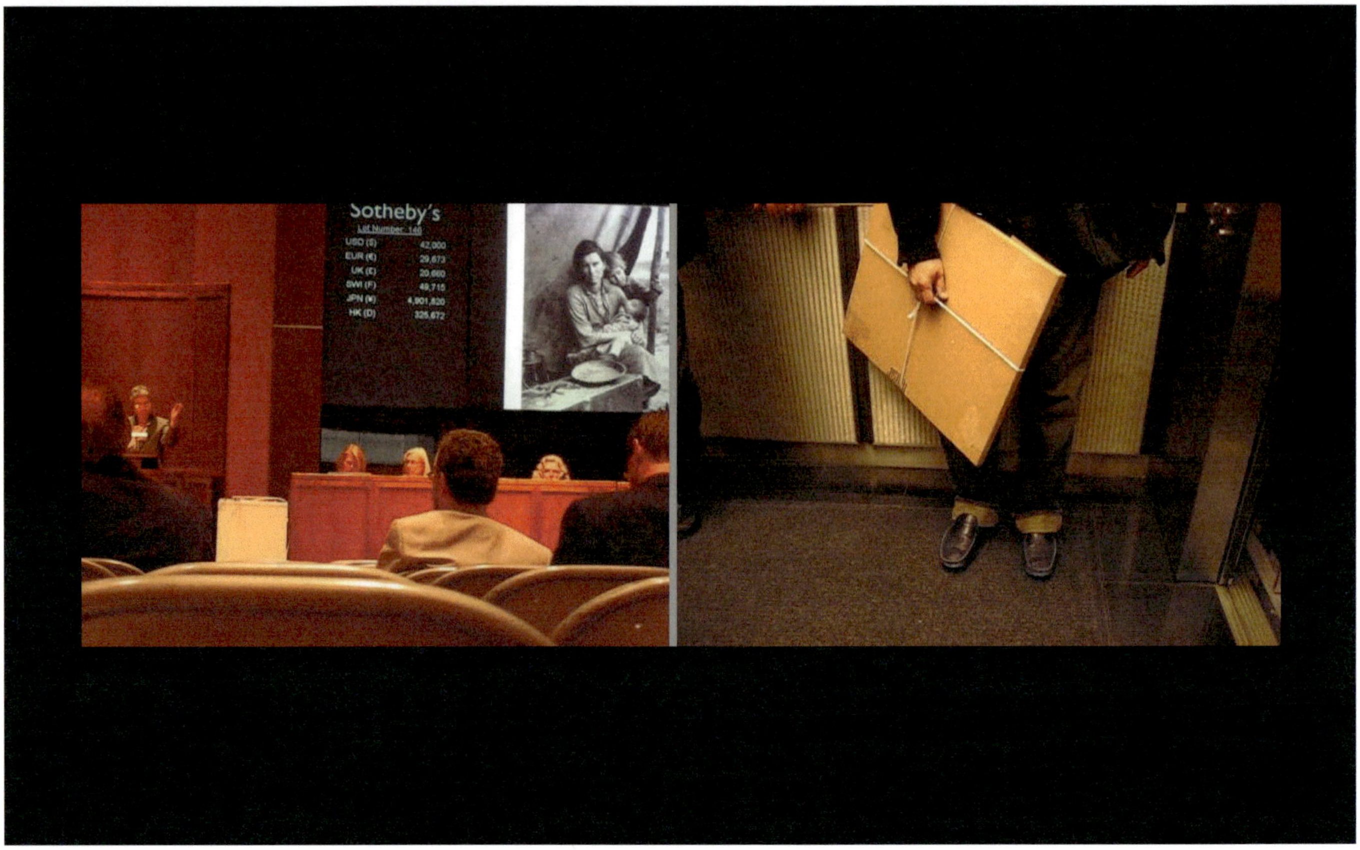

24
Take Me Home, 2005

25
A Day in the Life at the Andy Warhol Museum, 2006

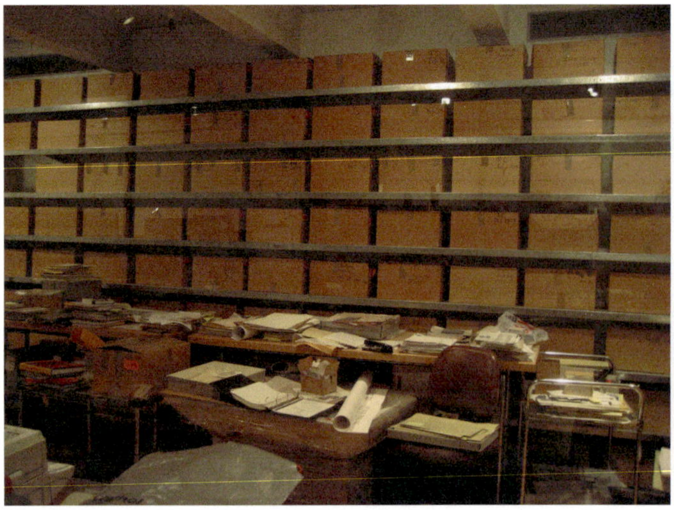

26
An Alphabet of Images, 2010

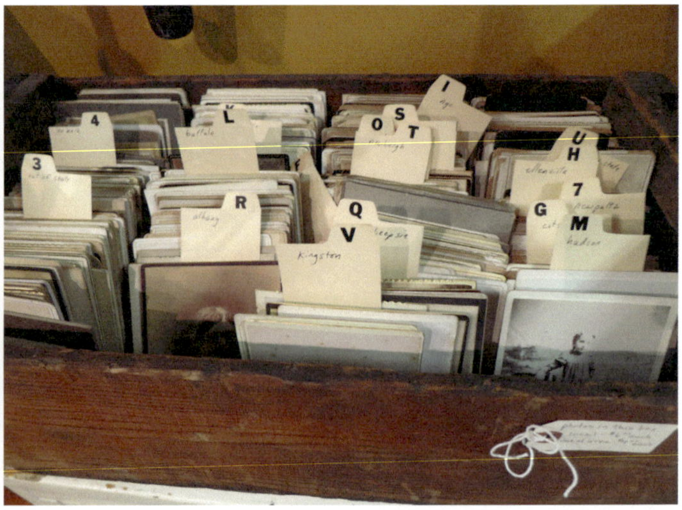

24 Photography is a history with buyers and sellers, archivists and historians, practitioners and collectors. A domain of claims and arguments and actual things.

Each box a time capsule, a possible narrative, a history of both the box and what's in it.

25 / 26 As a boy, German novelist W. G. Sebald was shown photographs at school in Oberstdorf and recalled that neither he nor any of his classmates knew how to give description or explanation to what these photographs were. They were photographs of the Holocaust. He would go on to incorporate found photographs in his novels, questioning the mnemotechnical processes that shape our memories, challenging the authority that photography has in the constructive of our narratives.

"His novels are notable for their curious and wide-ranging mixture of fact (or apparent fact), recollection and fiction, often punctuated by indistinct black-and-white photographs set in evocative counterpoint to the narrative rather than illustrating it directly" (*Wikipedia*). Photographs can lend themselves to a multitude of narratives. I wonder what the narrative of photography constructed by photographs is. Aren't all photographs from a certain vantage indistinct? Isn't photography itself an image?

We have moved from hard copy files to digital files, literally filed away, files away from us, in no particular place, in every place encoded and ubiquitous. Translated, transcoded, translation, is that what photography is, a productive and continuous misrecognition?

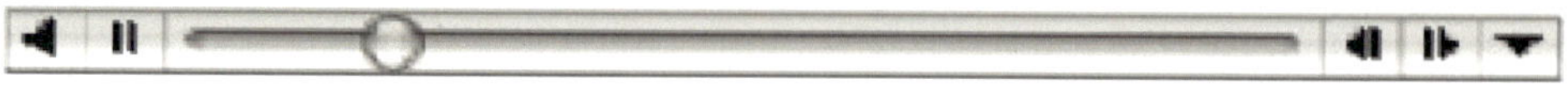

27
Sound and Image, 2005

28
Photography and Its Disappearance, 2009

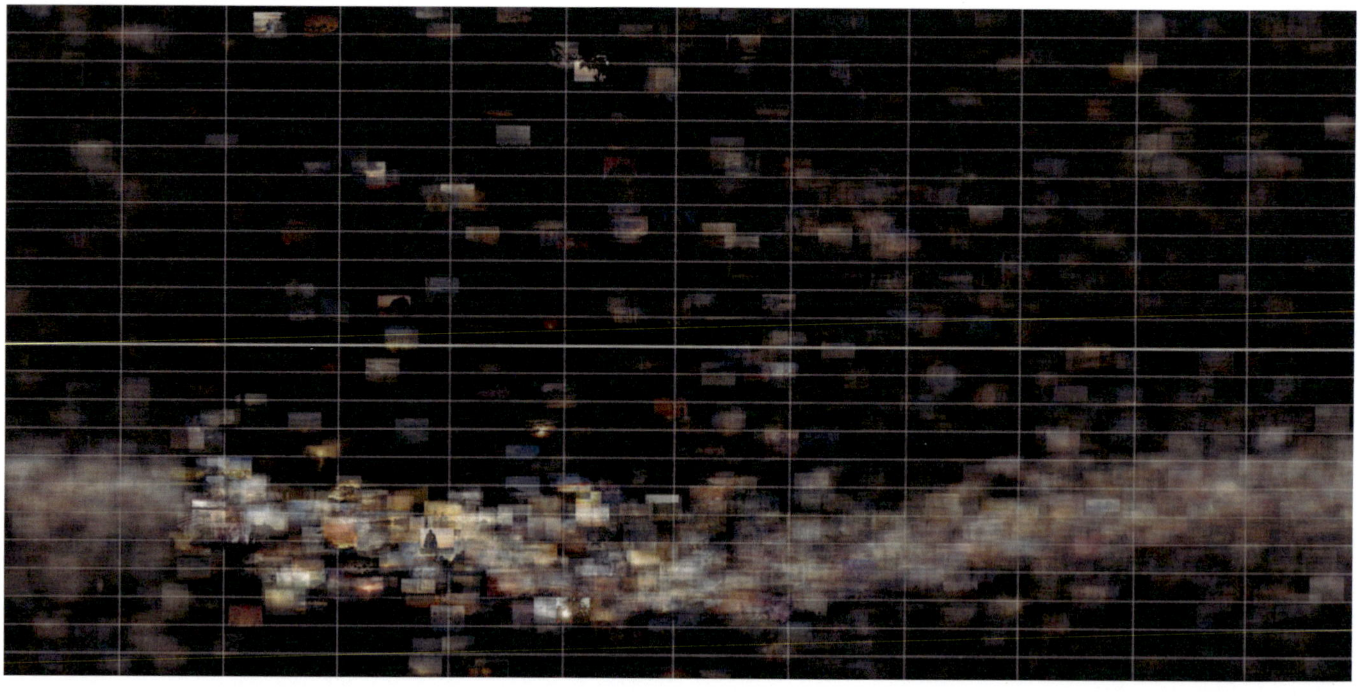

27 / 28 Indexed in a vast quanta of data, the image, a file of many characteristics, the photograph, becomes its metadata, its search tags.

I wonder what "indistinct photograph" as it was mentioned in the *Wikipedia* entry above means. Why is black and white both more indistinct and at the same time more distinctive than color? Black and white removes the particular of color to a gray scale of tones between black-black and white-white, creating an image at a remove from the analogue of the material world. It makes an icon of the image, an icon in the sense that the image is both the particular and a sort of ideal. It is both the thing it depicts and the thingness of the thing, or rather the ideal of the very picture it is. It is the abstraction of the event depicted.

But there is another kind of indistinctness that interests me, the image gradually moving from representation to abstraction to disappearance. The image, not as a site of memory, but of material erasure. It is free from history. Not lost as a file, but the recording itself works against photography as an analogue to the real and becomes noise and grain. It is the photograph that has already disappeared, the image of a disappearance, moving away from the figure, from representation.

Facts don't exist outside of interpretation, translation. The material facts of an image, what are they without a reader, a thing in this world whose codes, not known, become a mystery, an opening, a story, not something known unto itself, as in "a picture is worth a thousand words" but beckoning to be read. It will take a thousand words and more to fully describe what someone is seeing. The image is never alone, it does not speak itself. It is any possible fact, any possible history ... unless you know that history.

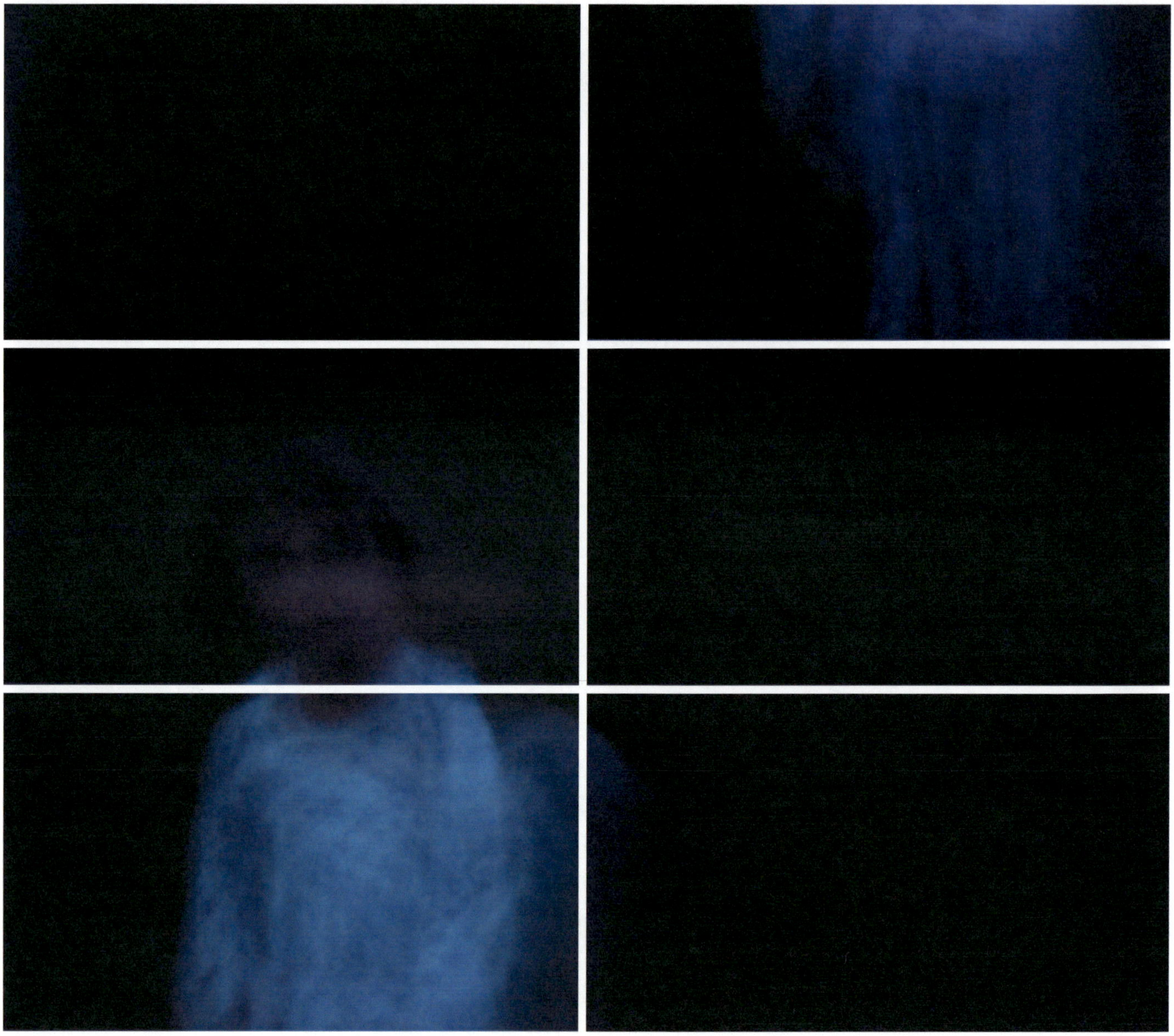

29
Midsummer Night, 2003

29 Here I am interested in the abstraction of material facts, to dissolve away the figuration of a material event and make it the source for a sensate visual mystery. The affect of a fact.

If the Bechers gave us an array of types, an indexing of particulars, their successors produced images of a single particular. Unlike the Bechers, they would produce such images to scale, or an idealized or hyperreal image at an even larger scale.

With the work of Jeff Wall and Andreas Gurksy we move from types or typologies to a singular idea, in isolation, in relief, not an array of variation of types, but one instant that stands for all types. From documentation to creation, from creation to ideation, the one instant takes on the style of documentation or "near documentary," as Jeff Wall would say. The work would isolate the typic, but it would not be one in an array, would rather seek out a singular moment. The moment, for example, that would express the global condition, not of so many factories all over the world, but the one factory that would represent this new condition, that would compress into one image the very idea of processes of globalization. In some odd sense the photograph would be a return to the decisive moment that never was an actual moment. It would be the unposed, posed. And then it would be made into an object. It would use photography, the salon, the museum, the collector's home to realize a photograph of outsized proportion, the image that summed up all others.

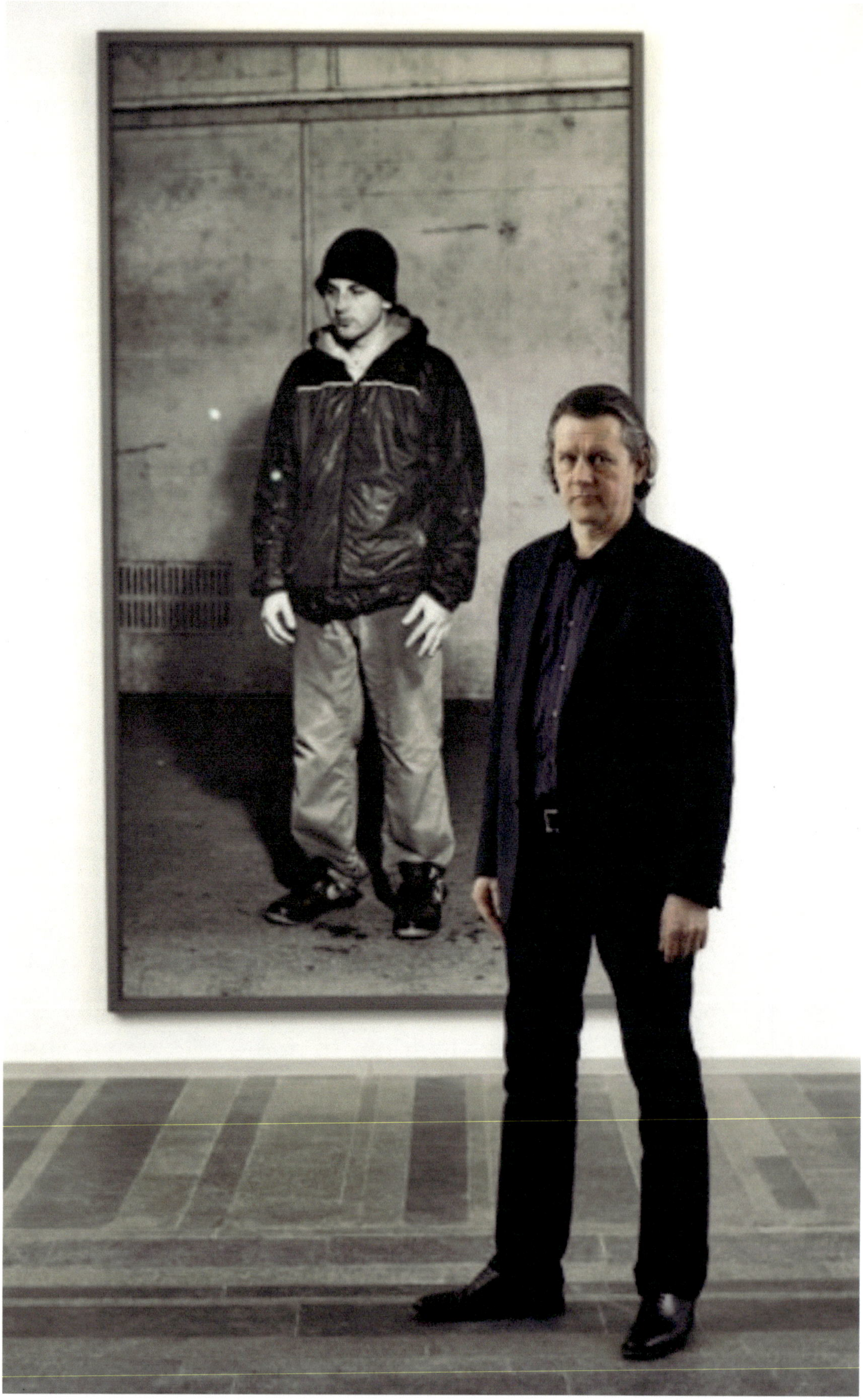

30
Jeff Wall in Russia,
Far Away
Document, 2010

30 The photograph printed at human scale would bring forth the fact of representation. We would behold it in relation to our human scale, we would have to reckon with the photographic object depicting someone our size, if not much larger, and its commanding presence would give presence to that which it depicted. The photographic object would be a being itself.

Photography's larger scale insists that we should be convinced of the fact of depiction or simply the fact of photography's scale. A scale that both creates the banal of something big and material, as well, yes, an über-real, the instance par excellence, a summation or condensation of all instances, the thing itself, an object that overwhelms the body that views it. I pursue the image that gradually moves from representation to abstraction and disappearance, all of it in plain sight. I must refuse large photography, as seductive as it may be. I see it as a conceptual conceit, though it most often is not read this way.

The image is not a site of memory or an elsewhere, but of contemplation, of reflection—a space all unto itself.

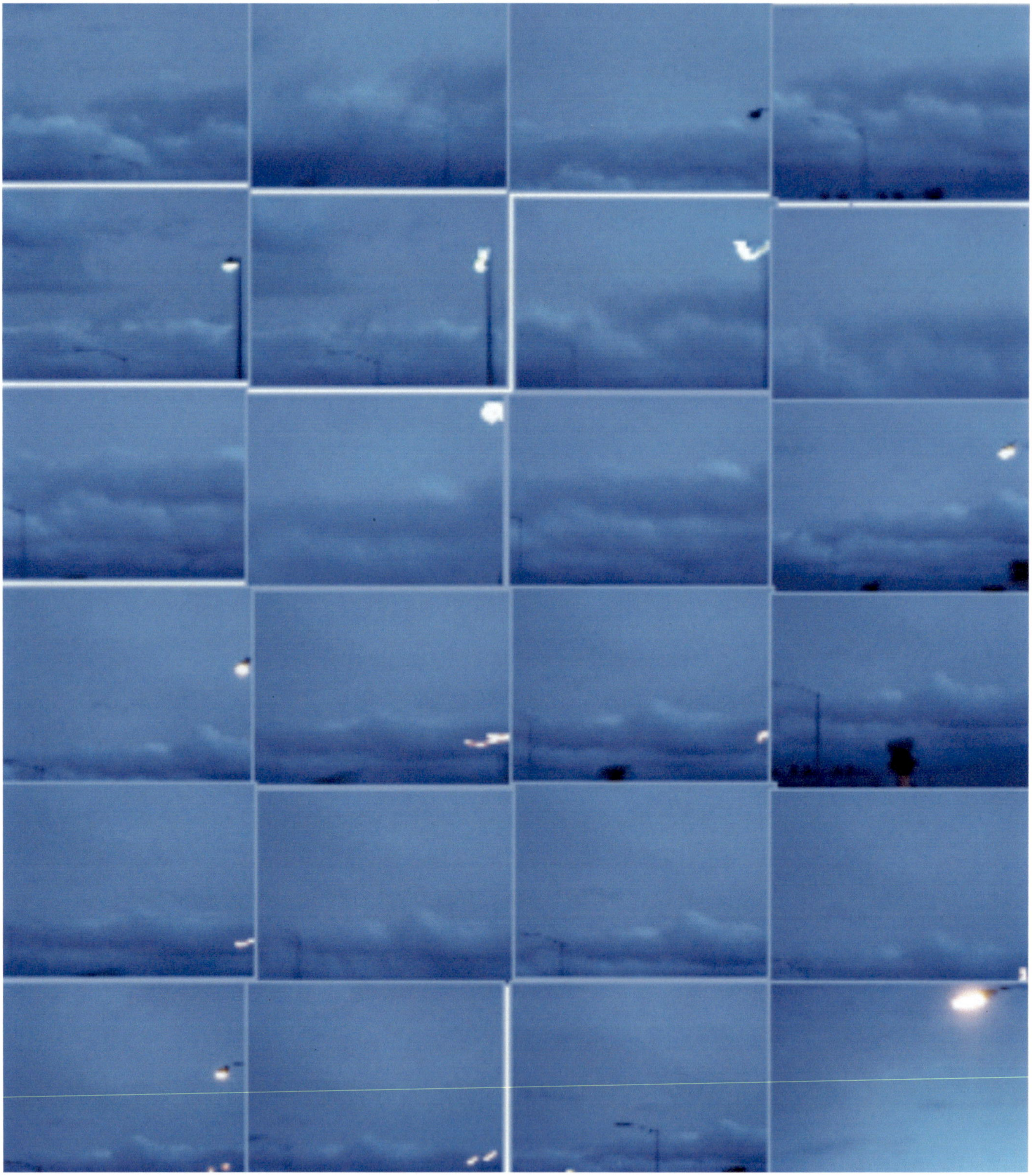

31
Computations, 2002

31 Seeing, not recording, not indexing, more precisely imaging—bringing forth a trace, an event of the camera seeing, not the eye behind the camera, in a sense, but accidenting the camera, or perhaps letting it see. The image as event.

Digital cameras are cameras, programmable cameras, perhaps more programs than cameras. It's uncanny and fascinating that they mimic the camera and photography but that they are also something else. It is this something else that begins to interest me.

The digital allowed us to see more immediately, more than the Polaroid, the instantaneity of our seeing.

Roland Barthes observed in *Camera Lucida*, "What the Photograph reproduces to infinity has occurred only once." But what is it that occurs only once, the moment in time, or the occurrence of imaging?

I begin to see this as an approach that I take everywhere in imaging, from environmental spaces to photographs, to friends, strangers, myself, video, cinema, books, objects, architecture, staged events—anything in my purview. This idea of the event of the image as an event of the occurrence of imaging.

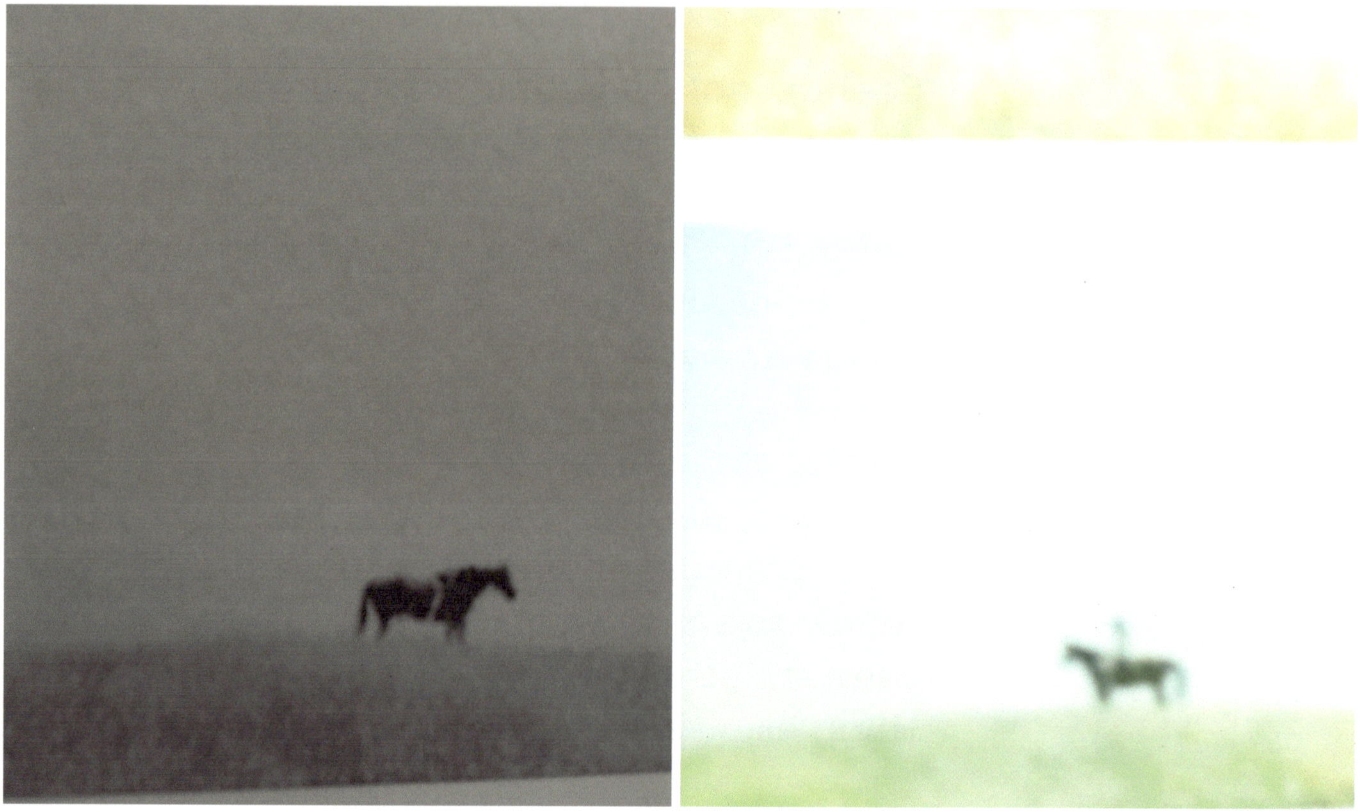

32
Black and White and Color, 2012

32 What the work is in pursuit of is not the image per se but the imaging of the event of myself with the camera on the occasion of these things being imaged. As such the images are presented always in continuum, or as a traversing of the event of these things becoming image. So much so that there are no longer these things, there are only images unto themselves.

What remains then of the presence in the imaged?

In modernism, artists explored the unique qualities inherent in photography, from composing the exact moment, finding varied subject matter, cultivating a signature, to of course exploring the very properties of light exposed by lenses and the properties of the darkroom. In the last thirty years, with the advent of conceptual art, artists moved away from photography's aesthetic or formal properties and used the photograph as an instrument of documentation—appropriated photographs, constructed photographs—and photography became not so much continuous with the world as much as an instrument for the invention of one's own world and, through appropriation, the recontextualization of the image and its very sense. In this sense the photograph became the already read photograph.

In the nineties, photography is recovered with the work of the objectivist school of photography, but photography, as in the domain of an art, stakes out positions in multiple and combinatory trajectories.

33

Instantly Instagram, Instantly Photographic, 2012

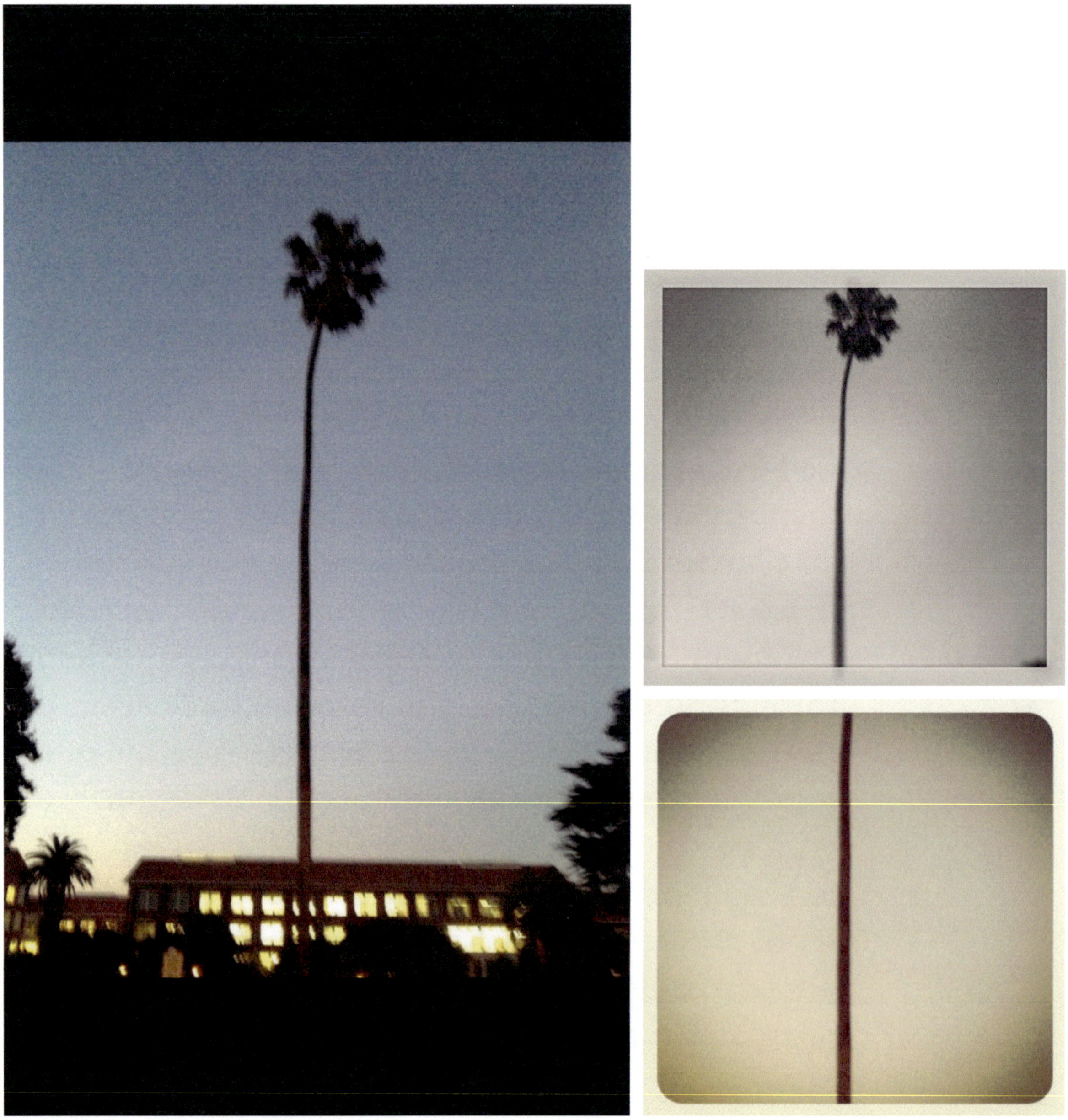

With the advance of digital photography and the vast repertoire of the camera in terms of effects, light sensitivity, image storage, and archiving—imaging is the very subject of images. The camera, a simulated, or software, camera, instructs itself, performs the camera—and is indeed something else. There is something about the image as file that heralds a new consideration of photography, something that both performs and exceeds photography.

Digital photography instruments become a way to examine photography, in a way similar to how video became a way for Godard to look at cinema. Today we need only think of Instagram, which mimics photography to become a new photography that we think of as a nostalgia for photography.

The digital both mimics and imitates photography, never quite being photography while also becoming something of the uncanny of photography. Digital photography is the image of the disappearance of photography, not of the world or the real. It is the recording of recording. What we see is the filter, the effects, the prowess of the digital, the signal, information, a possible sample, the beginning of a riff, a conversation, a disputation. Photography in the electronic ether cannot speak for itself, photography never really could, except perhaps, at the brief incendiary moment of its inception, when its "magic" brought us the world. Now it brings us its "magic."

33 All photography now is in a sense conceptual and about materialization, the materialization of something in the event of a kind of appearance.

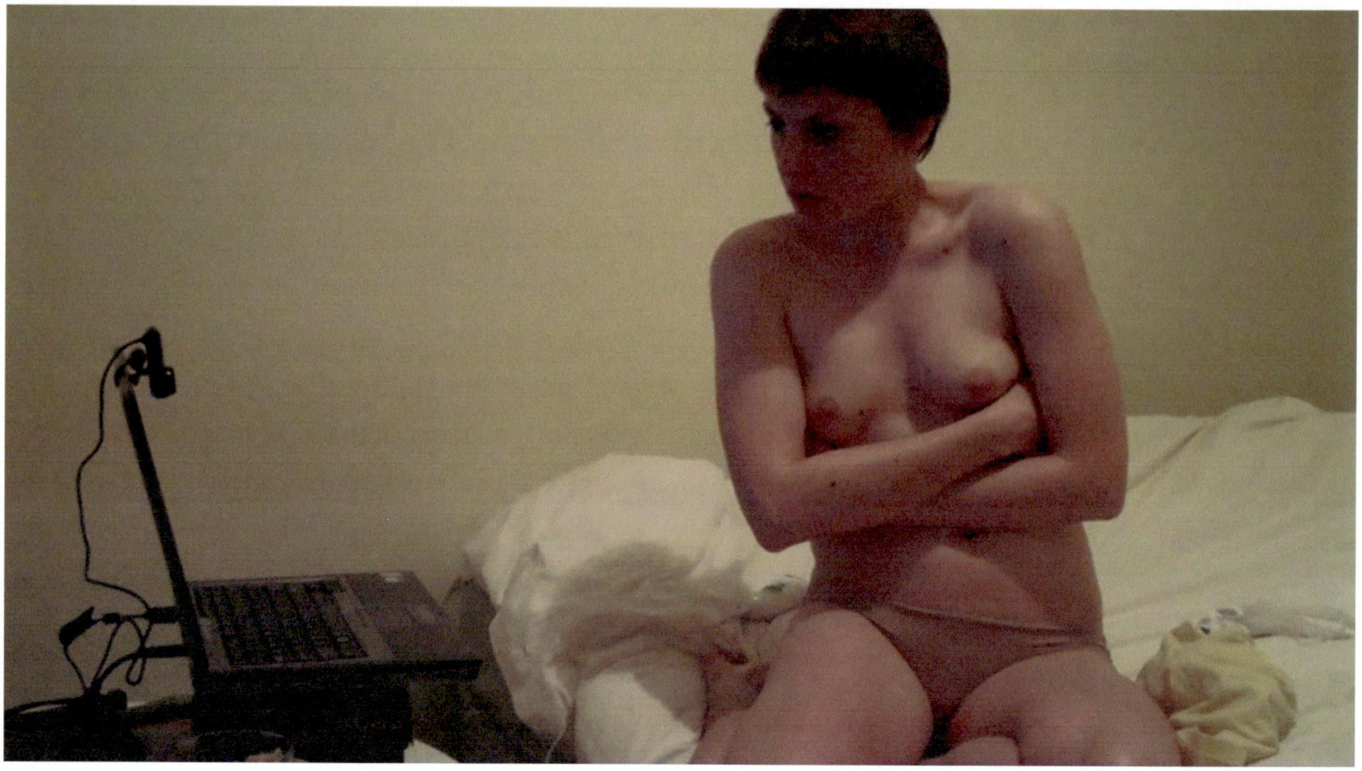

34
Hi, How Are You Guest 10497, 2012

Perhaps there is an image of the image, the image imaging. What could this mean? The idea of the image as indexical or as a scene of the photographic. Or perhaps it's me or someone, something, becoming imaged.

34 Yet in all of this I am absolutely convinced by the presence of the electronic image. Here, in an image from my project *Hi, How Are You Guest 10497*, I work with an actress to have her record herself over the course of six months as she joins the international sex workers site www.myfreecams.com. In this case the recording concerns how one comes to construct an image of oneself, how one sees oneself imaged.

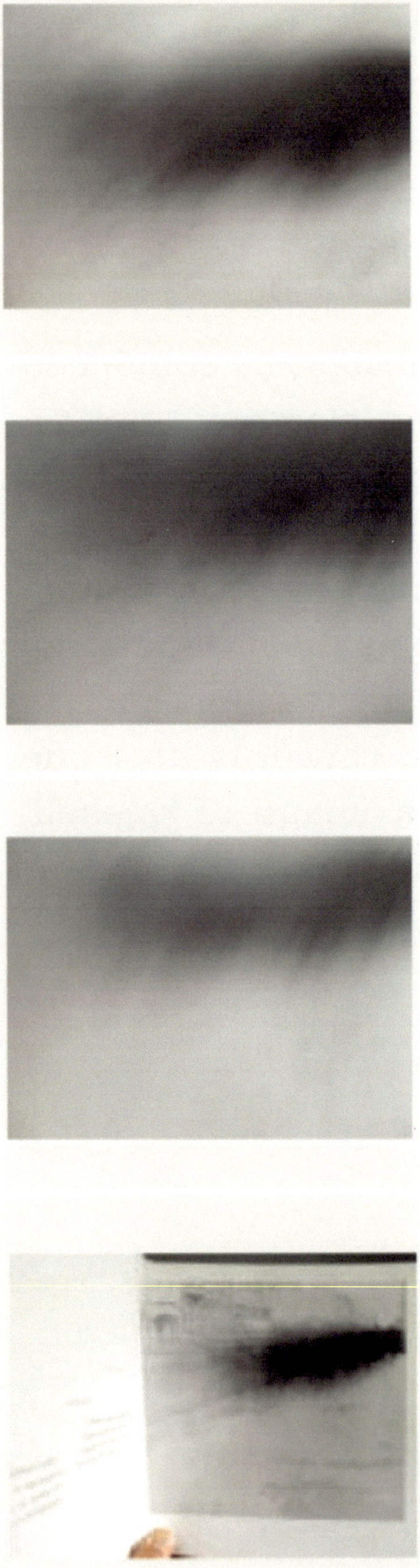

35

Three Acts of Erasure, 2012

35 Here the image is a trace of the image, but to look for the trace of the image, as if "the image" was out there, would blind one to what is here in front of us. Admittedly, the image in the book performs the idea of the trace of the image, of the mass dissolving away, the poetry of one lost in the crowd, an undifferentiated mass.

This same body, this one in the mass, that becomes singular, yes, like the woman in *Hi How Are You Guest 10497*, presenting herself to the camera, it is both the real in the image and its disappearance, its here and elsewhere, its contrivance and reality, like the yesterday so far away but so present in the narrative of history. Photography confounds us with its recordings pulled out of context.

My image is the image abstraction, my photography a reading of the photographic. I have to ask in all abstraction: do we look to recognize something of our world, something only we can see?

I wonder how bees see. I wonder how photography sees.

Photography for this moment is the visioning of the trace that becomes the thing itself. And conversely, at the same time, photography is the documenting of the individual's desire for self-presentation, the desire to represent oneself as a body in a network, to have presence.

This is my desire—to find photography. My idea of photography, like Gerhard Richter's of painting, is in working with the natural and the abstraction to find a stance of indifference. Richter's paintings, from flowers, nudes, cars, curtains, everyday life, snow-scapes, clouds , women, candles, buildings, Baader-Meinhof, skulls, to his abstractions, were the copying of photographs giving a demonstration of indifference, that indifference being his pursuit of painting. To see painting itself, indifferent to what is painted.

The photograph then is a recording, an occurrence, a complication, a fabrication of presence and time, a thing. The image as an index, particular to recording.

The moment of the image is not a special moment but one of many moments that involve the surveying of a site—the

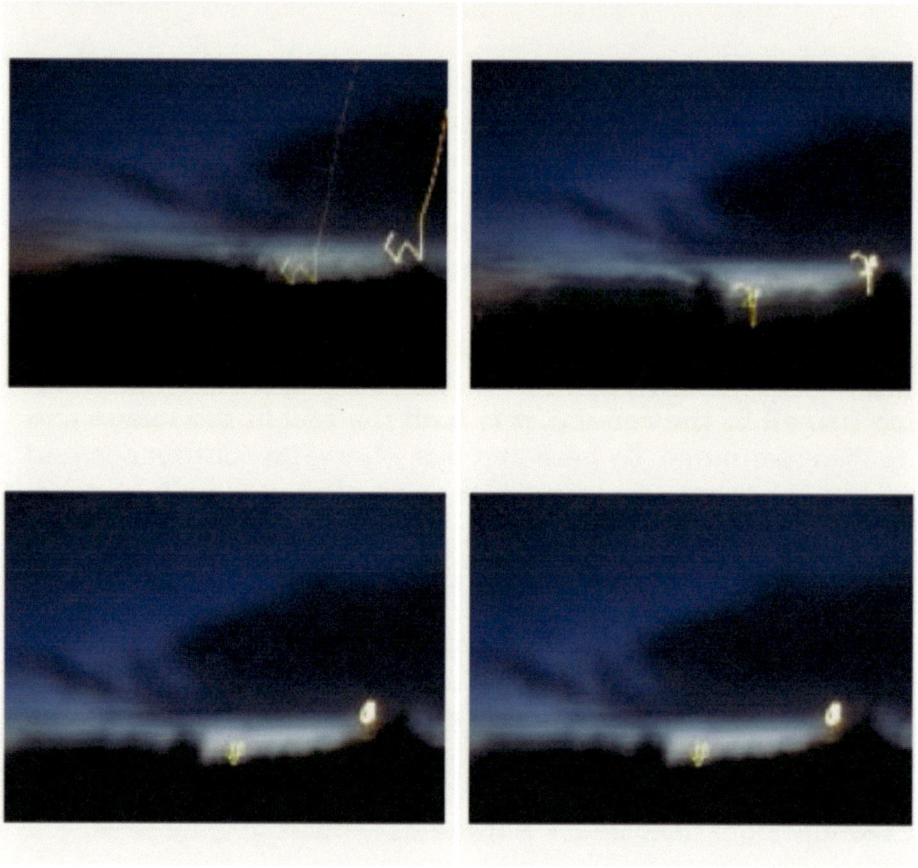

36
Kinds of Blue, 2004

37
For Yves Klein, A Solitary Blue, 2010

site being an event, a photograph, the cinema, the world, the desktop, everyday life, a software program—curating the archive, the image is always an event of photography, of instrumentation with or without an agent. It is also an archival event, its ability to be found.

This procedural approach, this rules-based formality, this consciousness moved me out of the picture and allowed for the getting on of imaging to proceed by way of approach and not result. The this or thusness of this work as photograph turns to imaging photography itself. It turns the occurrence of time to the occurrence of imaging. If it is an image, it reads backwards as a photograph or carries forward with the aura of the photograph—such are its attributes.

It is an idea about the event of photography—and my relationship with cameras, the archive, recording machines, software, accidents and intentions and their capacity to image.

36 Yves Klein spoke to the creation of a milieu within the limits of photography, of imaging: "The object of this endeavor: to create, establish, and present to the public a palpable pictorial state in the limits of a picture gallery. In other words, creation of an ambience, a genuine pictorial climate, and, therefore, an invisible one. This invisible pictorial state within the gallery space should be so present and endowed with autonomous life that it should literally be what has hitherto been regarded as the best overall definition of painting: radiance."

"One of Klein's favorite places for meditation was the basement of a business owned by a friend's father. To mask the claustrophobic quality of the windowless room, Klein created a false sky by painting the ceiling blue. This marked the first time he created a monochromatic painted surface using the color that symbolized limitless space and spiritual purity for him. By 1955, after establishing a Judo school in Paris, Klein committed himself solely to art. In 1956, he held his first major exhibition at the Galerie Colette Allendy. There he showed single-hued paintings which he considered metaphysical fields devoid of emotion" (Hirshhorn Museum).

37 Perhaps photography is our false sky.

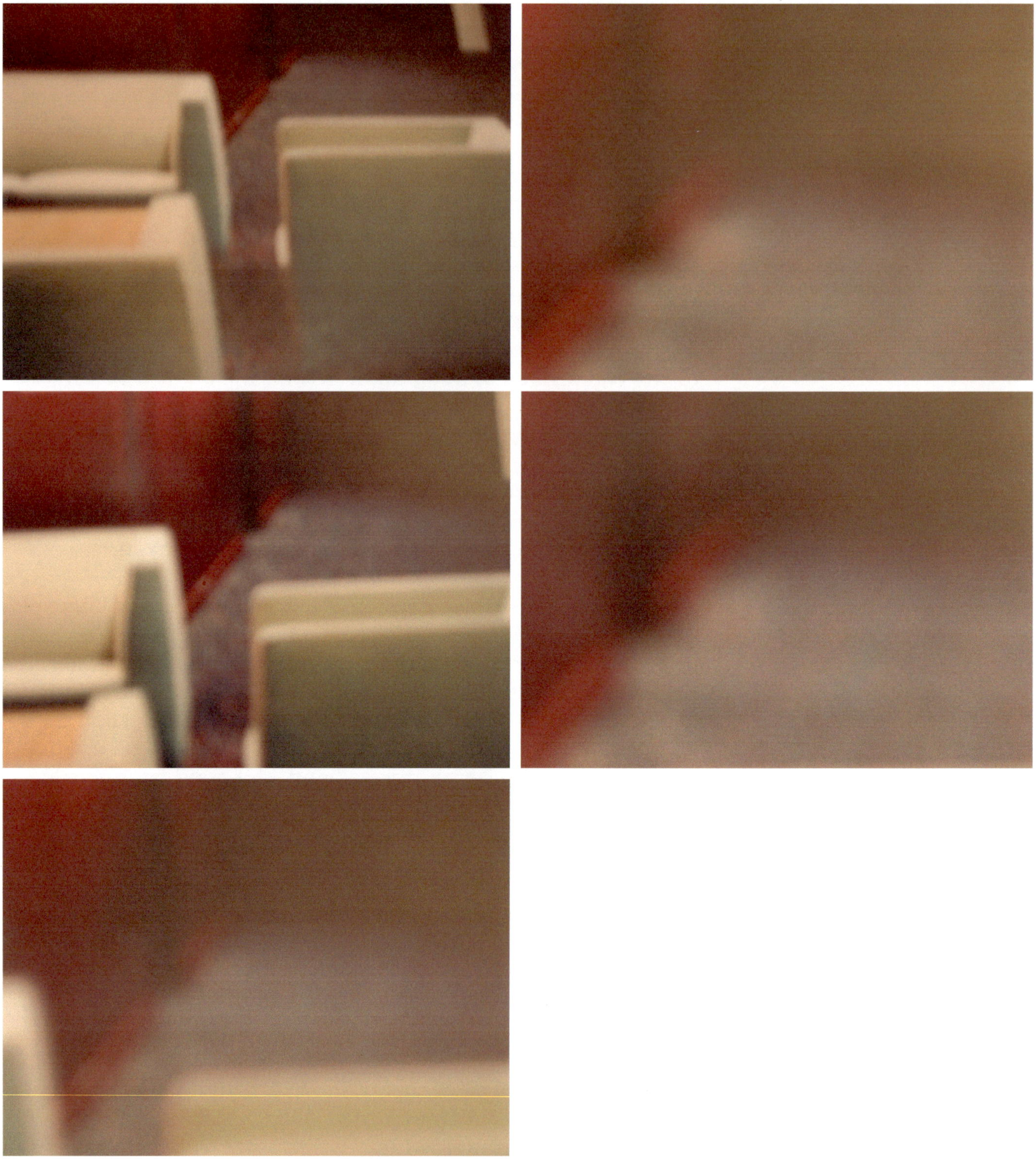

38
Into the Void, 2002

Seeing Again, seeing form in all that formlessness

38 The works in my book *Seeing* were not about distorted traces of reality but realities unto themselves. Realities of the apparatus of the camera, its program.

But in time I ask myself what would it be like to again use the camera to see through the lens an image and bring back through recording an equivalent to my human vision, something recognizable by sight, something that gives the coordinates of space.

What would be the minimal information needed to convey a sense of space, a geometry of corners and windows, of depth, of figure and ground, not light, not the flux of movement but fixity, boundaries, Cartesian dimensions.

Architectural spaces (albeit very small, corners, window frames) are marked equally by the rational as they are the formless. Even the formed, at a certain vantage, its shape disappears and the play of figure and ground give forth vertigo and uncertainty, ushering in disequilibria.

By photographing actual architectural sites and visualizing them at different scales and at different speeds of the photographic, the fragment becomes monumental and its continuous process of decay and regeneration is given vision. The pictures here are architectural secrets, an intimate architecture, a secretive architecture that destabilizes space, that gives forth the formlessness of form.

39
A Fraction of Myself, 2001

How far away I am from Candida Höfer, who prints images practically at the scale of the actual spaces she photographs. She photographs to-scale, straight-on, frontal-angle empty spaces of waiting rooms, interiors, offices. Such depicted spaces are said to depict the social psychology of space.

The photographic presents a double illusion, something seemingly both contiguous with the real and at the same time something real only unto itself. This is to say, the photograph can equally be an instrument of vision in the realm of reason, as well as an instrument that captures doubt and paradox.

39 Space at different proximities and varying scales suggests infinities, mysteries, and conundrums. How can this rationale be marked by sentiment? Perhaps it is that space is inherently perceptual and psychological.

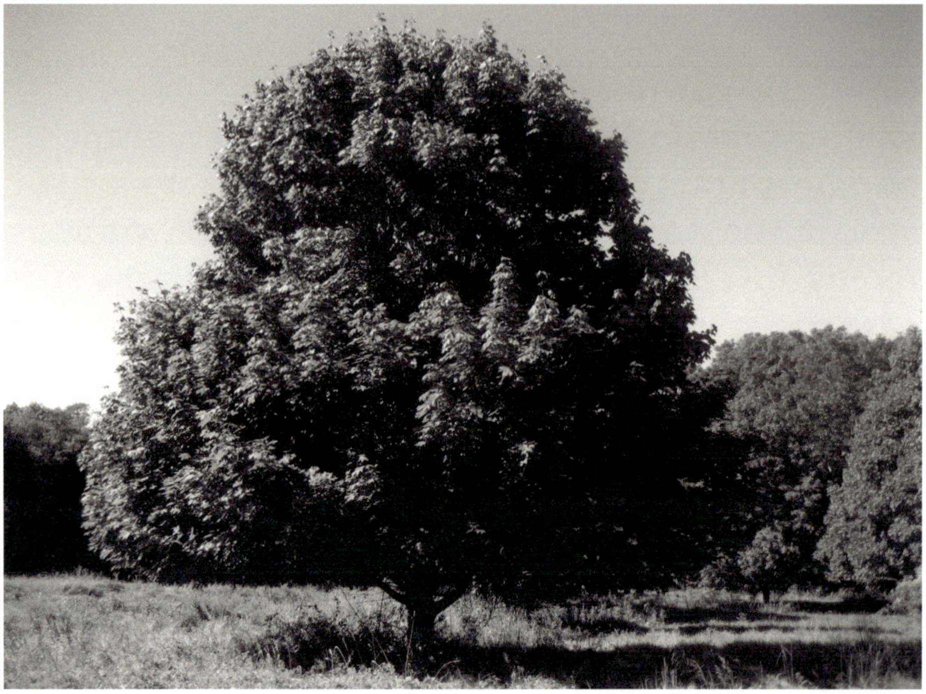
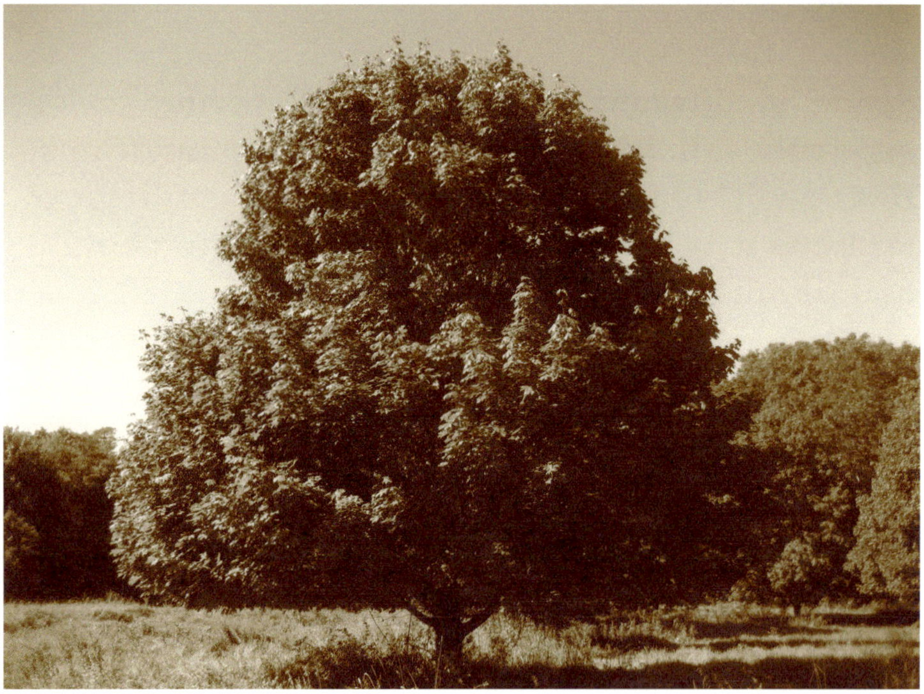

40
You Can See That I'm a Tree, 2007
You Can See That I'm a Tree No. 2, 2007

I no longer want to see traces of the camera apparatus, not blurs and swirls, nor obscure architectural elements. I want the camera to see like I see. I want it to be deadpan, forensic, a machine. What you see is what you get.

I must understand that machine seeing is indifferent to what it sees. This, the art of photography.

40 A tree, a rock, a bird, dead, alive, what's it to the camera? No wonder machines have an aesthetic. And an absolute one.

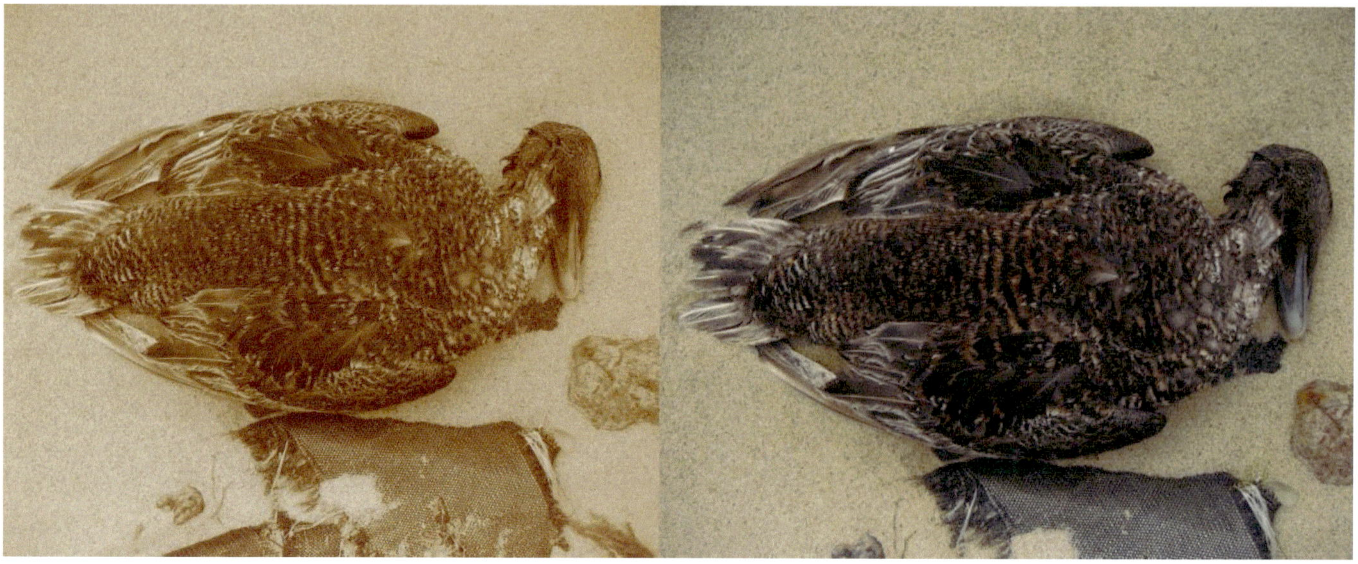

41
A Bird in Hand is Worth... 2007

41 Here the bird is dead. It is a fact, a closed life. A still life. An image.

What is the image, the thing in front of the camera, the thingness of the thing? In these images the camera is a forensic instrument and the objective style of presentation straight up—or is it?

What is it that the camera does?

I deny its straight-up-ness because objectivity and neutrality do not exist.

Three same-sized images seen through the camera lens are seen in different registers—sepia, black and white, and color. In the digital there is no objective camera (there never was), only a camera program that has program instructions. Though I know the straight up, the objective, as a style, as a mode of seeing, exists and can be absolutely persuasive.

Then again: "The photographer is committed to the exhaustion of the photo-program, and to the realization of all the virtualities contained there. The program, however, is rich and nearly impenetrable. The photographer is committed, then, to discovering hidden virtualities in the program. He handles the camera, turns it around, looks into it and through it. If he looks through the camera into the world, he does so not because he is interested in the world, but because he is in search of the yet undiscovered virtualities in the camera program enabling him to produce new information. His interest is concentrated on the camera, and the world 'put there' is a pretext for his realization of the virtualities contained in the program. In sum: he does not work, he does not aim at changing the world: he looks for information to be realized in a photograph.
—Vilém Flusser, *Towards a Philosophy of Photography*

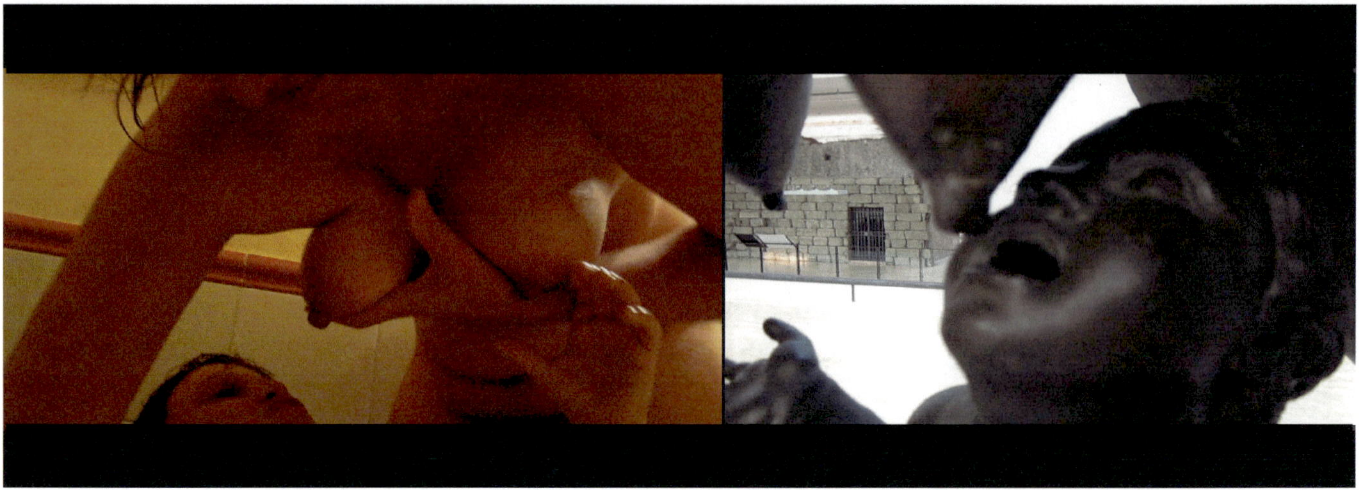

42
Roman Holiday, 2009

43
A Tree in Many Parts, 2007

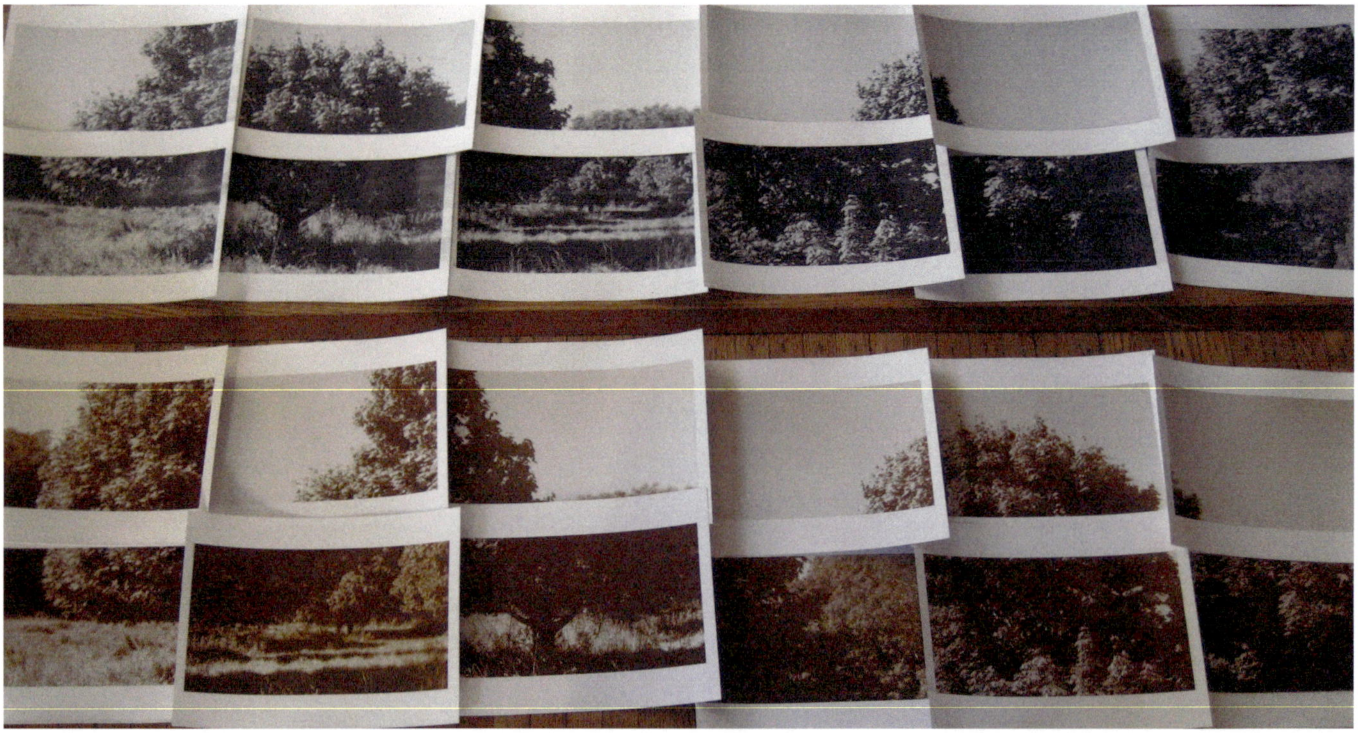

42 The image is an event of recording, the instrument of recording. Recording, nothing else. And yet it is always an image in the conversation of images, always put to work to say something, to mean something, it can never be itself.

43 But this desire for the camera to approximate what I see does not last long. I will not believe in the image, and so permute it, cut it up, reorient it. Here the one image of the tree becomes a permutation of a tree and is presented in twelve images made from the image tree, and so I produce a new tree image, a rearranging of tree.

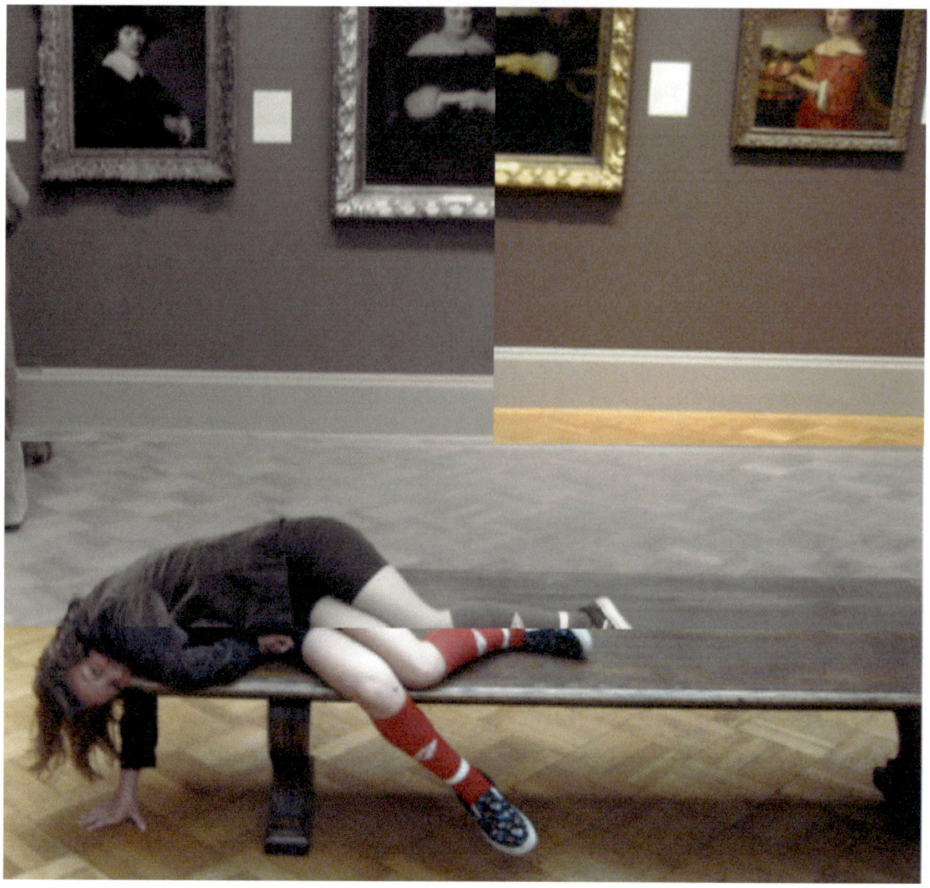

44
Double Dutch, 2007

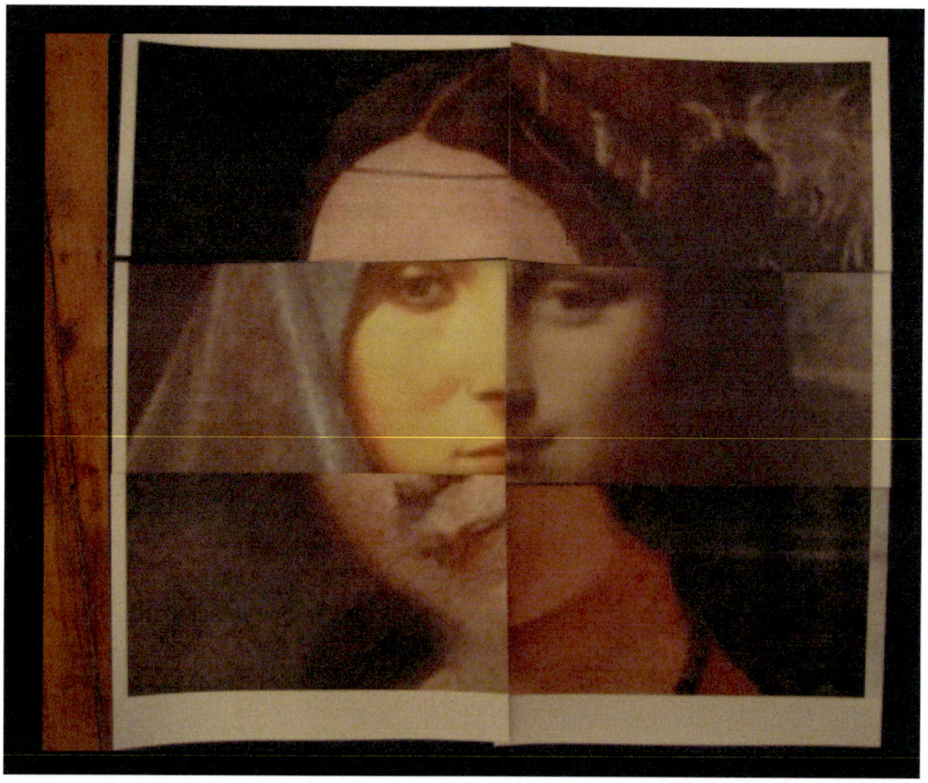

45
Portrait of a Woman, 2008

44 A single image is one thing; an image next to another is two things plus a third thing. The arrangement of images, of photographs for display puts in circulation something that hovers between and among the entirety of all select images. This process might be thought of as the other side of imaging, and indeed, a kind of imaging in its own right. As described by Roland Barthes in his essay "The Third Meaning," imaging as arrangement might be said to create meaning that "opens the field of meaning totally." It is this field of relations within the image that interests me.

45 A refusal of the one single perfect moment.

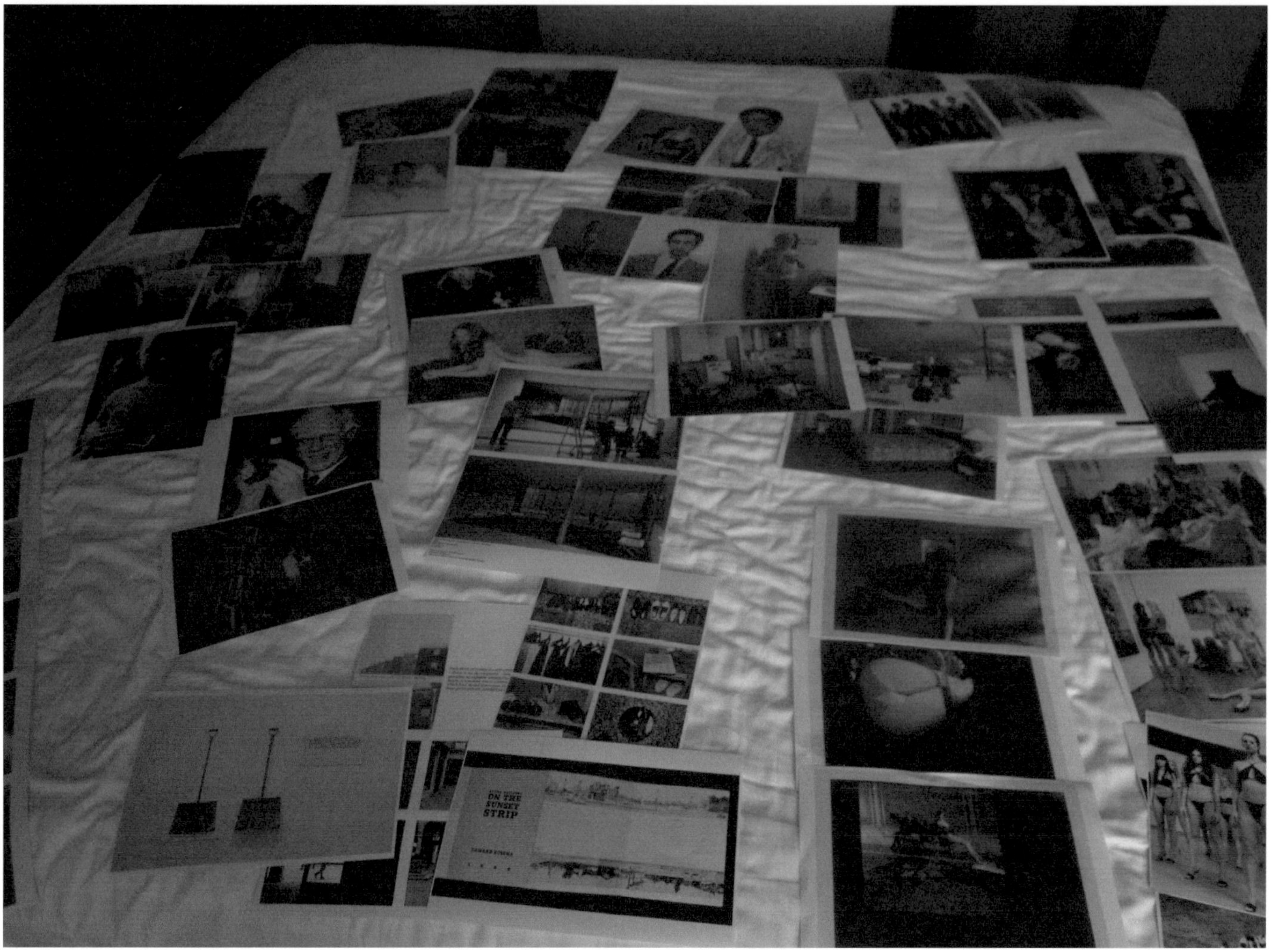

46
Print Copies of Photographs on Bed in Shanghai in Preparation for a Talk, 2012

46 Here, photocopies of images used for a workshop in Shanghai. It makes me think about what becomes the set of images for an exhibition. Why some and not others? And why this one, then that? Is it because such strategies come from an interior sense of the initial images, from a meaning that, Barthes writes, "seeks me out"? For artists, curators, and exhibition designers, the selection, arrangement, and presentation of images puts in valence the reading of any one particular image. An image is always an image next to another image. In that sense, the photograph "here" is one image and "there," another.

The finished work, either in a book or a series, or a period of work, becomes a set of images, and together seen, bound by a room or a publication, might be said to represent a performative reading-imaging, images across image.

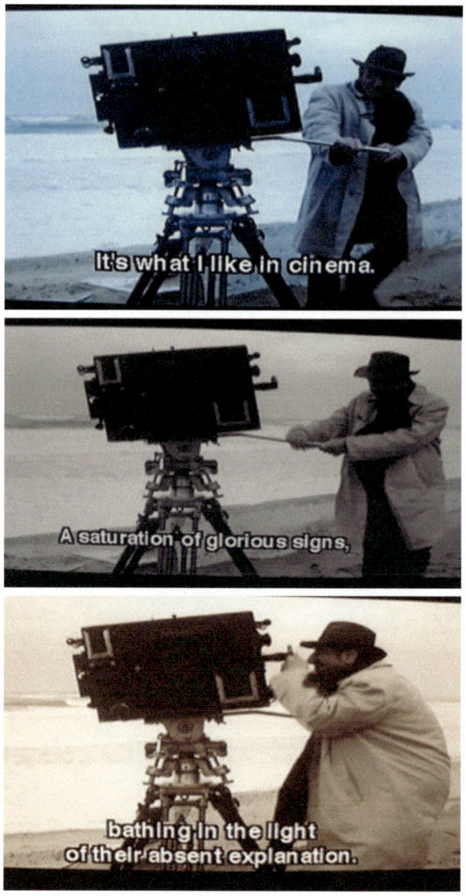

47
A Saturation of Glorious Signs, Godard in Three Colors, 2005

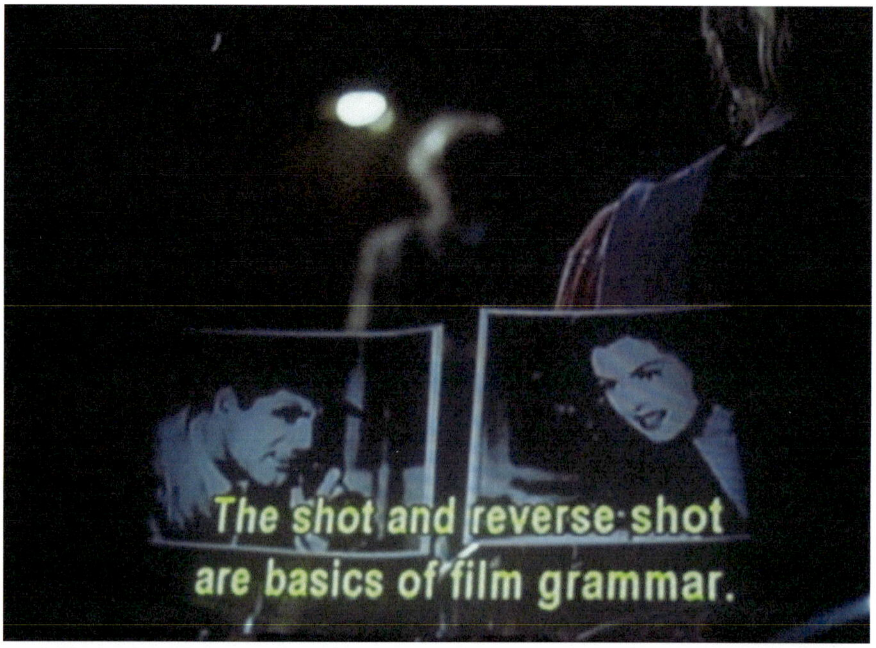

48
Shot Reverse Shot, Notre Musique, 2008

47 Like cinema, photography can be thought of in terms of shot and reverse shot—not one discrete image after another, but as a correspondence or relay of images. An image may be thought of as one in a flow of all images that one has seen and might have imagined. Perhaps, as William Burroughs suggests, it is surprised recognition that captures us in the image.

48 We can also say this same recognition happens within the image: foreground, background, dark and light, posed or unposed, the image orchestrates space and scale. What is it that can surprise us in images? Here we enter the domain of the photograph proper, its composition and methods, its forming ideas and metaphors, those things that make a photograph legible.

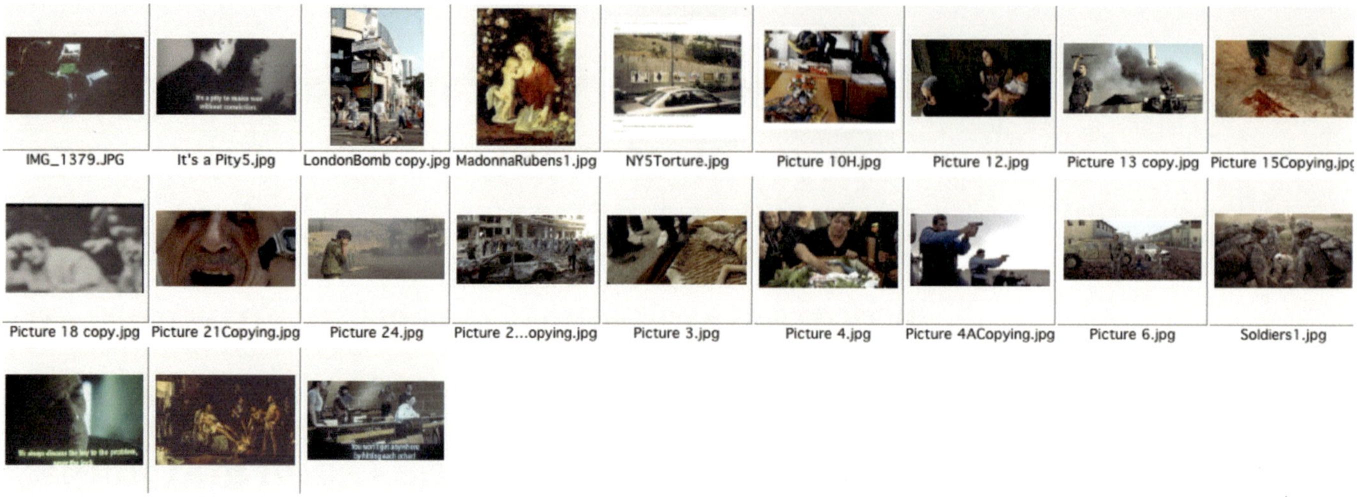

49
The Image Alone, 2006

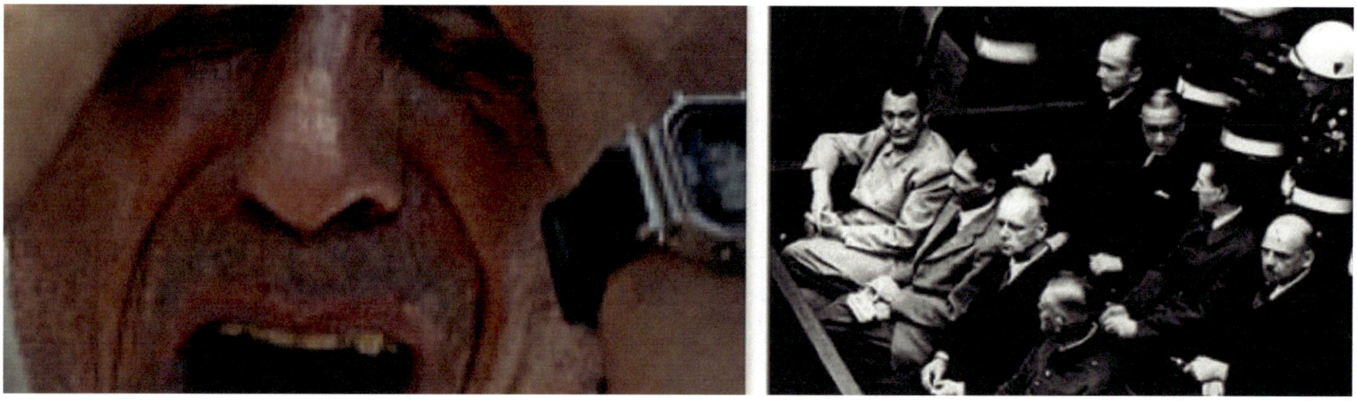

50
The Cries of Silence, What Am I Seeing?
What Am I Hearing? Who Is this I Am Looking At?, 2006

49 Seeing comes out of an enormous collective and cumulative training. We learn sight, and in that learning, in that habituation, in the domestication of sight, we learn not to look for certain things, not to see things, things it may never occur to us to see or perhaps no longer need to see. We know where they are, so we don't need to see them. Walk down the street with a seven-year-old and they will point out things, one after the other, that you just didn't see. There are so many things, so many social actions, that are right in front of us, that are out of vision, let alone those things that bring to sight our imagination.

Our seeing then is not at all open. It is predisposed in certain ways, cultural and biological. Yet it is this limit that is always the opening of imaging.

As Clive Scott of the Sainsbury Centre for Visual Arts has said in relationship to the use of photographs in W. G. Sebald's novels, "With photography, we are peculiarly shut out of the image; we have no access to it; it has already happened and nothing further can happen to it. It is quite beyond our control. The photograph presents us with a now that is then, a here that is there, something that is profoundly unaware of us and of any text that might be attached to it."

50 Yet in this closed quality, the image, all images, are extraordinarily open, to mean and be many things. In this sense a photograph presents countless possible narratives. They are events that can take on almost any narration, as they do in Sebald's novels.

Perhaps it is only images that will know how to see other images. As with sight, we see relationally. To see images is to see them next to others. Yes, shot, reverse shot, in ever continuing sequence.

The image that becomes our memory can become any memory. Photography is an art that gives us sight. That allows us to see.

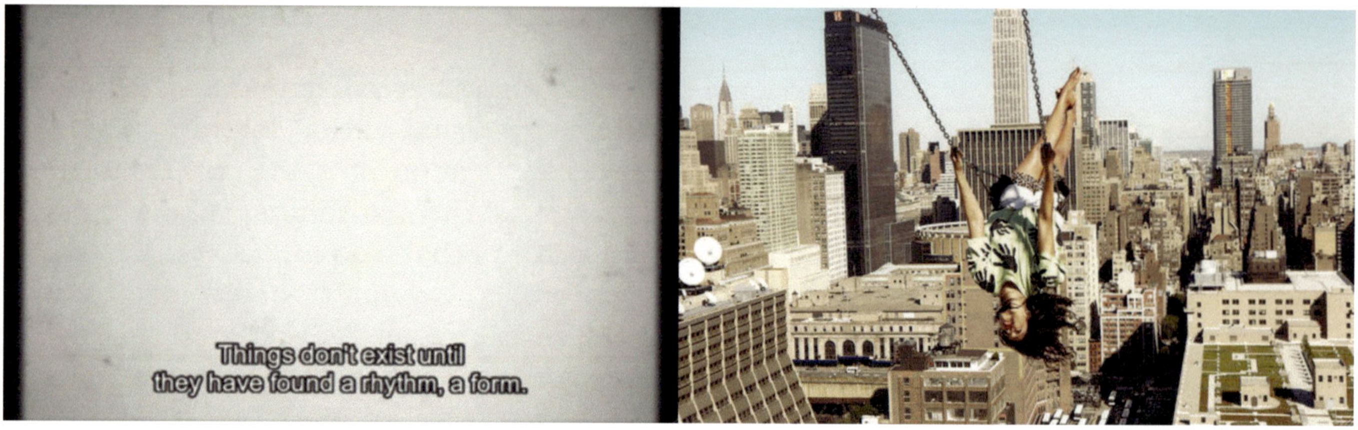

51
Things Don't Exist Until They Have Found a Rhythm, A Form, 2009

52
Double Feature, 2009

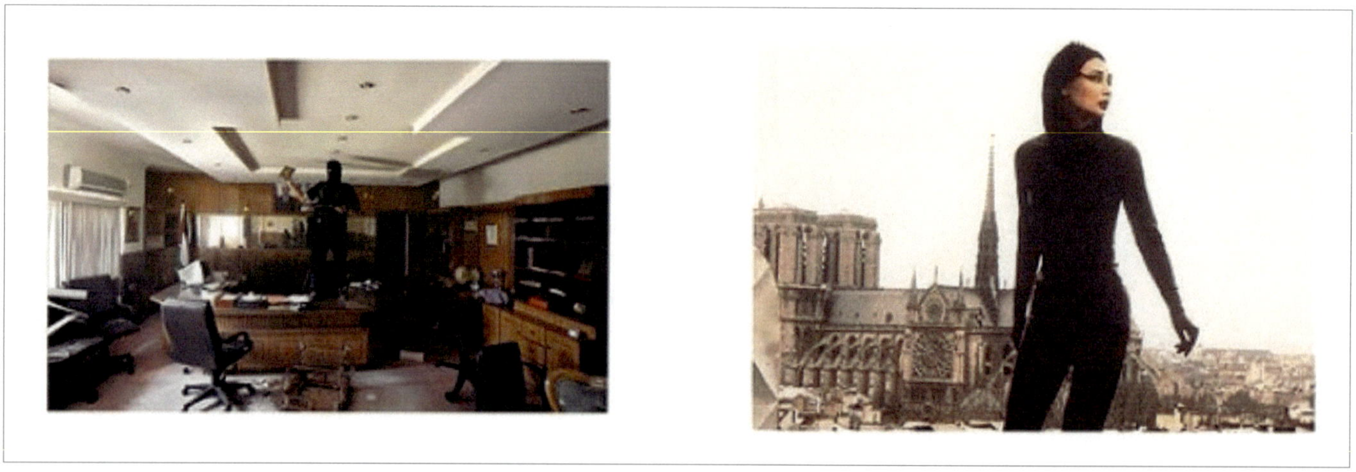

51 But it is also a form. And as the title card here says, things don't exist until they have found a rhythm, a form.

52 "Today there is a quarrel over representation that sets art and the official image of reality against each other; it is propagated by advertising discourse, relayed by the media, organized by an ultralight ideology of consumption and social competition. In our daily lives, we come across fictions, representations, and forms that sustain this collective imaginary whose contents are dictated by power. Art puts us in the presence of counterimages, forms that question social forms. In the face of the economic abstraction that makes daily life unreal, or an absolute weapon of techno-market power, artists reactivate forms by inhabiting them, pirating private property and copyrights, brands and products, museum-bound forms and signatures. If the downloading of forms (these samplings and remakes) represents important concerns today, it is because these forms urge us to consider global culture as a toolbox, an open narrative space rather than a uni-vocal narrative and a product line. Instead of prostrating ourselves before works of the past, we can use them....

"It is up to us to judge artworks in terms of the relations they produce in the specific contexts they inhabit. Because art is an activity that produces relationships to the world and in one form or another makes its relationships to space and time material."
—Nicolas Bourriaud, *Postproduction*

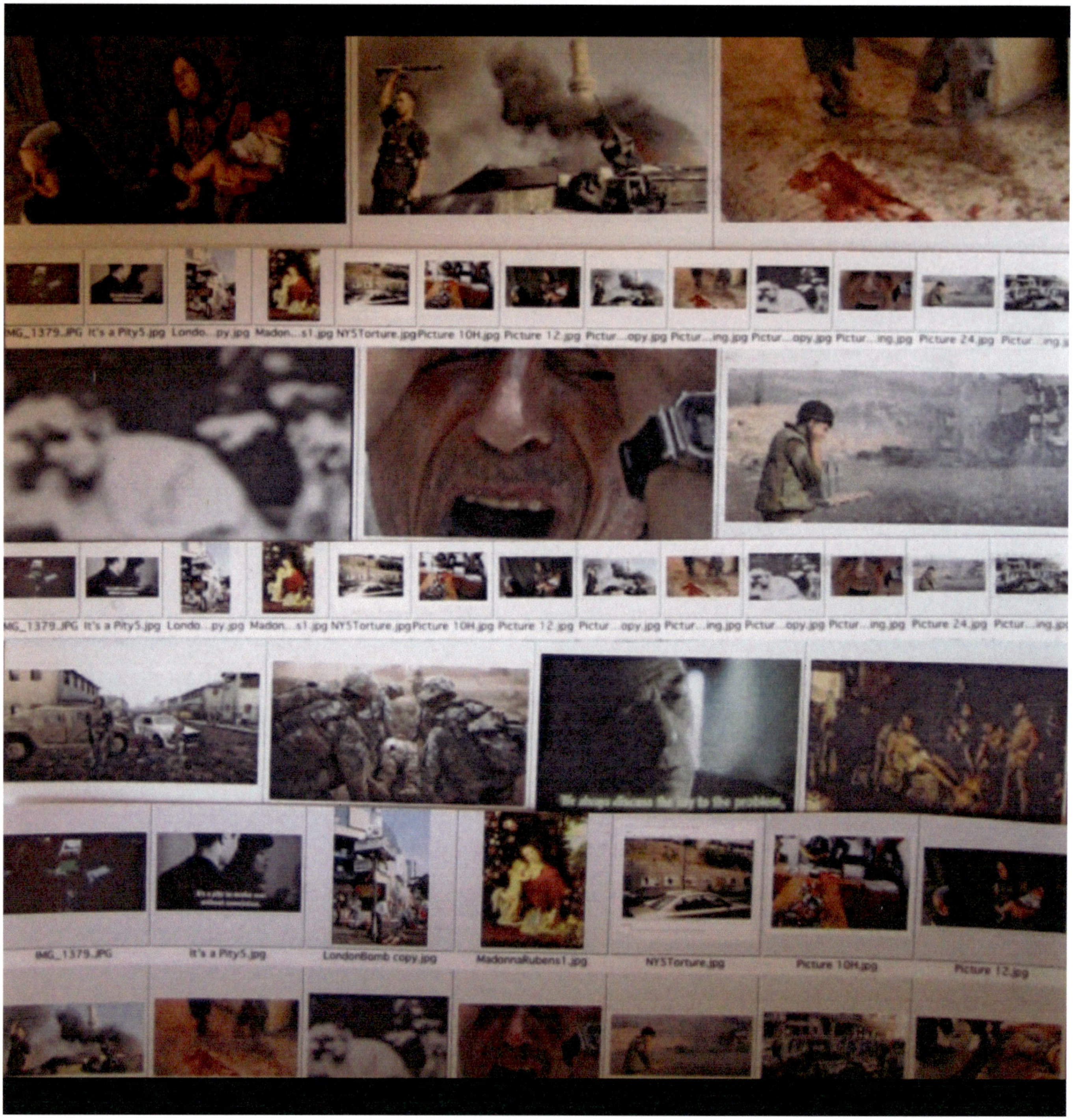

53
The Image, a Witness to What?, 2006

The Image, a witness to what?

Literature, painting, film, photography—all speak to things we know or can imagine happened, to an elsewhere that is here only by virtue of this telling, these signs. The image is a witness, a transcription, doubled, simulated, transcribed, transposed, that not only tells us about the apparatus but is an event in itself. An event of authorship, of a time and place.

The Image, Alone > The image is never alone.

53 In the image here, I found it impossible to present a single image and found the only solution was to compress the entire series into a single composite image.

I have often wanted to have all the photographs in a newspaper printed on one sheet, to be seen all at once, as shown here, without words. Instead of the *New York Times* using photographs to tell stories, like Sebald in his novels, I would be most pleased to simply be sent the pictures with the paper divided in three sections: Images, Writing, Ads. So no captions to photographs, and writing with no pictures, and the ads all by themselves.

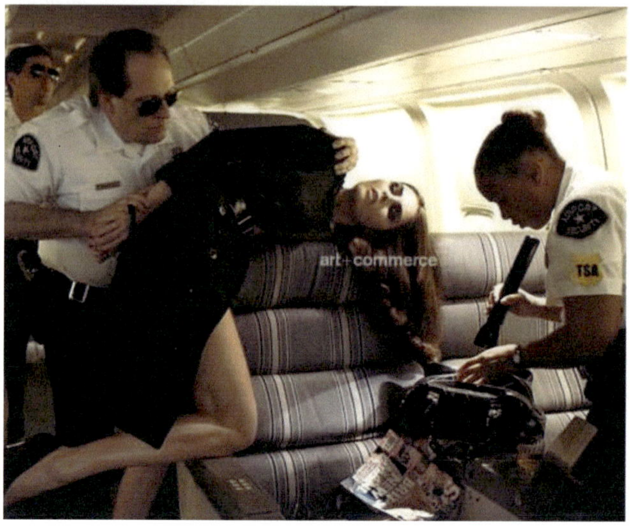

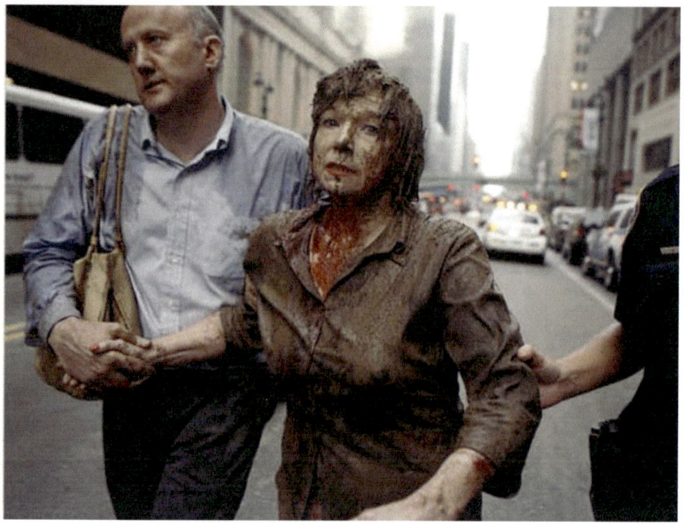

54
Fashion Journalism, 2009

Facts and Fictions. Doubling.

54 I often put images next to each other. Each presents itself and then tells us something about the other and then again something else as the two of them. The image already presents us with a condition of seeing, yet this condition is often, in time, no longer visible to us. Our conditioning and habituation blind us to things. Perhaps that is what photography is, another seeing. There was a film, *The Gods Must Be Crazy*—a wonderful title—in which a small tribe of Africans find a Coke bottle thrown out of an airplane. Having never seen such a bottle they spend the rest of the film trying to discern what it is.

A variation on this game is played by Vik Muniz, who will remake famous photographs from chocolate or dust. In some sense it is the same game played by Thomas Demand, remaking everyday objects and scenes as paper tableaux in miniature and then scaling them up in photographs.

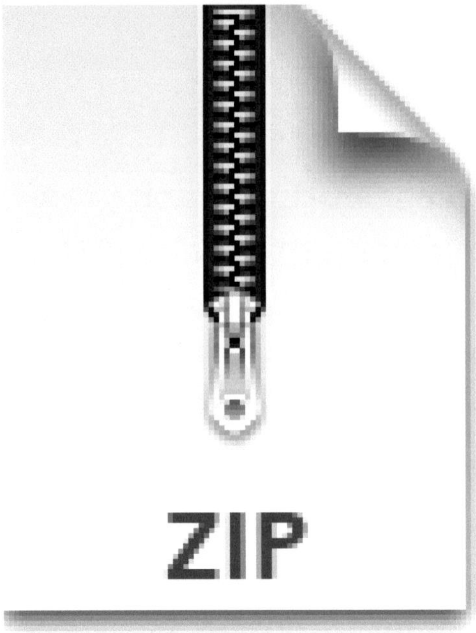

55
Zip, 2003

Seeing, then, is not a question of facts and science but a conditioning. The artist remakes our seeing so that things once not there, invisible to us, can be seen. But we, as readers, must remake the artist's seeing for us to see. Photography invites us to do that. To see photography is to grasp a way of seeing. It is to reclaim our sight, to bring our tactile sense back to sight. We must invite ourselves to use photography as a tool to read photography, its circulatory system and exchange value, its materiality, as image object and as a file.

55 In the electronic the image circulates as a file and can be processed, degraded, transmuted.

"So then how about a specific thing called 'image'? It is a complete mystification to think of the digital image as a shiny immortal clone of itself.... The bruises of images are its glitches and artifacts, the traces of its rips and transfers. Images are violated, ripped apart, subjected to interrogation and probing. They are stolen, cropped, edited, and reappropriated. They are bought, sold, leased. Manipulated and adulated. Reviled and revered. To participate in the image means to take part in all of this."
—Hito Steyerl, "A Thing like You and Me"

The photograph then is not only an image, making visible a condition of seeing, but it's also a mutable object, a thing, a file, a system of transport, a condition in perpetual transfer, forever in exchange, taking on new appearance, decay, and transmutation. As Steyerl goes on to say per the image, the JPEG file: "If identification is to go anywhere, it has to be with this material aspect of the image, with the

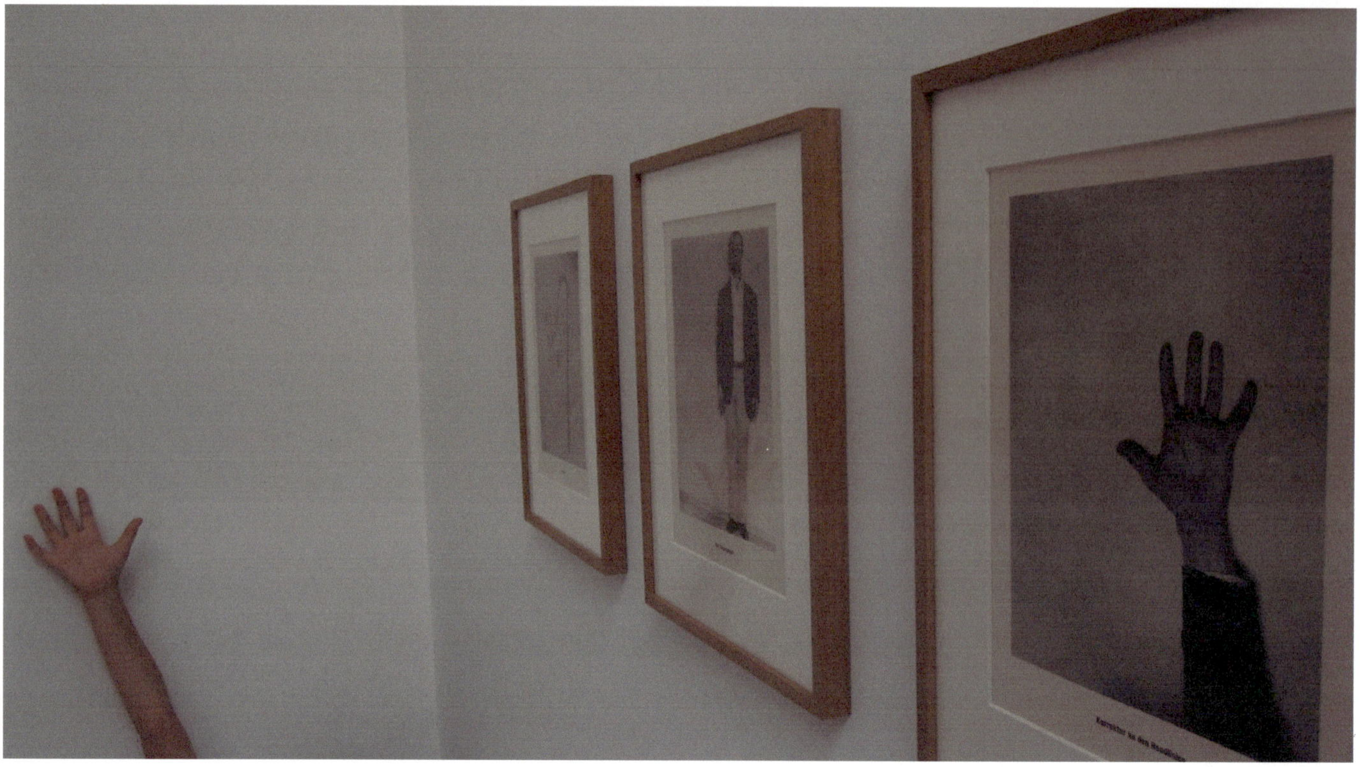

56
From My Hand to Yours, 2011

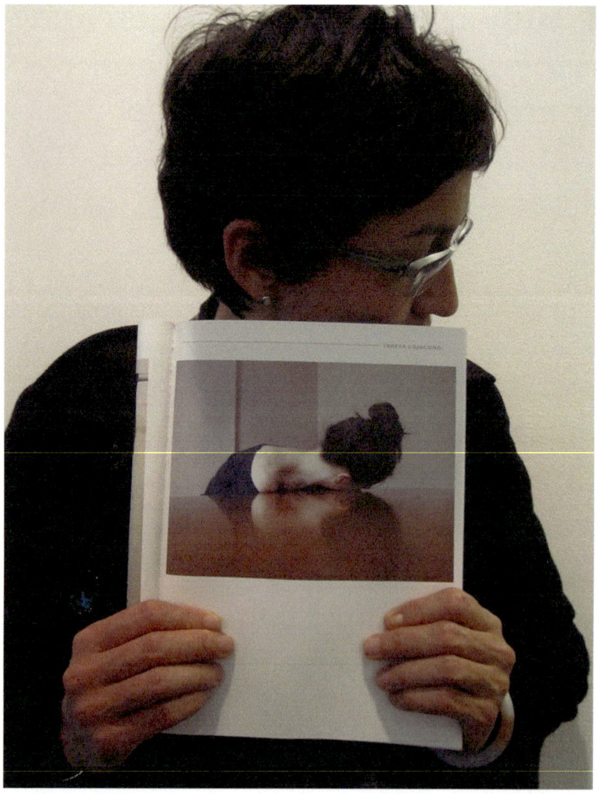

57
I See You Look Away, 2012

image as thing, not as representation. And then it perhaps ceases to be identification, and instead becomes participation."

56 But then what of the image as photograph, an object, a fact of scale, of being, stable for a moment, an instantiation of its file, as an object in space, outside a book, outside a computer screen, at scale at times in relation to ourselves in space and our embodiedness. The photograph is not the idea of something or a picture of something. It is a thing, an object. The printed photograph takes the image to something much more than what it represents—as Godard would say, "a glorious sign bathing in the light of an absent explanation."

If we could only hold back from naming and simply experience it. I always want to touch the photograph. Is this why I photograph, to touch the things I cannot?

57 Here the photograph the woman holds in hand is a kind of subtitle that announces photography itself. The image-photograph is a material fact inside the image. Photography confers a factualness, or is it here the publication that gives the fact of the photograph? Then again is it the woman's hands holding the object of the photograph that gives it its materiality? The book frames the image, the image redoubled by the photograph.

"The art I call conceptual is such because it is based on an inquiry into the nature of art.... Thus, it is ... a working out, a thinking out, of all the implications of all aspects of the concept 'art' ..."
—Joseph Kosuth

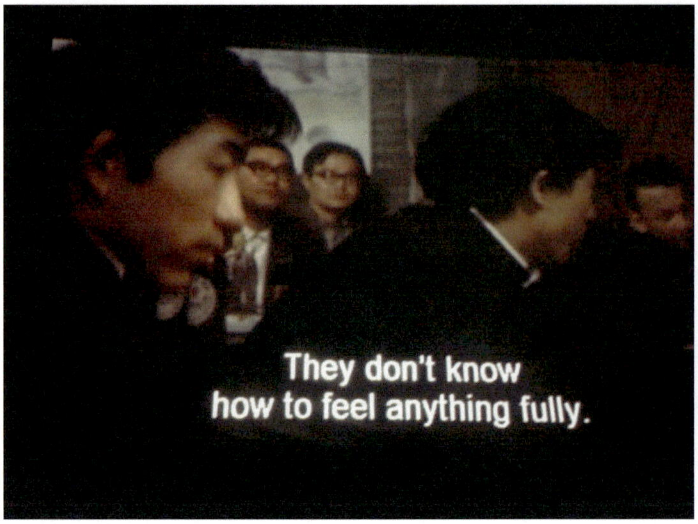

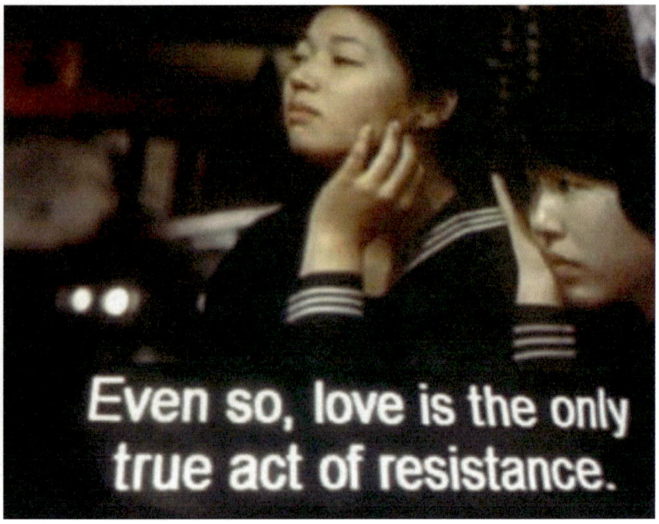

58
Words and Images, Oshima, Love Is the Only True Act of Resistance, 2011

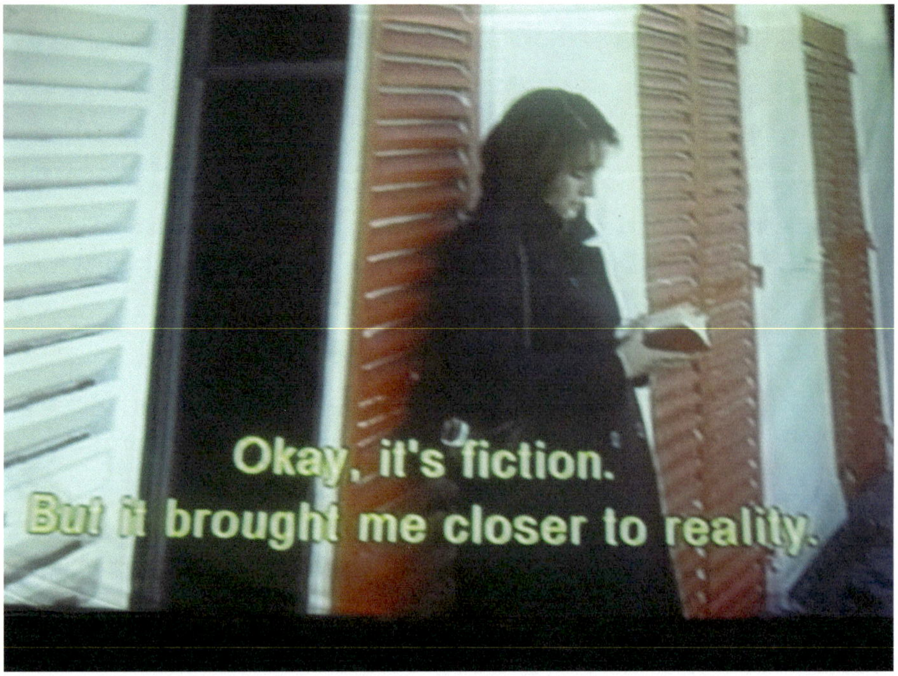

59
It's Fiction But It Brought Me Closer to Reality, 2009

58 I like subtitles as they narrate images. I like images as they narrate subtitles. The film still is like photographing the cinema. In this case the film still comes with narration.

59 For some time I photographed cinema images as stills in a series called *Film Stills, Still History*. The series of prints were screen and subtitle excerpts from Chinese, French, and Japanese films spanning the past fifty years. The sequence of stills creates a nonlinear reading of cinematic history by piecing together characters and themes across cultures and generations as a way to explore the relationship of the individual to society, but moreover the individual's personal revolution-evolution in relationship to societal revolution.

The cinema is always a sequence of shots, not unlike the photographer's series. But unlike the cinema, photography remained silent and suggests that the single image speaks. But how does the image speak? Or how can photography speak images like cinema? I am not sure, but I like the silence of the photograph. I like its aloneness, but I always meet it with the recollection of other images. And once one image is next to another, it's both itself and something else.

60

Meta Fictions, 2010

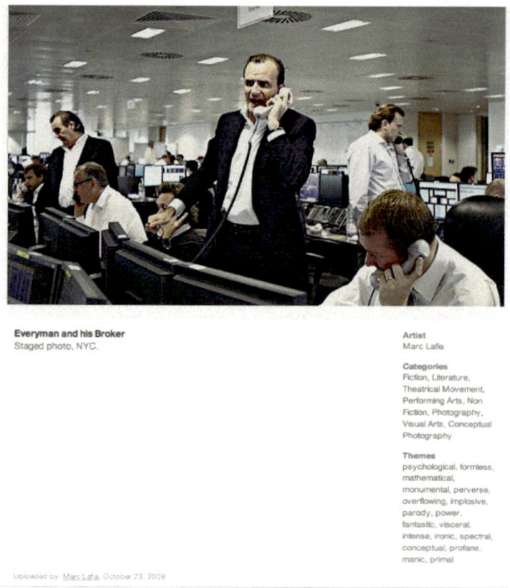

61

Meta Fictions, or, Index as Narrative, 2010

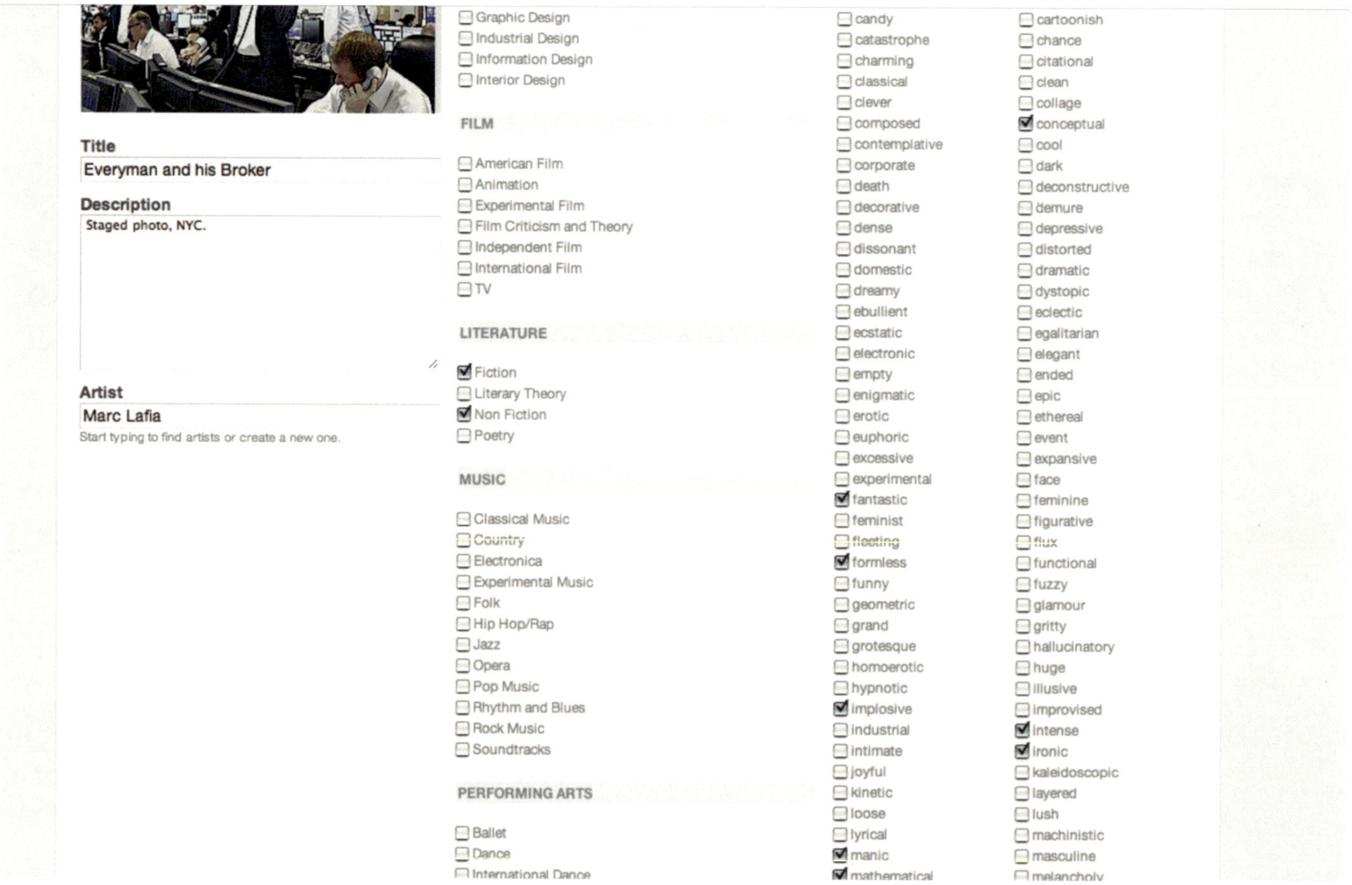

60 I am always intrigued by how we find images and wanted to create works that reflect the condition of search, which is often invisible to the photograph itself. In a series of works called *Forms Factor*, I wanted to construct photographs that revealed the data behind them, not so much the pixel data of hue and intensity but the narrative and indexing of keyword data. The photograph here, from the series *Meta Fictions*, is not an image above a series of key words and metadata. The whole of it is a single constructed photograph.

In the condition of network, in our electronic and digital archives, software forms, including key words, like subtitles, lead us to images, and read them before we ever see them. As software and users see and read images, then index, report, and narrate what has been seen, it is then metadata that leads us to the image.

In the vast archive of the network, the image is first a series of characteristics, of intensities, of hues and saturation, as well as tags, words, and then and only then are we presented with the visual artifact.

61 For *Meta Fictions*, I designed, with a team, the indexing form, the software program to tag and give description to images. The idea was to show that the software form is in its own right a camera indexing an image. The form factor is a filter creating a record of a file. I wanted the photograph to include such words as *perverse*, *intense*, *visceral*, *power*, *monumental*, *implosive*, all of the words you see in the photograph. It is a conceptual photograph pointing to the photograph as an object, creatively narrated by its indexing.

The digital allows for the creation of the form as well as the content. The software index form, as an information artifact, is commonplace in the world of Web 2.0, user-generated content. The form factor with social tagging including comment, like, share—all become part of the image.

The image is the design, the software, the social system of circulation, the photography, the tags, the context.

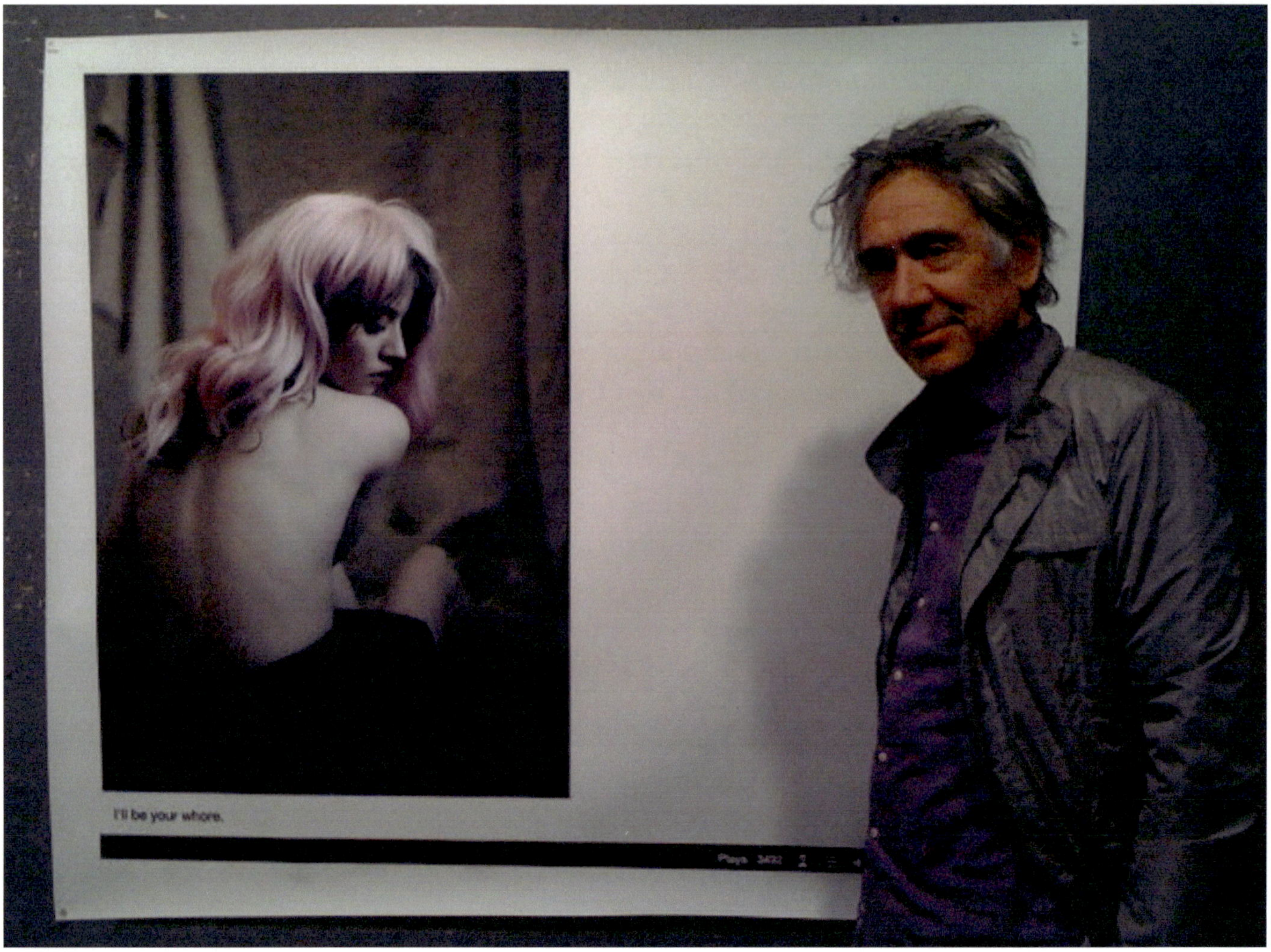

62
I'll Be Your Whore, 2012

Increasingly I find myself photographing our electronic culture online, the way it moves and speaks, its protocols and social etiquette. I have had a number of Tumblr blogs and there are a great many fashion and photography Tumblr blogs I follow. I set about to photograph the milieu of it, as a kind of club, as a social space, as an actuality, as a social set.

The currency of Tumblr is the visual—visual imagery, attended by annotations and exchange. It is images that set in motion networks and social relations that shape and form the sociality of this particular social media. Here in the tendrils of the network, within Tumblr, images of fashion, celebrity, pornography, anime are circulated to express feelings of desire, abjection, fear, loathing, and joy, and many networks and social relations are then formed.

If much of photography allows us to see a great variety of subcultures, religious, sexual, drug related, social classes, neighborhoods, then how to photograph the intimacy of bloggers, lonely, sexy, abject, in love, tentative, brazen, and bold, all these affects and emotions as they are expressed through the annotating and circulating of images. The Tumblr blogger often has a passion for images and expresses it in likes and comments, in their very postings.

I wanted to capture this sense, not the image alone, isolated and monumentalized, but the annotated and public/private attendant to the circulated image. Such images are possessed by everyone, and yet, paradoxically, both as photographs in the art world and on Tumblr, they are owned singularly.

62 / 63 I want to represent the feelings expressed through comments and tags that then constitute a social milieu around images. I want to see the bloggers not seen, in the way that only photography can see and make things seen. So using file scans, I printed the very small images as large photographs, sometimes as large as fifty by forty-two

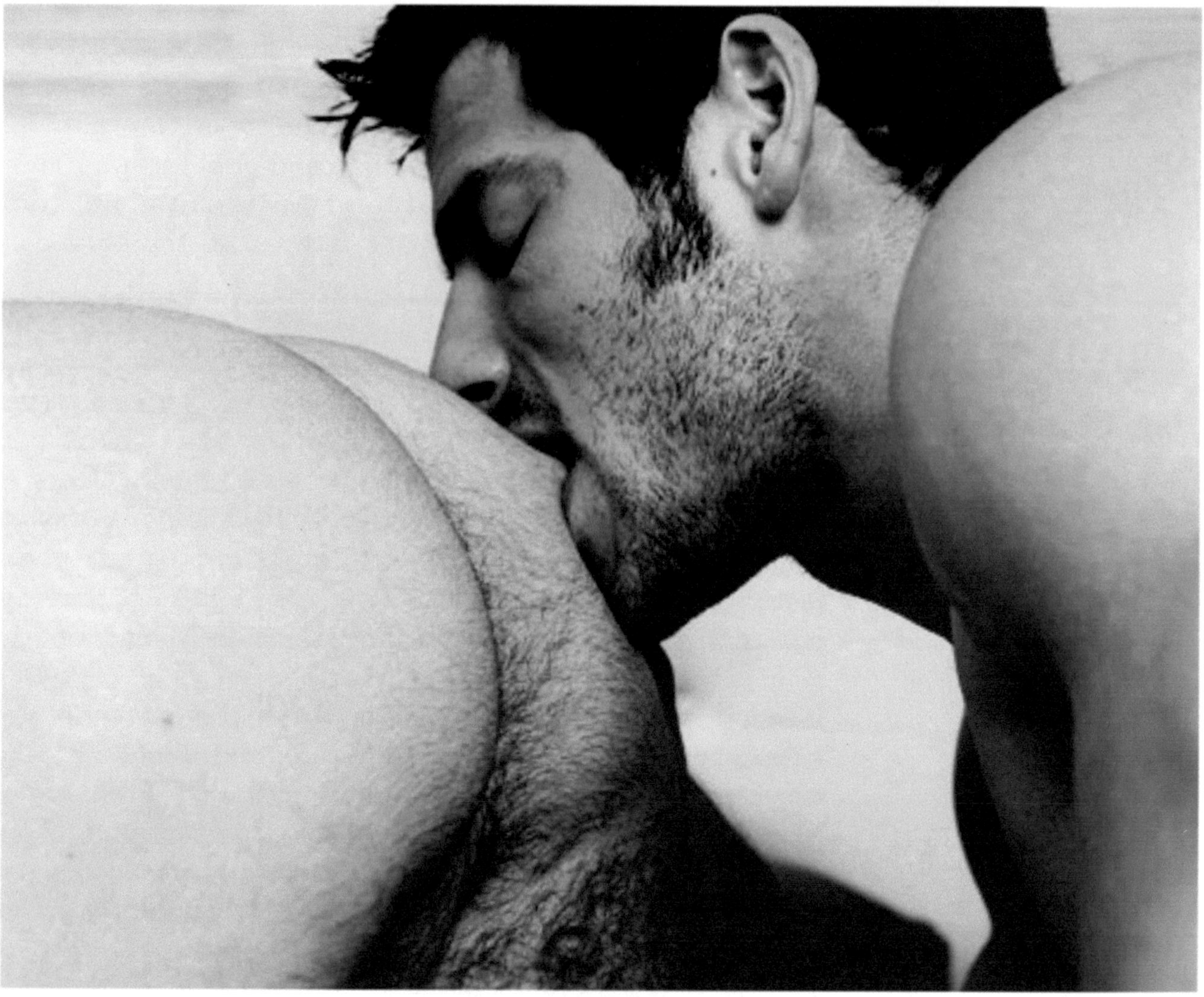

love doin' it and have it done on me :P

Reblogged 2 months ago from nudebeat (originally from averagejoeguys) 597 notes

Source: averagejoeguys

Love Doin' It And Have It Done On Me :P

inches, thereby taking what is ordinarily seen at a remove out of their electronic environment and then presenting them as photographs at close to human scale in the physical world. Here the intimate and private is made large and public. Like the series *Form Factors*, I show the text of bloggers next to the images, the likes and comments, the reblogging, the conversation around the images. Like off-screen space in cinema, the blogger would not be seen directly; and if they were, it would be in the presence of their name and a comment.

Isn't that often what photography does? Makes the private public, takes a moment out of time, puts something in a very altered context, a war in a newspaper, a forgotten social class in a museum? But here something is different: rather than being at a remove, perhaps voyeuristic, it brings into the image its social construction, depicting the construction of the social around the image.

The image archive is now infinitely reproduced and owned by everyone. We use it to explore our private desires, one to one, one to many. In *The Tumblr Room* I want to photograph the social discourse and groups that are shaped around photography and images, reveal how in our electronic spaces, intimacy is lived in public. We are always already photographed; we see by rephotographing; we exist by being imaged.

How we see and read, how we write privately in a chat or on our blogs, is very intimate yet strangely public. The screen gives us a certain courage and a certain shamelessness, and our emotions are more intense in the anonymity of the screen, our self-loathing, our sense of grandness, sexuality, hurt. We are all behind the screen now, behind and in front of the camera, not only in social media but in our medicine, our warfare, our finances, our phones. The screen, the viewfinder is the instrumentation that gives us, and through which we produce, our realities. Photography can see this for us.

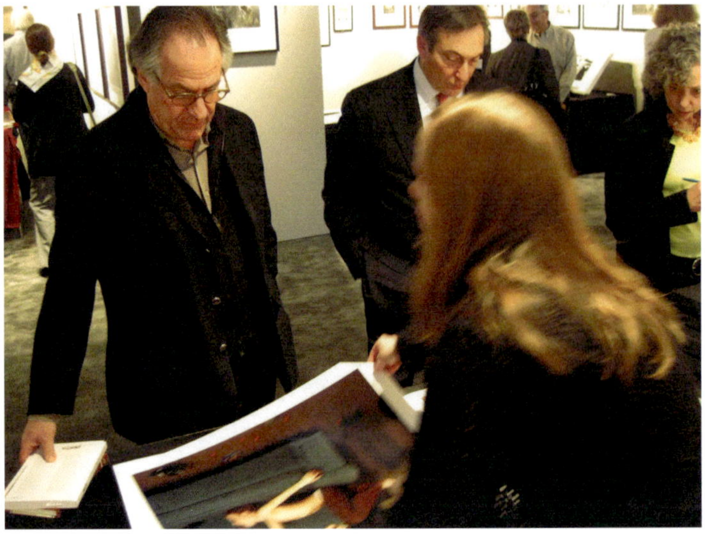

64
The Photography Collectors, 2006

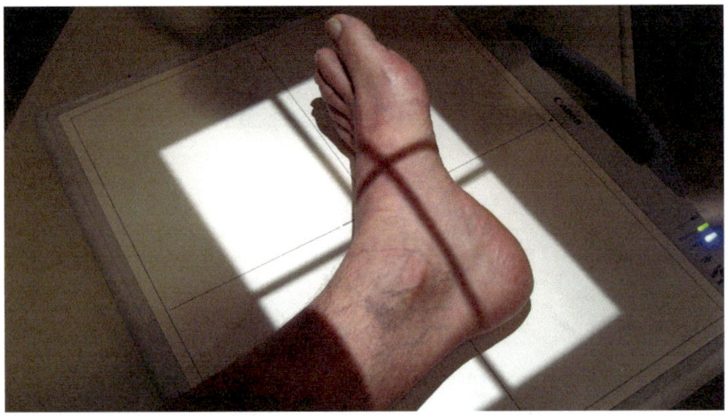

65
Ready for My Close Up, 2010

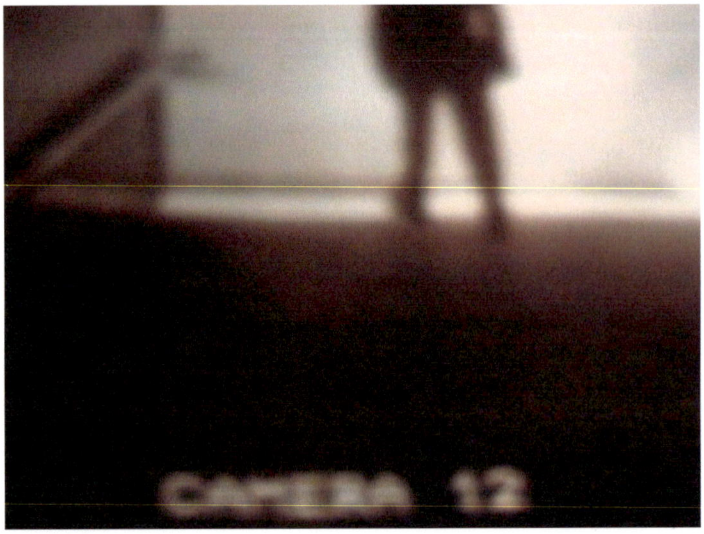

66
Camera 12, 2004

64 Here image is a print, a thing to press all your senses up against, something you can take possession of, something singular (even if editioned). The collector more than the photographer collects photography. Few photographers work to produce photographs, most images. The photographer does not collect images, she finds them, uncovers them, forges the image, creates and constructs the image possibility, that which might be a photograph. The photographer who produces photographs does not see an image but a photograph.

65 Like an x-ray, the substance of representation is already our predisposition to see in a particular way.

66 What are we looking for in looking-scanning an image? What is there but the desire to see? To see what? When we look for one thing we don't see something else. Our sight blinds us, our predispositions have us not see the things we don't want to see or invent things that are not there. We must use photography to see photography.

In the film *Blow-Up*, we can't see "it," the primal scene, the image the protagonist keeps blowing up, the photograph he has taken that he suspects is a murder in the garden. We keep blowing it up, further and further, but "it" is not to be found.

In the last scene of the film we see the pantomimes on the tennis court "playing" tennis. We "see" the imaginary ball. We imagine we see what is not there.

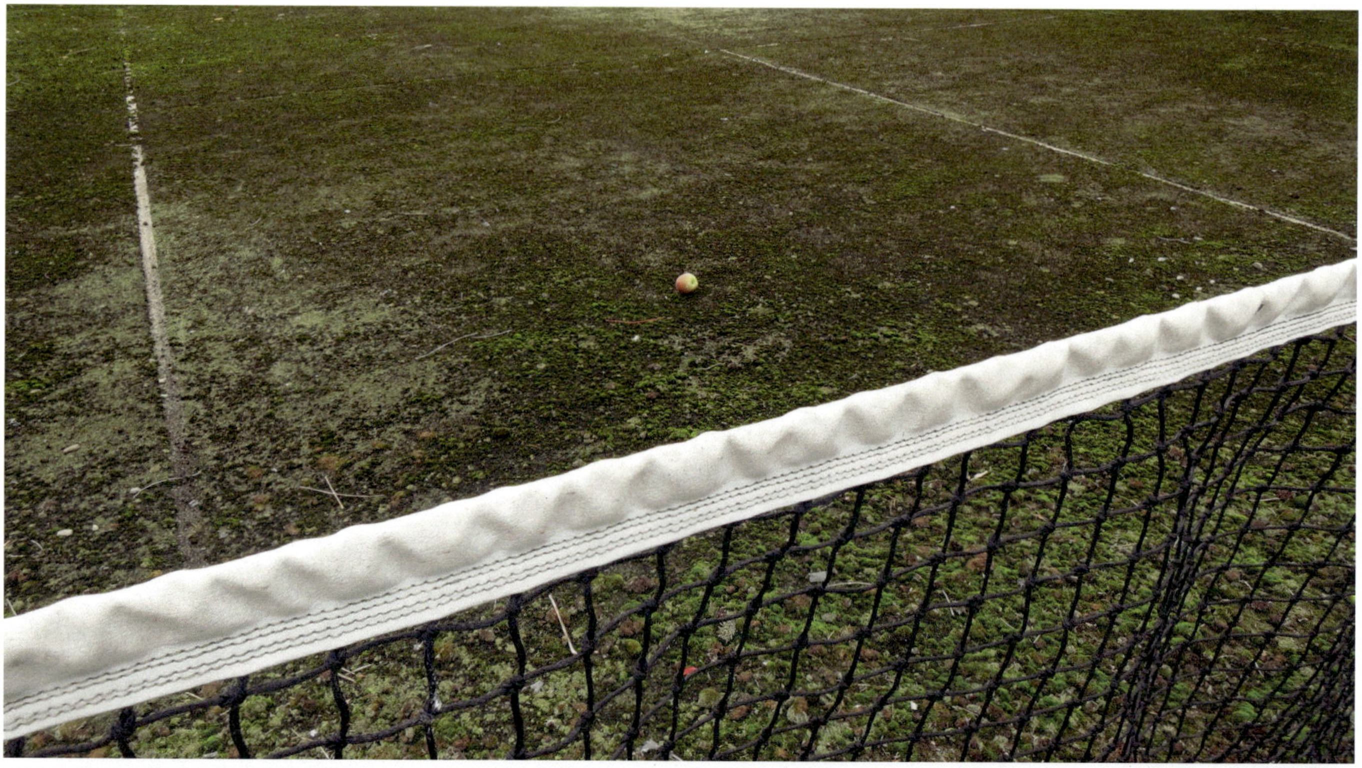

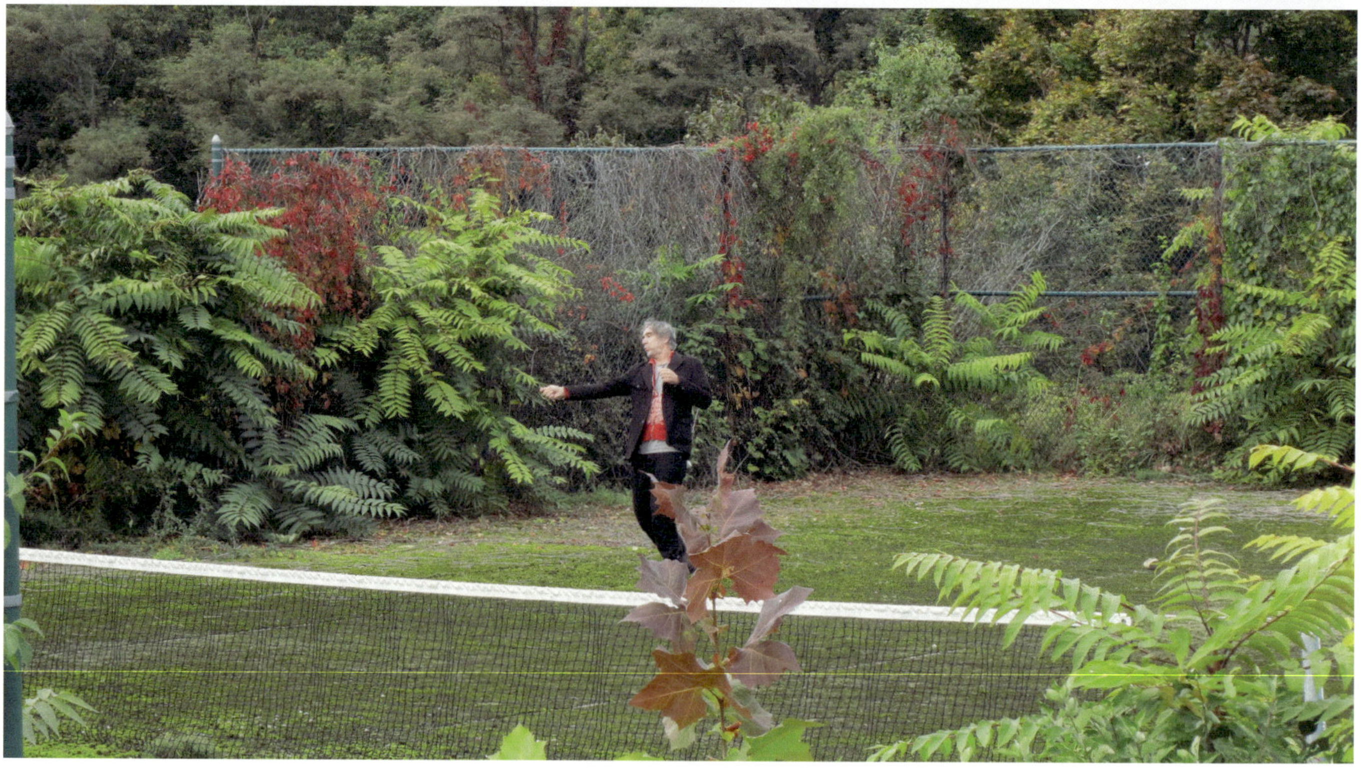

67
A Game of Knowing, 2011
Match Point, 2011

In the film *Blow-Up*, we can't see "it," the primal scene, the image the protagonist keeps blowing up, the photograph he has taken that he suspects is a murder in the garden. We keep blowing it up, further and further, but "it" is not to be found.

In the last scene of the film we see the pantomimes on the tennis court "playing" tennis. We "see" the imaginary ball. We imagine we see what is not there.

67 Here I photograph myself in the tennis court that is the garden. And instead of a tennis ball, on the other side of the court I place an apple, the apple of the primal scene, the scene of knowledge. Photography is an instrument of sensuality, an instrument of knowledge.

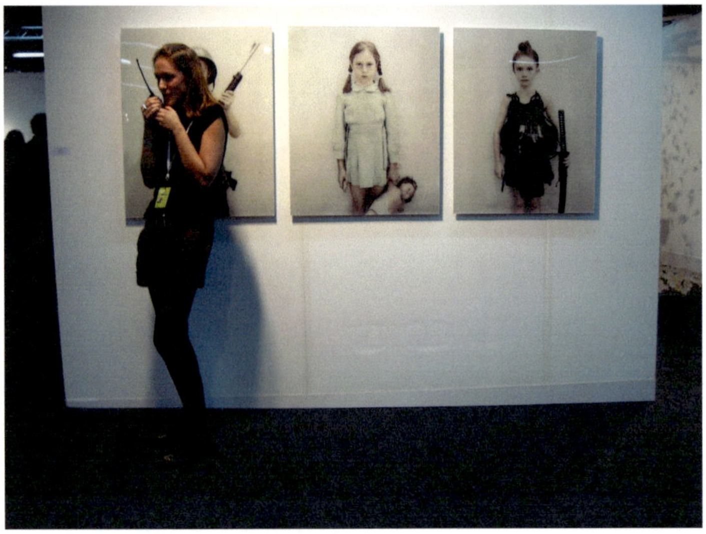

Portrait Times Four, 2009

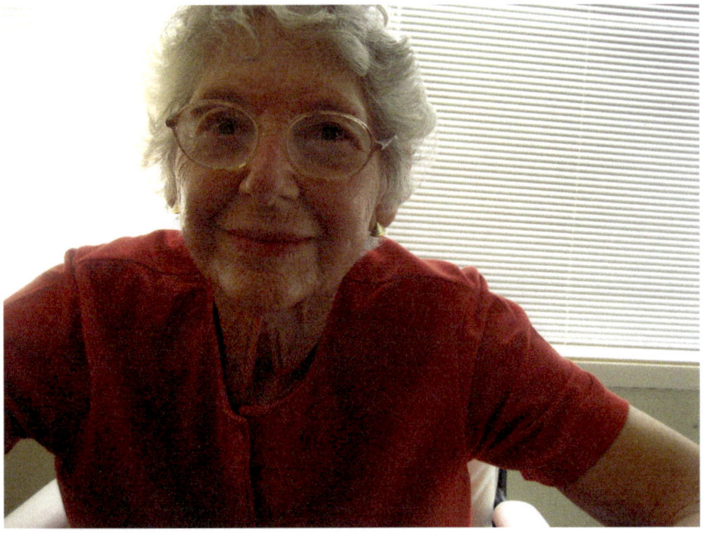

Gertrude Lafia, 2008

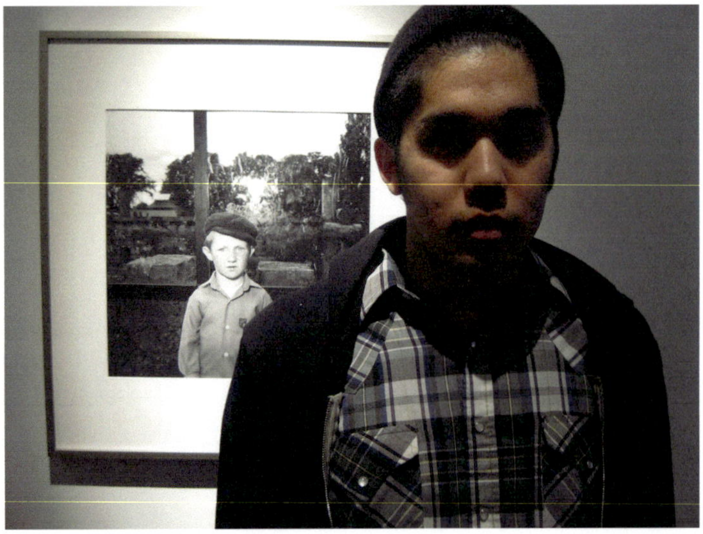

Boys, 2010

68 The portrait is a complex and complicit act. Let's take it to mean that the person photographed knows that they are being photographed and is complicit with the photographer. The subject of the photograph and the photographer align themselves to each other, yes and no. The subject wants to present herself as such or imagines herself already seen as such. That is, she has prepared and prepares herself to be seen and wants to be seen in a particular way, while the photographer sees what the photographer sees.

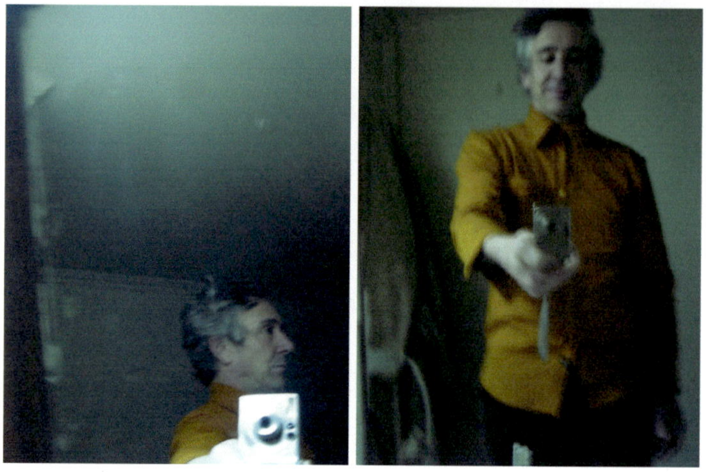

69
Camera in the Mirror, 2006

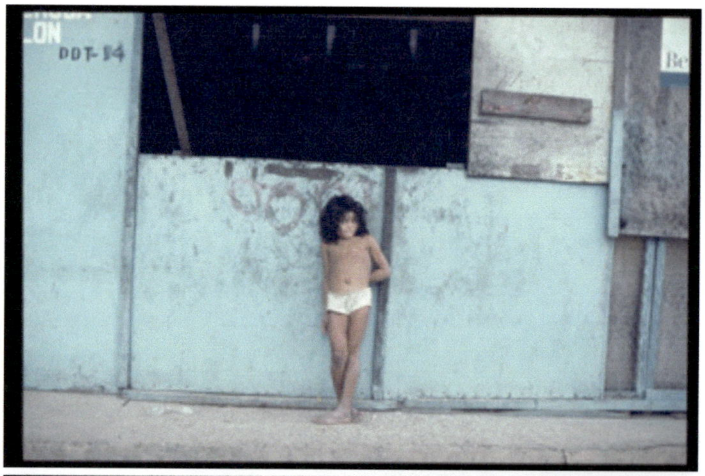

70
Young Girl, Andes, 1983

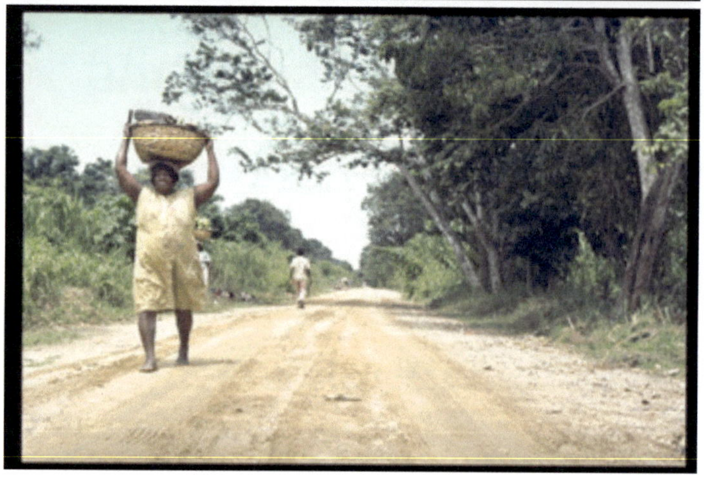

71
Woman with Basket, 1983

69 Here the subject is myself. What am I in the image of me? No, I am not an "I" in the image. There is no "I," only the eye of the image apparatus.

70 But isn't the picture here an image of someone, something tangible? Is this an image about the image instrument? No, it's an image about an encounter. It is an image of this young girl, how she is dressed, where and how she stands, how she presents herself to be seen.

71 When I first started taking photographs, I wanted to concretize what I saw. I wanted to make manifest my seeing, to go about seeing, and to create a record of that seeing. Photography was uncanny in that way, in the way that very easily, very immediately, something particular to me could not just be seen, but recorded. I could see what I saw. And it would be there to be seen again and again. Not that I went back to the images (though I did in my first darkroom printings). Yet I had recorded and materialized a way of being in the world. Not being in the world really but apprehending the world, going through it, touching it, seeing it, being of it. My seeing constitutes a way of being in the world. It tells me I have seen these things. This is my seeing of things.

But, as I said, I stopped taking pictures. I stopped printing photographs. What I wanted to see, what interested me, was recording itself, the event of recording, the possibility and the instrumentation of recording. How does a picture come about? What is picture taking? What is an image and what is a photograph? How can it come to be, or what exactly comes to be a photograph?

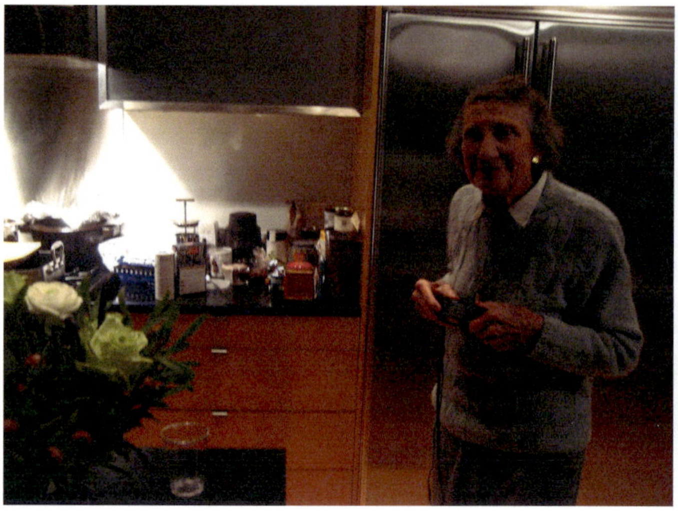

72
Woman with Camera in Kitchen, 2007

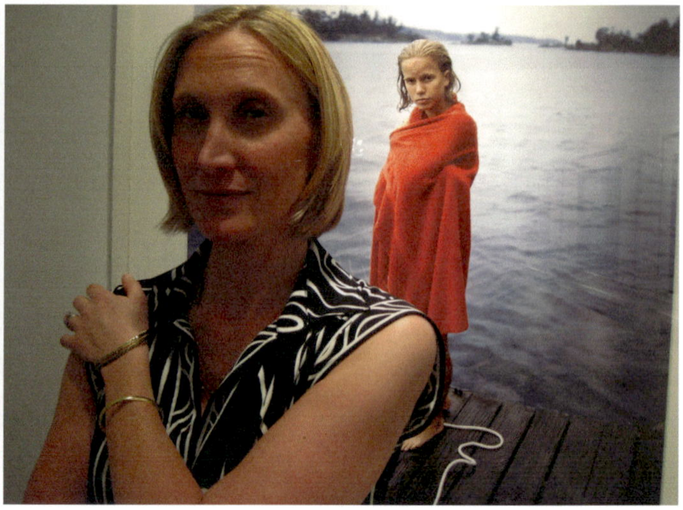

Portraitress and her Portrait, 2009

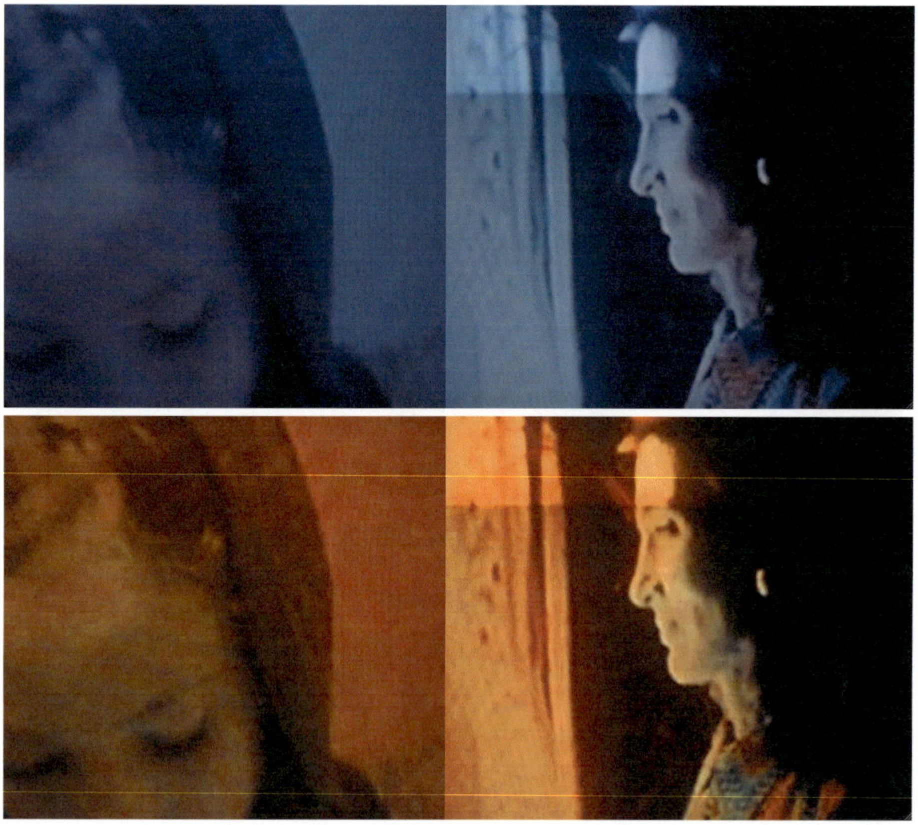

73
Mother and Daughter in Two Colors, 2007

But, as I said, I stopped taking pictures. I stopped printing photographs. What I wanted to see, what interested me, was recording itself, the event of recording, the possibility and the instrumentation of recording. How does a picture come about? What is picture taking? What is an image and what is a photograph? How can it come to be, or what exactly comes to be a photograph?

72 The portrait as a knowing complicity.

73 I can no longer take a single photograph. But I continue to construct a relationship between photographs, between imaging.

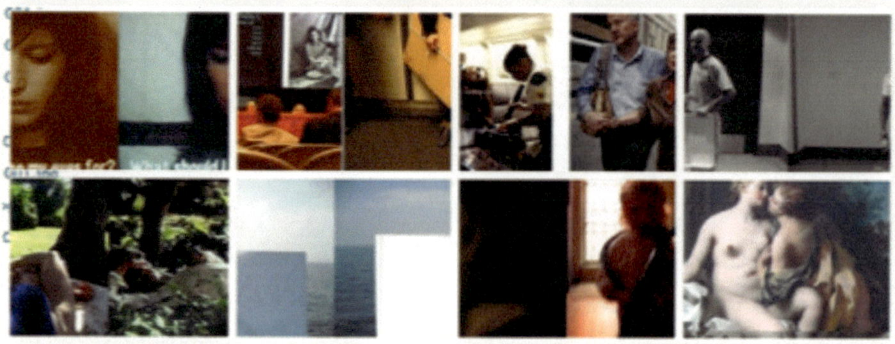

Still of photographic works

still of varied photos. more photos can be found here:
http://www.metabolichouse.com/marclafia/Artist_Statement.html

Artist

- Marc Lafia

Categories

Photography

Themes

playful, event, intimate, repetition, self-reflection, citational and conceptual

Uploaded by: Marc Lafia, Wed Apr 29 18:02:28 UTC 2009, 79 views

74
Archive Narrative, 2010

Making photographs is curating the archive.

"The archive is a door to the future which is waiting to be uncovered or rearranged to create a new logic."
—Jacqueline Steck on Derrida's *Archive Fever*

74 It would be impossible to estimate the amount of photographs that are produced everyday or even every second on this planet. Websites and services such as Flickr, Google Instagram, not to mention the numerous online stock photography agencies, blogs and more, archive much of the world's image production, yet there is so much more. Everyone with a camera-enabled cell phone, the media industry, our medical, military, research industries, all are incessantly imaging and producing images.

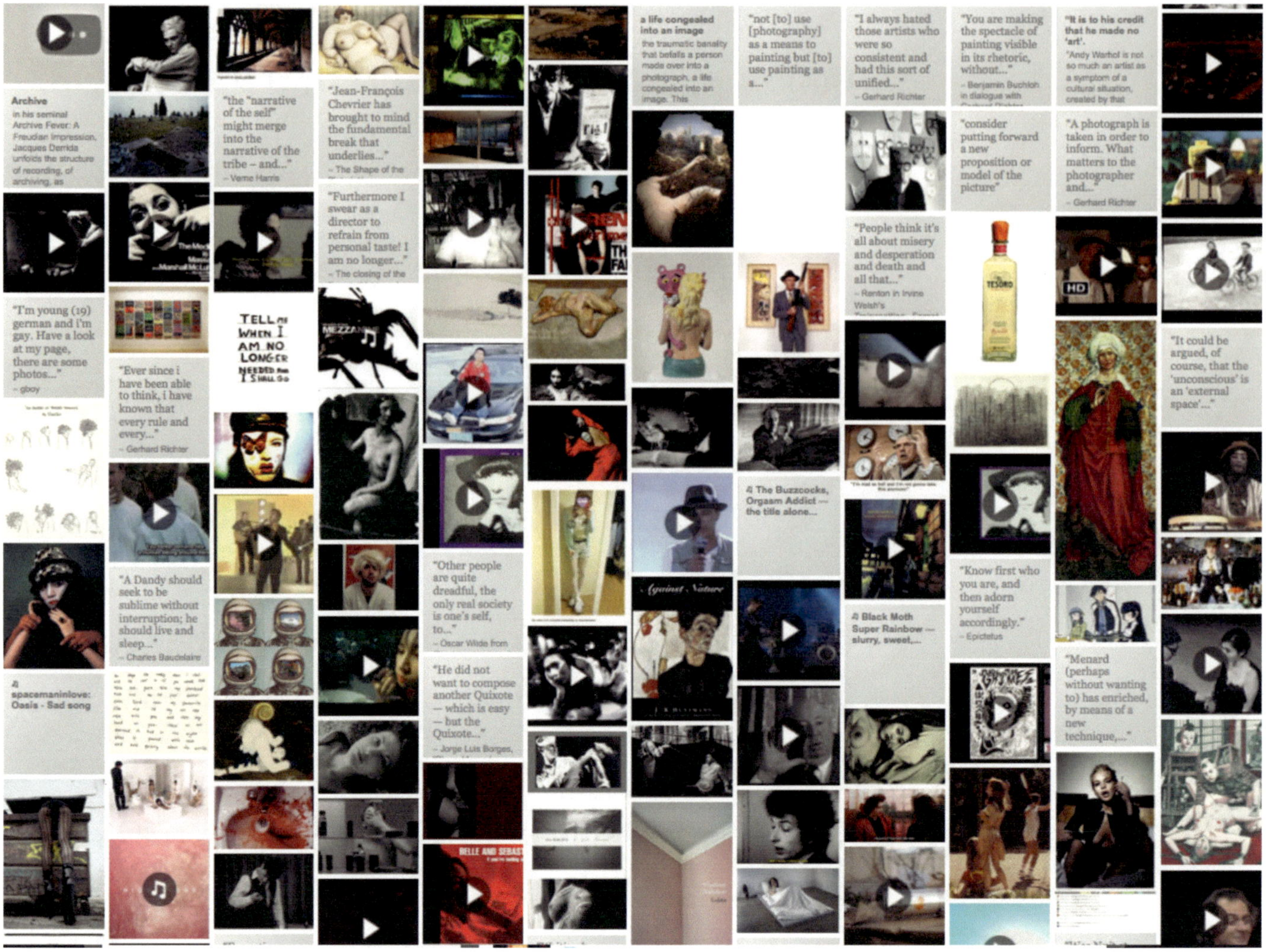

75
The Esthetes, My Archive, 2011

75 Here, an image from the archive view of my Tumblr blog *The Esthetes*. The composite image is an image in of itself. All images today become part of a flow of images, parts of other images, continually recontextualized and mapped to one's own curating. We easily take possession of the world's images today and put them in our own archive, creating an extraordinary and ever-mutable portrait of us, our tastes, our interest. The desktop, the mobile phone, each is a window into a plethora of image. They are like the commonplace books of old where one wrote recipes, weights and measures, poems, quotes, medical information, a hodgepodge of useful information, only now we can reproduce them and share them openly.

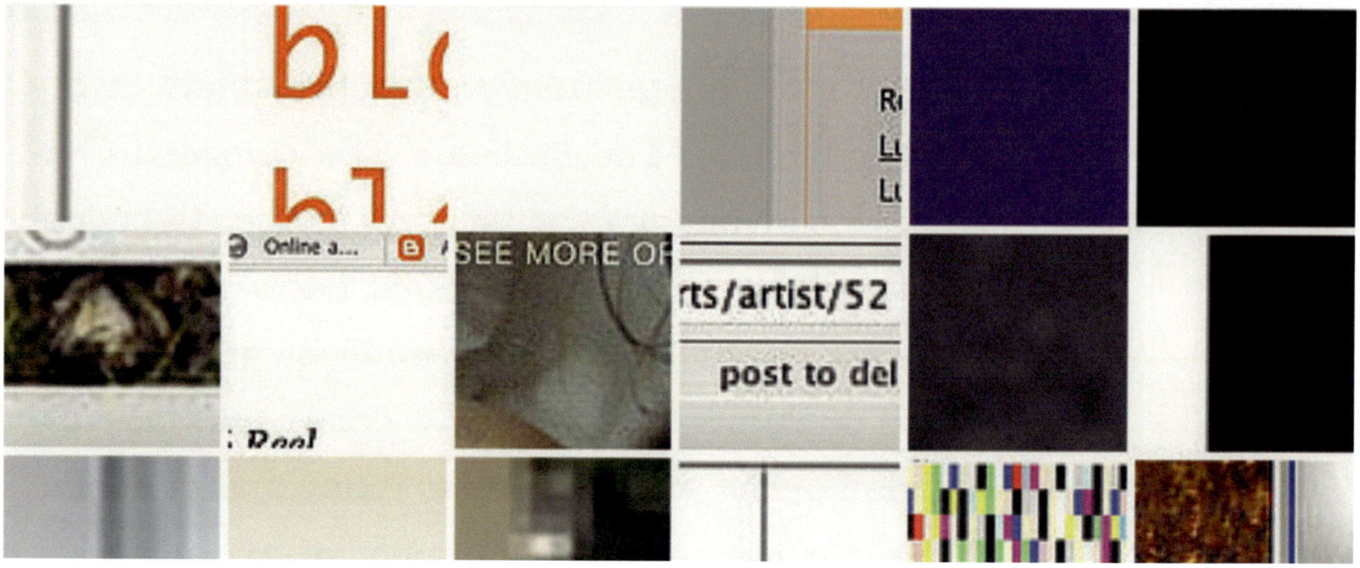

76

F4, Accidenting the Frame, 2007

76 The desktop is also a camera. From this superfluity of archive and image, not only do I drag images onto my desktop, into my possession, I also take pictures. I rephotograph. And as in all photography, taking pictures often results in the hazard, the accident of the shutter going off when we don't want it to. Here the shutter is shift command four, right at the desktop.

To record is to frame. Framing invites as well as conceals. It can suggest more than what we see. At the same time, it is what it is. To see the archive is to frame it, index it, copy, photograph, reuse, remix it. The desktop screenshot is my new camera. And as such it produces accidents.

The accident of the "shutter" sizing the frame. The variable lens which has no depth of field but only size. In dragging out the viewfinder onto the surface of the screen one frames the shot, and at times, the dragging out happens before it should.

77
F4, No. 23, 2007

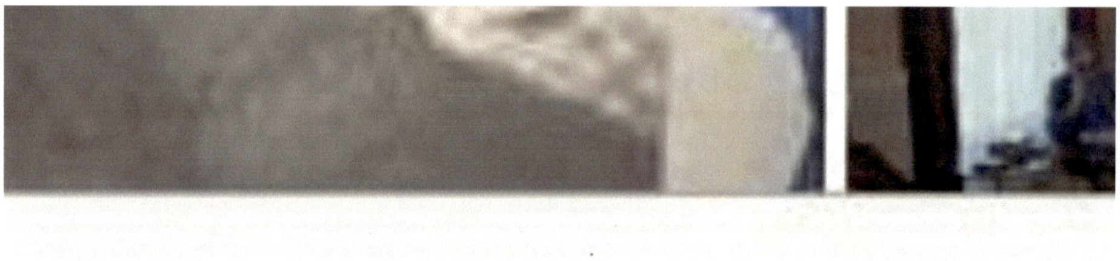

78
F4, No. 12, 2007

79
Word, 2004

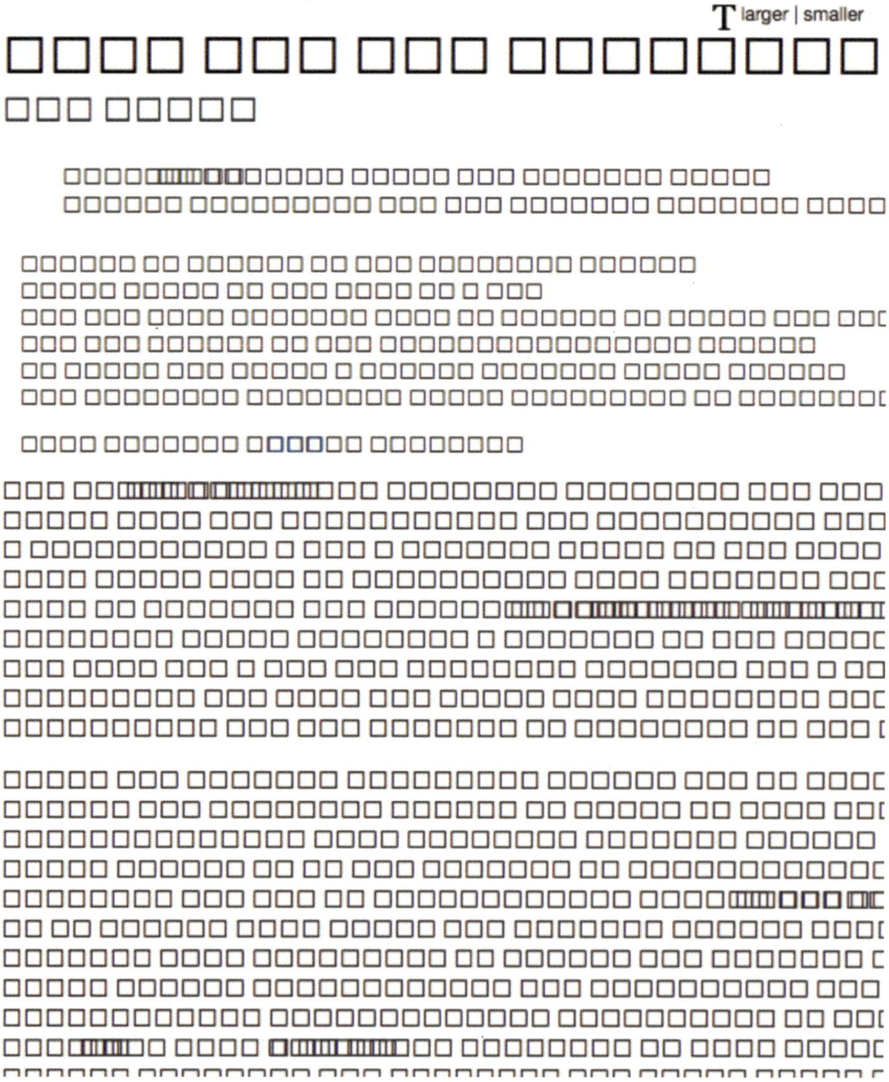

77 There are errors in every endeavor of recording. I place all these "accident" desktop pictures into a file for a year. And in these errors, there is an abstraction and fragments that take hold of me.

In accidents of recording, when the shutter commits before it is intended to, what it captures is a fracture of the screen, not quite a glitch, but partial markings, lines, and gestures.

The accident cannot be planned. Its result is unknown until it happens. Yet when we see it, we can take hold of the accident and make it a procedure to produce what we liked in the accident. That knowing and not knowing exactly what will happen becomes a method to go forward.

78 The sense of accident becomes a procedure, an algorithm, a controlled chaos, an event of possibility. As I continue with the desktop camera, recording the desktop's surface, I have become more and more interested in flatness, in the deadpan, in erasure, not by masking or an elaborate procedure of concealment but simply in the gesture of dragging out the framing device of the desktop recording instrument, shift, command open apple, number 4 or F4.

79 The desktop camera rerecords in a very confined surface, in and on the flatness of the screen.

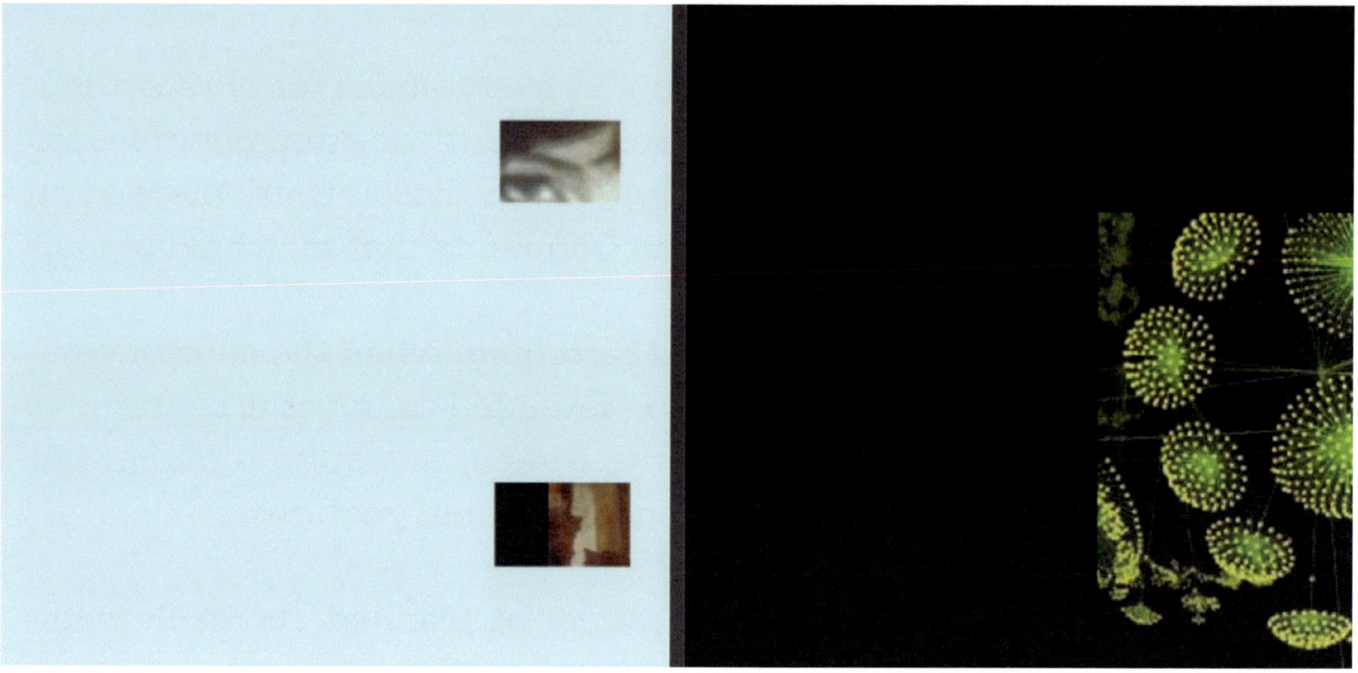

80
Sites, 2005

81
Twitter is Over Capacity, 2011

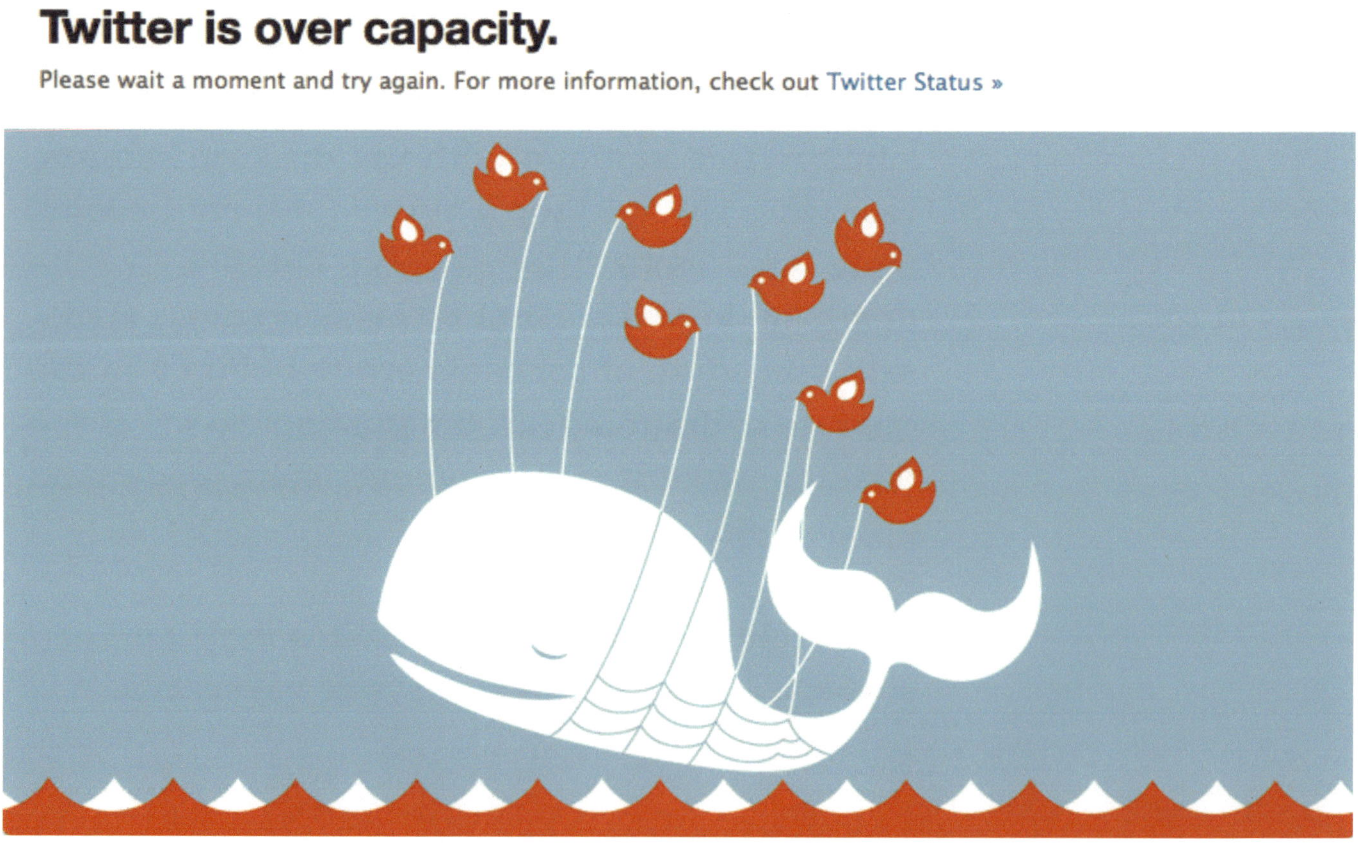

80 Here the image accident becomes a design, a grammar, no longer an index, but a reading of lines of force.

Following the accident of the desktop's recording modality I find a new opening to imaging.

81 There is also another kind of accident or error often sighted in the network. "Twitter is Over Capacity," a vernacular sign in the network. I like the idea of photographs in the electronic as homages to the beautiful vernacular photos of Walker Evans.

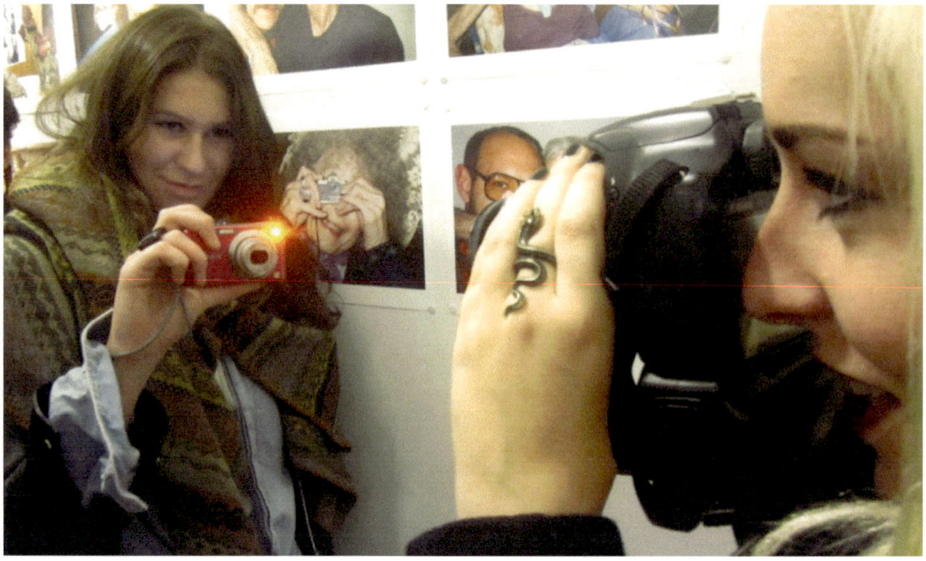

82
Looking for Terry, 2012

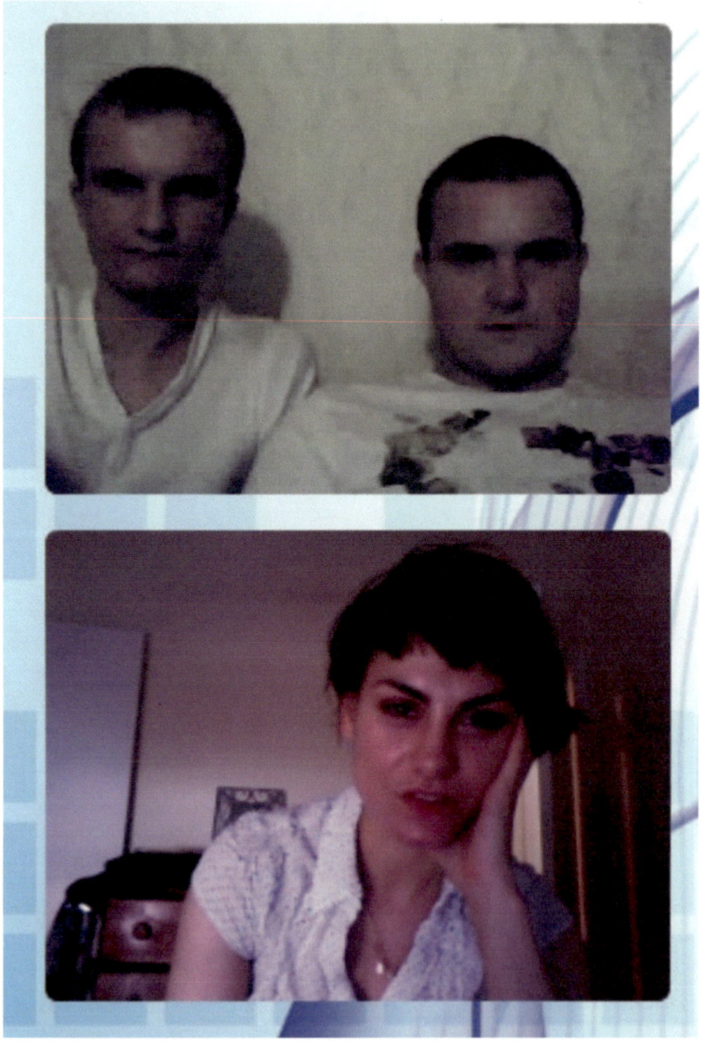

83
You Me and Everyone Else,
Hi Guest, 2010

82 / 83 In the electronic network, image taking / photography / recording is ubiquitous, happening all the time and at many levels and scales—typing here, using ATM machines, credit cards, blogging, Skyping, chatting, on the network live, under the surveillance of cameras, while shopping, walking across the street, under the instrumentation of a physician, in devices inside our bodies, our homes and cities under the sights of satellites.

Warhol early on gets fixed at the sight of seeing through the camera. There is no need of mise-en-scène, no boredom of seeing, just an endless fascination and compulsion to see as recording sees—not necessarily to play back, but to see and in that moment of the shutters release, to possess.

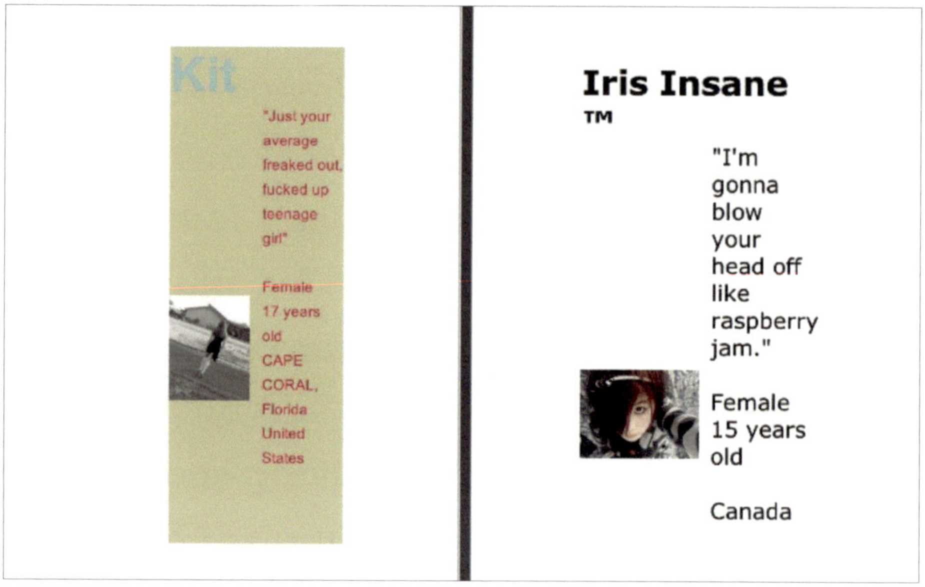

84
Kit, Iris, 2005

84 If photography was a way to image the world, to narrate the recording event, to create an event that would allow us to see, recording now turns on us. In recording, we are forever seeing and imaging ourselves, in a networked digital saturation where in some sense recording has superseded the seeing of images. We can almost say taking the photograph is the moment of seeing the photograph. It is seeing the world as a photograph that interests us, not photographing the world around us. Like the touring couple going down the Grand Canal in Venice all the while looking at it through the recording frame of their iPad.

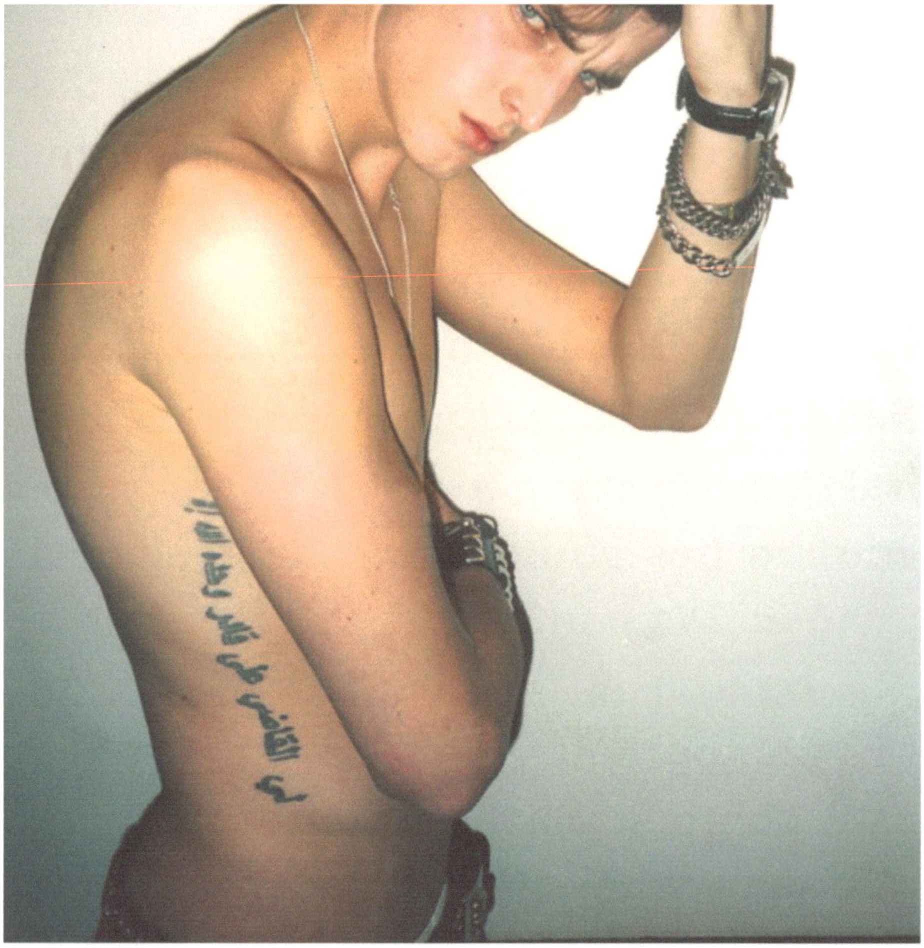

ANONYMOUS: *when did you find out you were physically attracted to men ?*
I've known since like first grade really.

ALEE-SWEATSHIRT: *Dude srsly, I am gonna be there and we should totally go to Disneyland! It will be fun. For realz.*
Yea! I'll have to see how classes and everything are going, but it would be so much funsies :)

ALEE-SWEATSHIRT: *Can we plz go to Disneyland together when I am in LA (in like three weeks) ?*
OMG! Yes :*

85
Can We Plz Go to Disneyland Together, 2011

85 "In our cultural landscape of blogs, webcams, profiles, live journals, and videosharing sites, the intimate lives of everyday people are on parade for all to see. One could say that a new culture of erotic exposure and display is on the ascendance, fueled by the impulse to reveal the self, and streamlined by DIY media technologies. In many ways this culture would seem to be less a representational than a presentational one, where we are compelled to solicit the attention of others, act for unseen eyes, and develop new forms of connective intensity—as if this were somehow the very condition of our continued existence, the marker of our worth.

"Within these presentational environments, performance and role-playing reign supreme, and new forms of subjectivity and identity emerge.

"These new cultures of self-display challenge us to rethink foundational concepts in film and media theory and, consequently, to rethink the very conditions of our approach. For clearly these cultures are not necessarily those of mastery and visual pleasure. They do not resolve easily to questions of perception, power, and language. They are cultures of showing as much as those of watching. Instead of a reliance on questions of spectatorship, representation, and scopic power, we are challenged to foreground issues of performance, affect, and display."
—Jordan Crandall

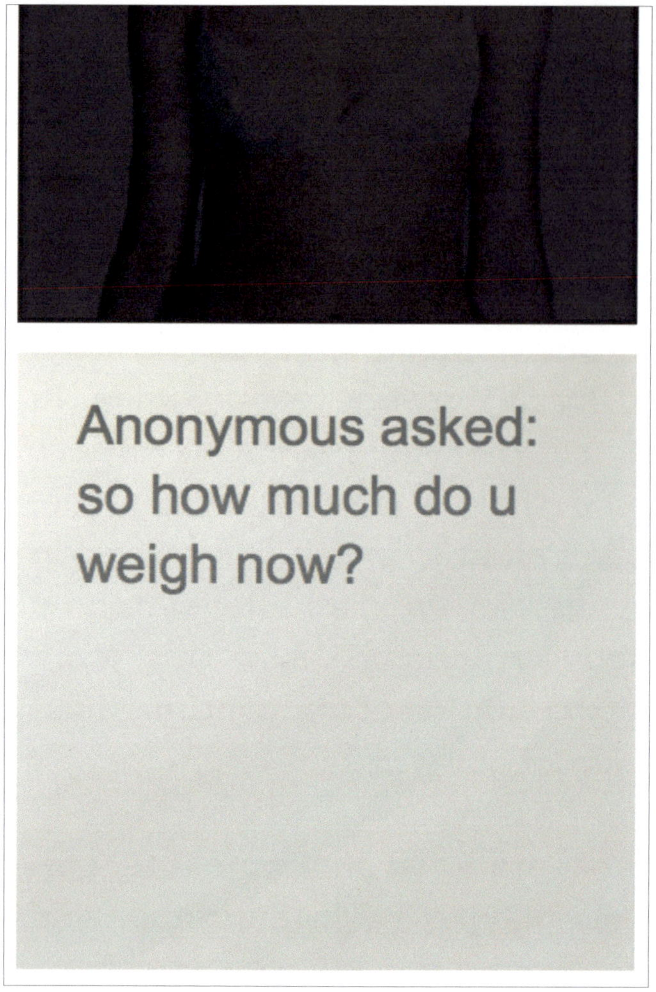

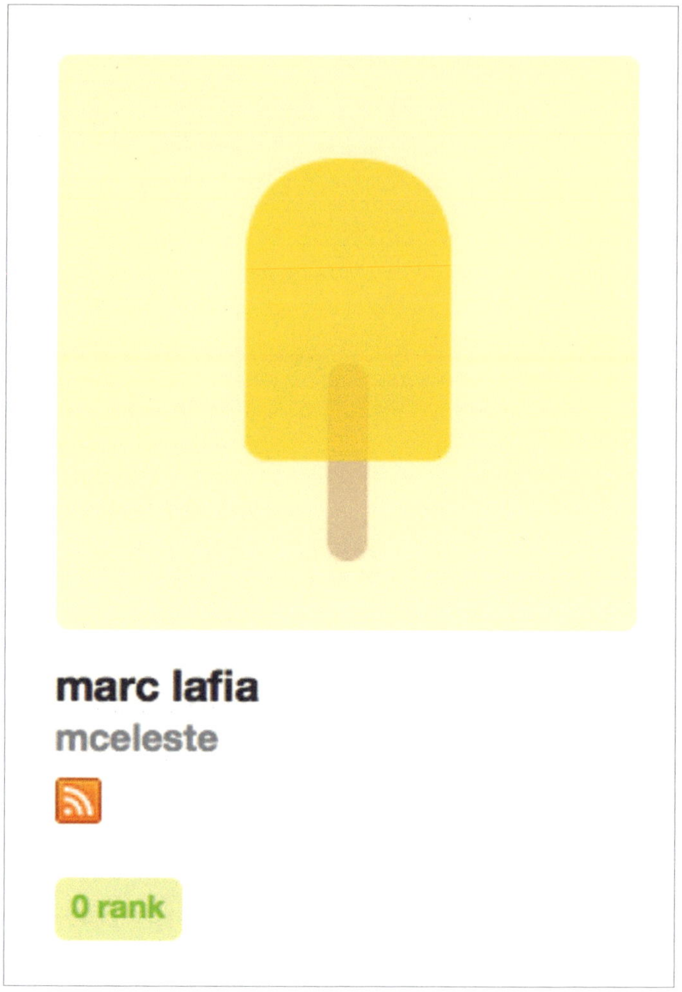

86
Anonymous Asked, 2011

marc lafia mceleste, 2011

86 Performance, affect, and play: in the milieu of the vast archives of electronic networks, we are continually asked to construct and put on a visual presence.

We are to be seen, to be imaged. Wanting to be watched on camera. In Michael Powell's film *Peeping Tom*, to see is to predate, to devour, to consume, to be erotically charged. To frame is erotic, to murder and orgasm while framing consummates this moment of taking a picture. It is a techno-social prosthetic for social discourse.

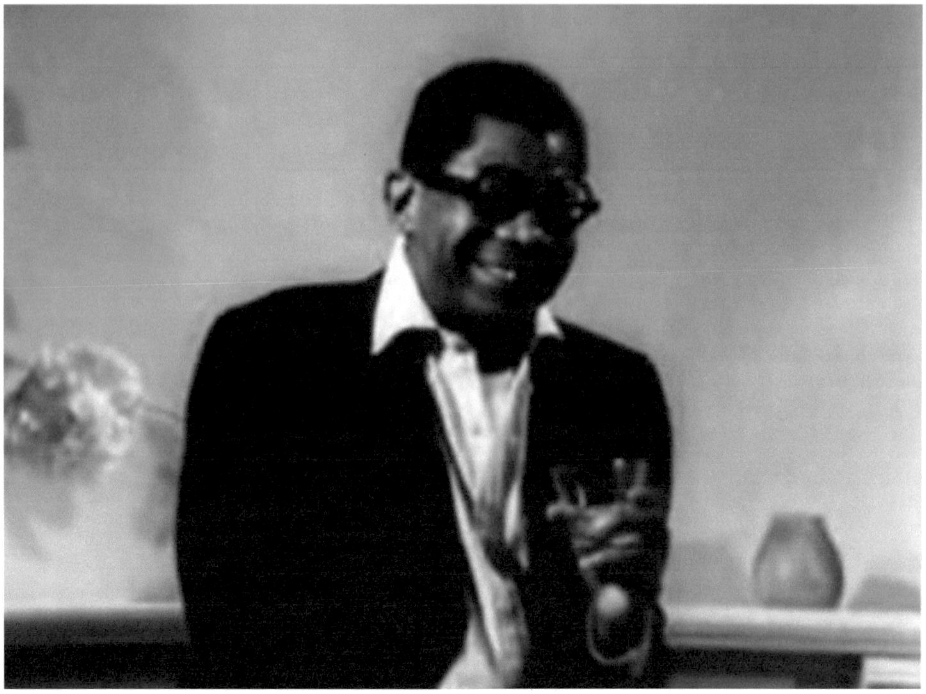

87
Still from Portrait of Jason, Shirley Clarke, 1967

In *Sunset Boulevard*, the once regal star of silent cinema Gloria Swanson, at long last under the klieg lights, says, "All right, Mr. DeMille, I am ready for my close up." How long she had to wait and exhaust herself before director Cecil B. DeMille and his camera crew of hundreds appeared.

87 In *Portrait of Jason*, Jason had the luminous director Shirley Clarke record his story, plying him with drinks as he revealed his lush life as a homosexual hustler.

No longer. One only needs to open one's computer, cell phone, and there the camera and the entire world are, ready for their close up.

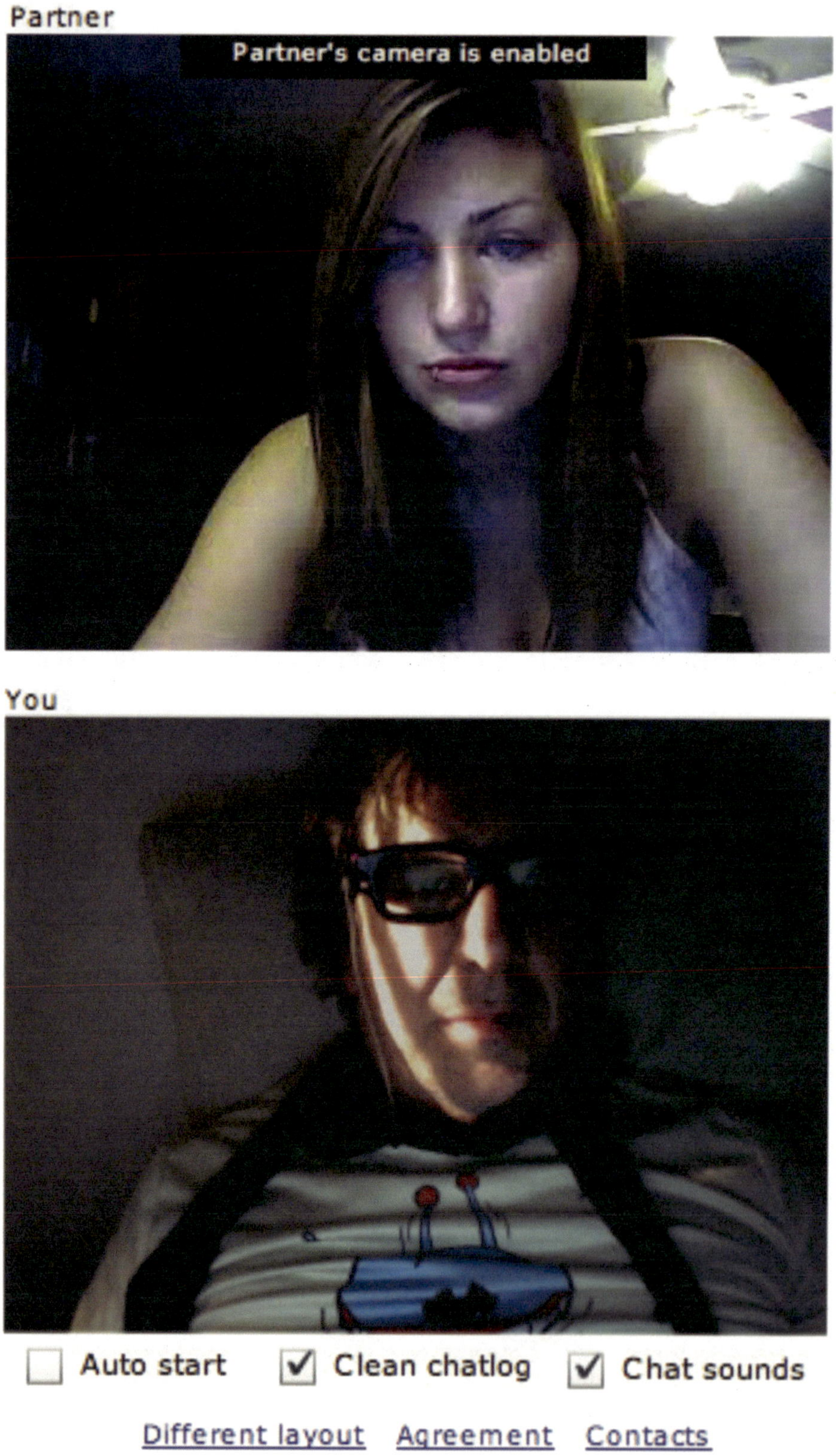

Chatroulette, No. 23, 2010

In front of the always-on camera, photography returns today to its beginnings of the long exposure, where we perform ourselves, to a new kind of self-exposure. We construct, perform a role, a pose, a circumstance, as Cindy Sherman does in her *Untitled Film Stills* and other series. But here in the instantaneity and archive of the online world, the role we play is us. Around this play we are urged to be authentic and present our true identities.

88 / 89 Once I feel myself observed by the lens, everything changes: I constitute myself in the process of "posing," I instantaneously make another body for myself, I transform myself in advance into an image for consumption, for pleasure. I take on the pose as my defense and assault against the many images that try to constitute me. Here I am the photographer's eyes, her viewfinder. I am

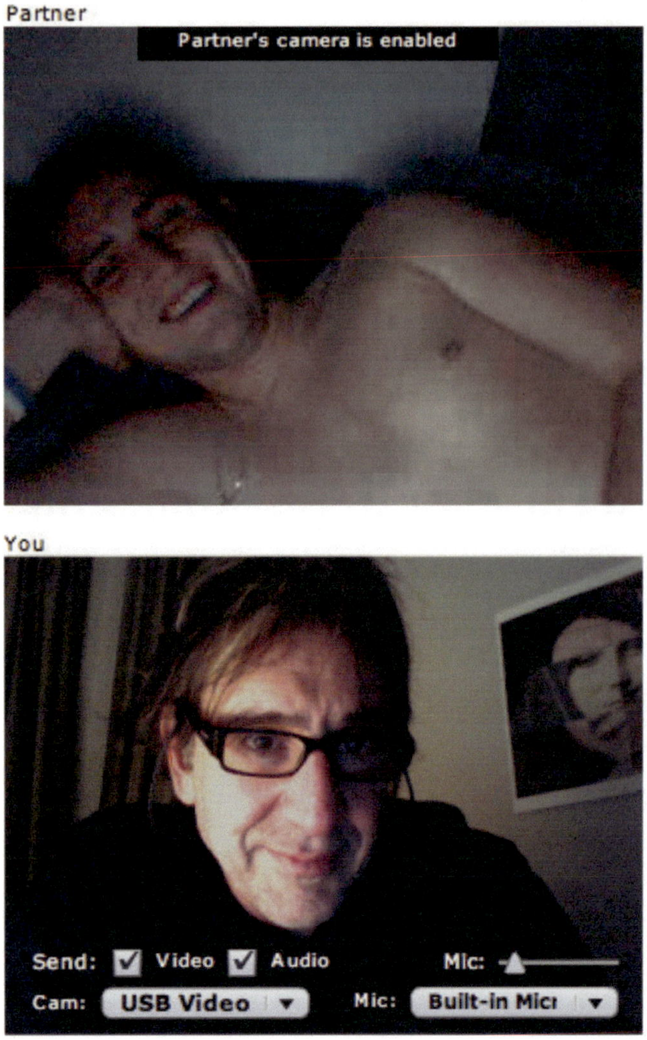

89
Chatroulette, No 123, 2010

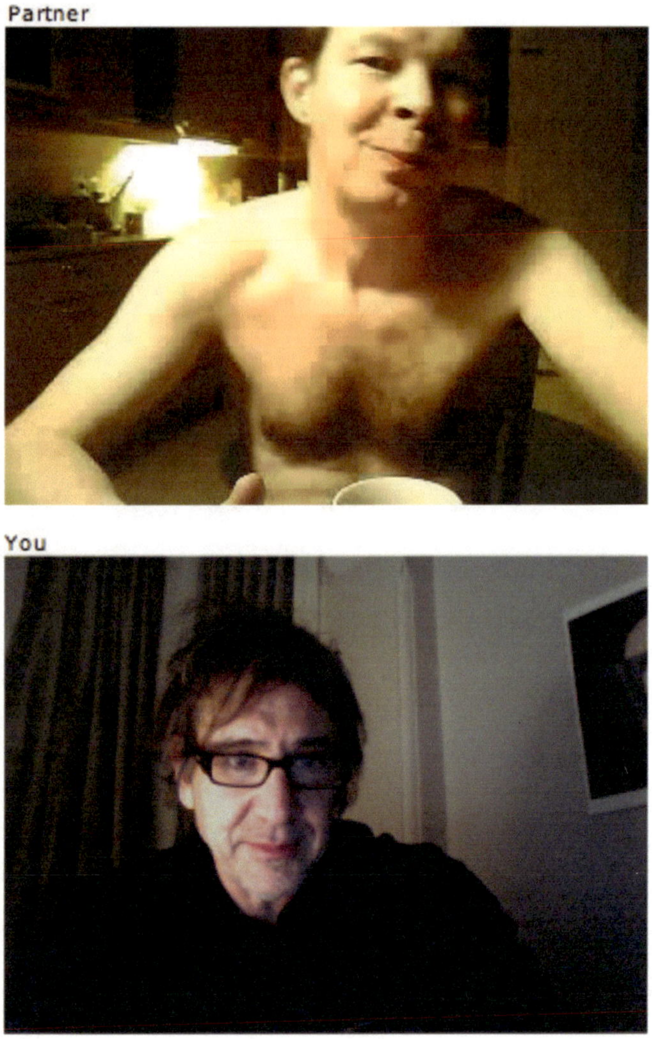

Chatroulette, No 213, 2010

the object and its double, the subject that constitutes myself for its own consumption. I affirm and author myself. I arouse myself. I narrate myself. I become myself in the image. I use the tropes of the pose as a kind of carnival to myself, of myself, for myself, to supersede any possible other definition of me, to indeed define myself.

88 / 89 In the vast online world I find a new kind of studio portraiture, a new kind of "street" photography, a new kind of camera that simultaneously photographs the photographer and the subject at the same time. A kind of sublimated peeping Tom who peeps and is peeped.

In our network culture, the camera is an always-on camera, we are already recorded, always to be recorded—so what is it to make an image, when one is always on or has a camera?

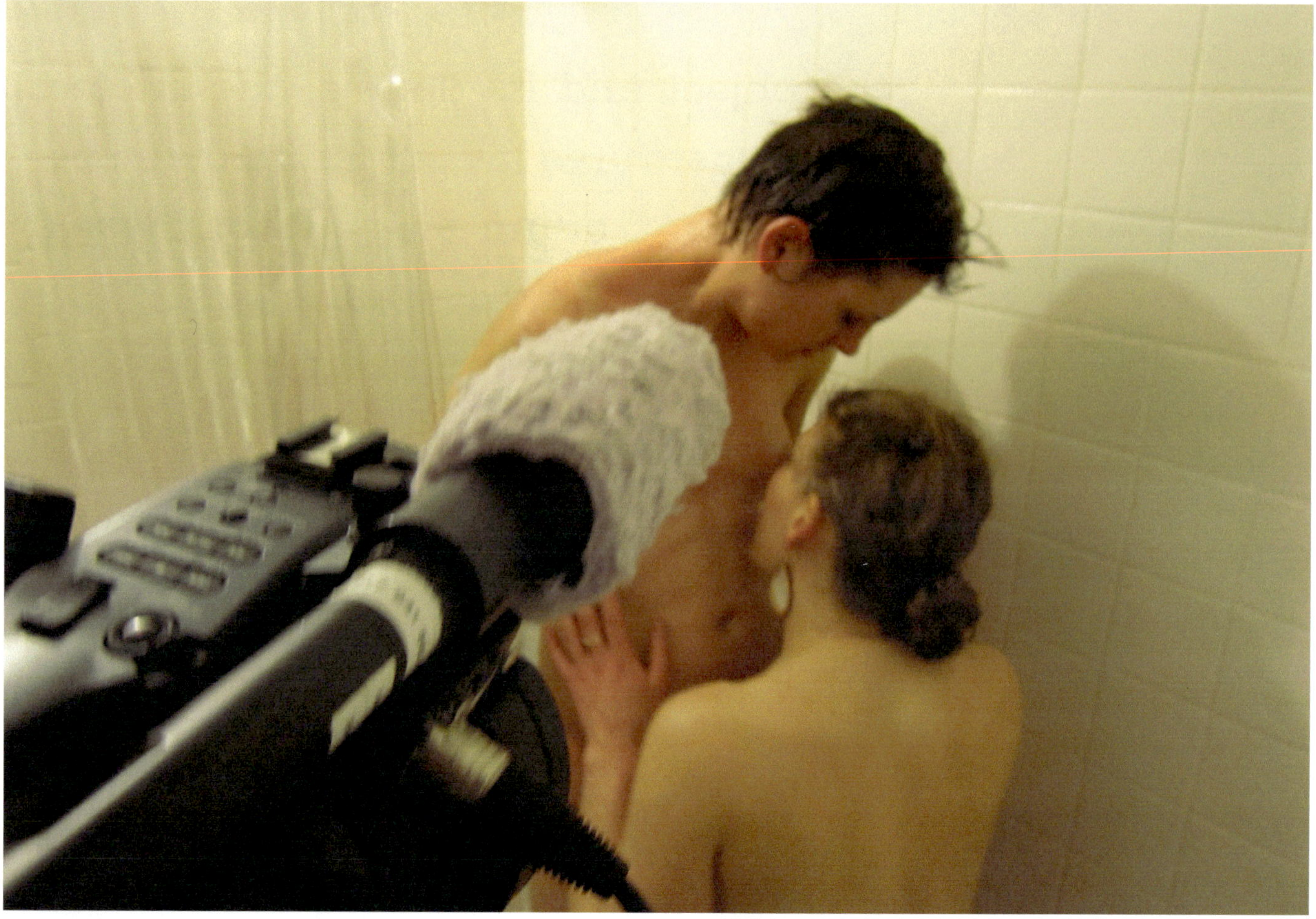

90
Revolution of Everyday Life, 2009

91
Girls on Film, 2010

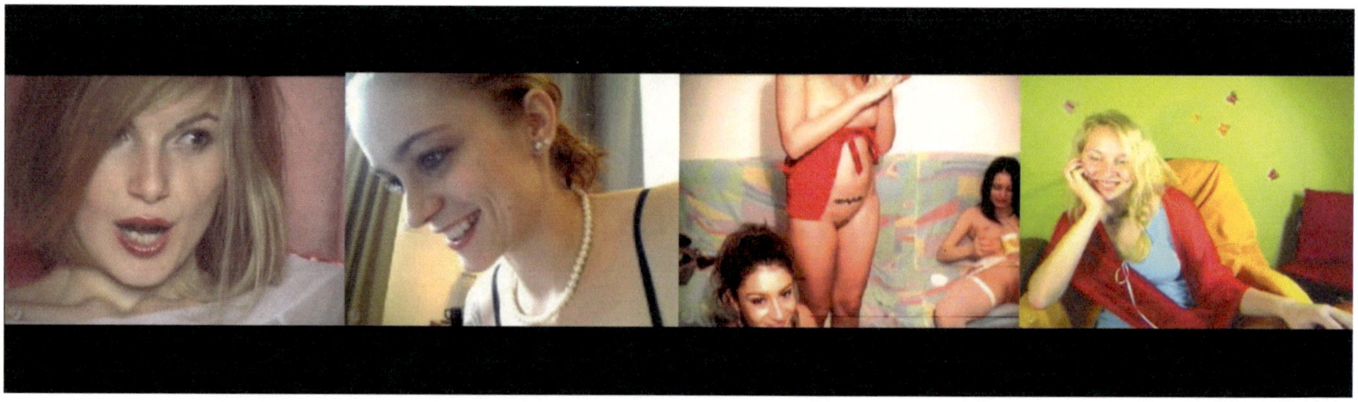

90 How does the presence of the camera create a situation? How does it activate the senses, the body, an erotics? There is something in being watched that heightens our sense of self, that can arouse or can make us timid.

91 Sex in the network reminds us of how much of our pleasure comes from sight, and that sight, as a sense, is close to touch. Live sex sites such as myfreecams.com, though they present bodies at a remove, are extraordinarily intimate and visceral. There is a circuit constructed there where the distinct spaces of the participants in some way increases the immediacy.

Chatroulette is another such online service, but even more open in its one-to-one televisual affordance that allows one to present oneself to any possible person playing the game. Like roulette, chance will choose whom you on camera will connect with also on camera. You never know where you will land, you never know who is on the other side, what they may want, and you may not even know what you want.

Chatroulette is performative of many things: the network, photography, performance art, cinema, and more.

It is the possibility of crossing borders, making connections, being moved beyond our comfort zone, taking risks, reaching out; it is about the desire to "see" beyond one's confines, the desire to com-

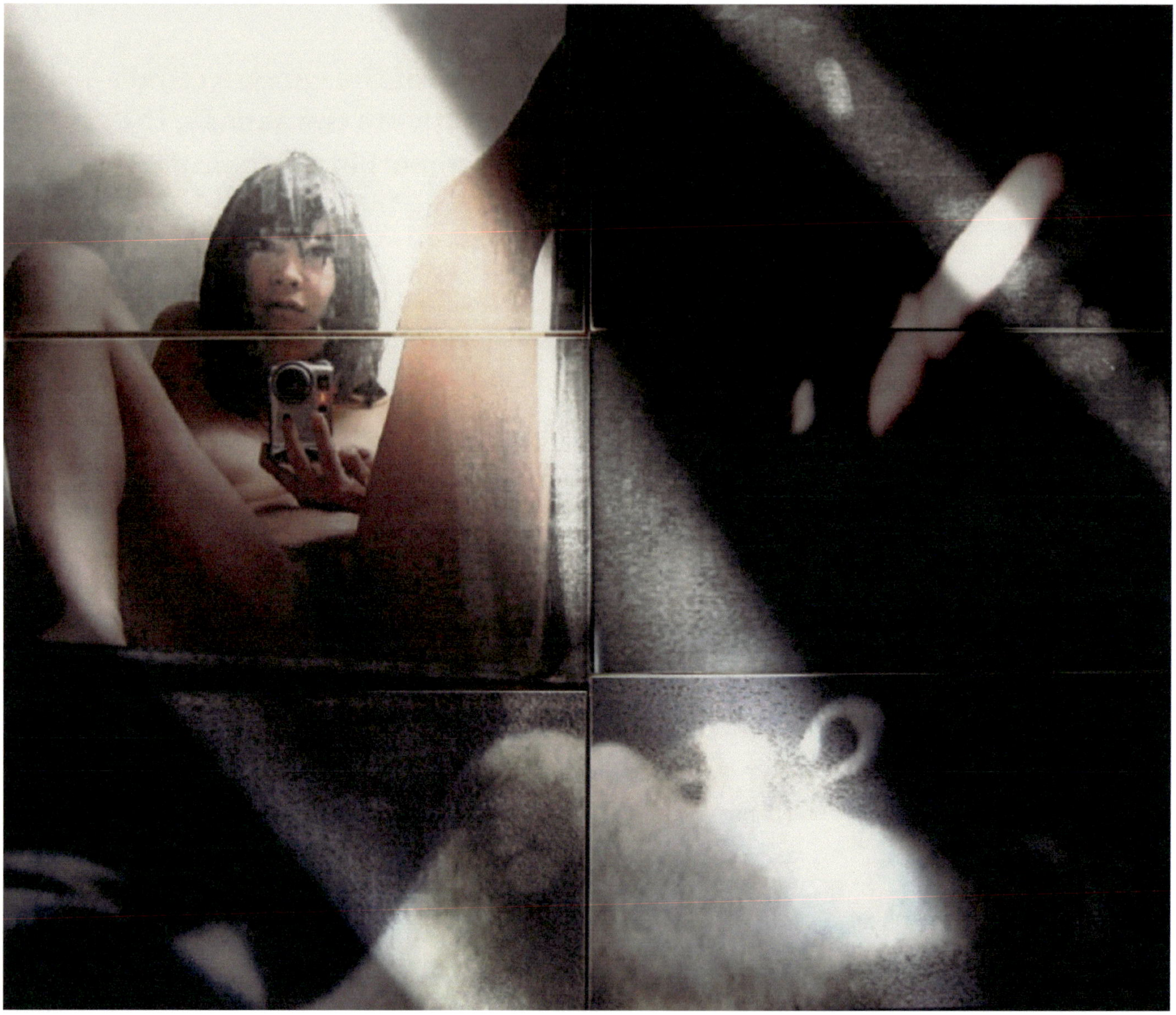

92
Me You, 2003

municate. All of it turning on the erotics of seeing and wanting to be seen. It brings forward the fear, abjection, and euphoria of sight. The anonymity of the camera. The desire for the unknown, for pleasure, not face to face but image to image, in the circumstance of being not in the same room, but in the same psychological space.

Is it then the sexual, the sexual maneuvering, here that can be spoken of more easily, without the kind of consequence one might find in the physical realm? Is this what makes Chatroulette so uneasy and loaded? That it is in a sense a carnival, an inversion of rules, the permission within tele-presence, within a closed circuit of imaging, to be at a physical remove yet present, that allows us to drop the social etiquette of the physical realm yet at the same time take on its pleasures? Is it that it allows us to act in a transactional way with another, without the conditions of transaction, but the permission of transgression? In Chatroulette, what is permitted, where the limits are, one is free to discover, to find a limit to this tele-presence.

I wanted to put myself in this environment, to document Chatroulette as a social space, as a formal medium, to performatively come to it and reflect upon it, and so made these pictures.

92 In the world of always-on cameras, the edit is left to the archivist, to the viewer, the reader. It is they who find images and declare them photographs.

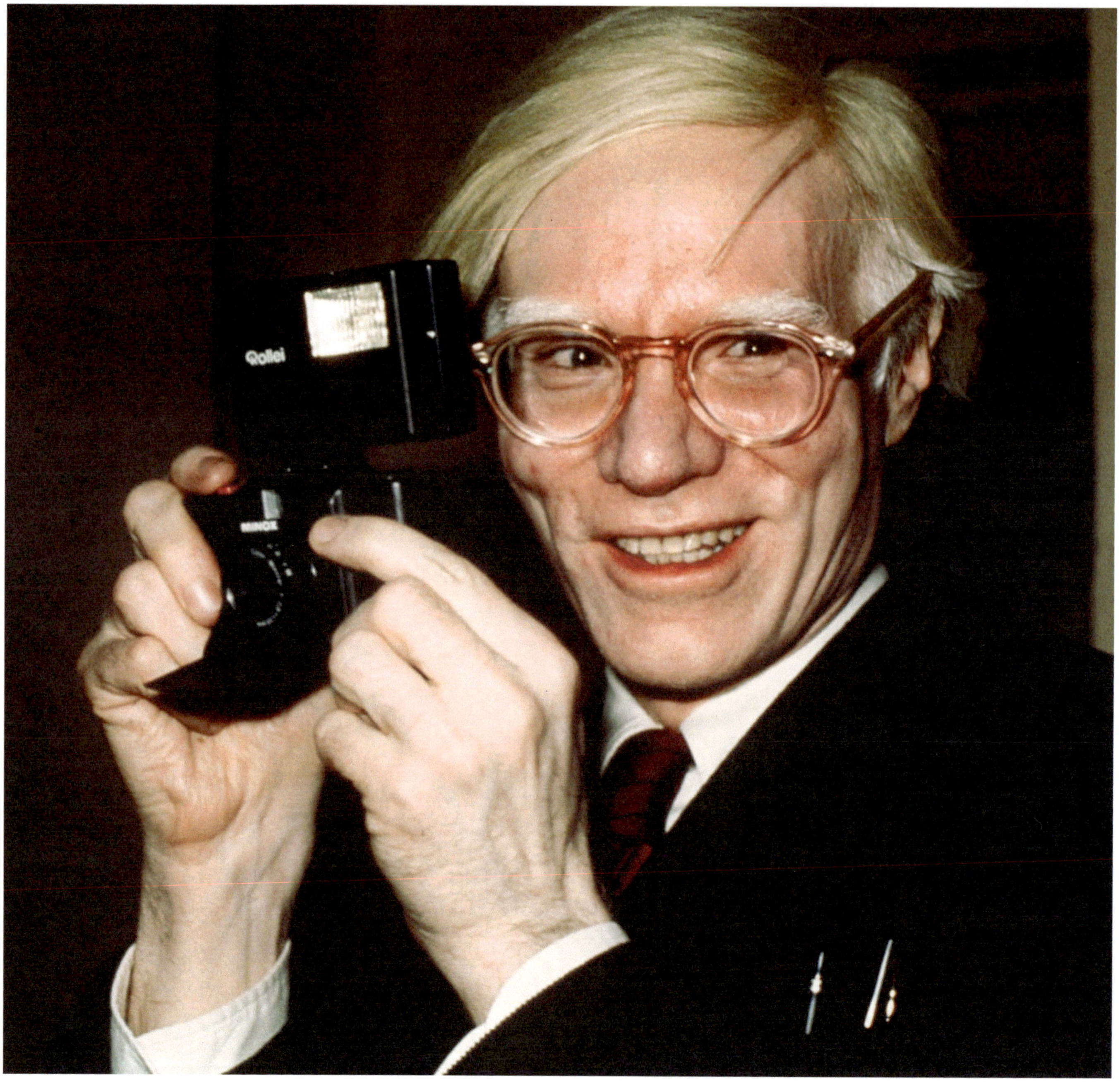

93
My Desktop Camera, After Andy Warhol,
2010

93 The relationship between the recording and the edit is most exacting in the films of Andy Warhol. The recording is the film, there is no edit. It is a pure recording. A one-to-one relationship.

His work is a prelude to a condition of always being photographed, of always being on camera, always recording. In a world of one-to-one recording, in some uncanny sense there is photography without photographs.

In a conversation with David Bowie, William Burroughs observed that Warhol was uncannily unpresent in his own body. He was not directing. He could only record. There is no mise-en-scène. There is no one shot followed by another shot. There is only the camera on. There is only recording. There is no interest in taking the recordings to another place. And that is their fascination and power. They are time, recorded.

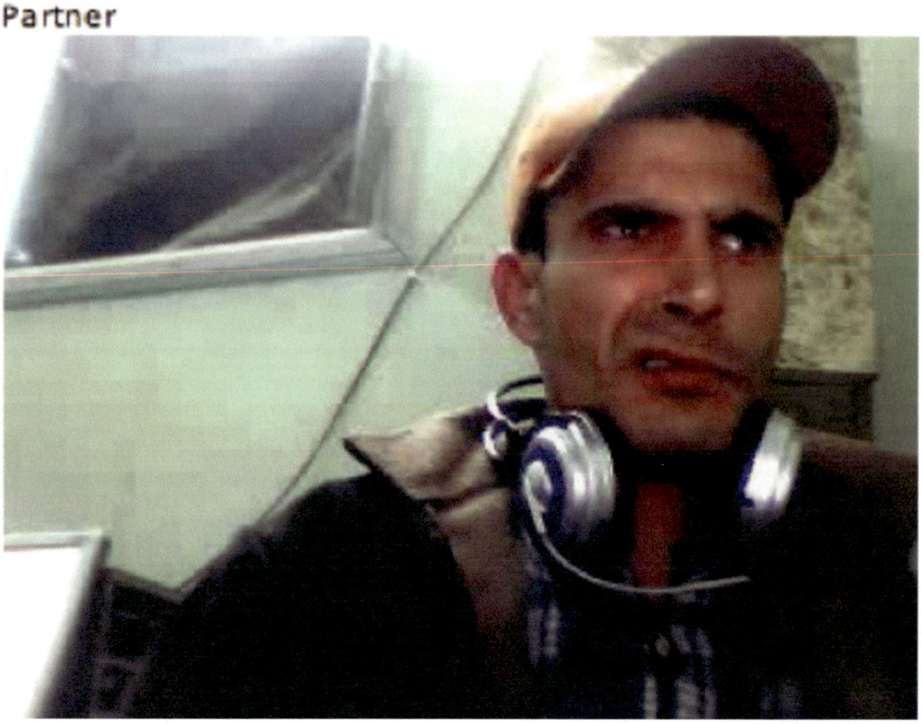

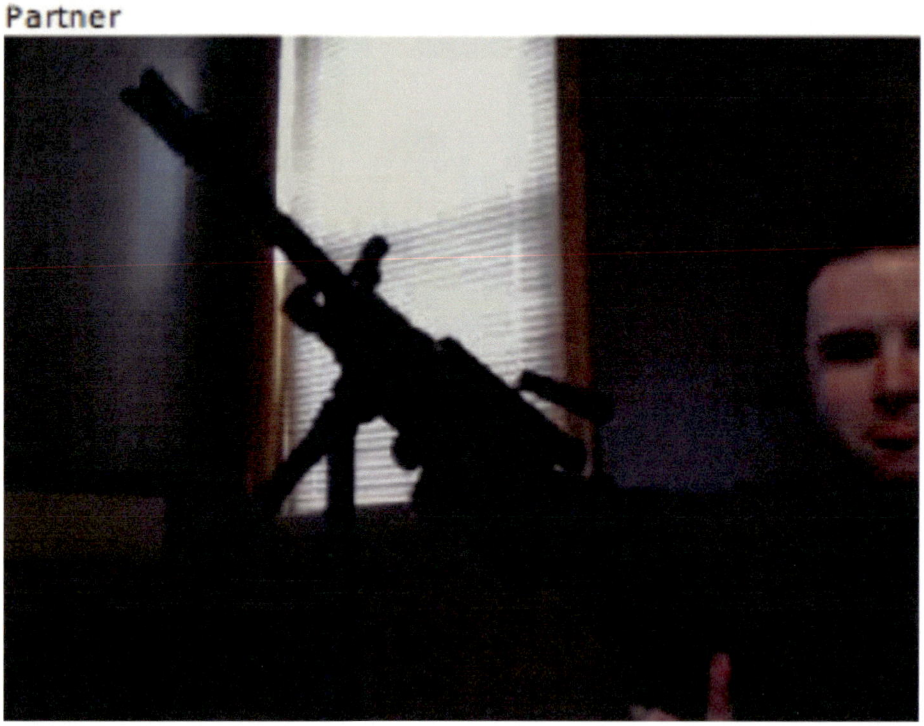

94
Chatroulette, No. 83, 2010
Chatroulette, No. 97, 2010

94 Chatroulette untethers us from the old networks of nation, class, job, all the indices that have come to define us in so many social networks. Here the encounter is not mediated by capital or the old metaphors of identity. Not the editorial assignment that gives one access to celebrity or fashion. There is no meta-explanation. There are no key words. There is no permissioning of "friends" into your network.

There is simply the possibility of encounter. There is simply the photographic that doubles, that reciprocates, that goes on multiplying, continuing without end. This is the condition of photography today.

The "self" is projected to answer the glance of the other. The photographic is a conduit of a conversation. It is like the early video artists who would bring their presence into the world in recording. Video gave forth a fact of being, the very time of being, the seeing of the body in space. The being of the body in recording gave us and put forward presence in the sense of doubling us, letting ourselves see ourselves. We are all video artists now in a perpetual recording. Recordings never to be looked at.

To enact the fantasy that is prohibited in reality is to create a space that enacts the fantastic, like a dream, the body touched but not touched. What touches the body is auto-affection, words and imaginings and the sight of the other.

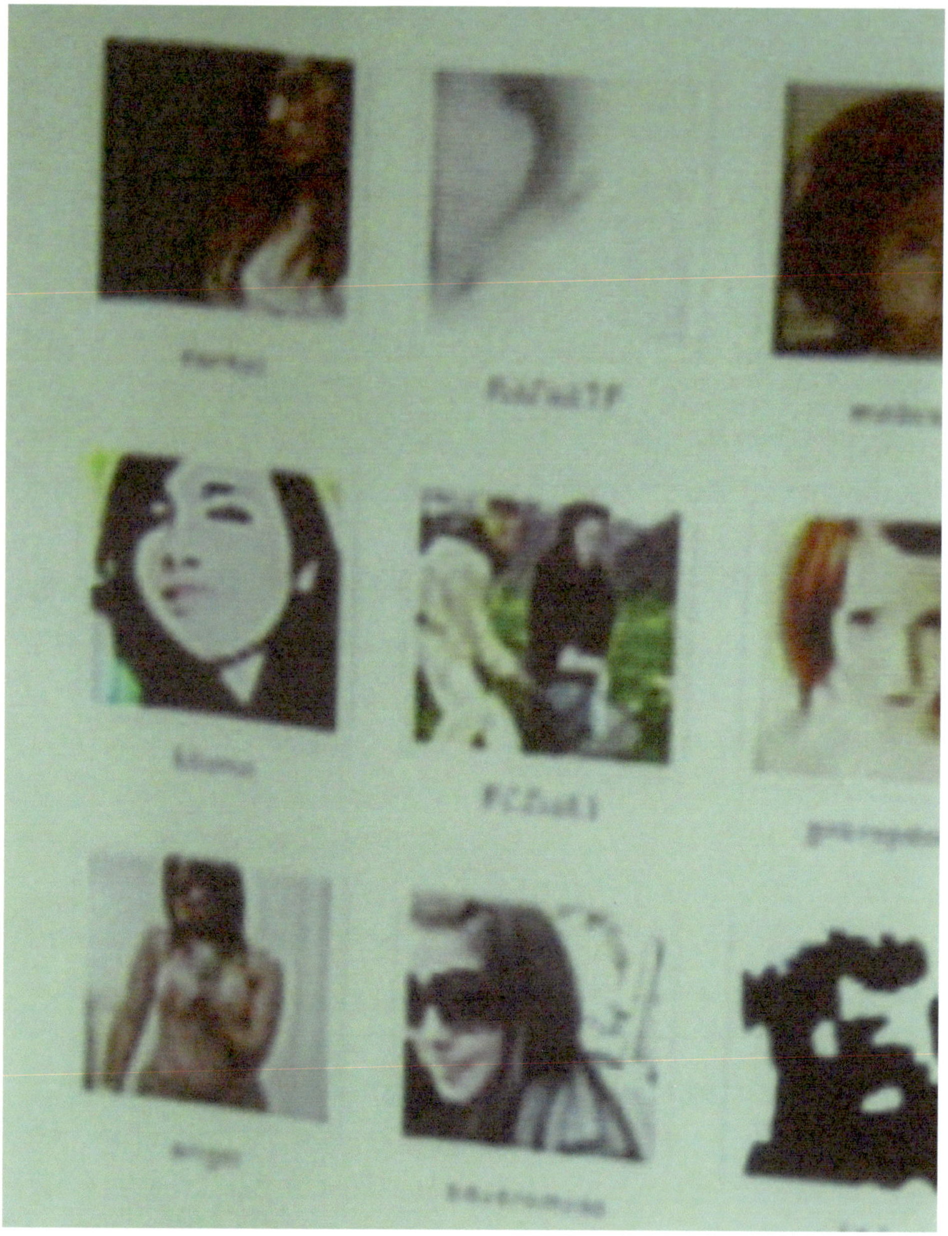

95
Here I Am Virb, 2009

95 Though seemingly without trace, without consequence, Chatroulette amplifies connection, becoming a space to meet the world, the communality of the world.

The world from each to the other, one to one. Here we are staged and unstaged, more alike than unlike. Not knowing what you are going to see, surprise, blink.

After so much time in the network, finding its many spaces of images, making such images, photographs, I think once again of the materiality of photography.

As cameras and phone cameras became increasingly software, they became for me the pleasure of seeing various repertoires of photography's history. That is, all the techniques of years past, in terms of aspect ratios, depths of field and film stocks all become instantly visible.

Every photograph, every photography is a particular seeing.

Photography is the location and discovery of any possible image. It is the image of imagining. Photography wants to show us how pervasively we are imaged. What is the image of this seeing going to do for us, to the idea and practice of photography, now but a small subset, in a vast world of visualization and imaging, that exceeds photography?

If I could not see the photograph until I saw it again through the lens of the camera, I could now not see the image until it became a photograph. I would look to see images as photographs.

Following the large print photographs of the Tumblr series, I turned my attention to 'history pictures'. Starting with the genre of history painting, I would make photographs constructed of images. They would be photographs of both a texture and an event. They would be constructions made of images; images of paintings, lithographs, photographs, drawings, graffiti and all kinds of reproductions.

If images could only be seen in the continual appearance and disappearance of the electronic scroll on the screen, the print image, the image written on paper, the photograph, would give a new life to the image. It would make of the image what photography conferred on all things, stillness, not as an arrested image, but more than that, object hood.

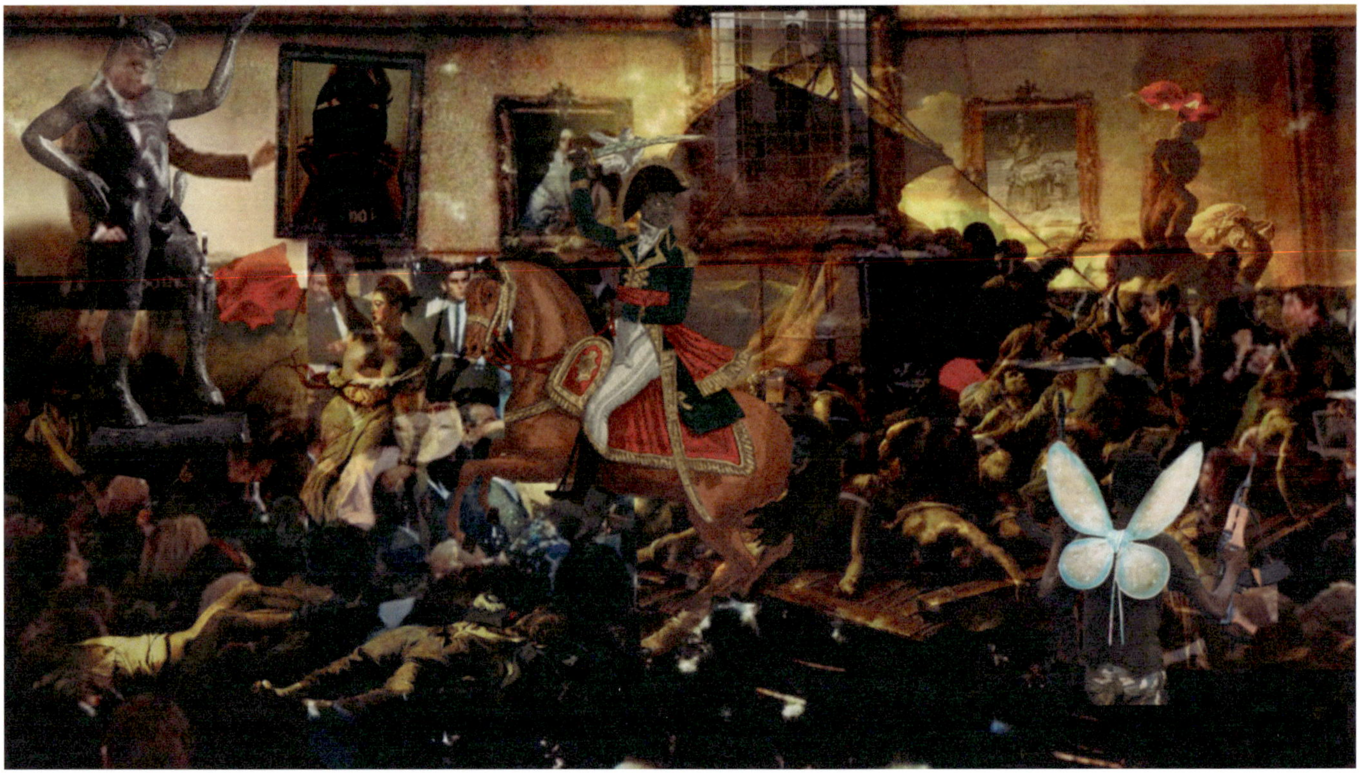

96
Auction, 2015

In this stillness, the image would become a photograph and would have a life that would be part and parcel of its new host, its carrier, be it paper, aluminum, glass or what have you. It would have object hood just as a book has object hood regardless of its contents.

The image photograph insists on the materiality of the image. It announces itself as something more than pixels on the screen. As the image moves to the photograph, it announces itself as a new kind of object in this world.

The photograph presents to us something to be seen in or as image besides the image captured by the lens or constructed in a software environment. The photograph is an event of an object, not simply an image, but a construction, a fabrication. As an object, as a material fact, it has unique properties coming into being with ever-new printing and mounting technologies.

This transmutation of image to object is at the heart of Post-Internet art where in often images, any image, is given an object hood, a thingness, such that image is simply another material, a physical thing of color, form or shape. It doesn't really matter what the image is, as much as, how it can be surfaced and shaped and take on materiality.

When printed on any variety of paper, aluminum or glass, the image, used as a kind of marking, is stretched, scrunched, scattered or presented in huge rolls or part of a design element. Here image becomes a substance beyond representation. The once image becomes a materiality of a photographic object, shaped into a new material form, a kind of sculpting with images.

96 The History Pictures would try and work against this, wanting to present in the object-photograph, both a history of various textures and techniques, and at the same time representation. Rather than a kind of disappearance, the History Pictures would be about appearances, appearances of inscriptions.

This was similarly my attraction in working with books and re-photographing the images within the books, placing them next to the reproduction images bound in the source books. These books I put through a saw to emphasize their object hood. This way the book would be a carrier of the image and its erasure and the entirety of books would become armatures for new inventions.

There was no longer book nor image nor photograph bound, but the collapsed book-image-now-object all commingled into one thing, a presence unto itself. A thing used now both as tableaux and patterning, part and parcel of its armature.

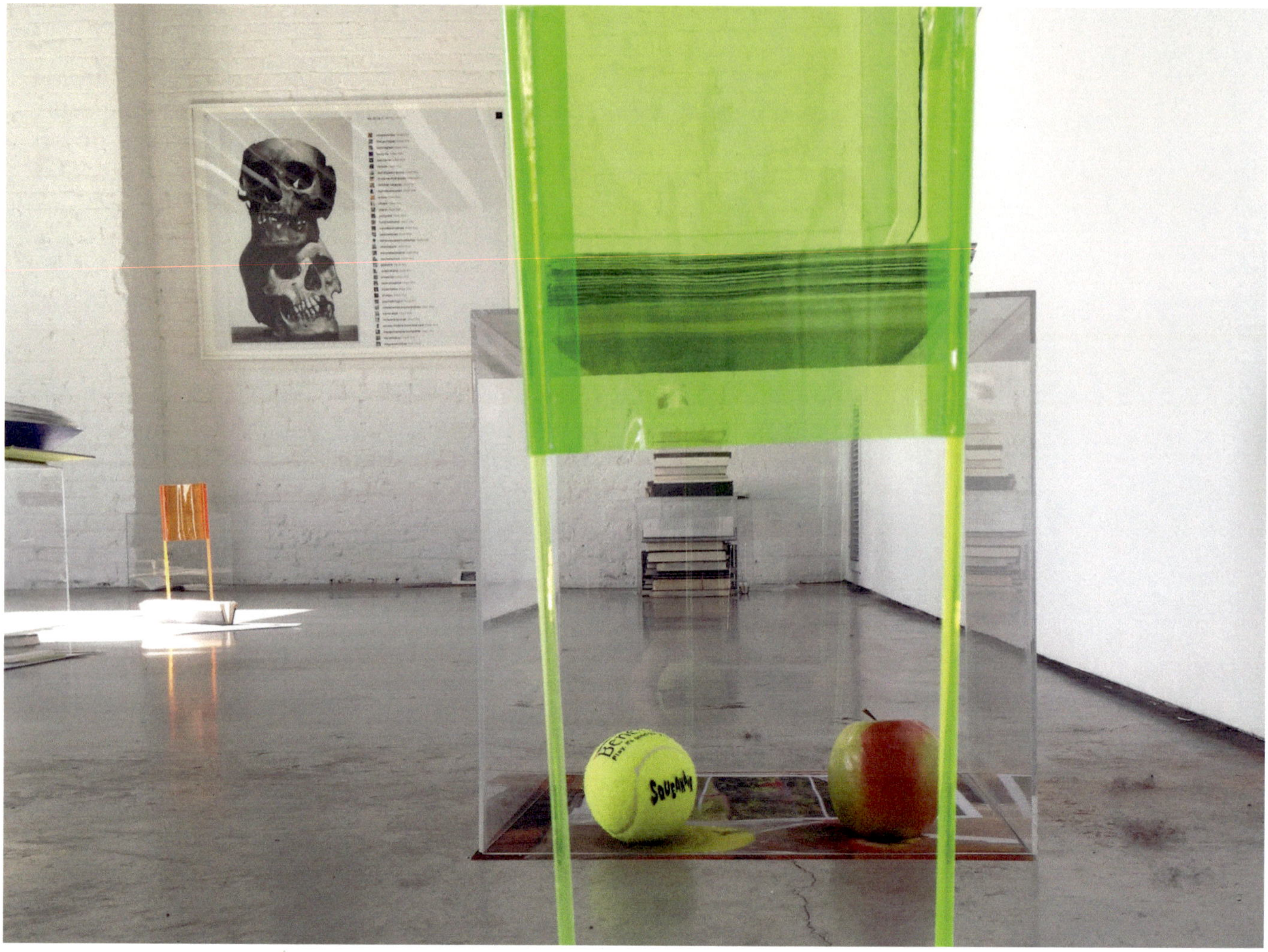

97
#Image, Paper Sculptures, 2014

97 These Paper Sculptures were framed by transparent plexiglass cubes with books sawed, cut, (re)framed into elaborate postures and juxtaposed with other books and objects. The cubes themselves act like containers, transparent like a lens, like a picture frame, they frame these unbound books, creating a new kind of image.

Books, of course, were the original Internet, the printing press, the pre-digital digital. Books were the way to reproduce the same images, even if just words, and disseminate them in discrete containers. Then along came the digital and literally blew the covers off the books, undid their binding, sent the images within every which way. The individual book sculptures are quite elaborate, their content inflecting their arrangement, what they sit with and how they've been framed.

The Paper Sculptures would hedge image and object, referent and thing, to become the presentation of a kind of disappearance.

In taking images from Tumblr, printing them large, something done also now by Richard Prince and his Instagram series, photography uses the materiality of the photograph to see a new condition of imaging.

The electronic image is not so much light, but any possible values, whose values can only be believed in the instance of their appropriation, their transformation, their deletion, their ruin or their decay in the nth layer of Photoshop, hardly seen or turned off and then turned on and off again. Struggle as we may to see the image in the photograph, we can't, even though paradoxically it's right there in front of us. Ah, but is it?

If there is no image, there *is* a photograph and we can see that. We can touch it, walk up to it, and stand close to it.

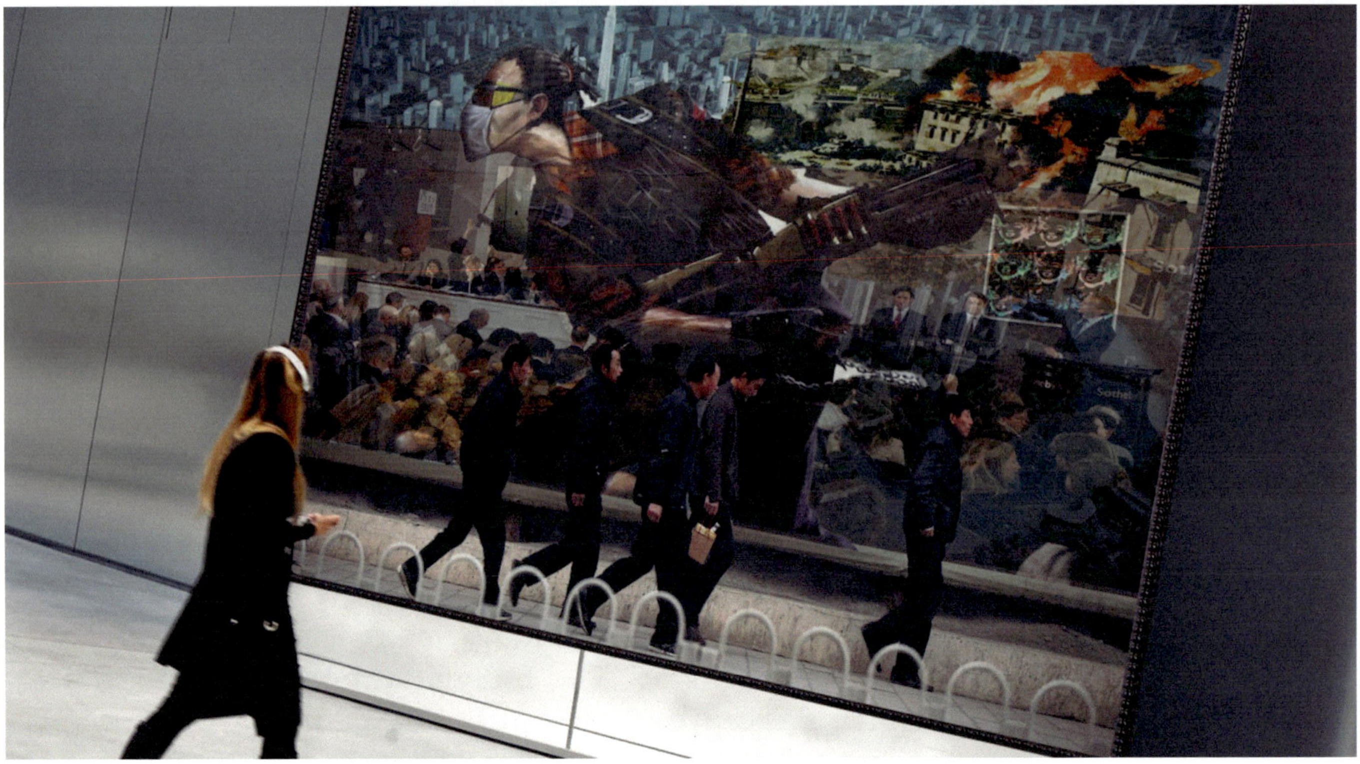

98
Tibet Tianjin, 2015

98 Photography fixes the image in transit. It is a stop along an exchange of back-and-forth, it brings stillness to our immersion in a constant and bewildering piece of theater, a ceaseless shape shifting that is indefinable and unstoppable.

In all of this imaging we are continually transacted. Though we knowingly participate in much of it, much more is invisible to us. From our social media, to our credit card transactions, to our biometrics, we are continually producing data as we avail ourselves of user services that have us imaged.

What is decisive in our society and what shapes much of our everyday lives is this pervasive imaging, which has almost totally withdrawn itself from the visual plane and escapes traditional representation techniques.

If photography once gave us narrative closure, both remove and intimacy, knowledge of and from a distance, the always on image-photograph gives us this realm in which we are always in photography, in a regime of visualization, in a regime of constant sight.

The image-photograph is a continuum and it is this larger sense of imaging and how it has evolved that we look for in our photography. We want photography not to show simply images but the image of our imaging. And yet, in saying this, it seems photography is over there, enclosed and encircled, when in fact it is pervasive and everywhere, only waiting to be named as such.

IMAGE
PHOTOGRAPH

Pictures

Text # Archive

27 seconds ago

In his seminal Archive Fever: A Freudian Impression, Jacques Derrida unfolds the structure of recording, of archiving, as involving a trace (text, information) being consigned to a substrate, a place (and it can be a virtual place) of consignation. So that for Derrida the archive is a conjoining of trace and substrate – writing on paper, painting on rock, cut on skin, even a configuring of brain particles in the psychic apparatus. Does the latter mean that 'archive' and 'memory' are conflated? No. The need for exteriority (ultimately) separates 'archive' from 'memory':

...since the archive doesn't consist simply in remembering, in living memory, in anamnesis; but in consigning, in inscribing a trace in some external location – there is no archive without some location, that is, some space outside. Archive is not a living memory. It's a location – that's why the political power of the archons is so essential in the definition of the archive. So that you need the exteriority of the place in order to get something archived.[14]

female body tied up with ropes, fixed in obscene positions. Things condense power and violence. Just as a thing accumulates productive forces and desires, so does it also accumulate destruction and decay.

So then how about a specific thing called "image"? It is a complete mystification to think of the digital image as a shiny immortal clone of itself. On the contrary, not even the digital image is outside history. It bears the bruises of its crashes with politics and violence. It is nothing like, say, a carbon copy of Trotsky brought back to life through digital manipulation (though of course it could *show* him); rather, the material articulation of the image is like a clone of Trotsky walking around with an ice pick in his head. The bruises of images are its glitches and artifacts, the traces of its rips and transfers. Images are violated, ripped apart, subjected to interrogation and probing. They are stolen, cropped, edited, and re-appropriated. They are bought, sold, leased. Manipulated and adulated. Reviled and revered. To participate in the image means to take part in all of this.

Photo

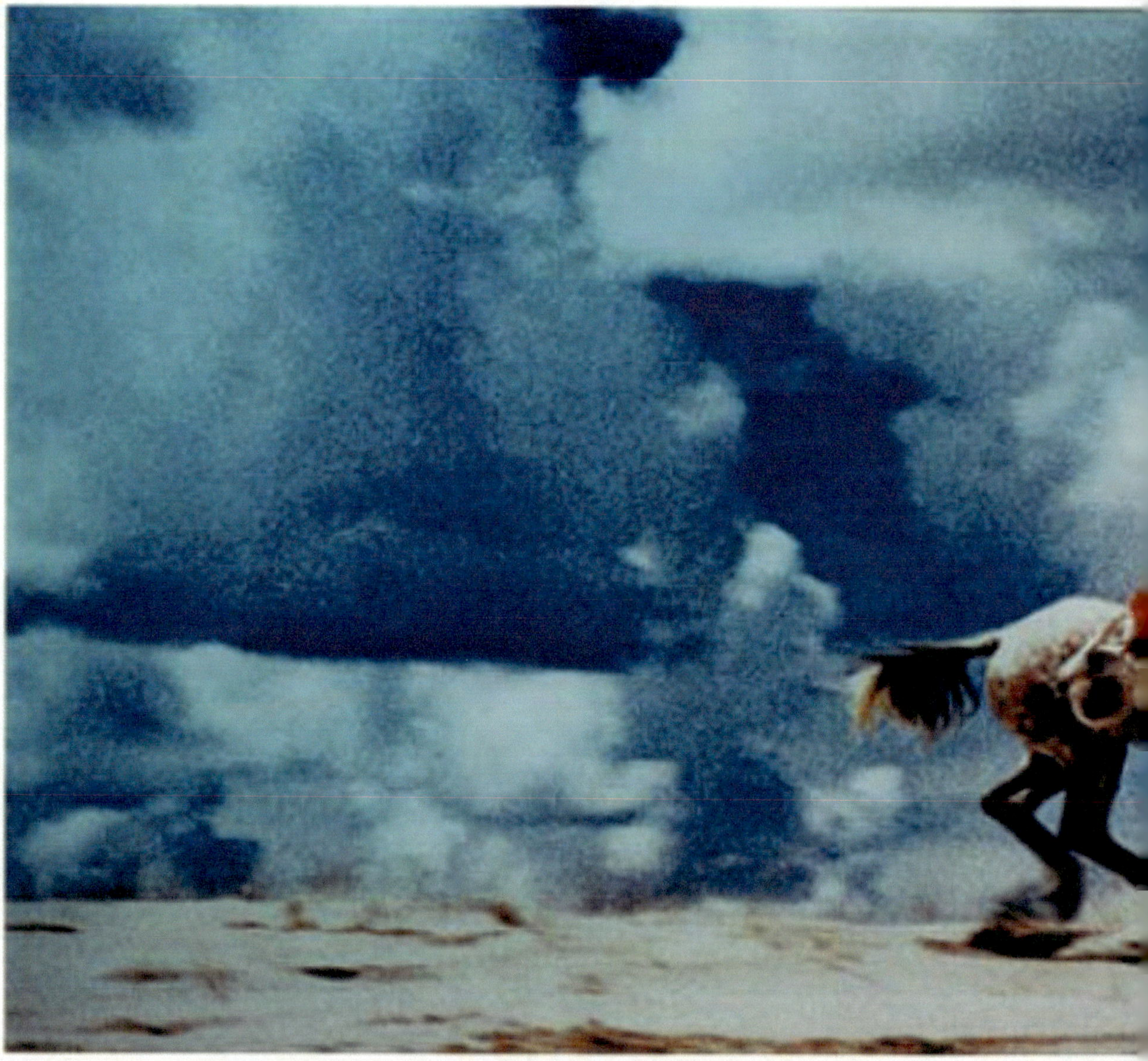

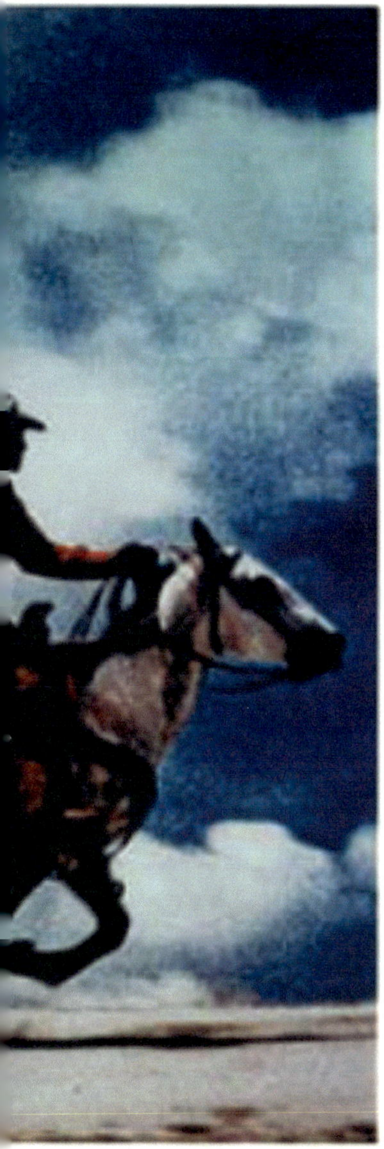

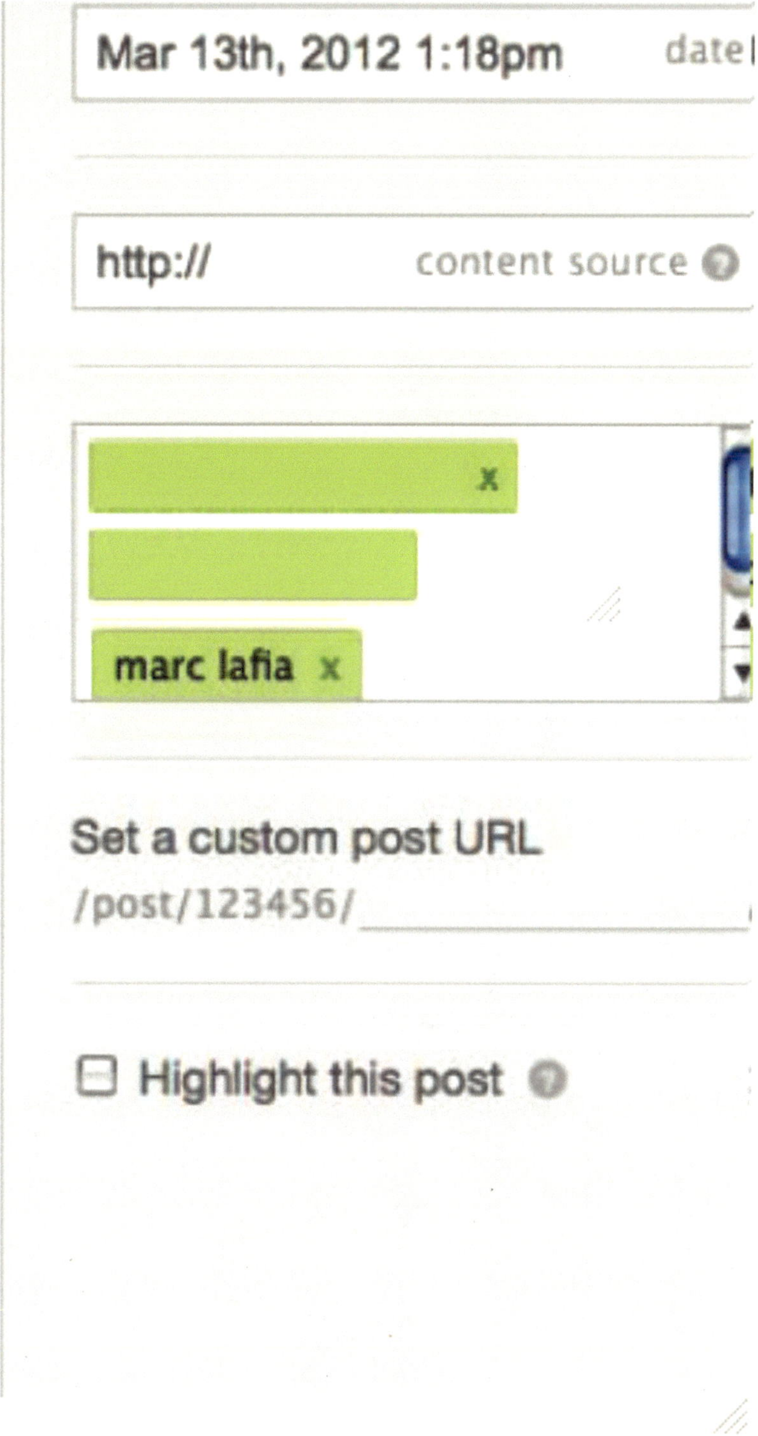
Mar 13th, 2012 1:18pm
date
http://
content source
marc lafia
Set a custom post URL
/post/123456/
Highlight this post

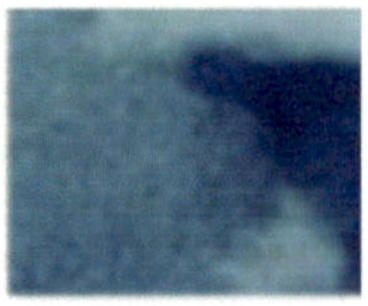

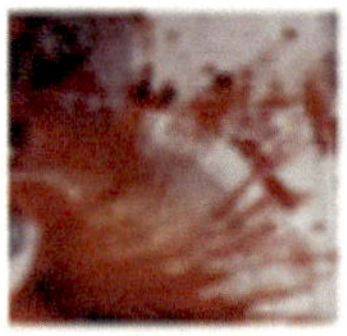

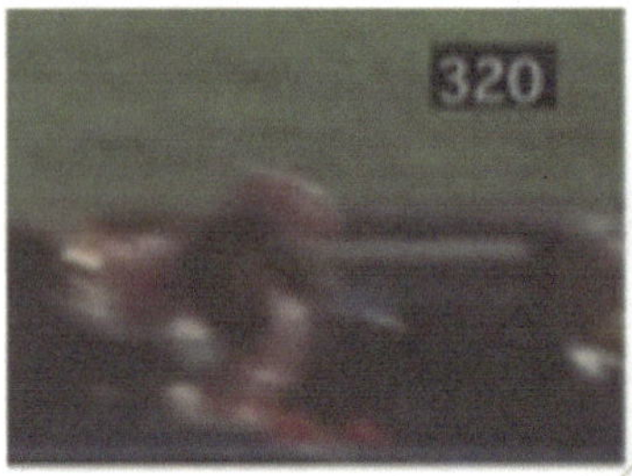
320

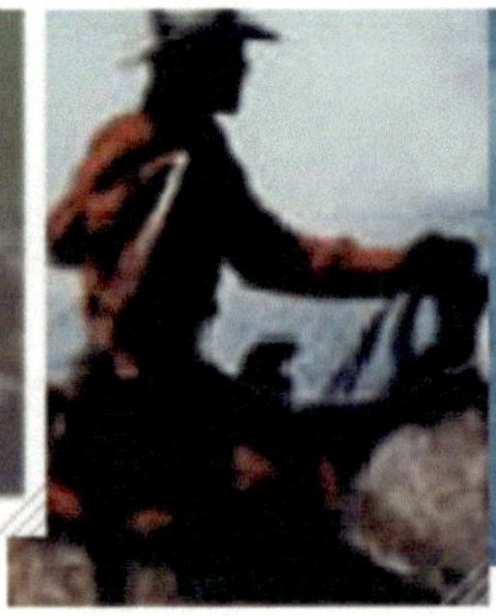

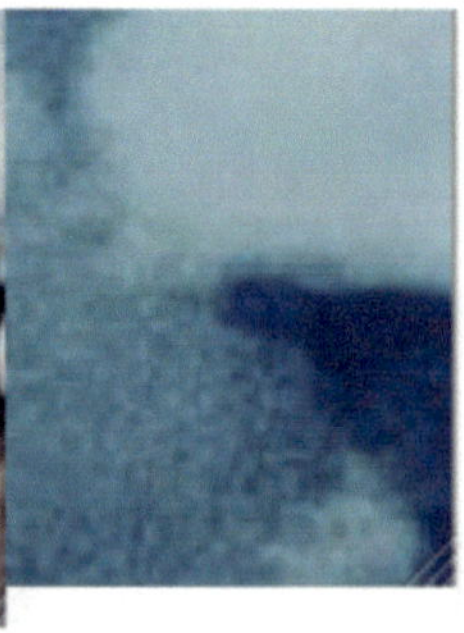

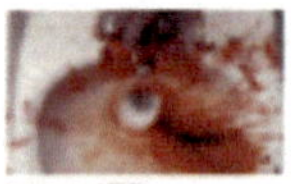

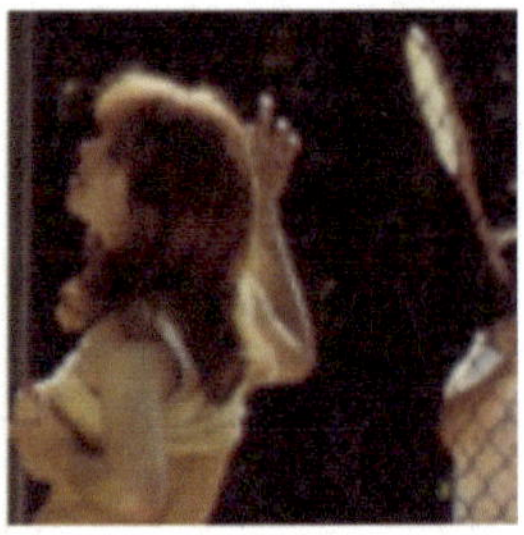

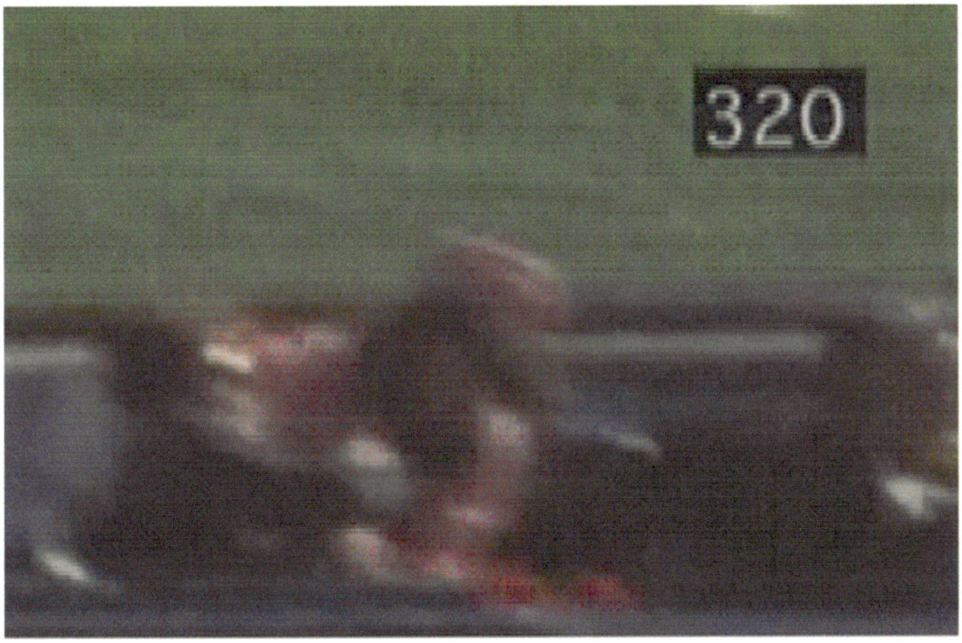
320

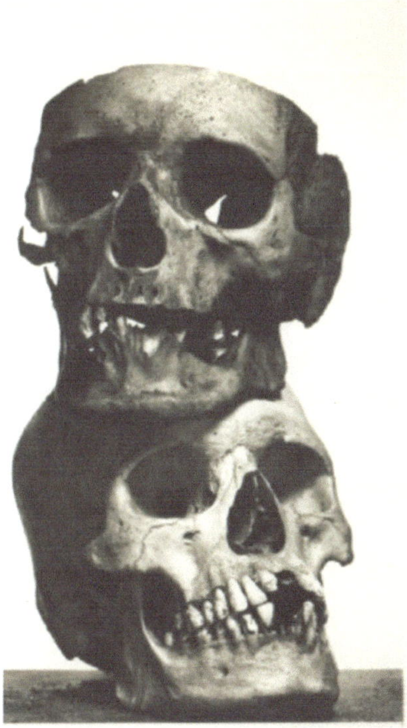

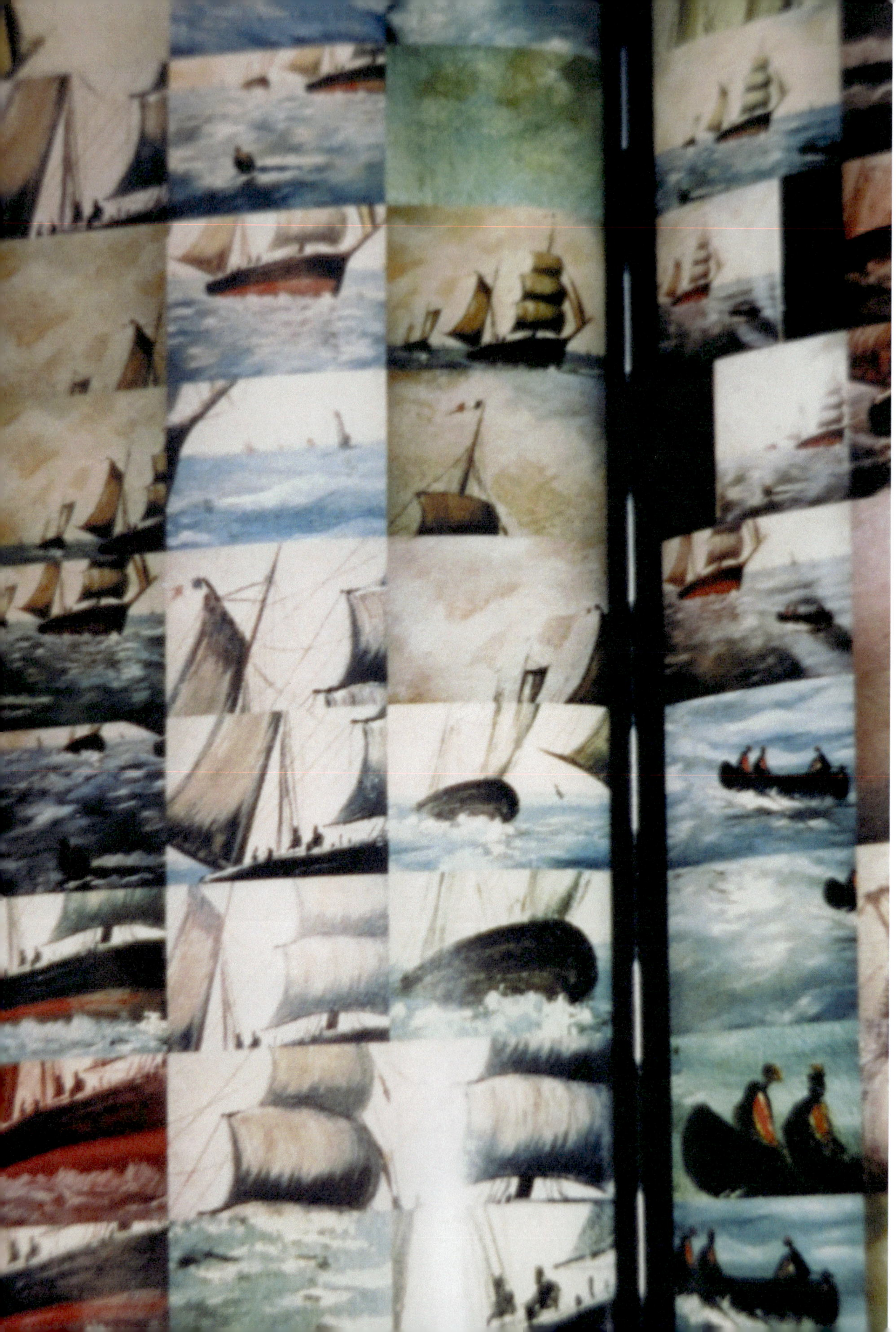

MARCH 2012 242 POSTS

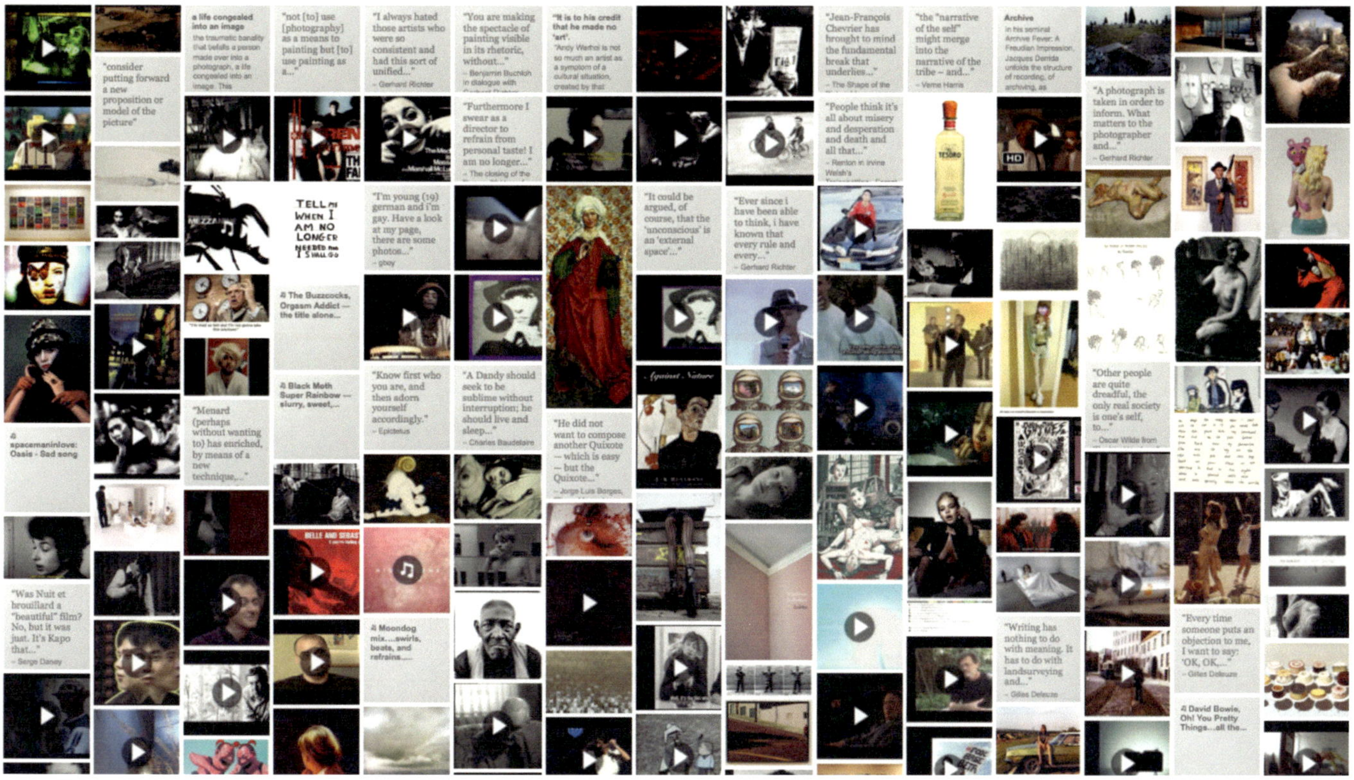

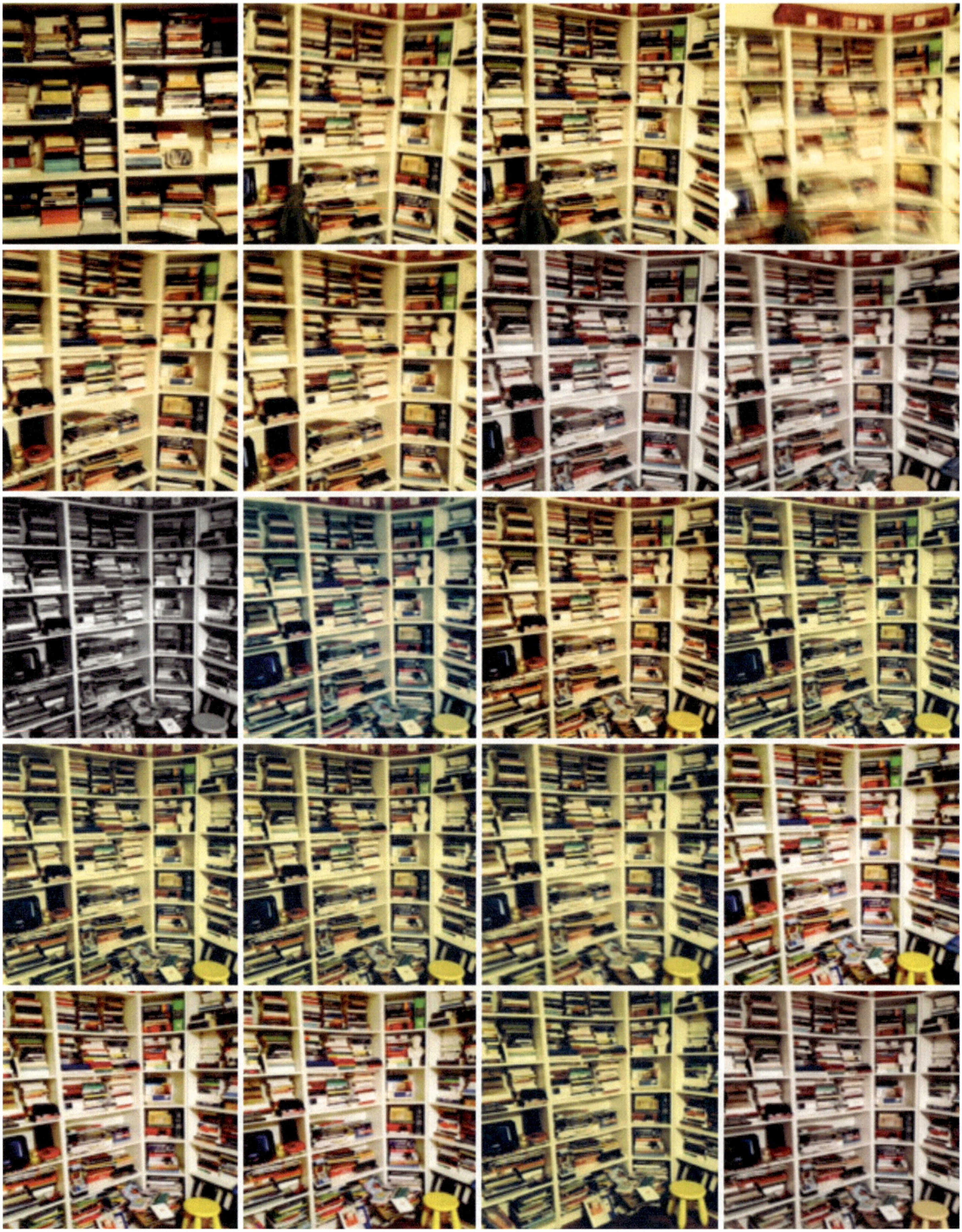

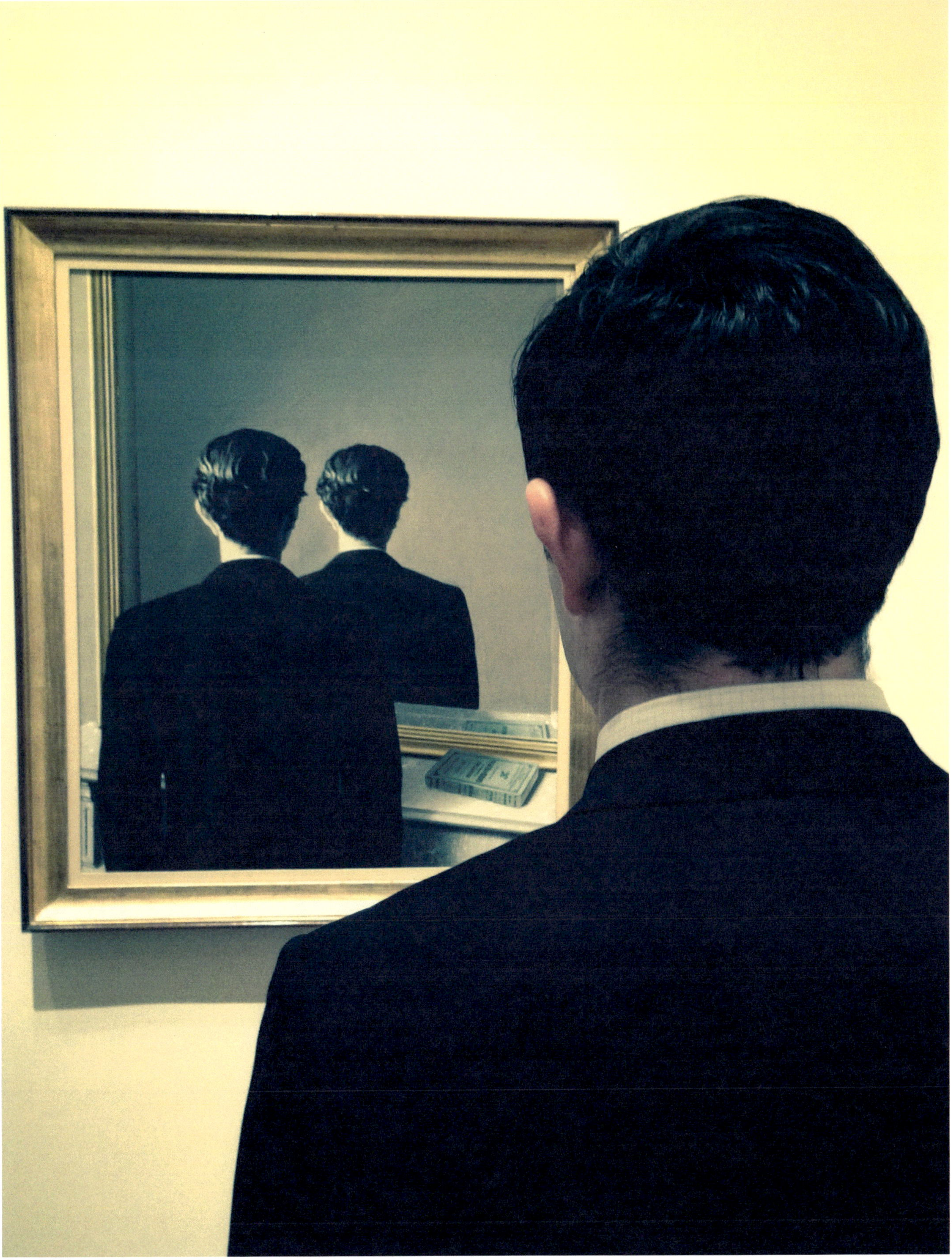

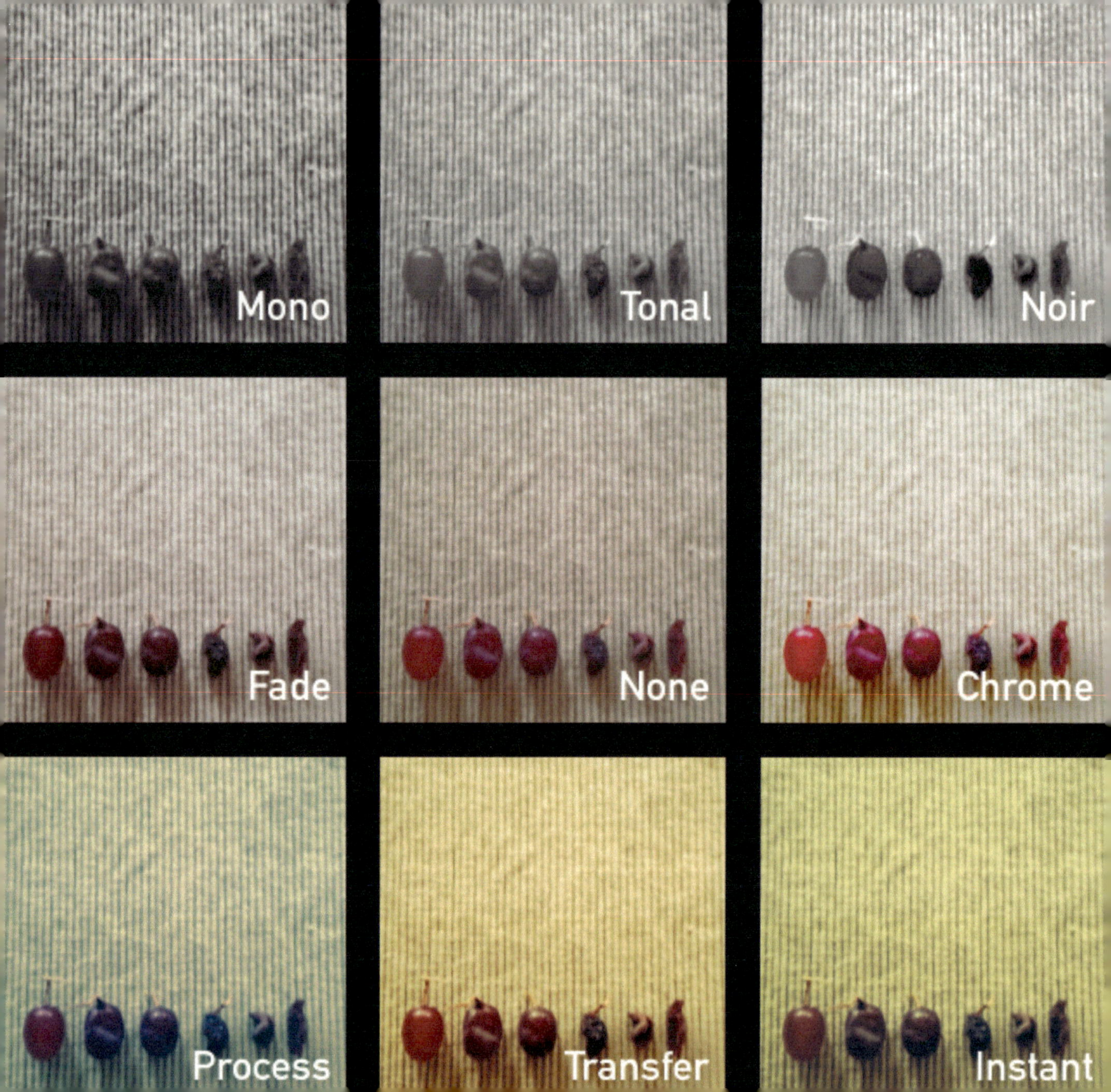
Mono
Tonal
Noir
Fade
None
Chrome
Process
Transfer
Instant

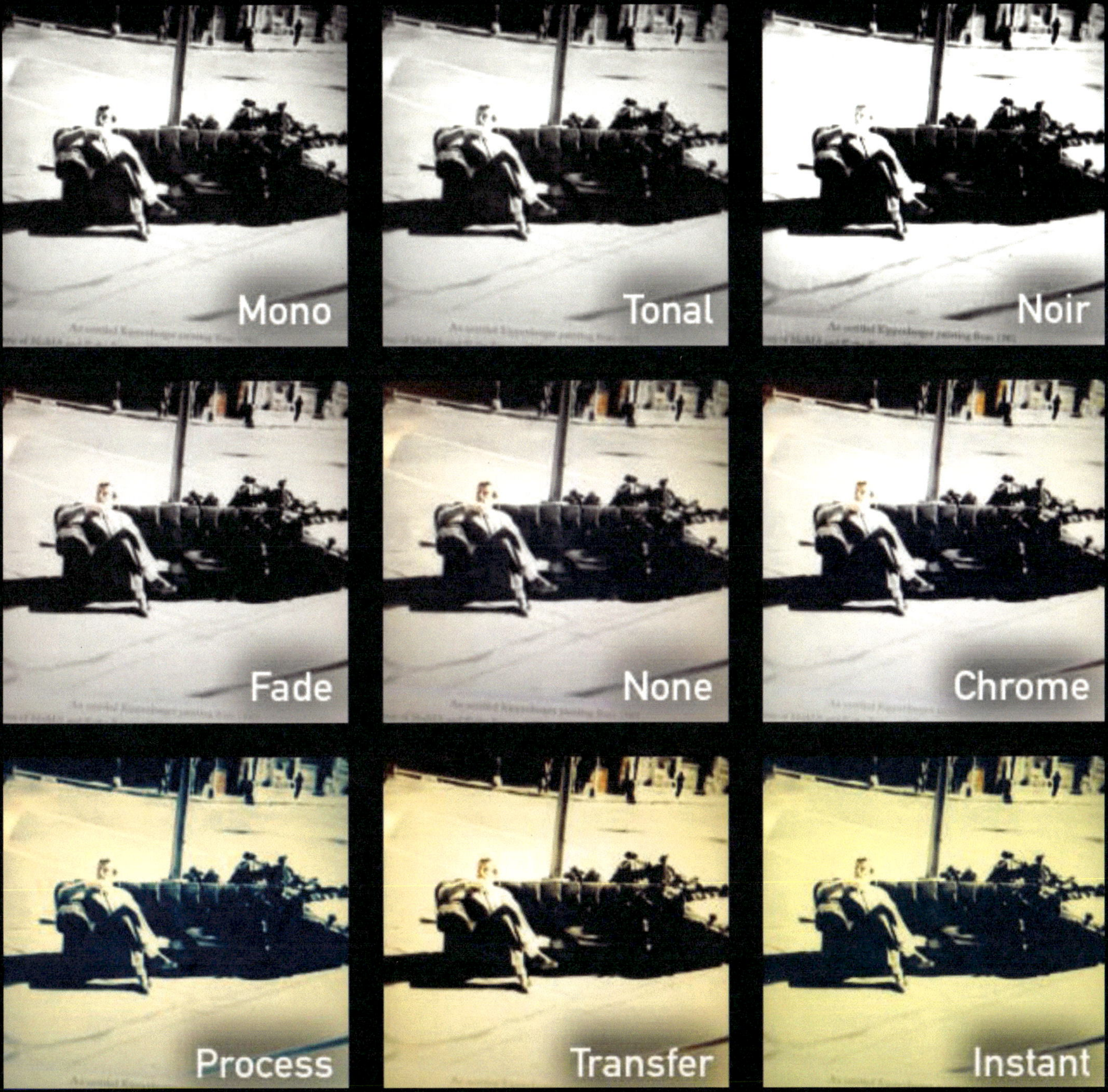
Mono
Tonal
Noir
Fade
None
Chrome
Process
Transfer
Instant

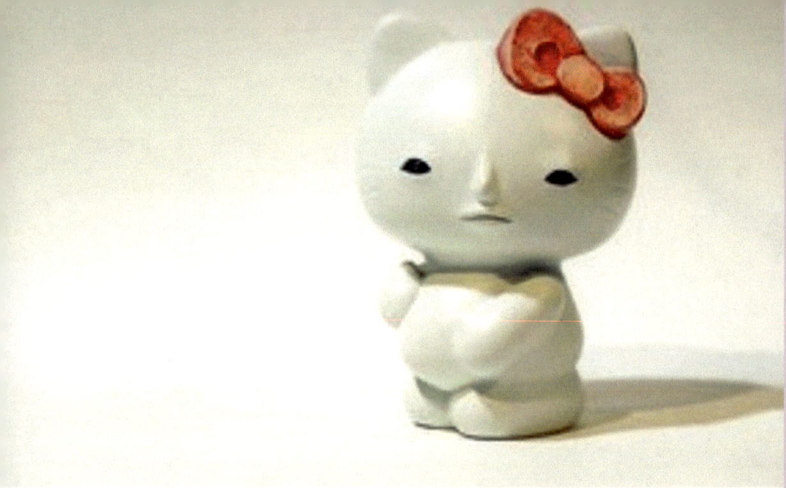

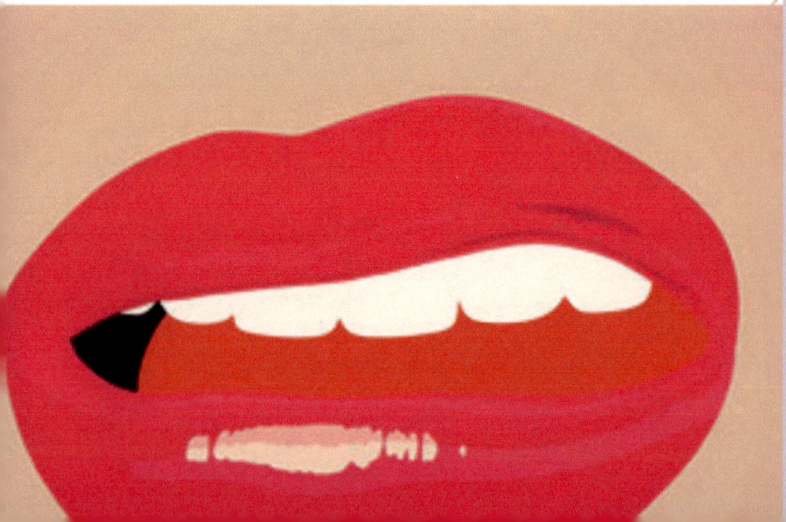

TELL ME HOW
CAN I LET GO
OF ALL THE THINGS
THAT SHOULDN'T
EVEN MATTER?
BECAUSE IT REALLY SHAKES
AND FUCKS ME UP INSIDE AND
MAKES ME THINK ALL THESE
LOUSY THOUGHTS.

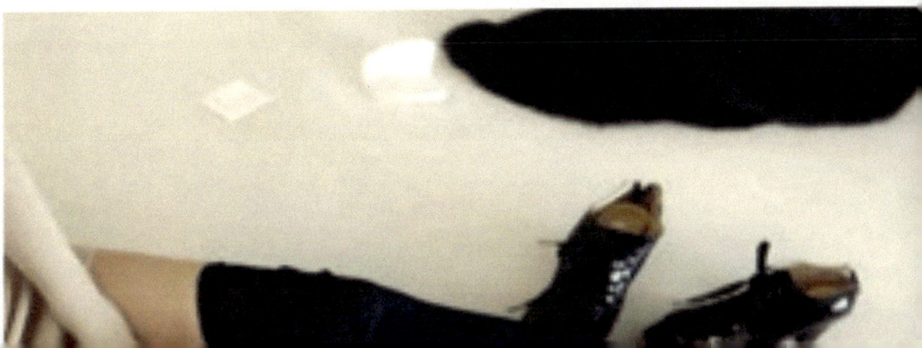

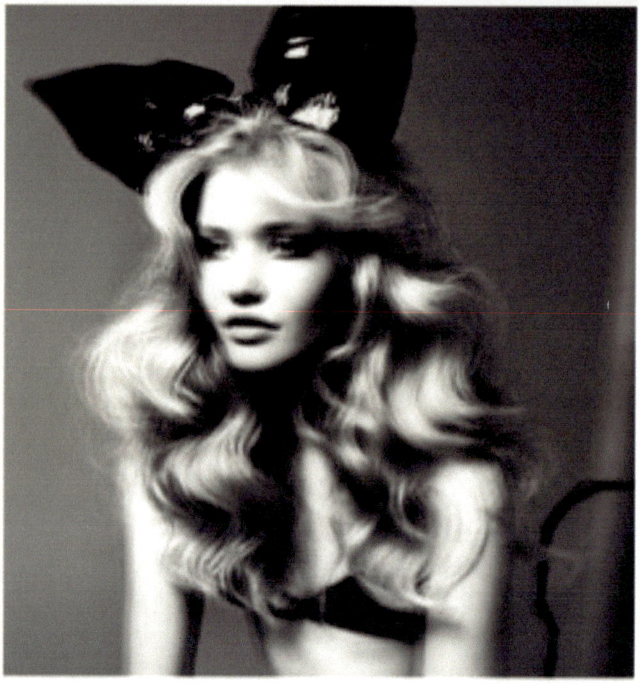

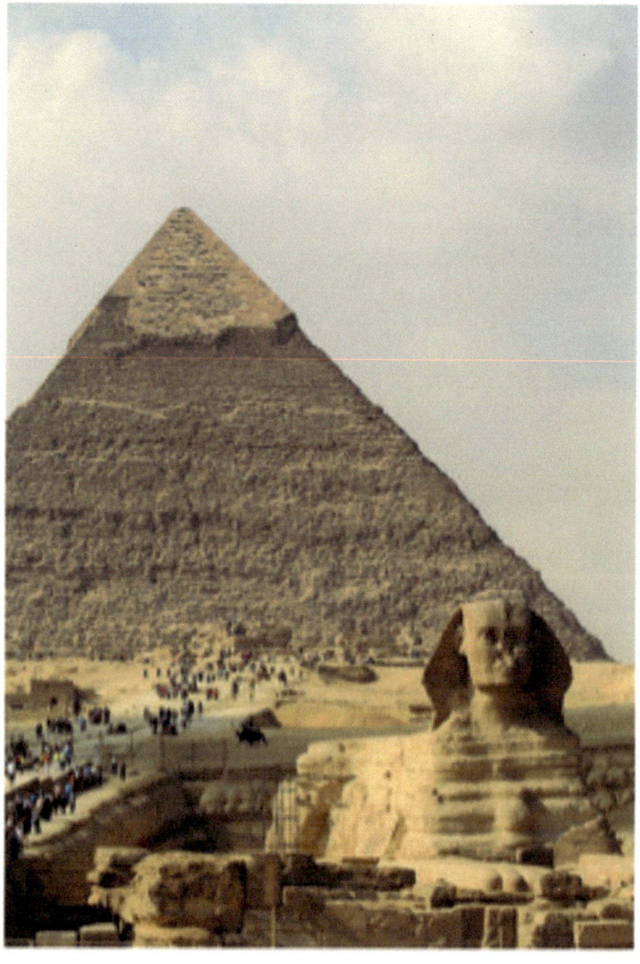

?A kiss is a lovely trick designed by nature to stop speech when words become superfluous.? ***written by*** **Ingrid Bergman**

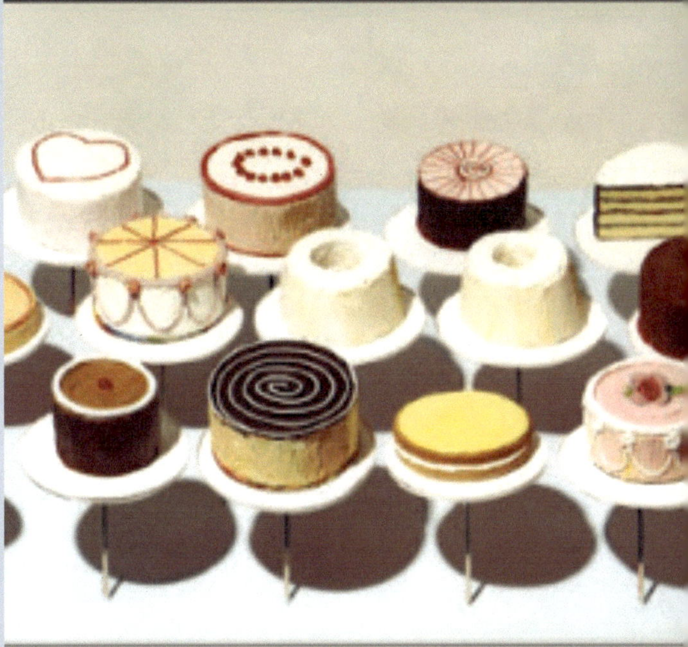

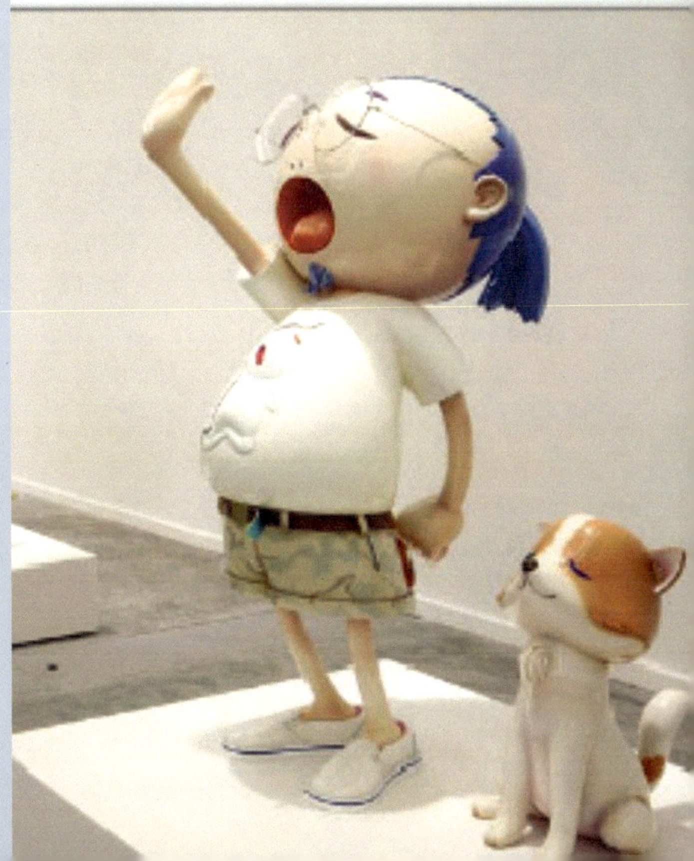

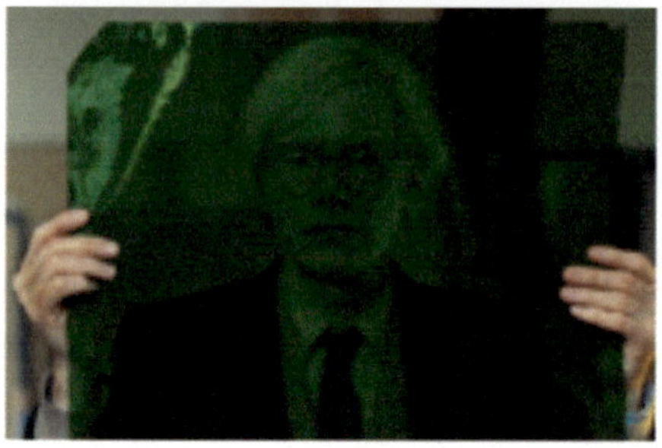

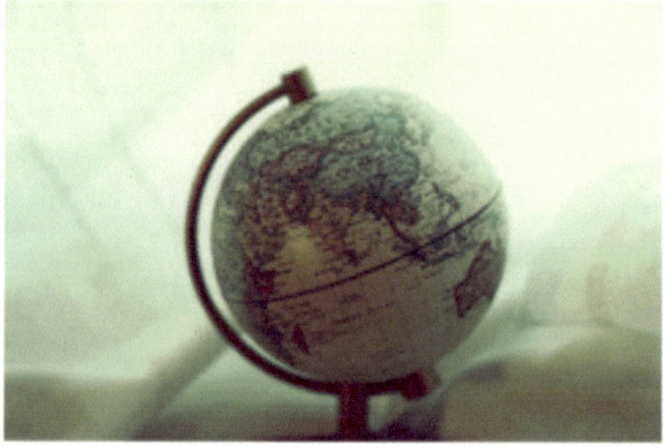

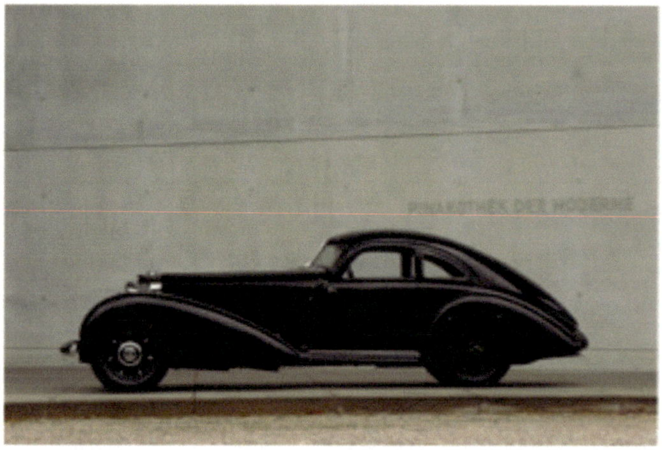
PINAKOTHEK DER MODERNE

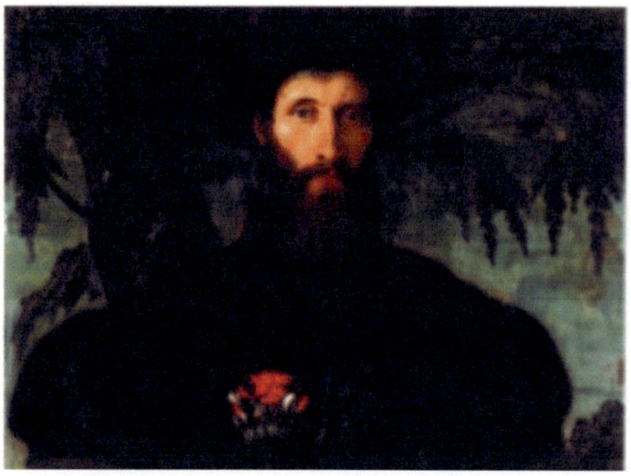

adventure,
bless,
and don't be sorry.

1,080 notes) Originally posted by typewriterword

(77 notes)

my life is just a text post that doesn't get any notes

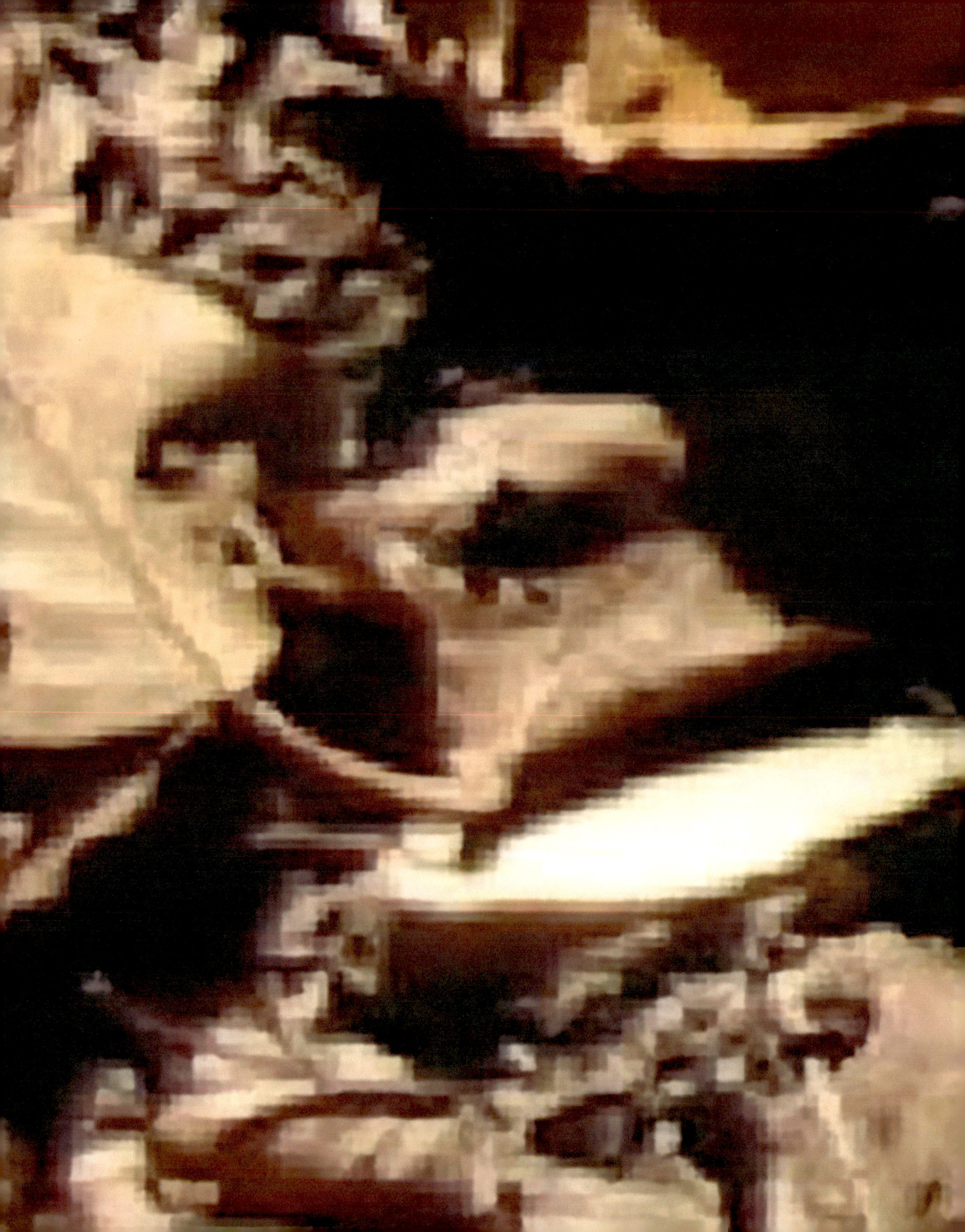

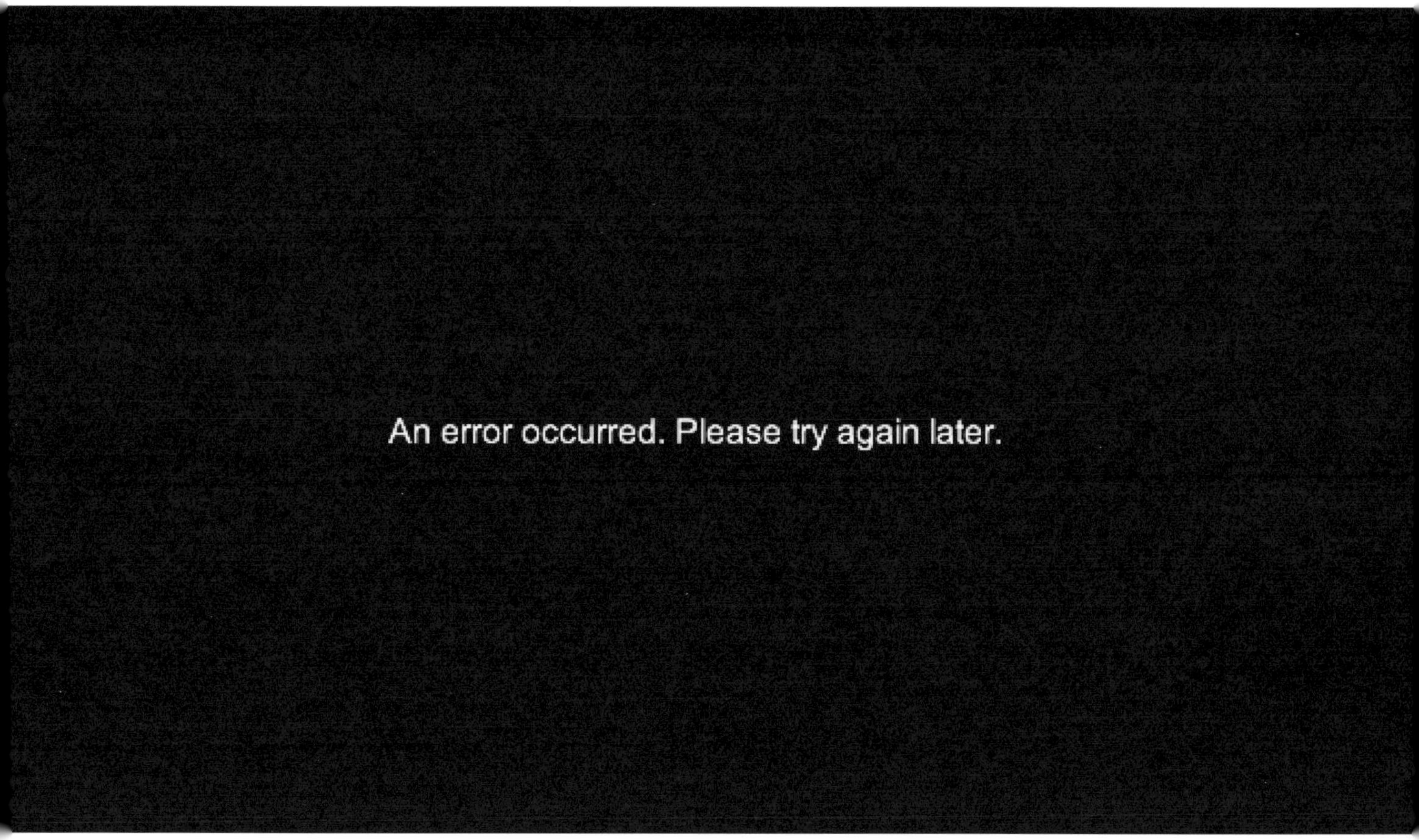
An error occurred. Please try again later.

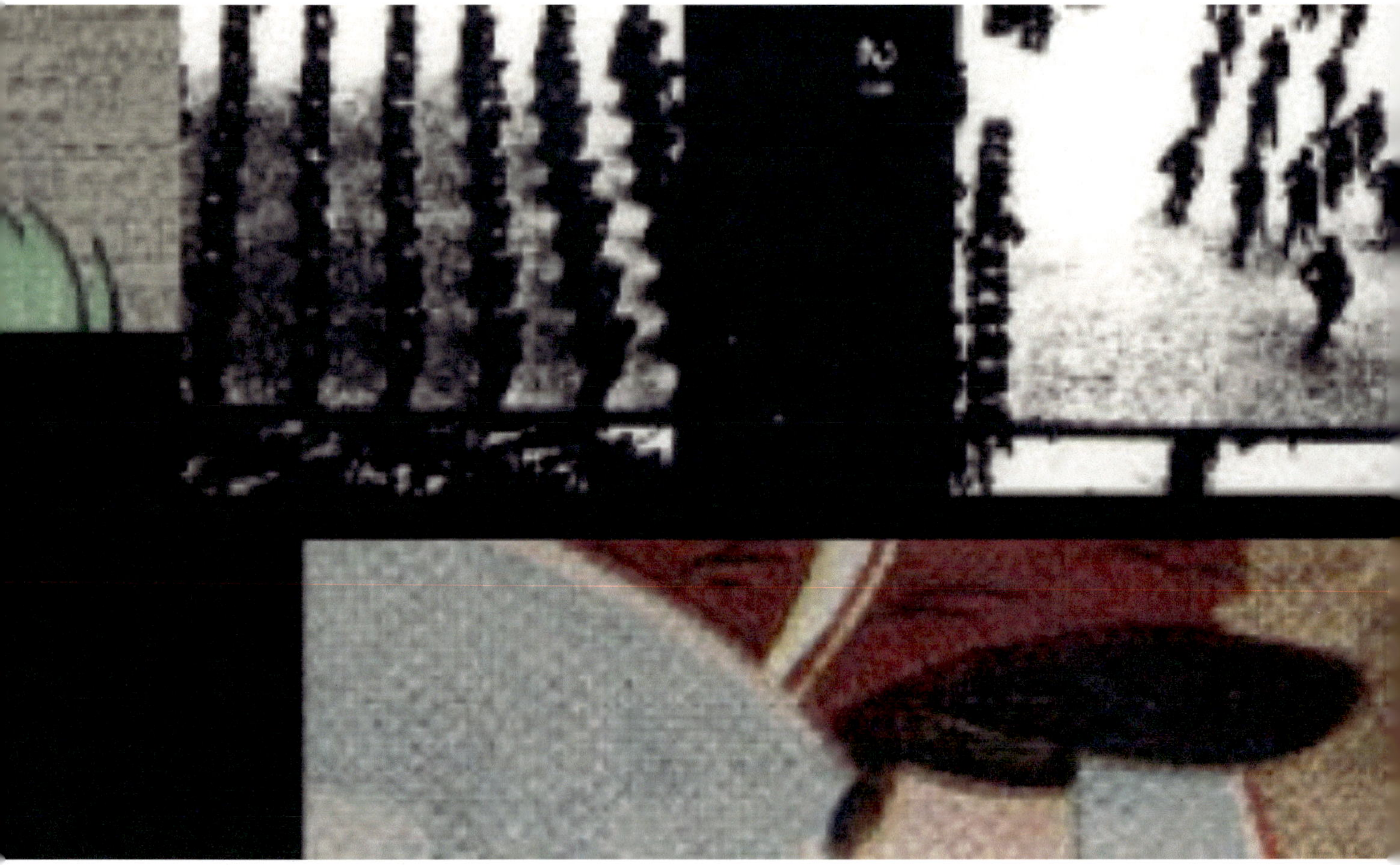

ECT

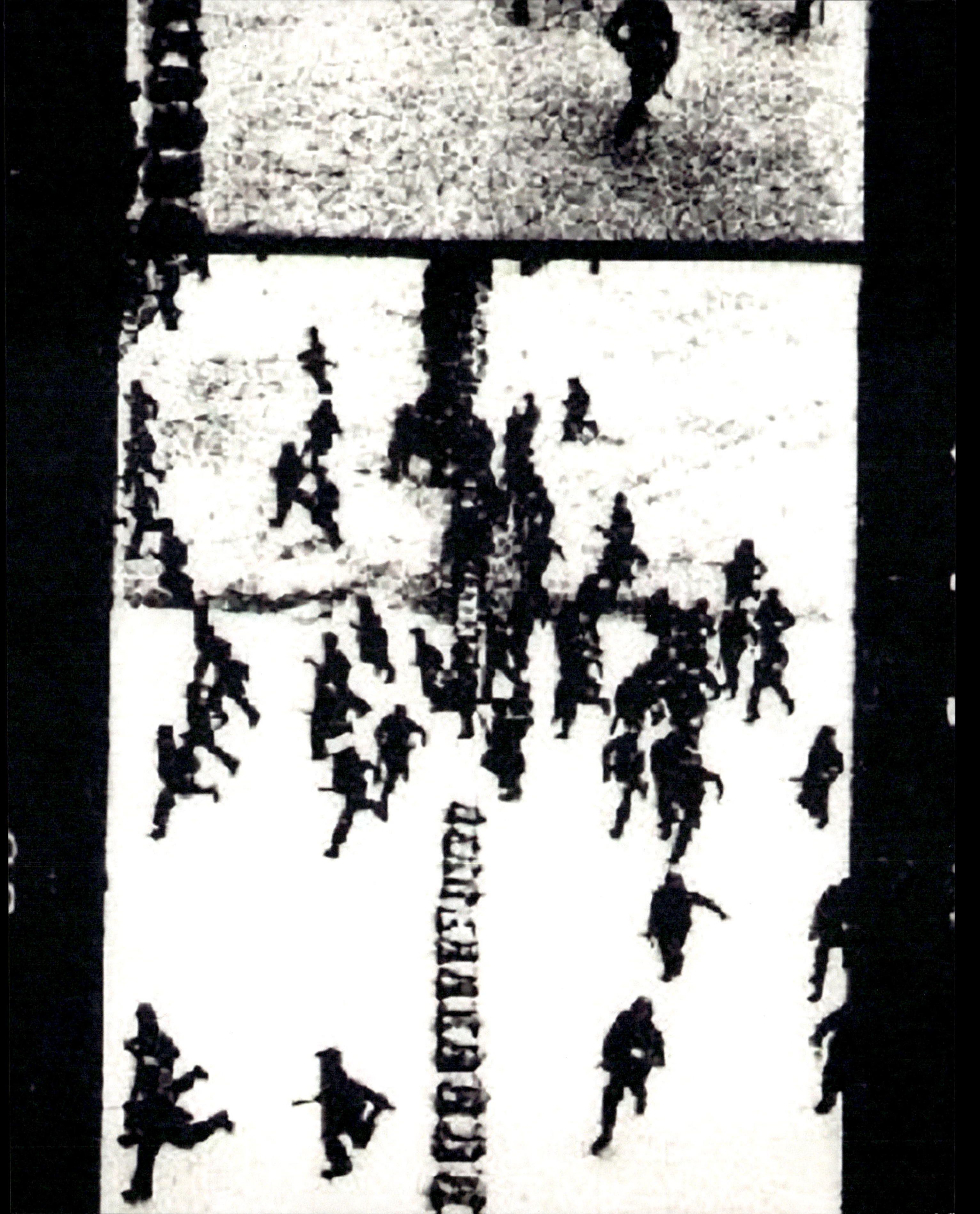

facebook

Please confirm your identity

Challenge 4 of 5

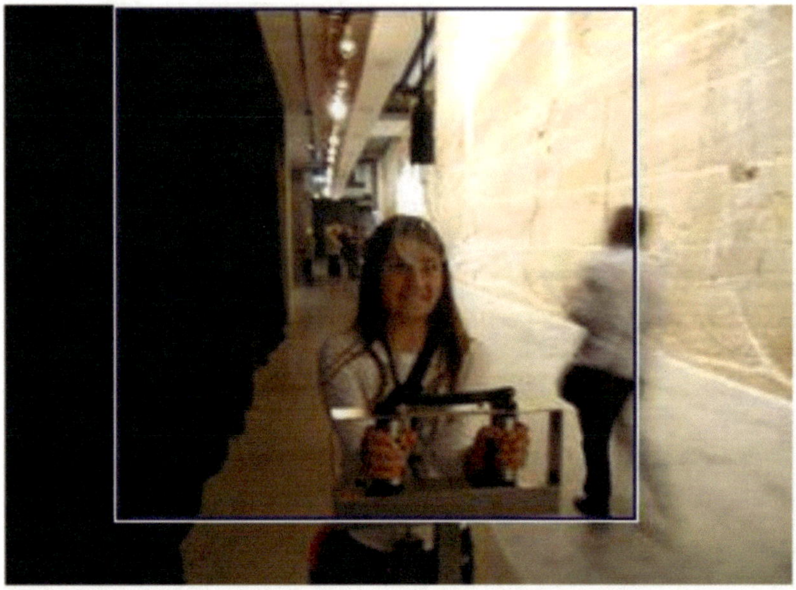

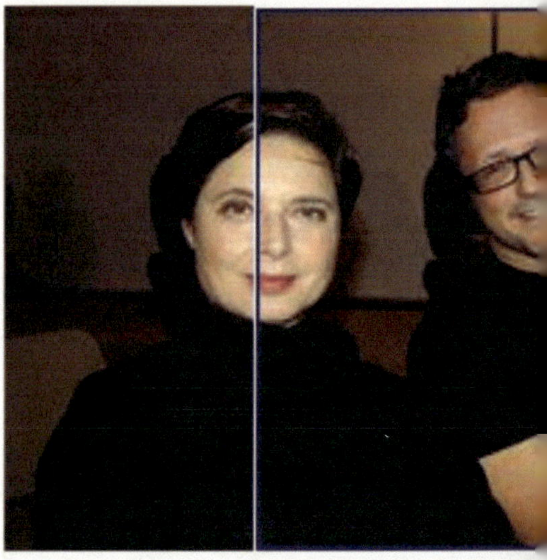

This appears to be:

- (●) Rafael Lozano-Hemmer
- ( ) Yoshi Sodeoka
- ( ) Paul Clay
- ( ) T David Downs
- ( ) Vuk Cosic
- ( ) Belu-simion Fainaru

Submit **Skip ▸** (2 skips left)

Confirm identity another way

Log Out

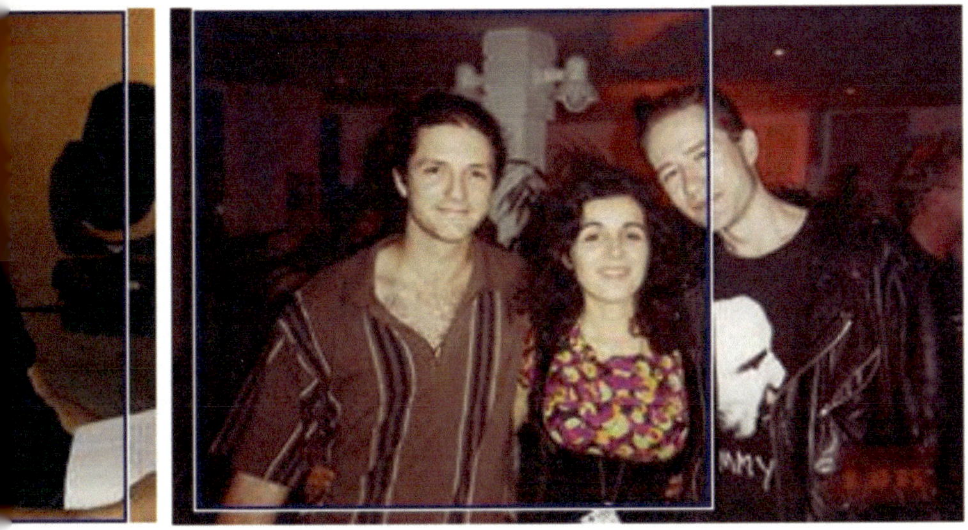

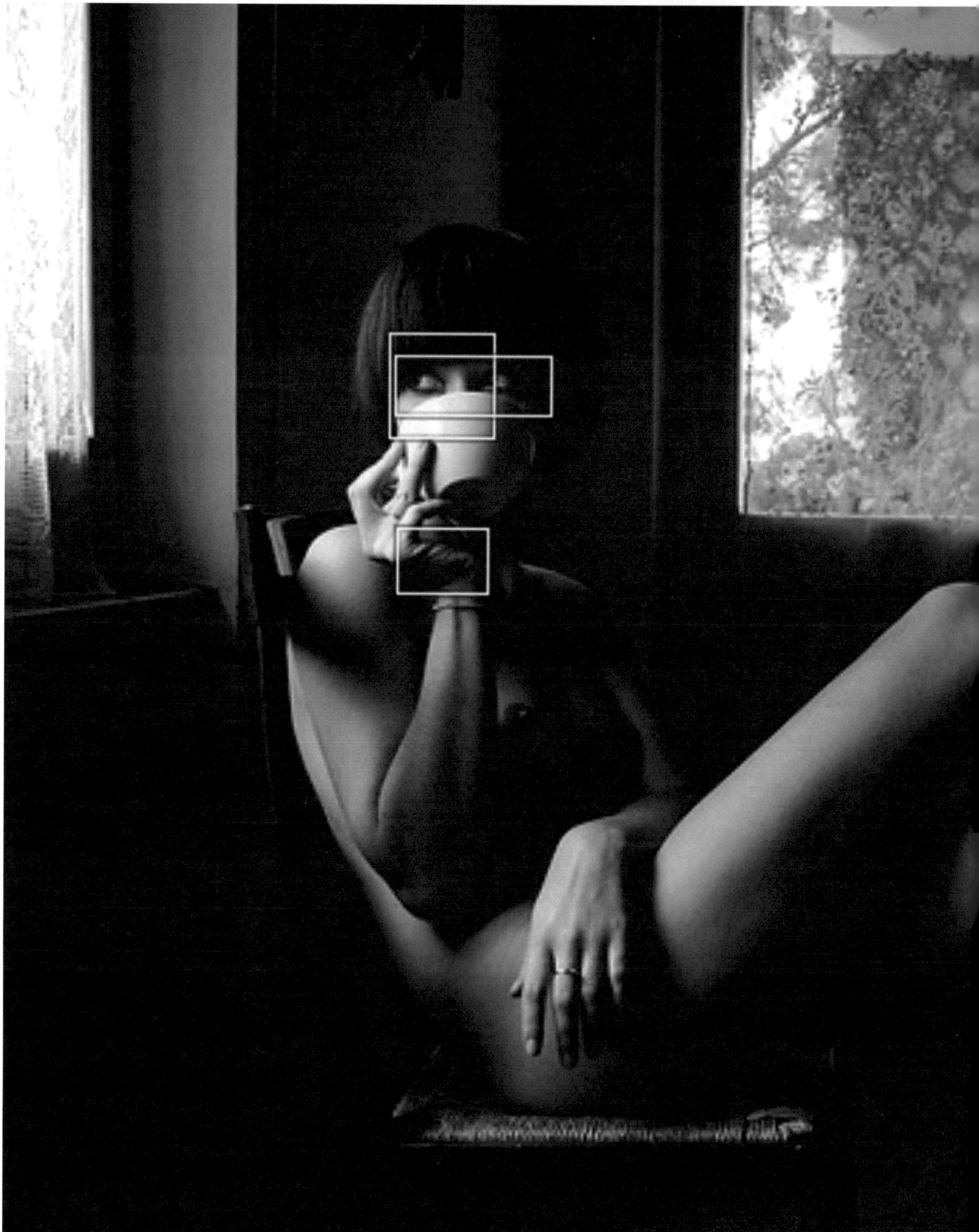

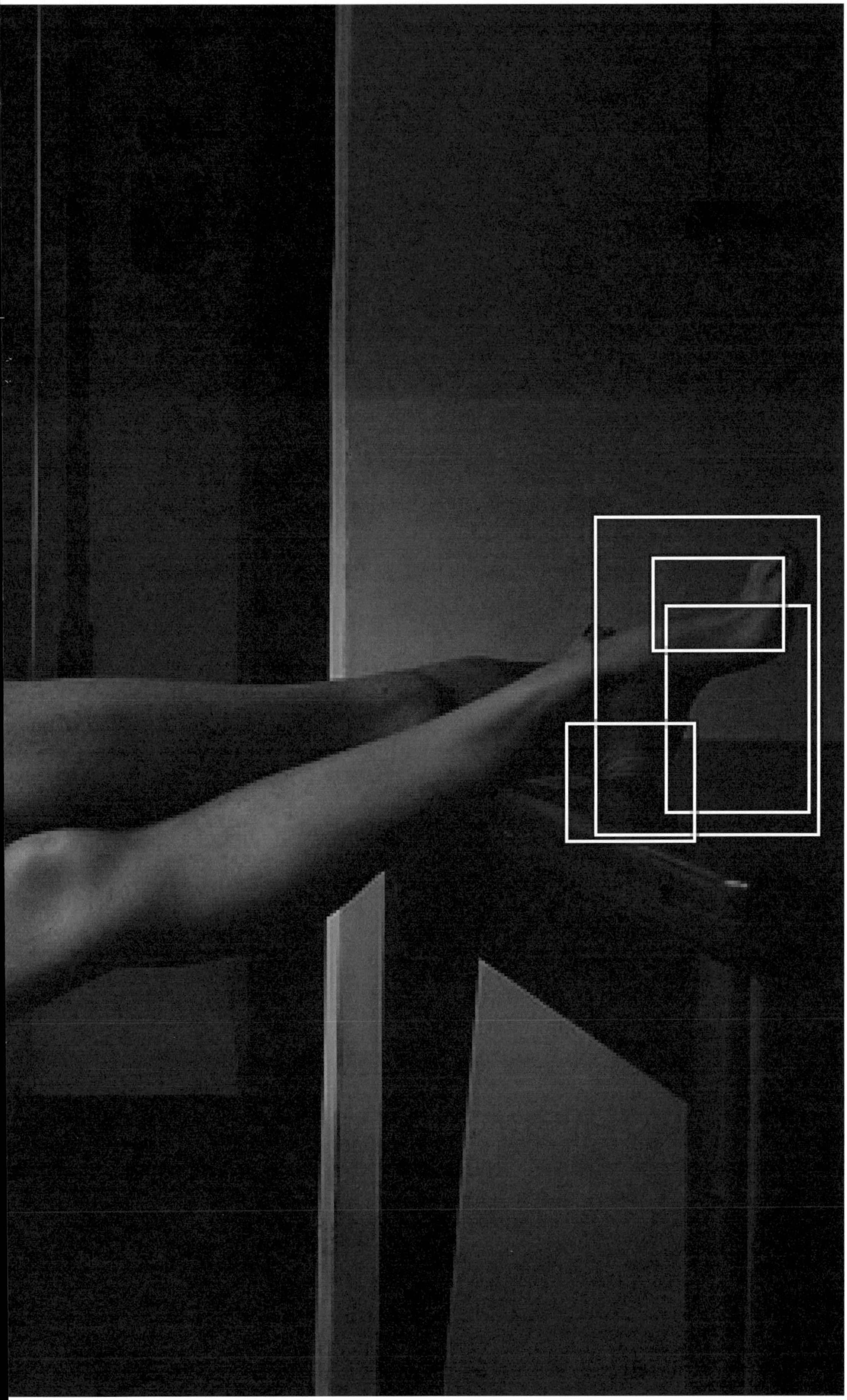

YES PLEASE, SHOW ME THE PHOTO

Or, actually, no - **take me home**.

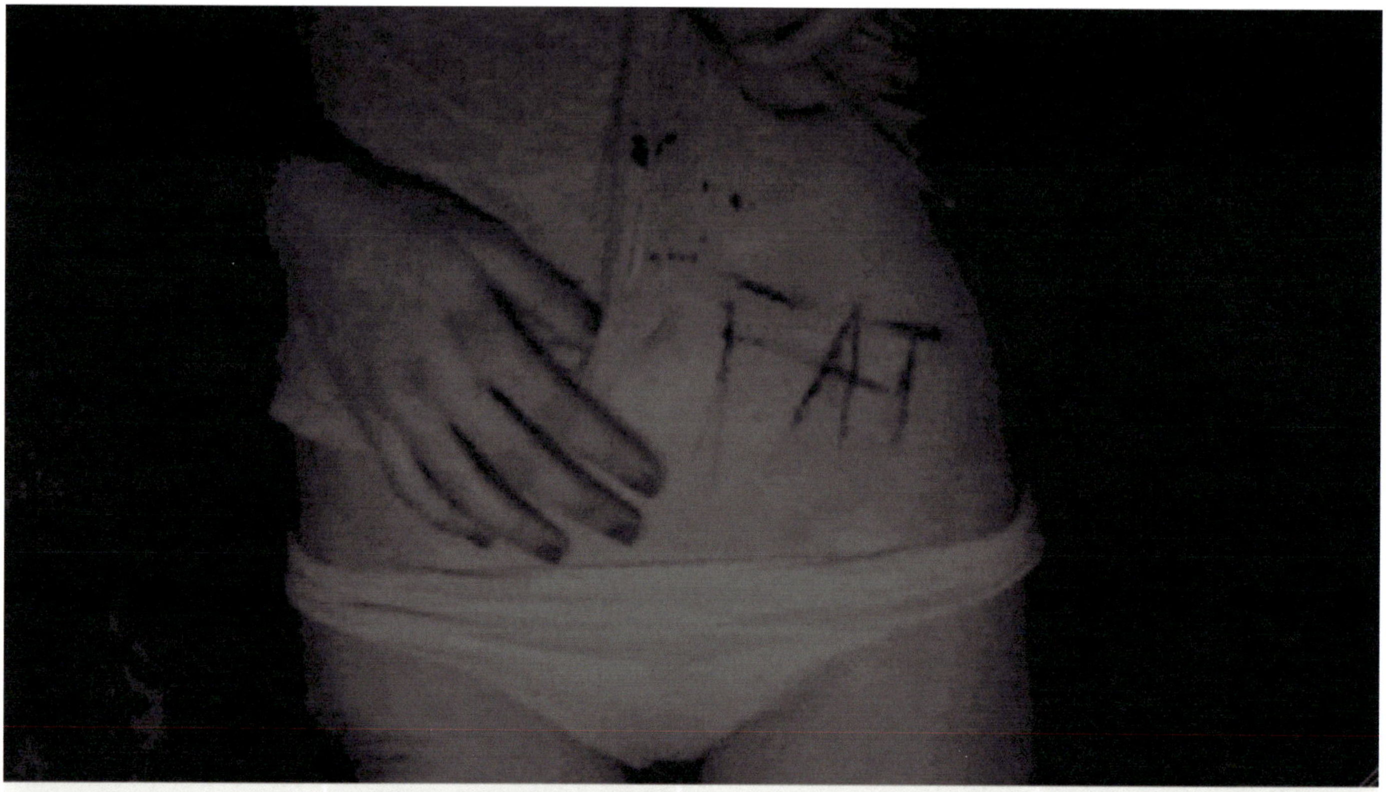
FAT

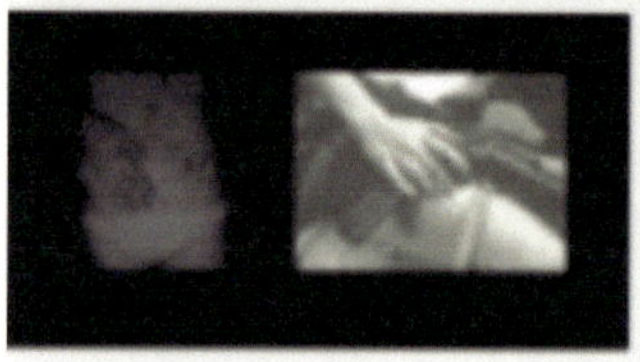

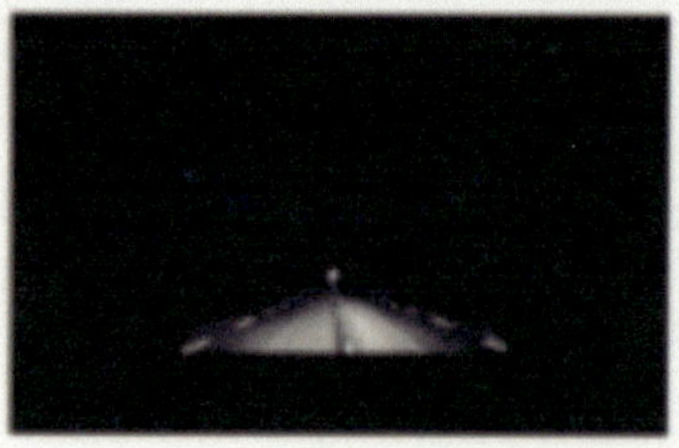

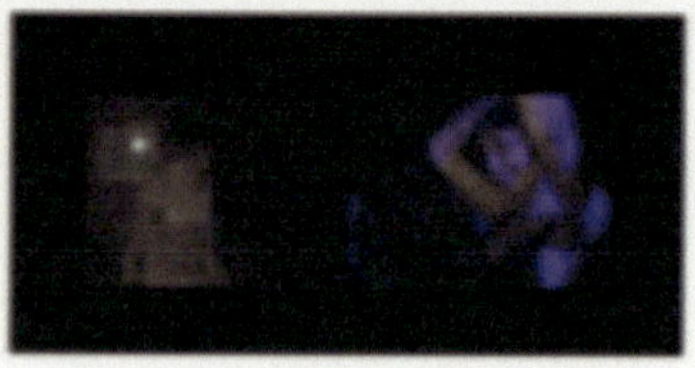

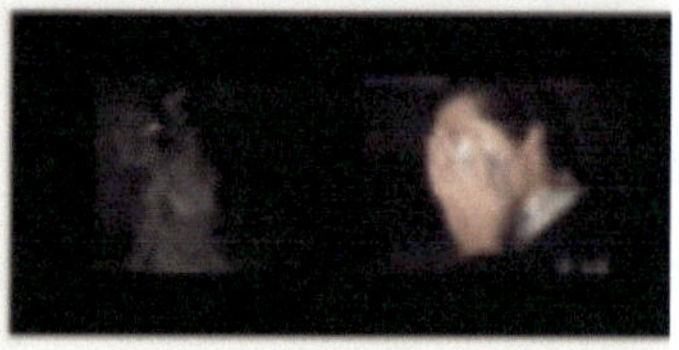

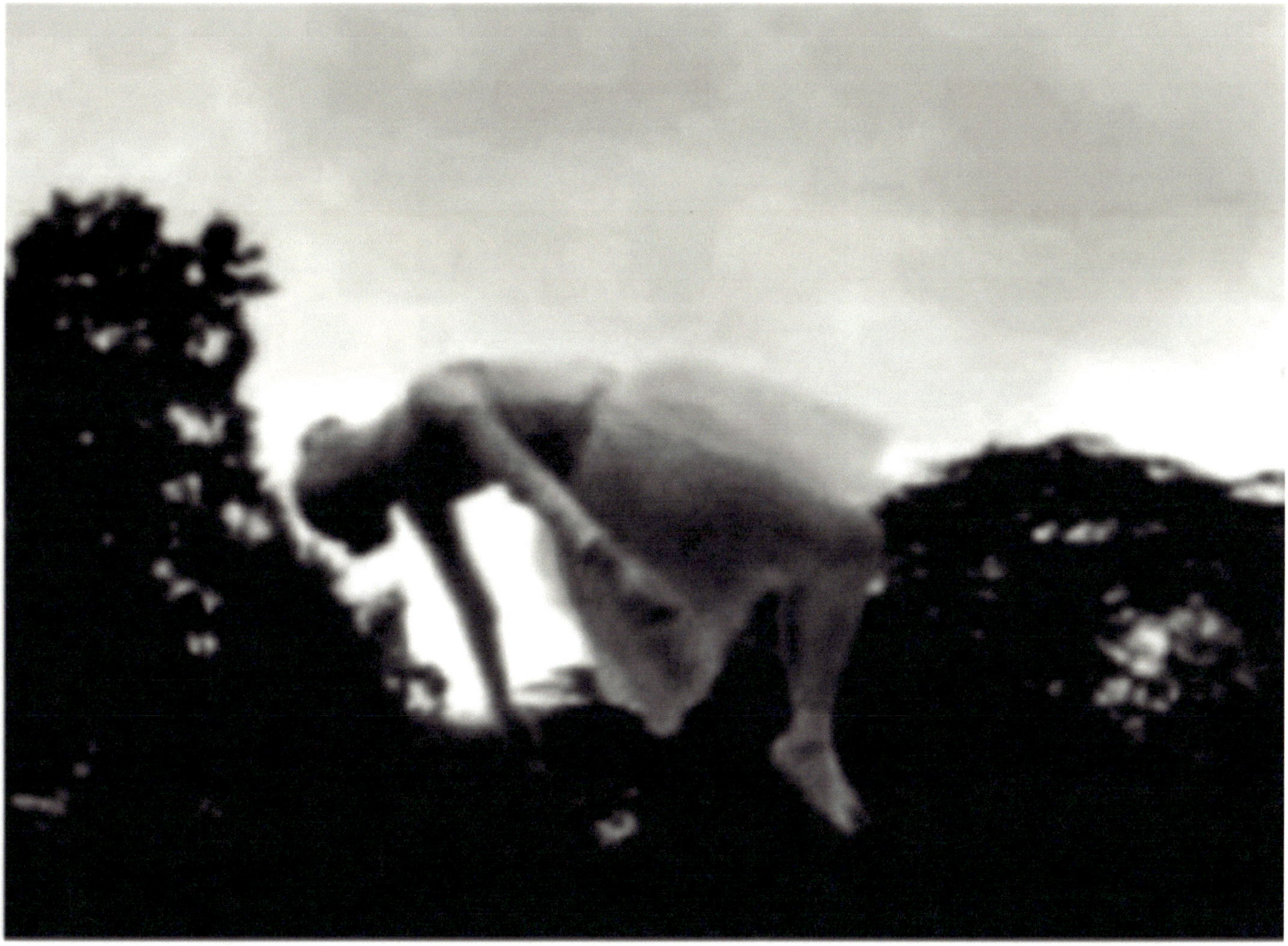

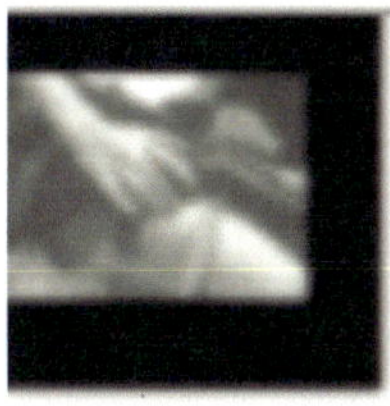

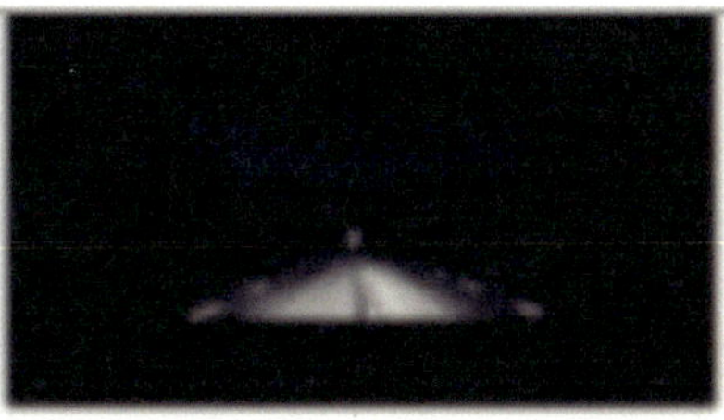

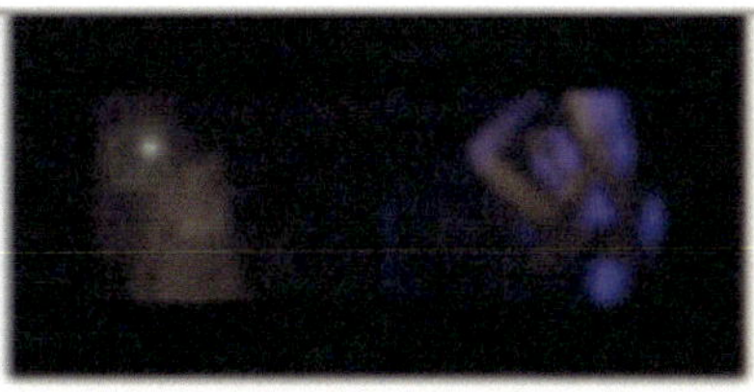

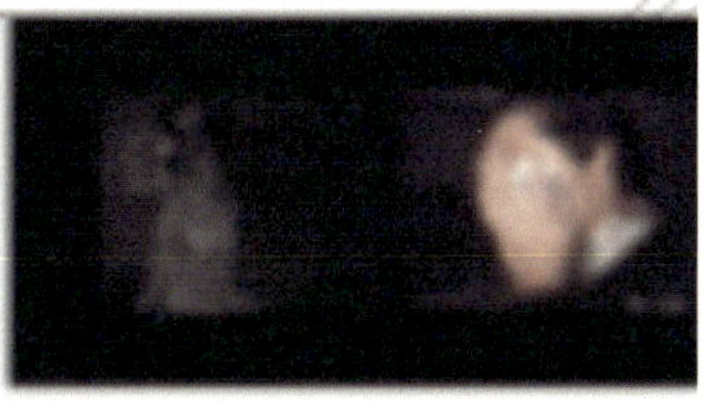

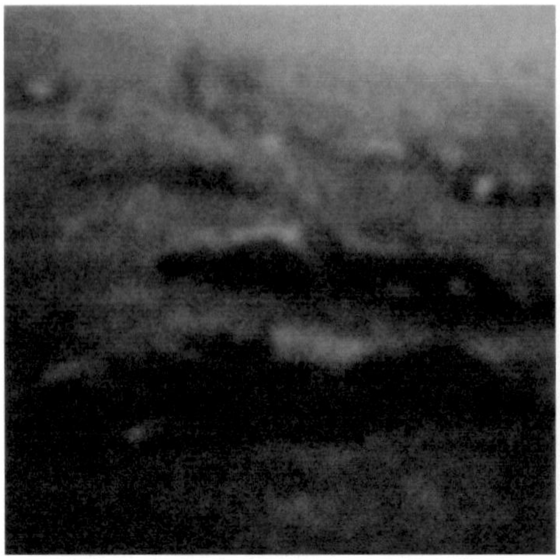

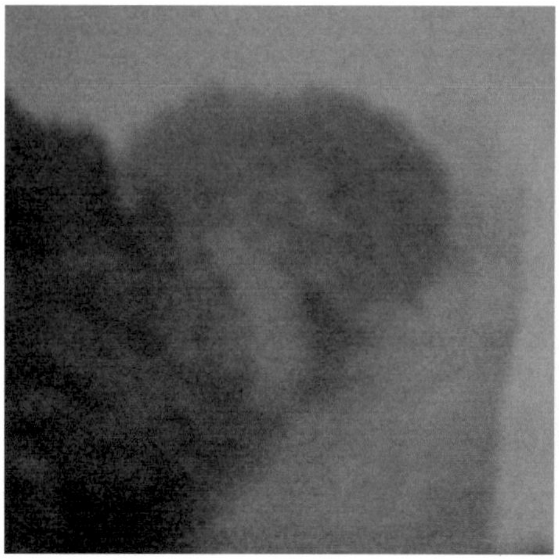
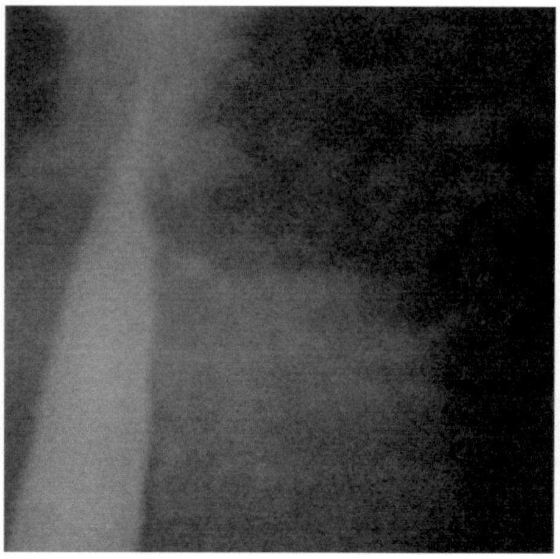

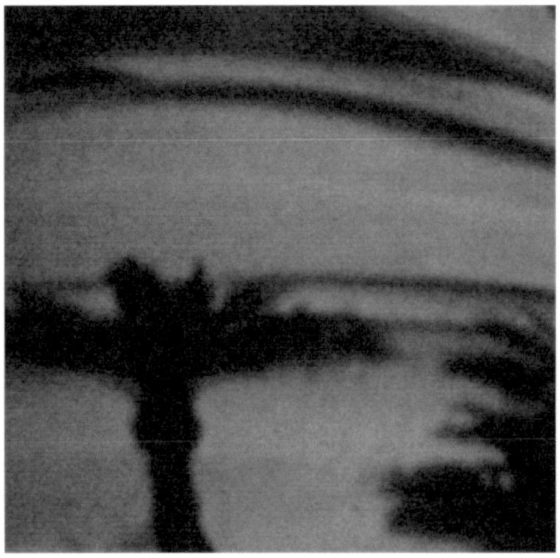
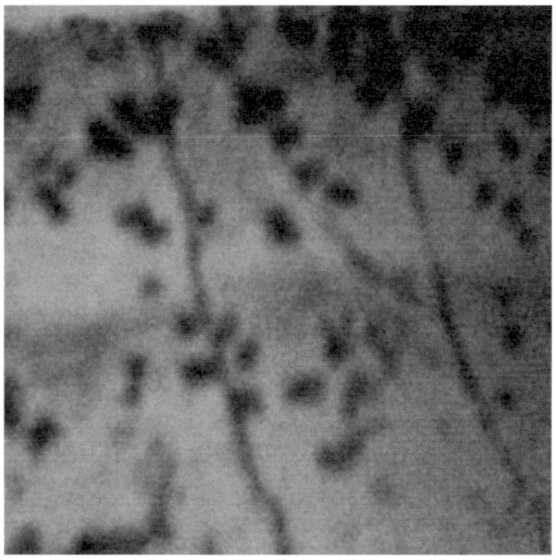

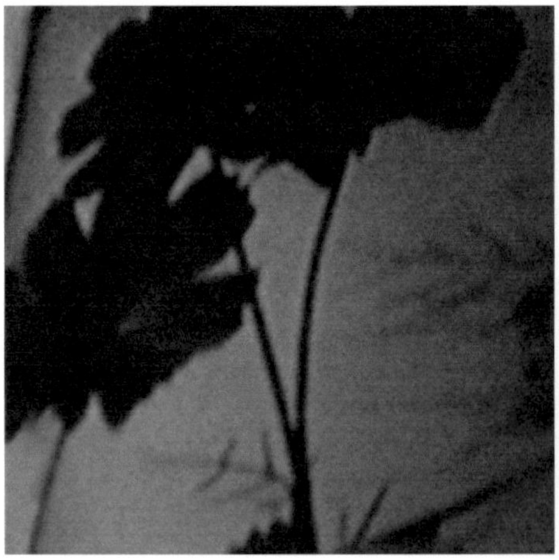
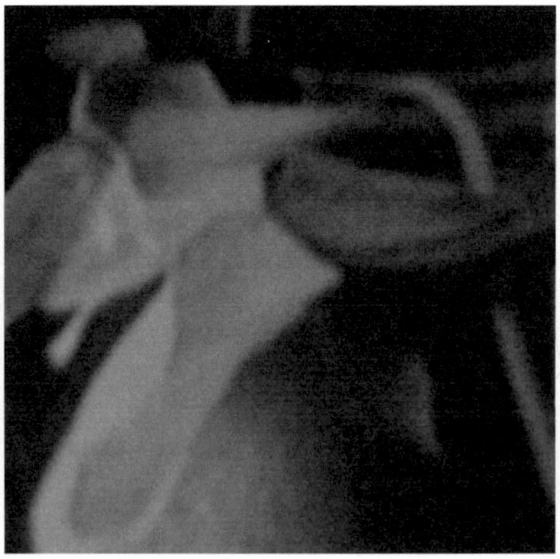
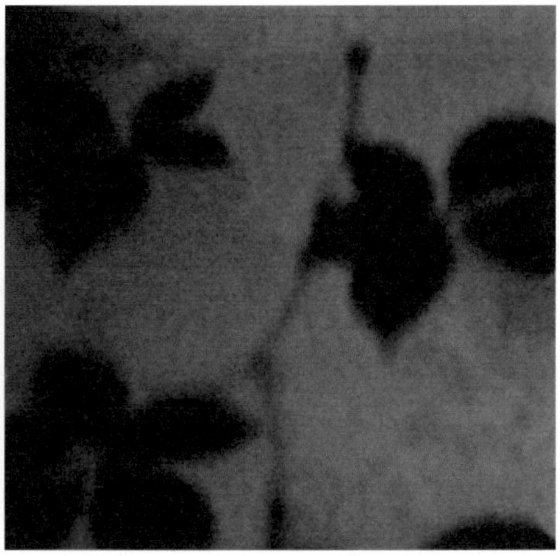

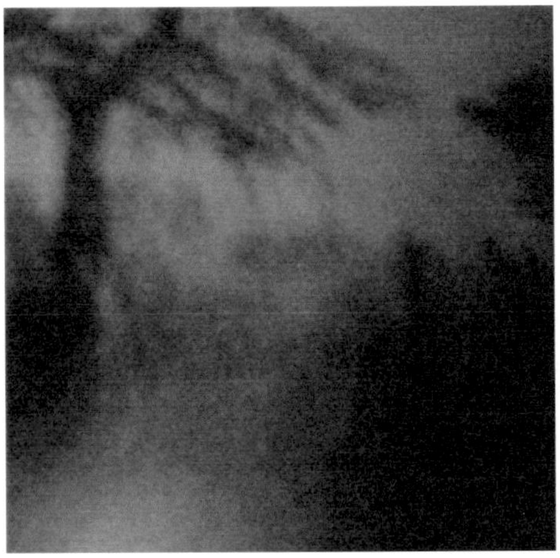
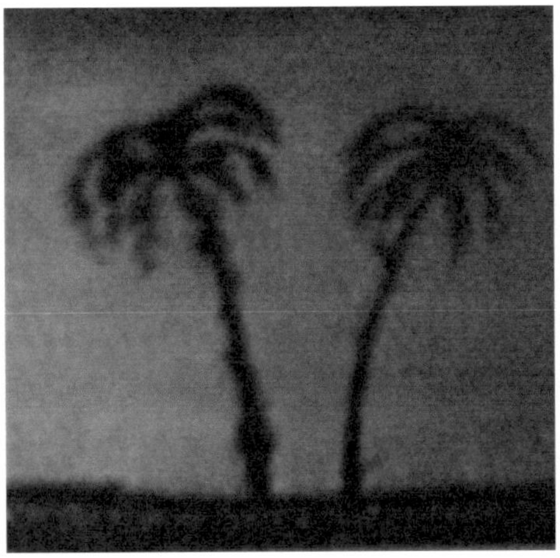
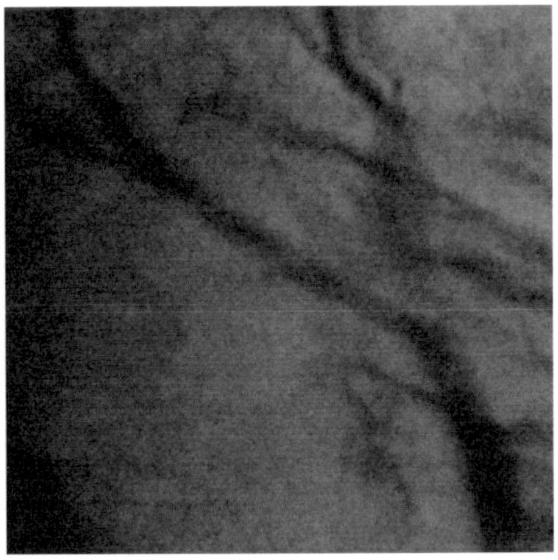

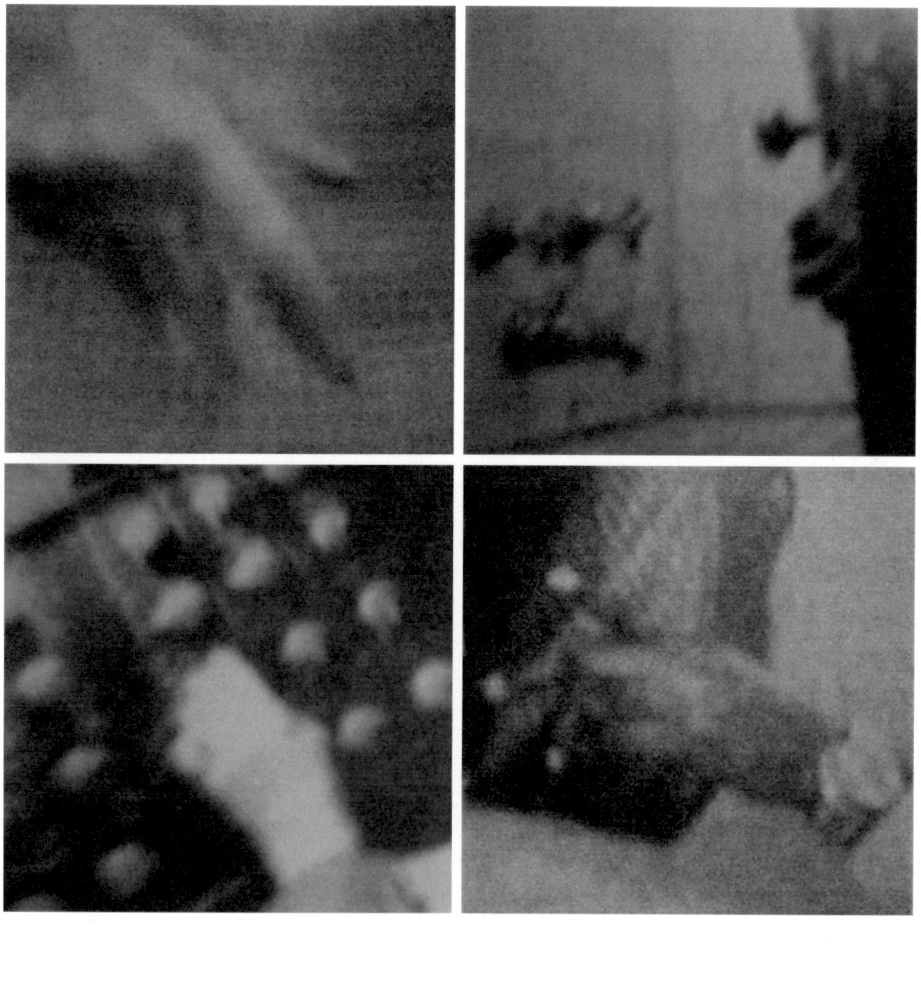

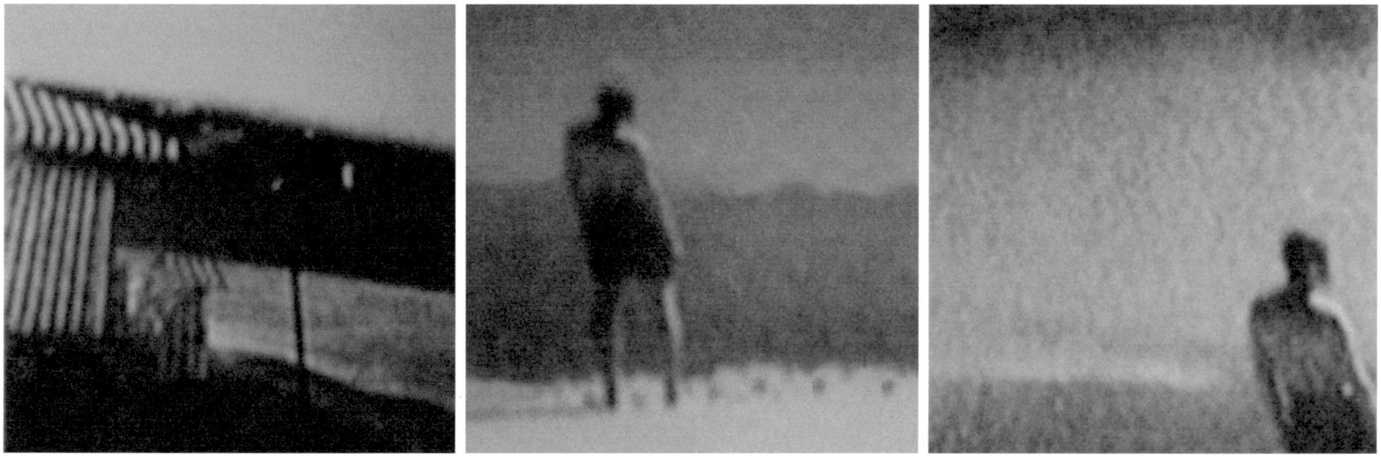

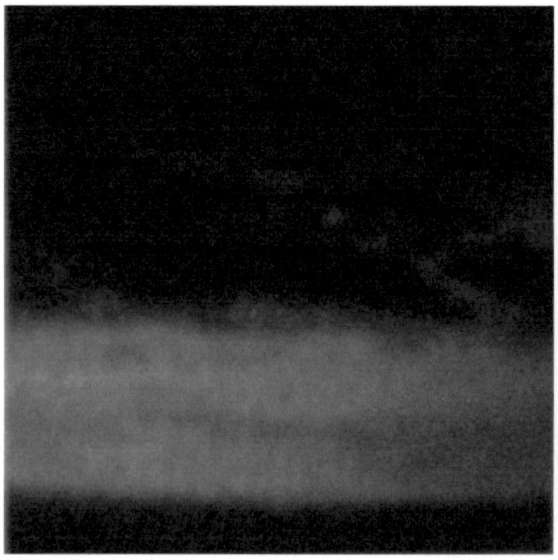

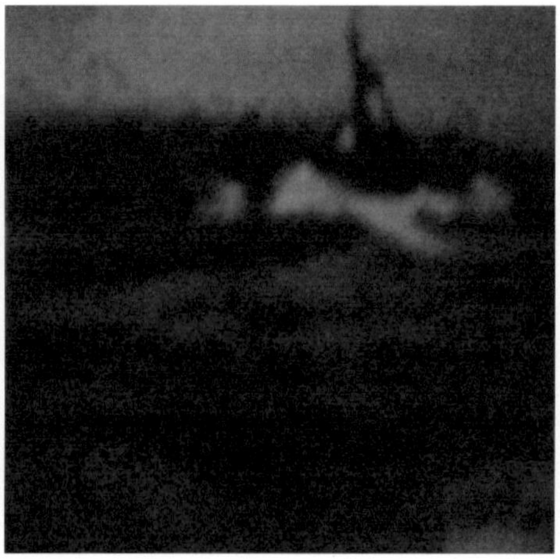

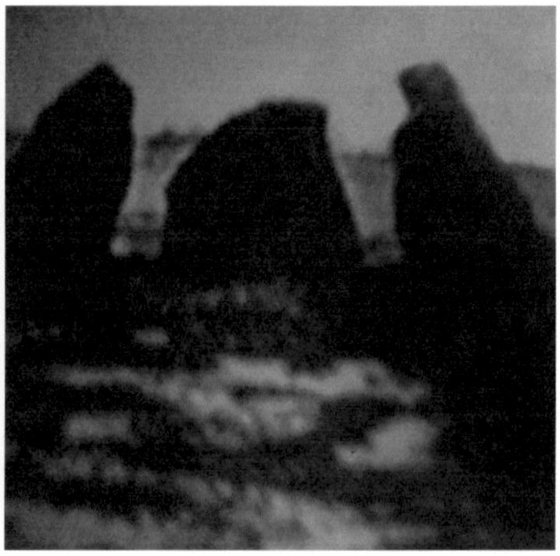

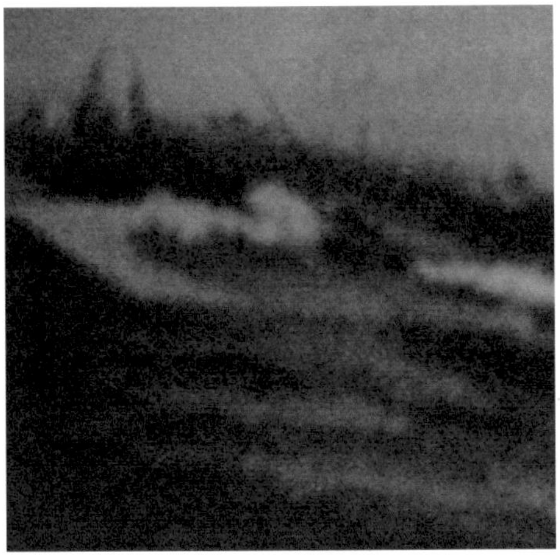
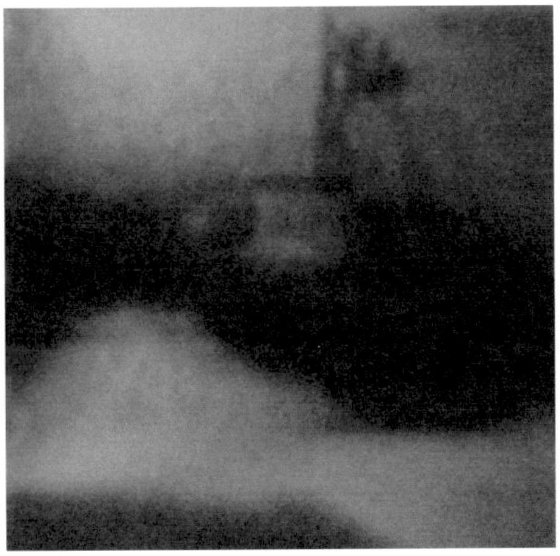

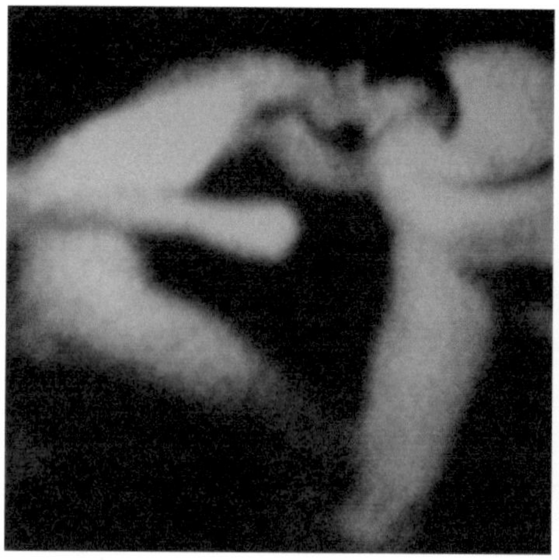

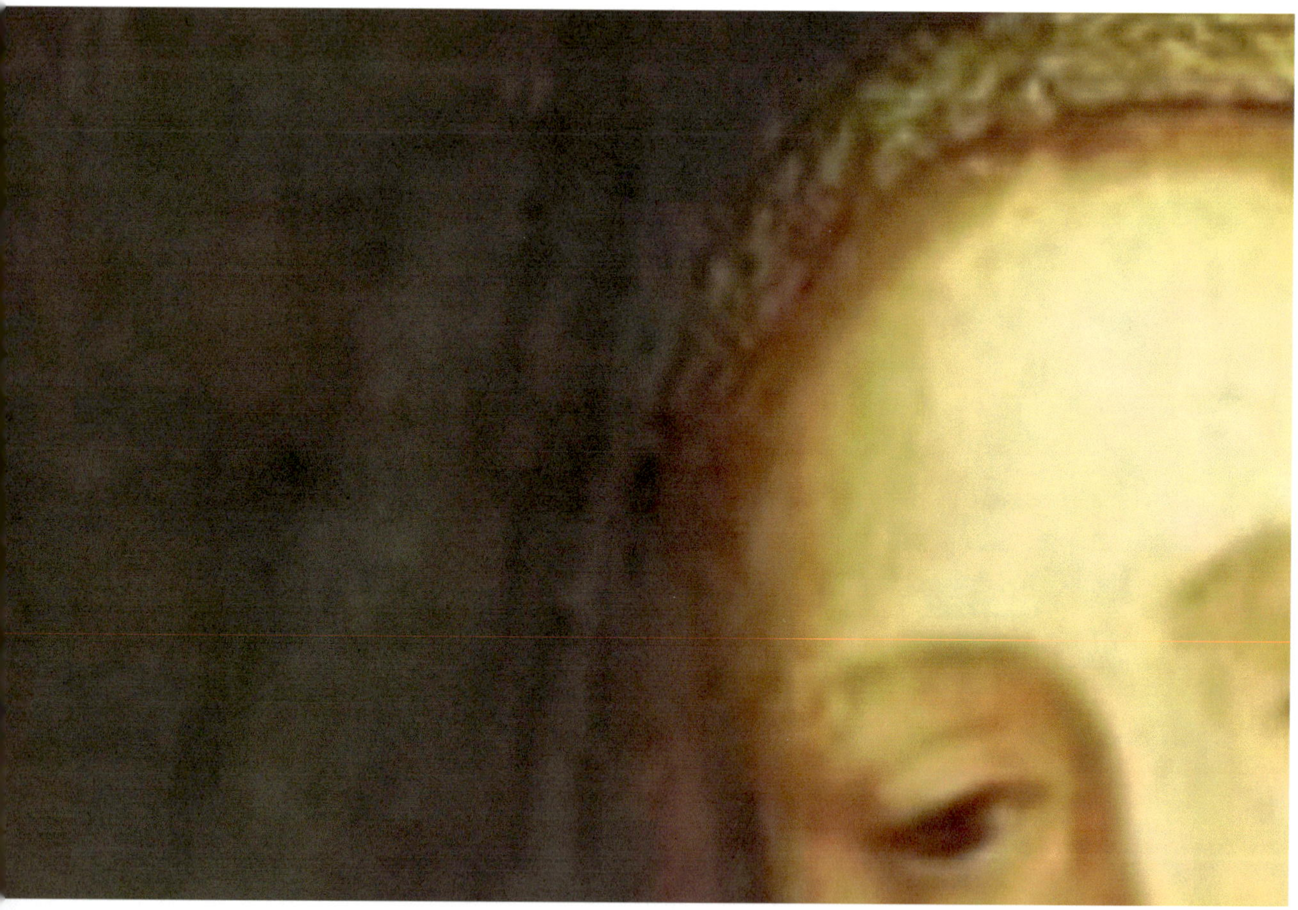

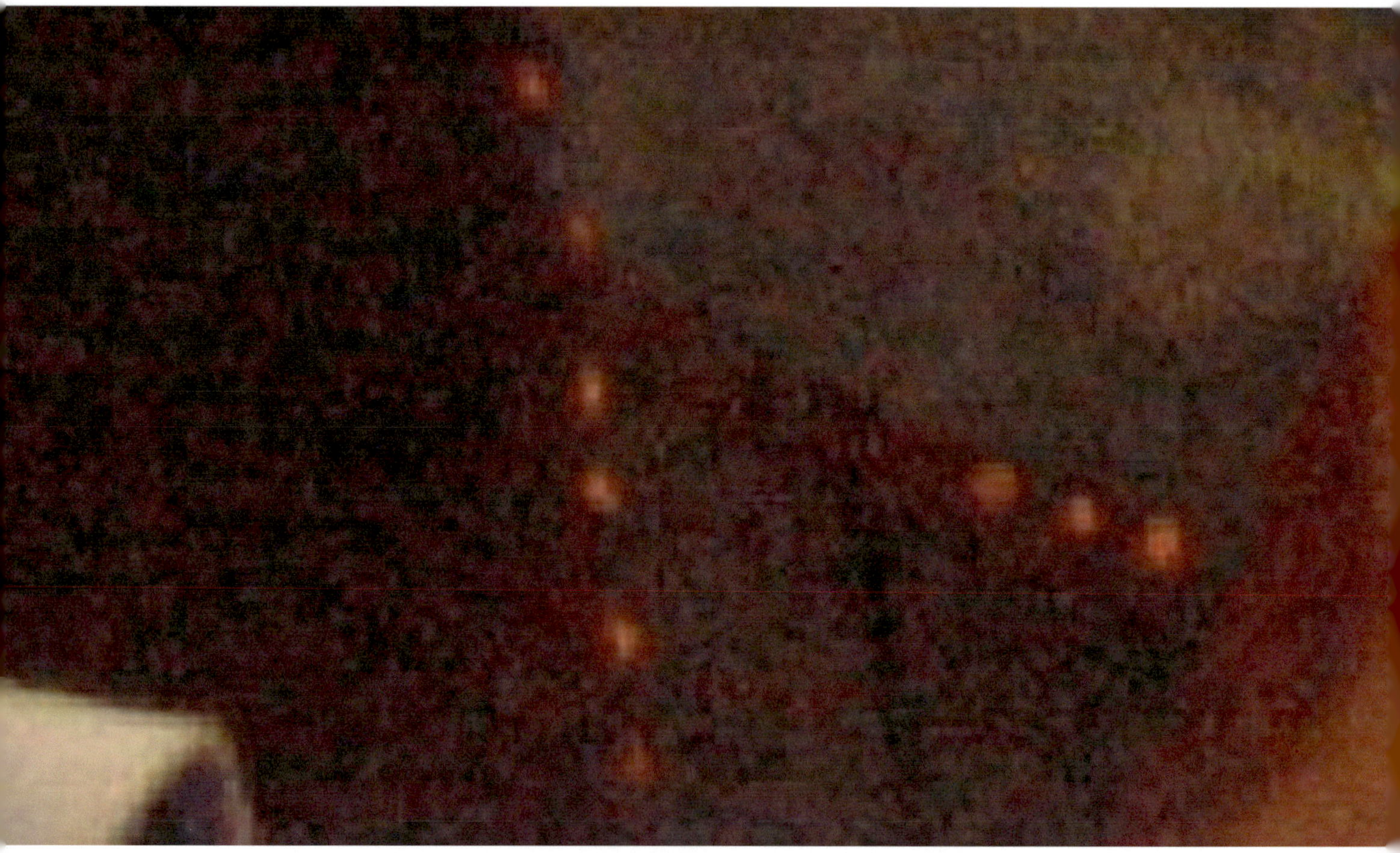

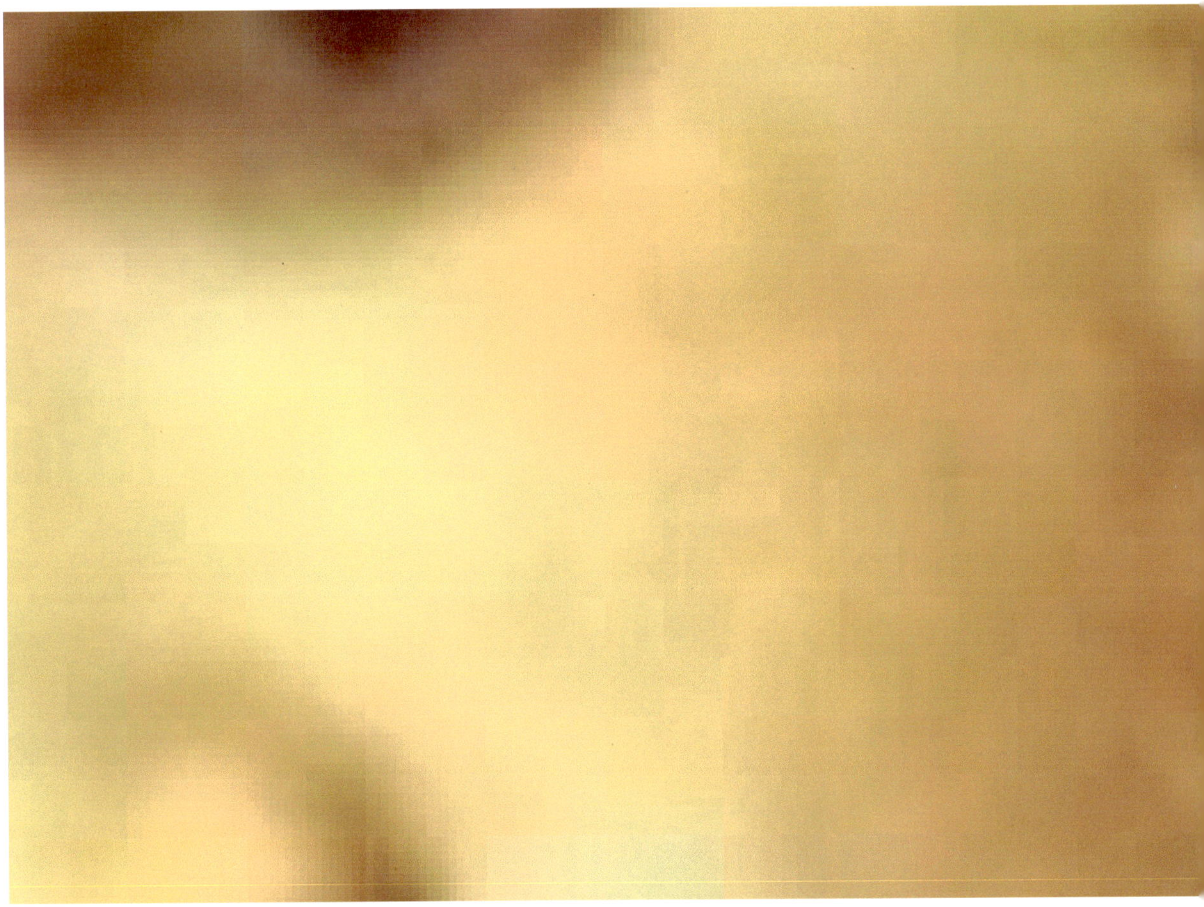

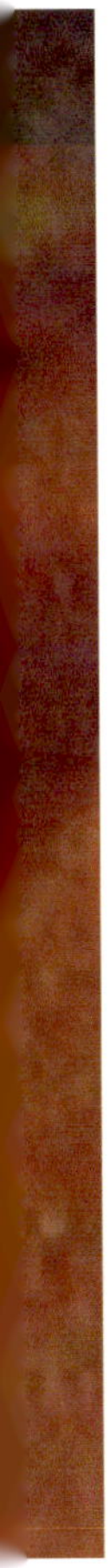

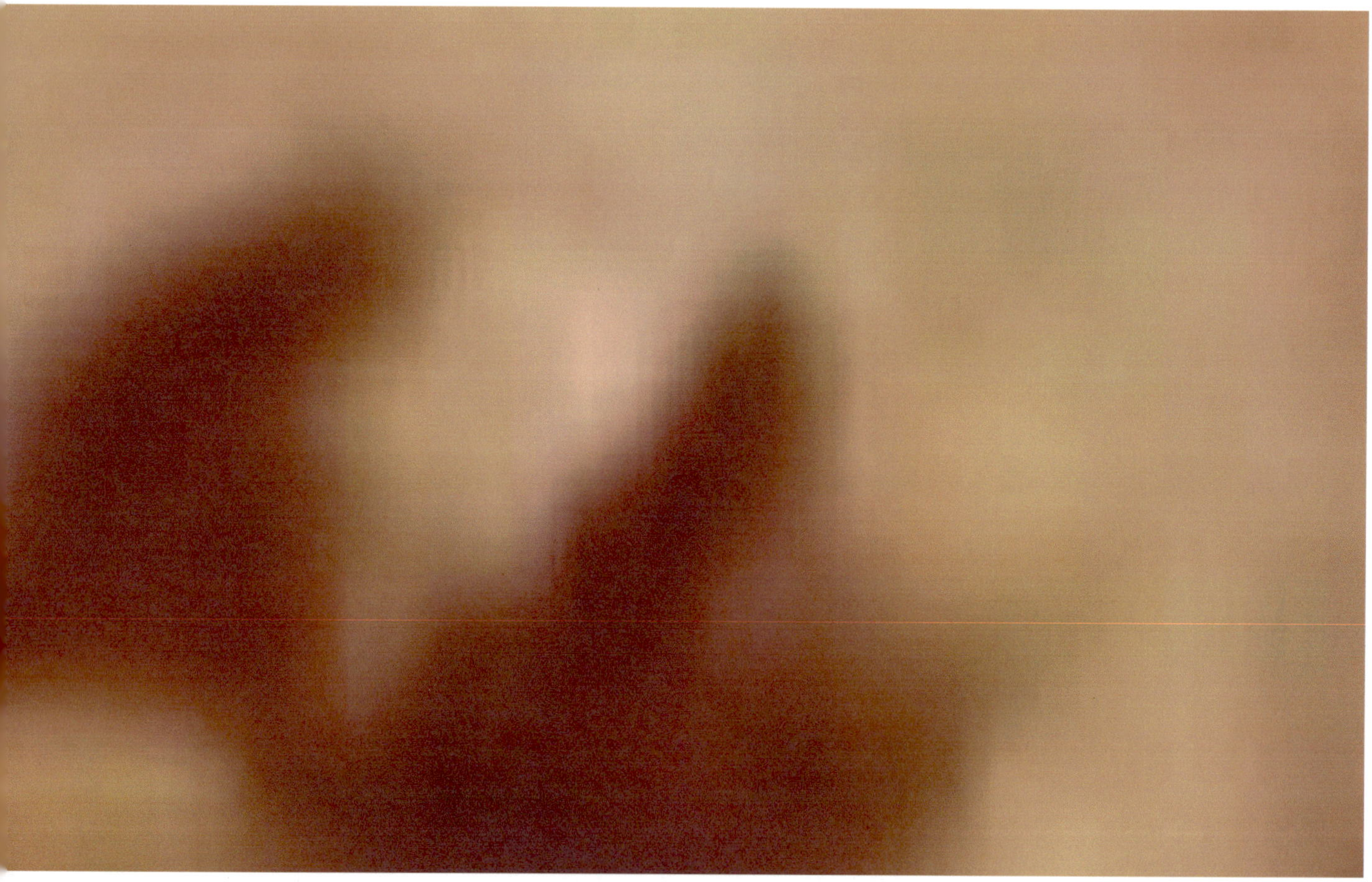

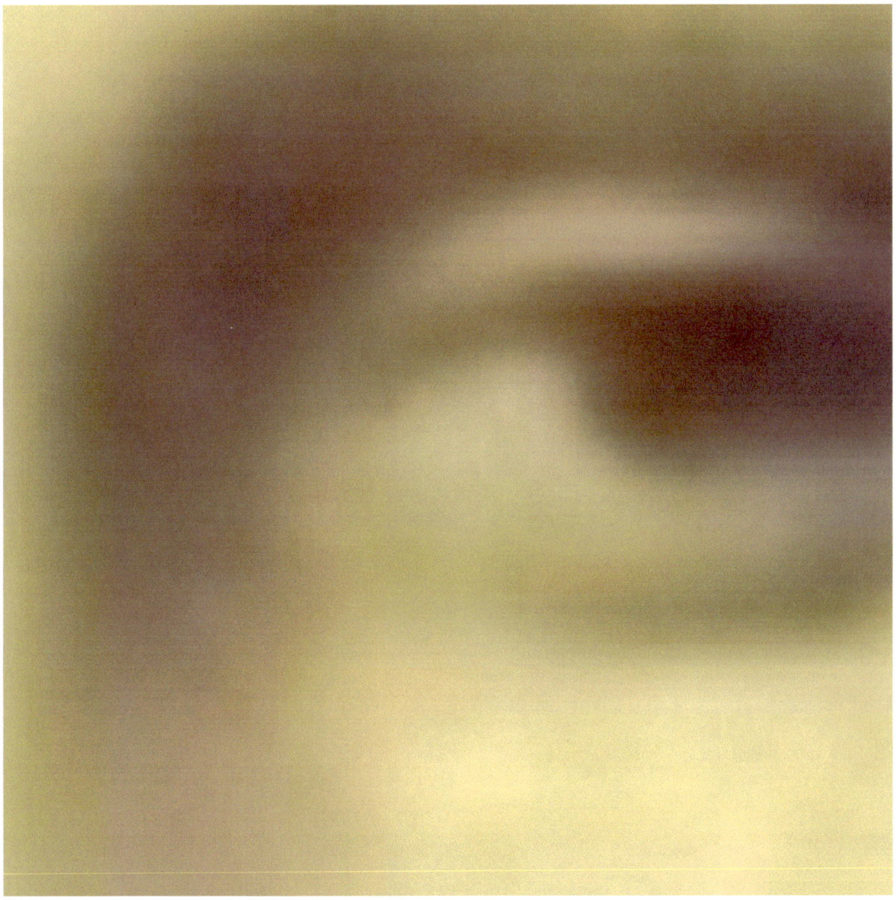

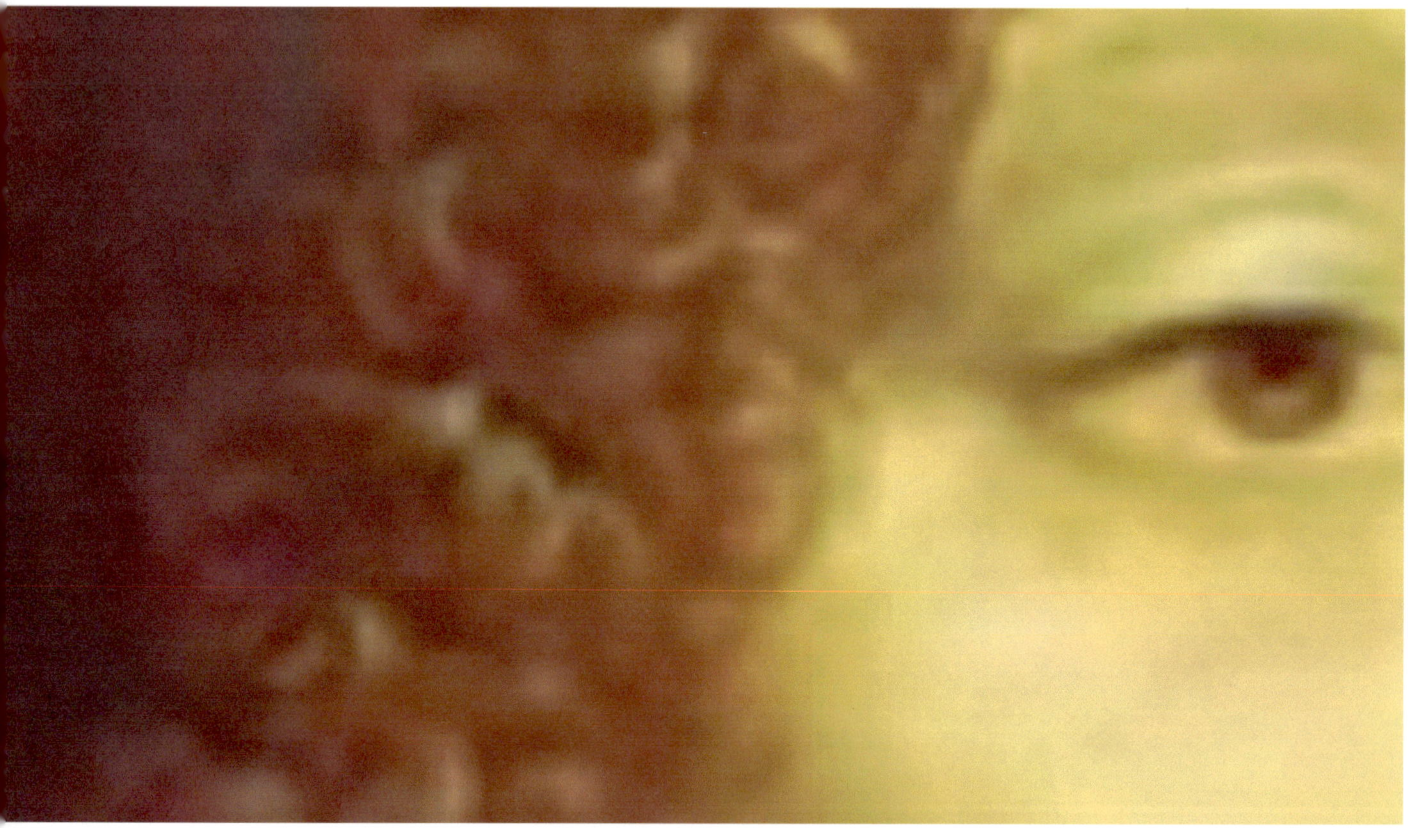

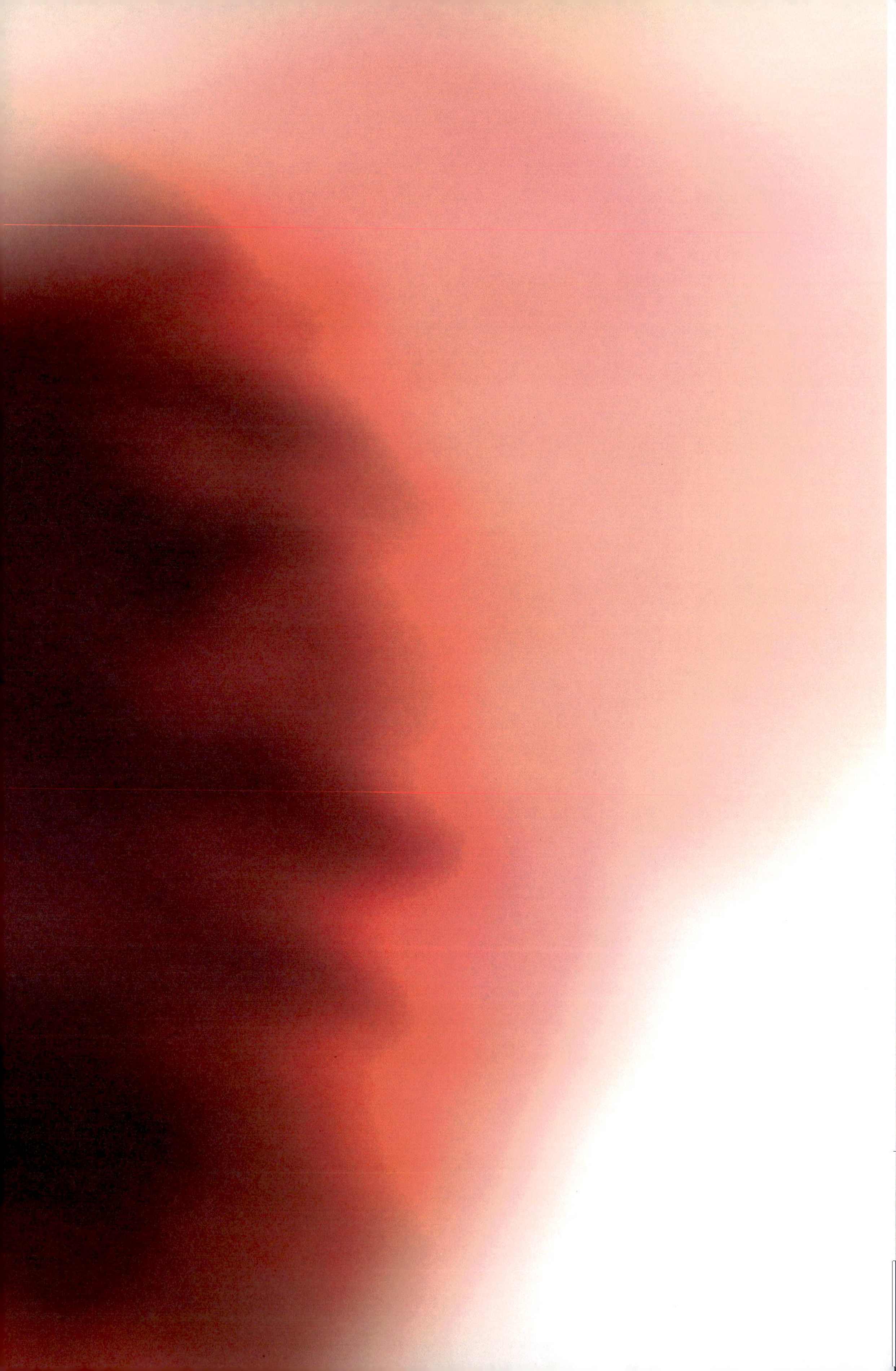

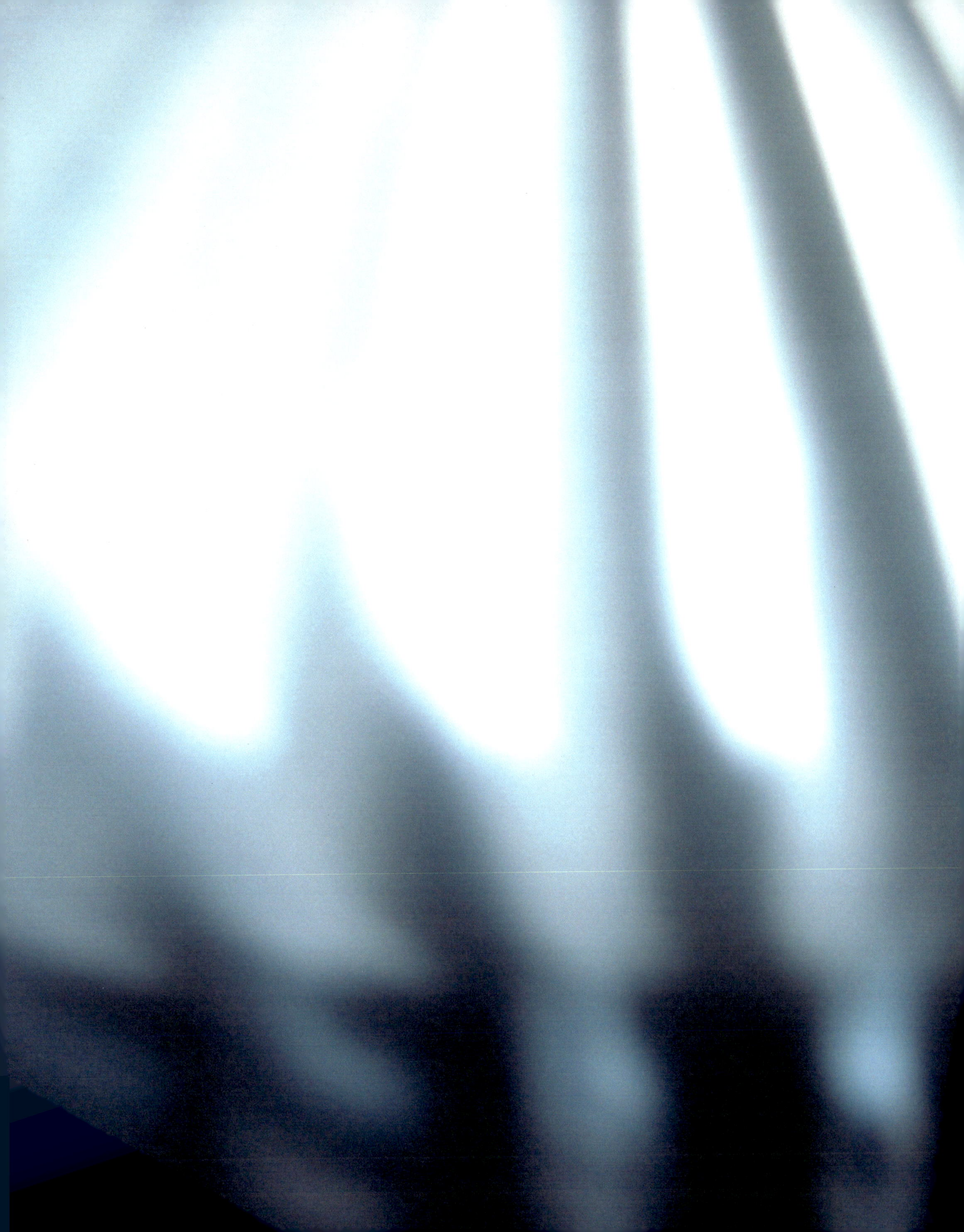

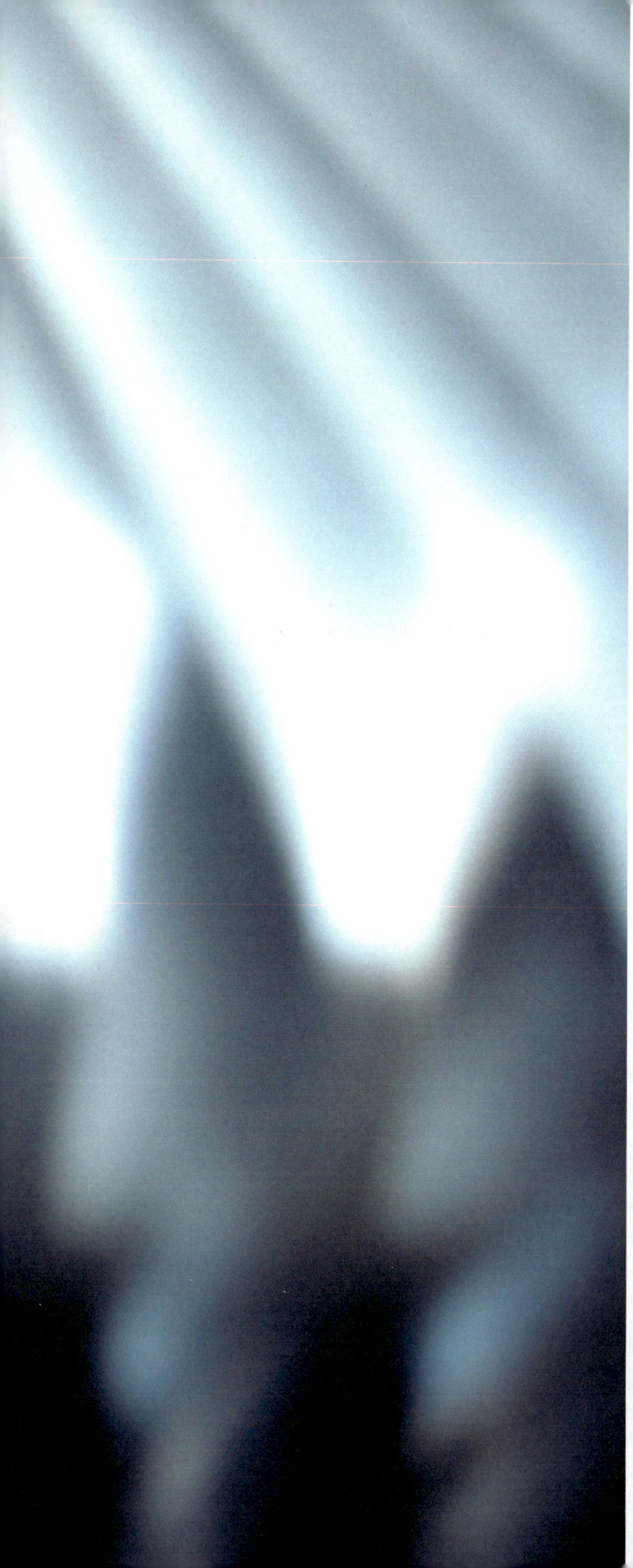

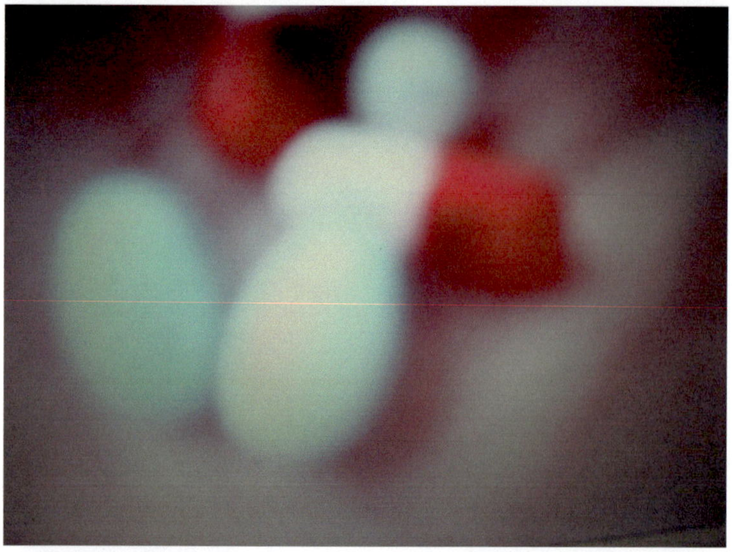
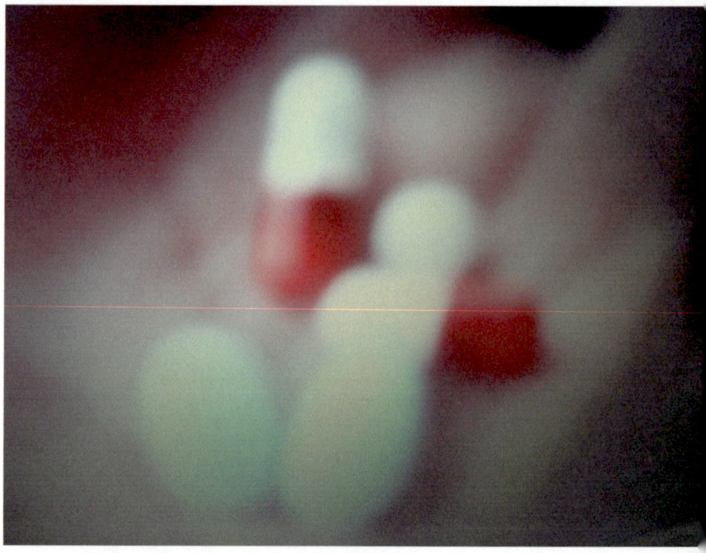
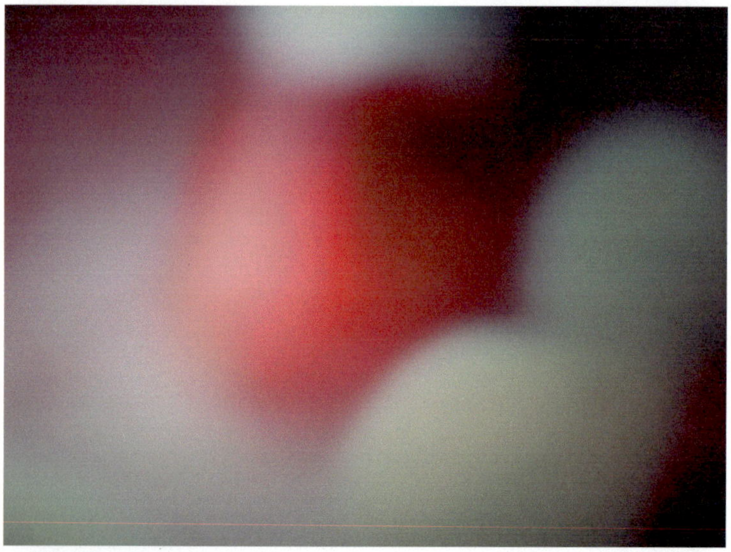

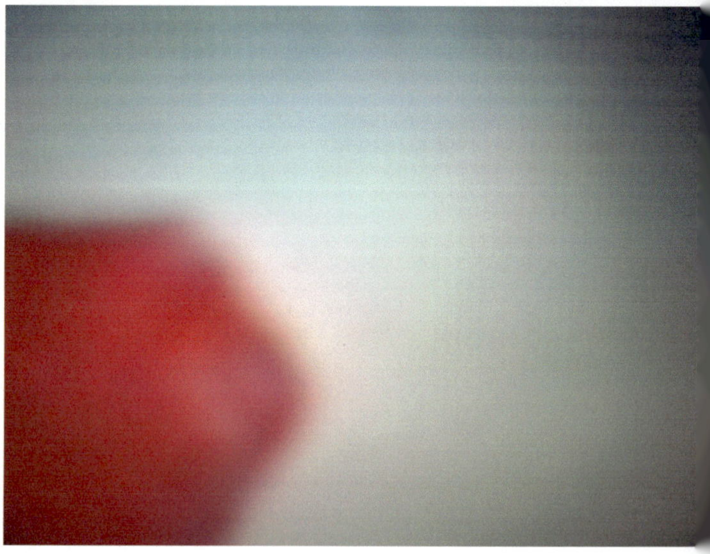

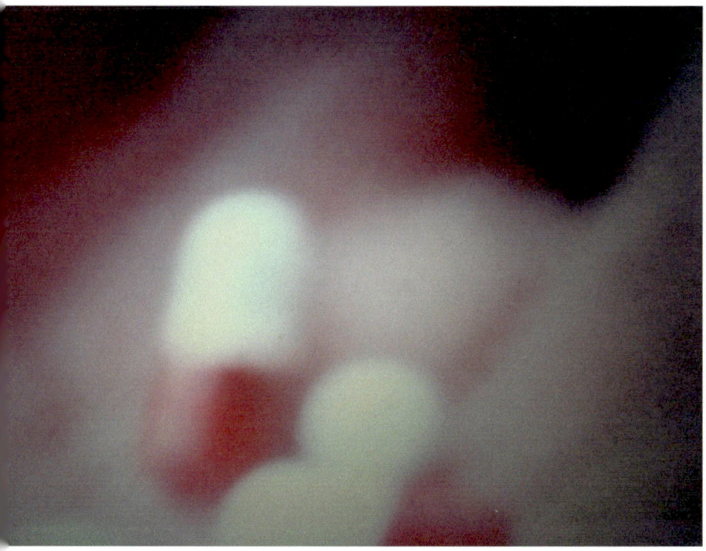
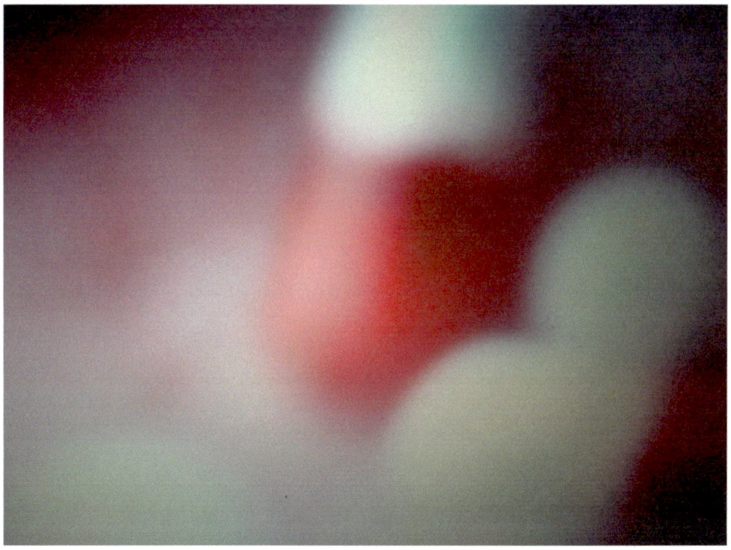

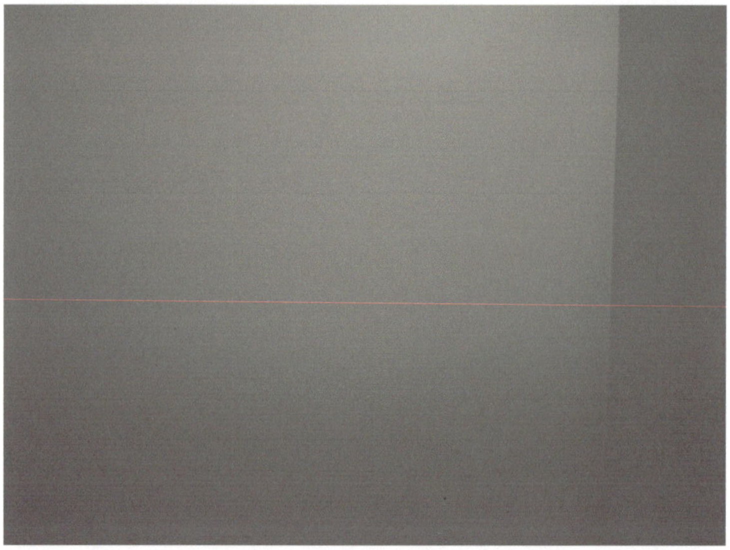

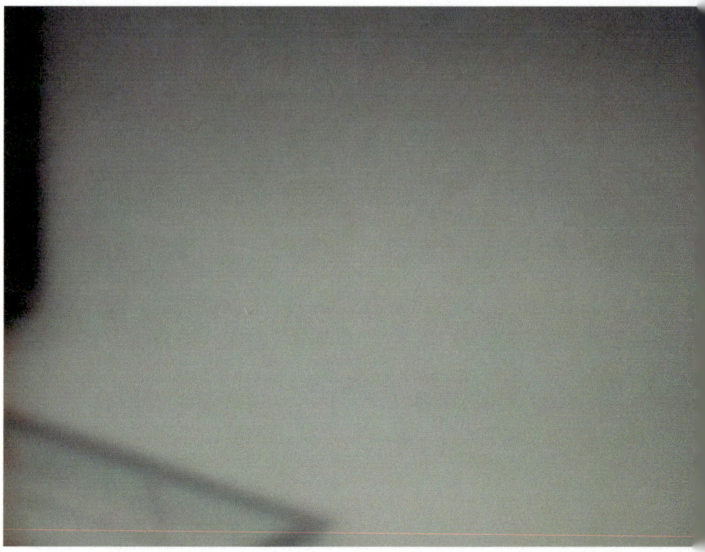

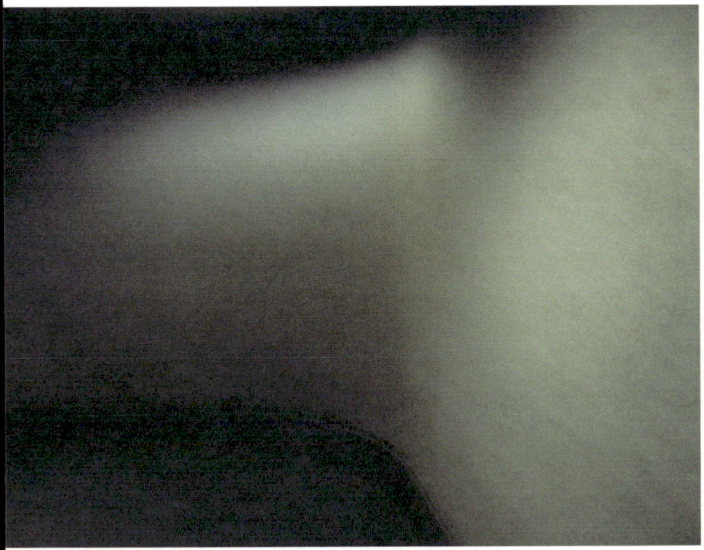

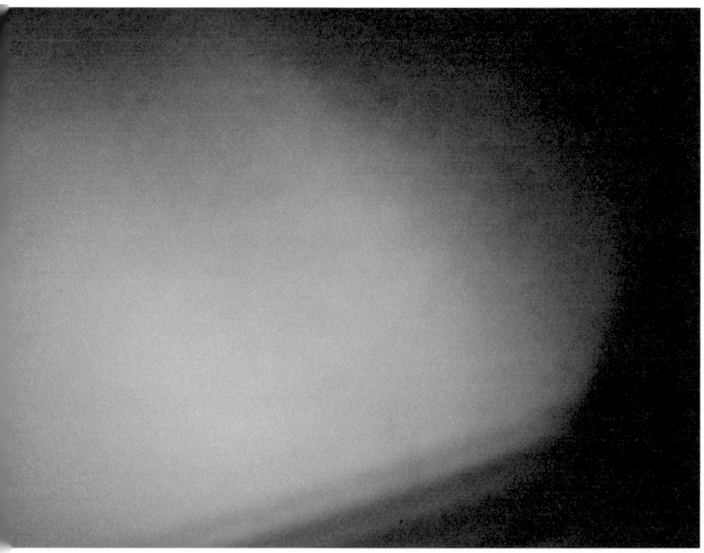

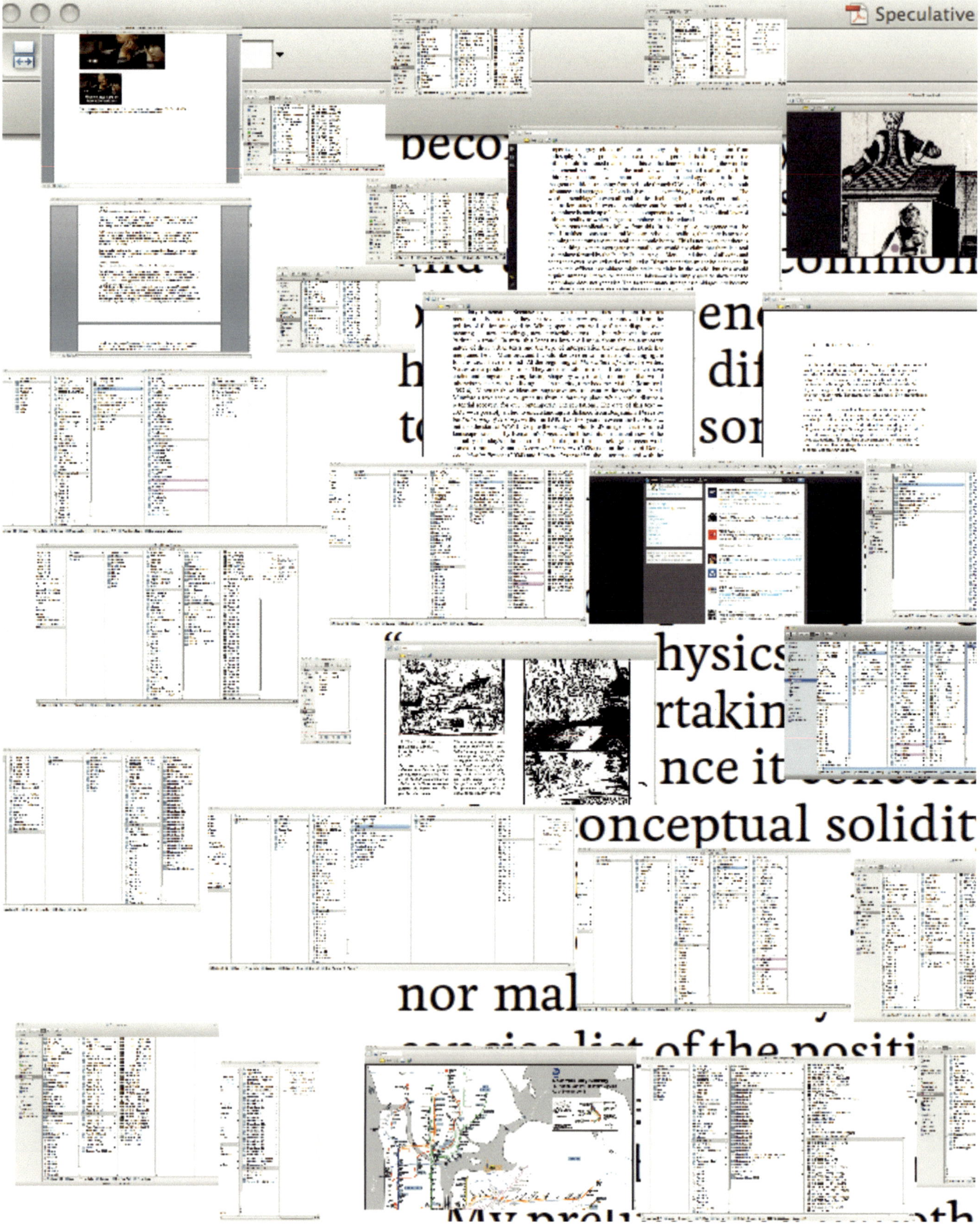
Speculative
beco
hysics
rtakin
nce it
onceptual solidit
nor mal

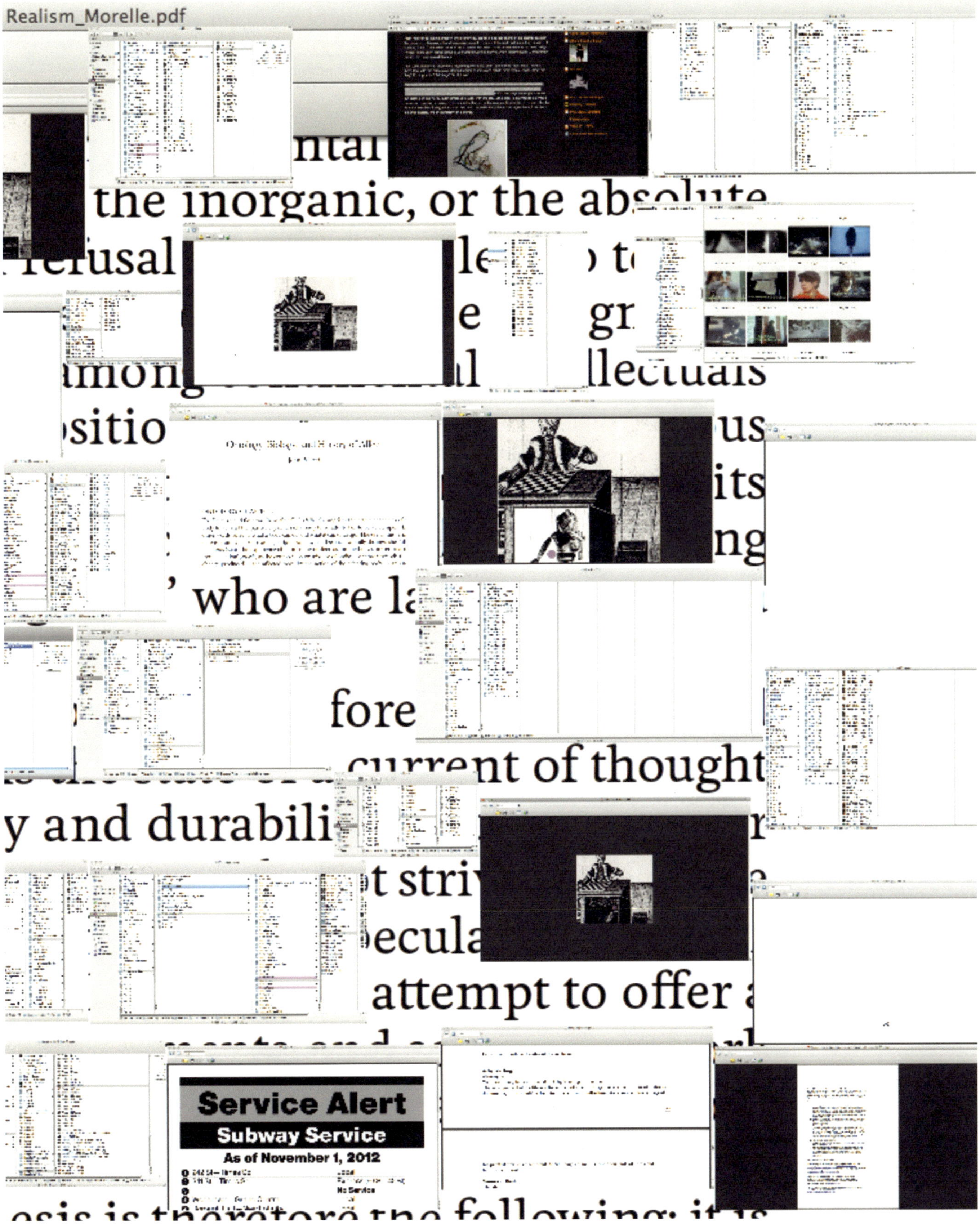
Realism_Morelle.pdf
the inorganic, or the absolute
who are la
fore
current of thought
y and durabili
attempt to offer
Service Alert
Subway Service
As of November 1, 2012
No Service

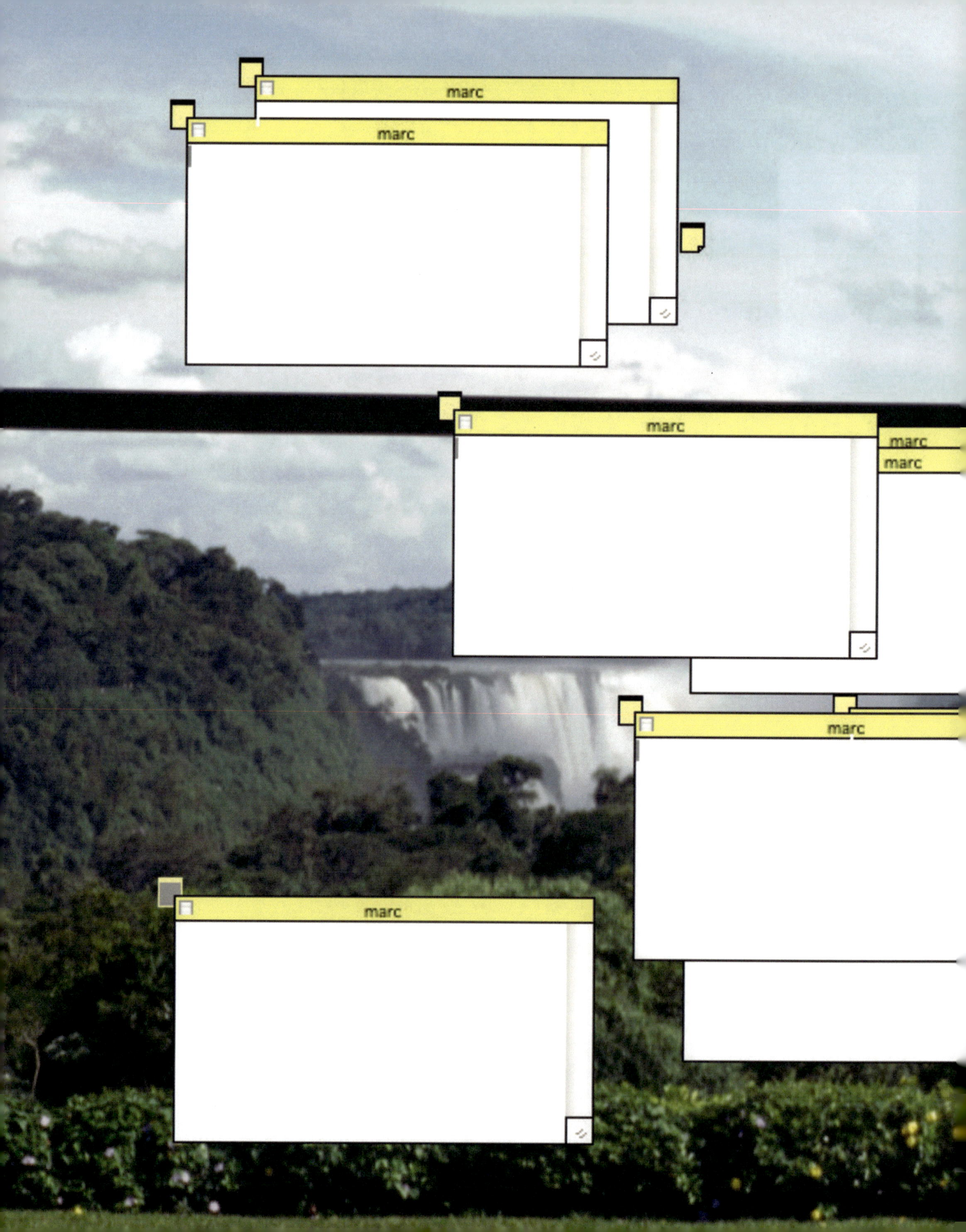
marc
marc
marc
marc
marc
marc
marc

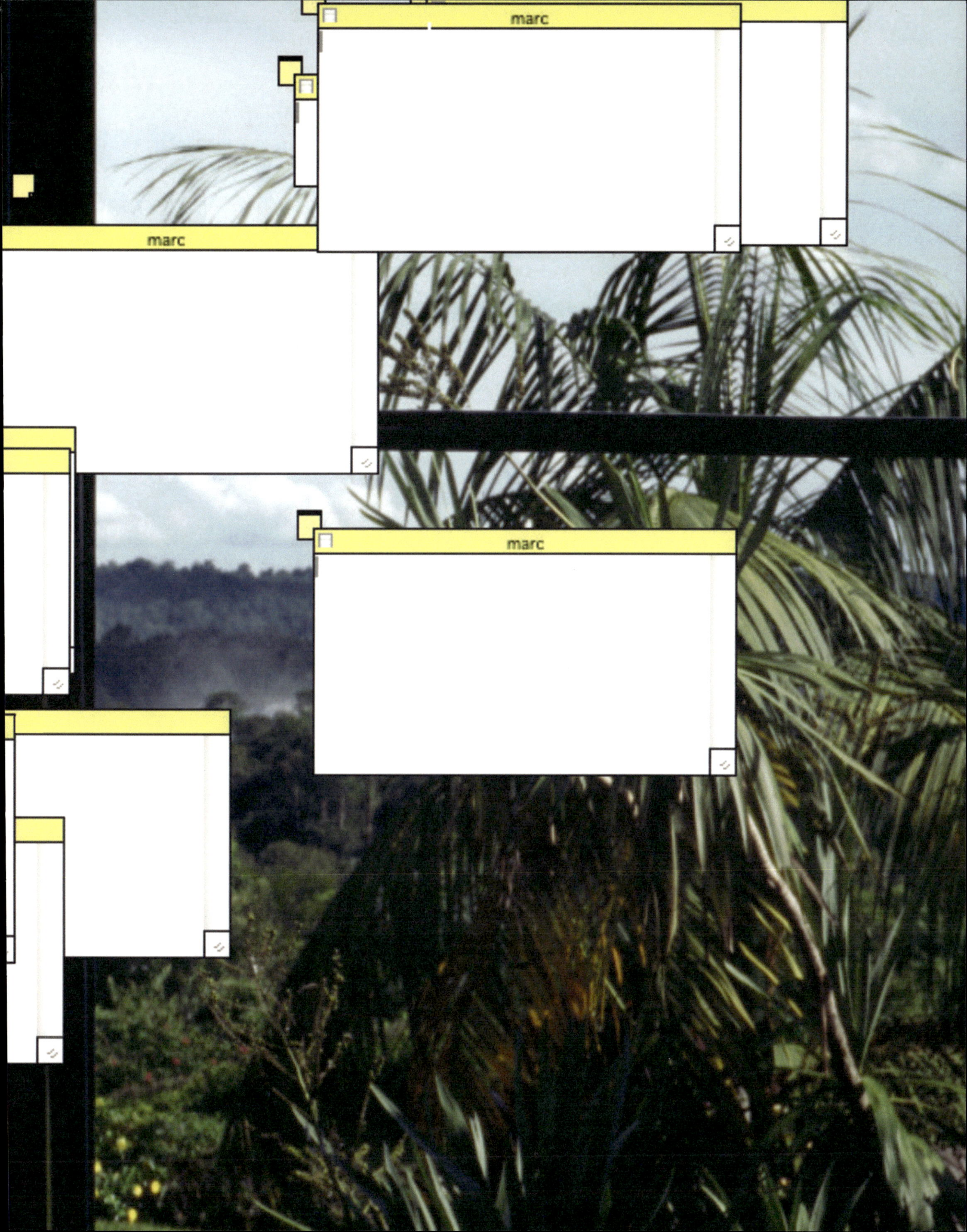
marc
marc
marc

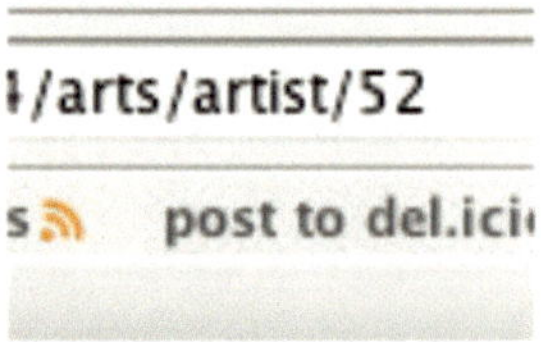
/arts/artist/52
post to del.ici

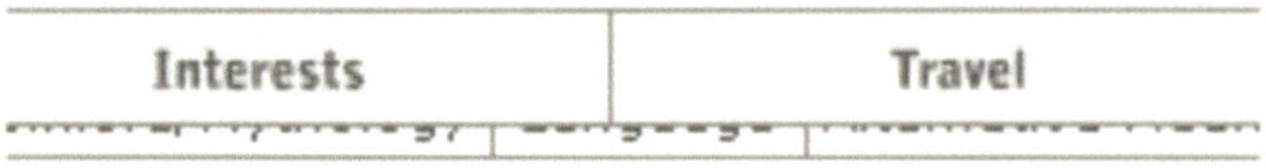
Interests
Travel

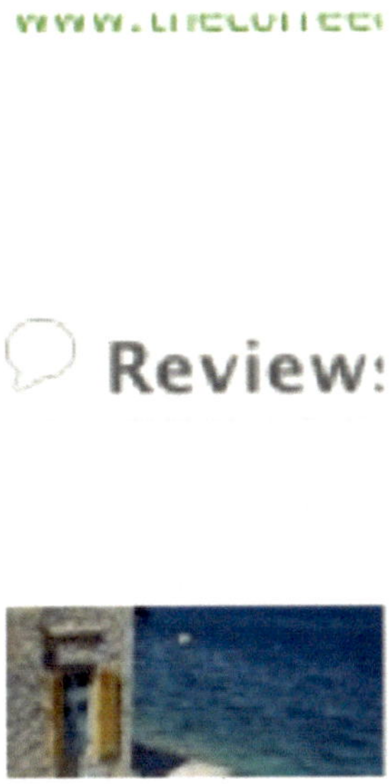
Review

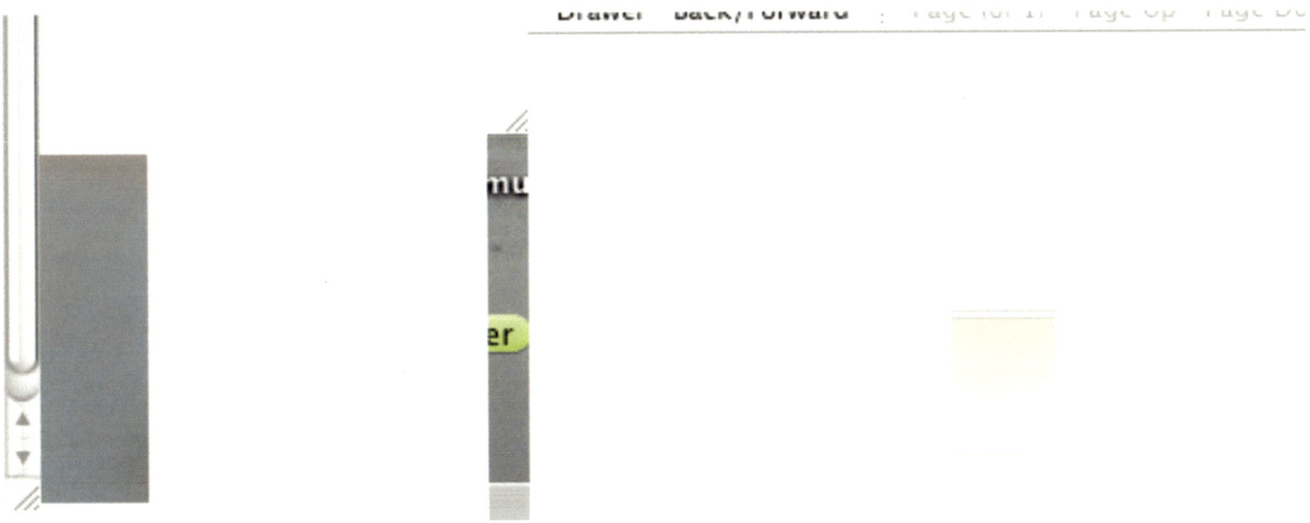

4: Gerhard Richter, or the Photogenic

"Andy Warhol is not so much an artist a
situation and used as a substitute for an a
November 4, 1989, more than two years
'art'; that he touched none of the methoc
(thus sparing us the great mass of 'artisti
However, in a 2002 conversation concer
something to Warhol. He legitimized the
way of letting details disappear, or at lea
voiced in these comments is telling. On
position of Warhol as true to the change
in his "mechanical" technique that Richt
Richter sees Warhol as a "symptom" wi
this ambivalence Richter effectively affi
Hamilton and Lichtenstein do, but sugge
way" indicated by Warhol—a way that l

Not restricted to painting, Richte
numerous installations and several sculp
practice is complicated and capacious en
painting, from the representational to the

:e
:e All Windows
ndow

e

;heet Split

een Mode

vans.pdf
rations.pdf (SECURED)
FECTTHINGS.pdf
'115923.pdf
ober 1977- Gerhard Richter's Work of Mourning and Its New Audience Author(s)- Rainer Us
8cd3537004a0b27067b9febf62.pdf
.pdf

nonmaevalopt.pdf
_Fever.pdf
df
Richter's October 18 1977.pdf
RTIST_PHOTOGRAPHS_251011.pdf
f
n.pdf
Real_Press_Kit_en.pdf
MarksofIndifference.pdf
odwinResearchPaper2011.pdf
ESSAY_BY_MIRANDA_LASH.pdf
esis_lowres.pdf
_Filmprogramm3_4_2012en.pdf
chersNotes_GerhardRichter.pdf
Mirror.pdf
ArroyoCT2011.pdf
h_essay.pdf
final.pdf
9.pdf
ng-and-stammering.pdf
nd-4921.pdf
df

".[19] [ ]

1971, 169-262.[5]

[19] 1862-92, 1973, [20]

1811-1838), 1995, [25]

[24]

984)25-32.[32]

,89-98.[22] 1862 1984)

116.[30]

[7]

1970, 135-206 (2003)

[1]

1789

] 1968, 215-229 195

21, 1997, 463-480 [26]

1884-87, 322

,787.[15] 166], [16

(

,13 12

14

20

[1]

[11] [21]

[3]

106-107), [4]

47(1837) 295-326.[

,337(1990), 220-228 (1991)

,23(1811), 145-154

[22]

17

51-65

,10(1959),2091

[5] [1]

[32]

1971, 196-226 [2]

10

u u u v u

.(13) 1960 u é :1960 :1979 u (1

993 14 (1893) u

u21."

[3] u [4]

:1979(7) .23 ." 15

[2]

[15] [17]

18) .436

4 -8

[8]

[9]

[19]

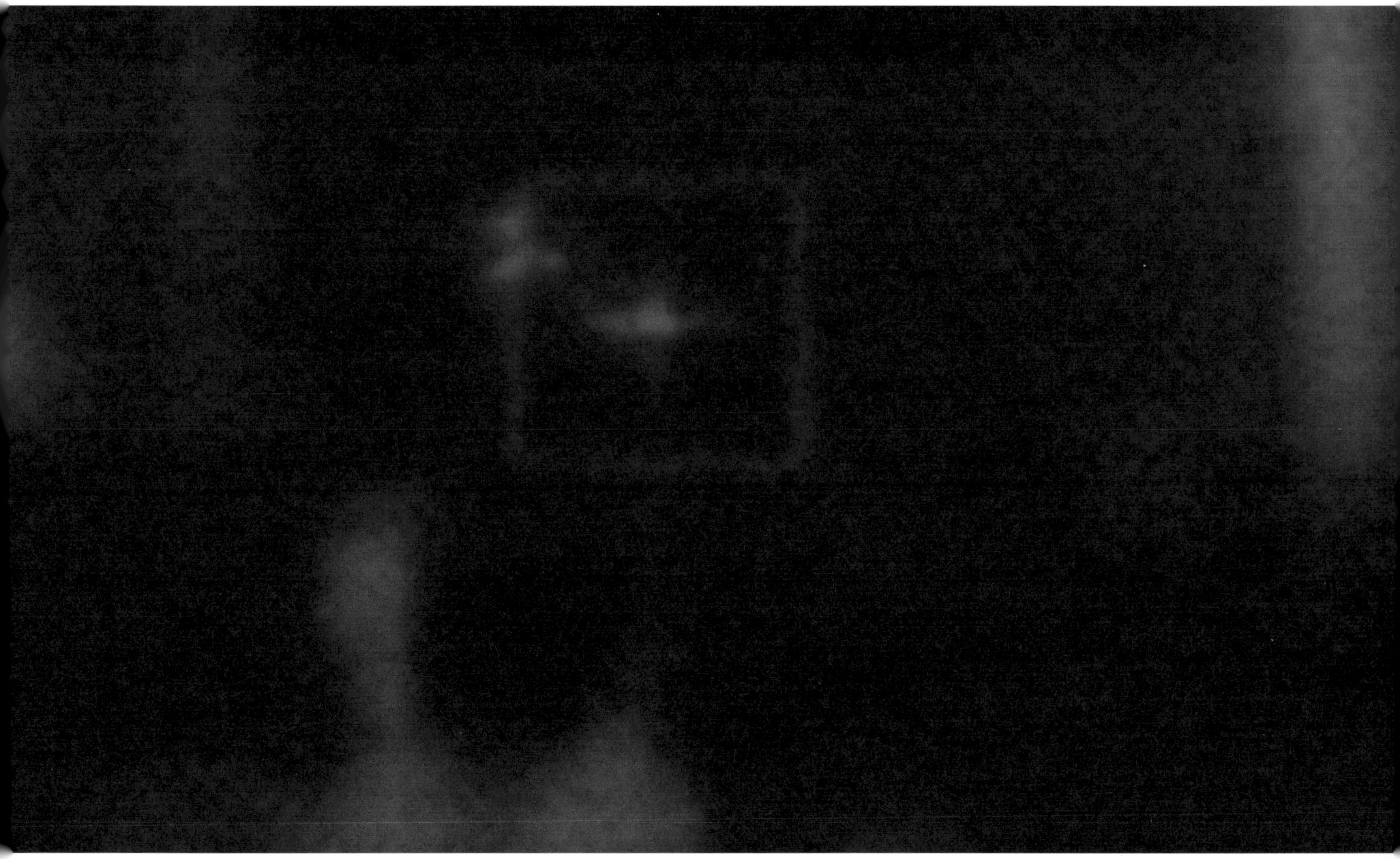

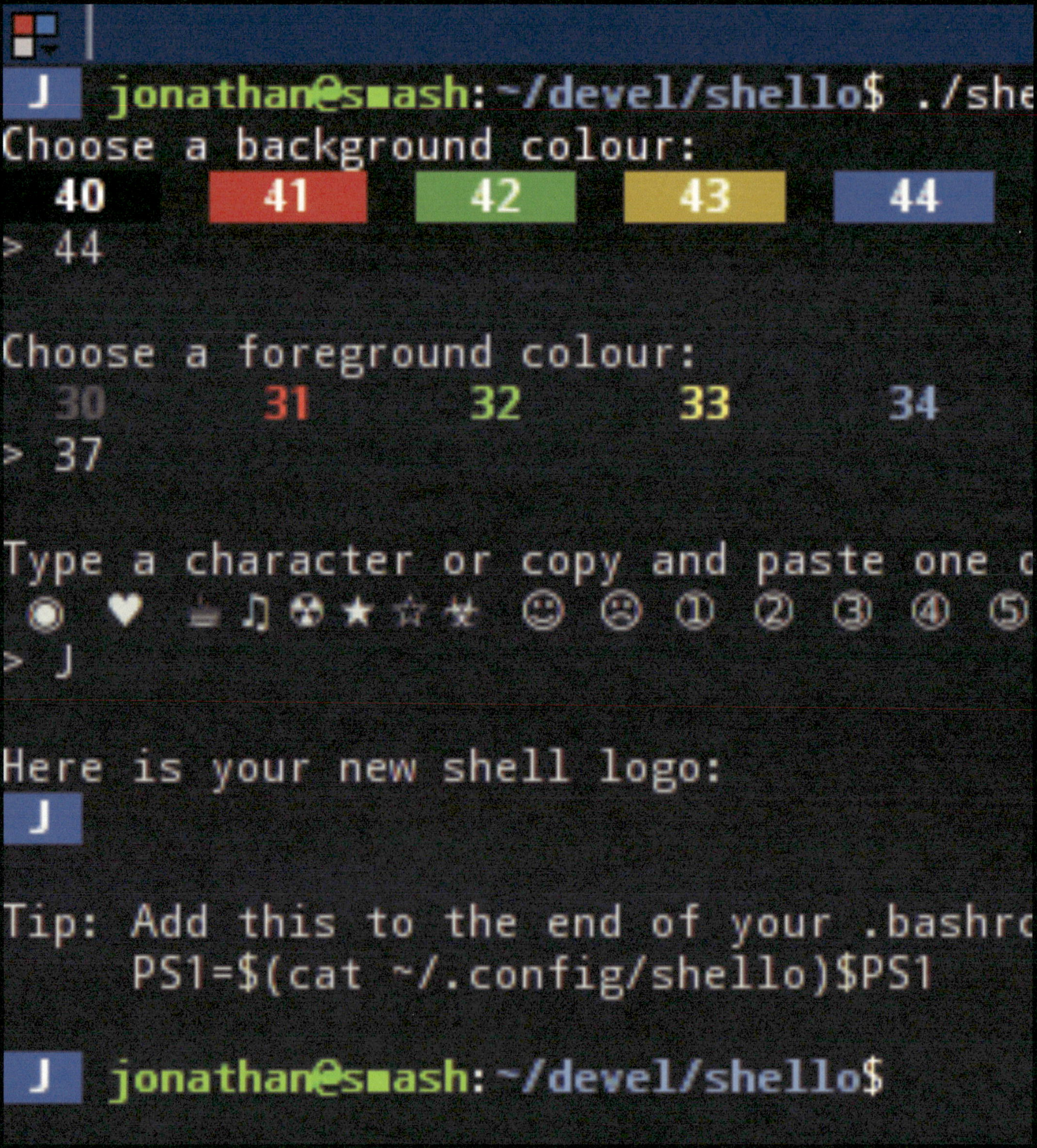
J jonathan@smash:~/devel/shello$ ./she
Choose a background colour:
40 41 42 43 44
> 44
Choose a foreground colour:
30 31 32 33 34
> 37
Type a character or copy and paste one o
◉ ♥ ♫ ☢ ★ ☆ ☣ ☺ ☹ ① ② ③ ④ ⑤
> J
Here is your new shell logo:
J
Tip: Add this to the end of your .bashrc
PS1=$(cat ~/.config/shello)$PS1
J jonathan@smash:~/devel/shello$

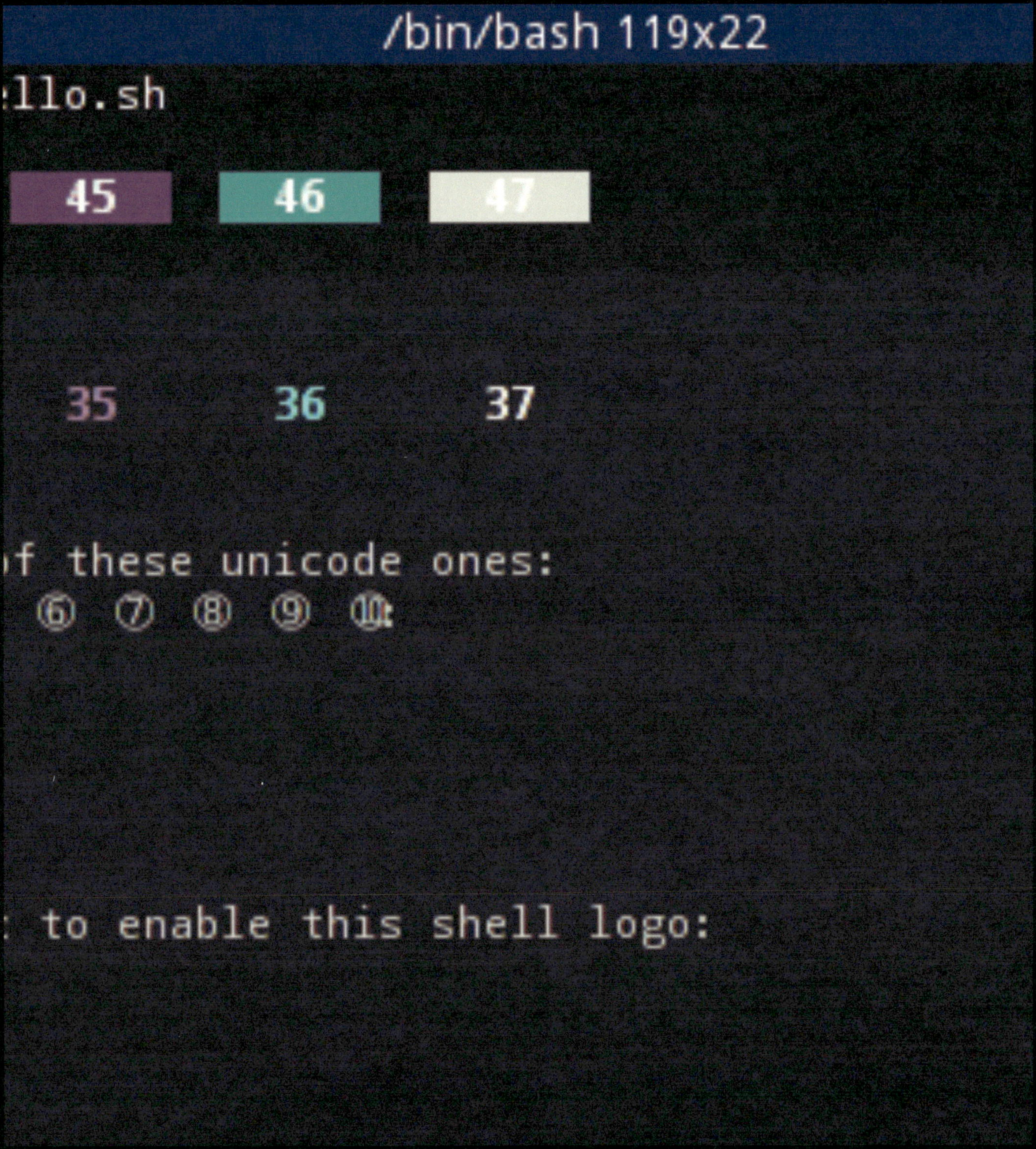
/bin/bash 119x22
llo.sh
45
46
47
35
36
37
f these unicode ones:
⑥ ⑦ ⑧ ⑨ ⑩
to enable this shell logo:

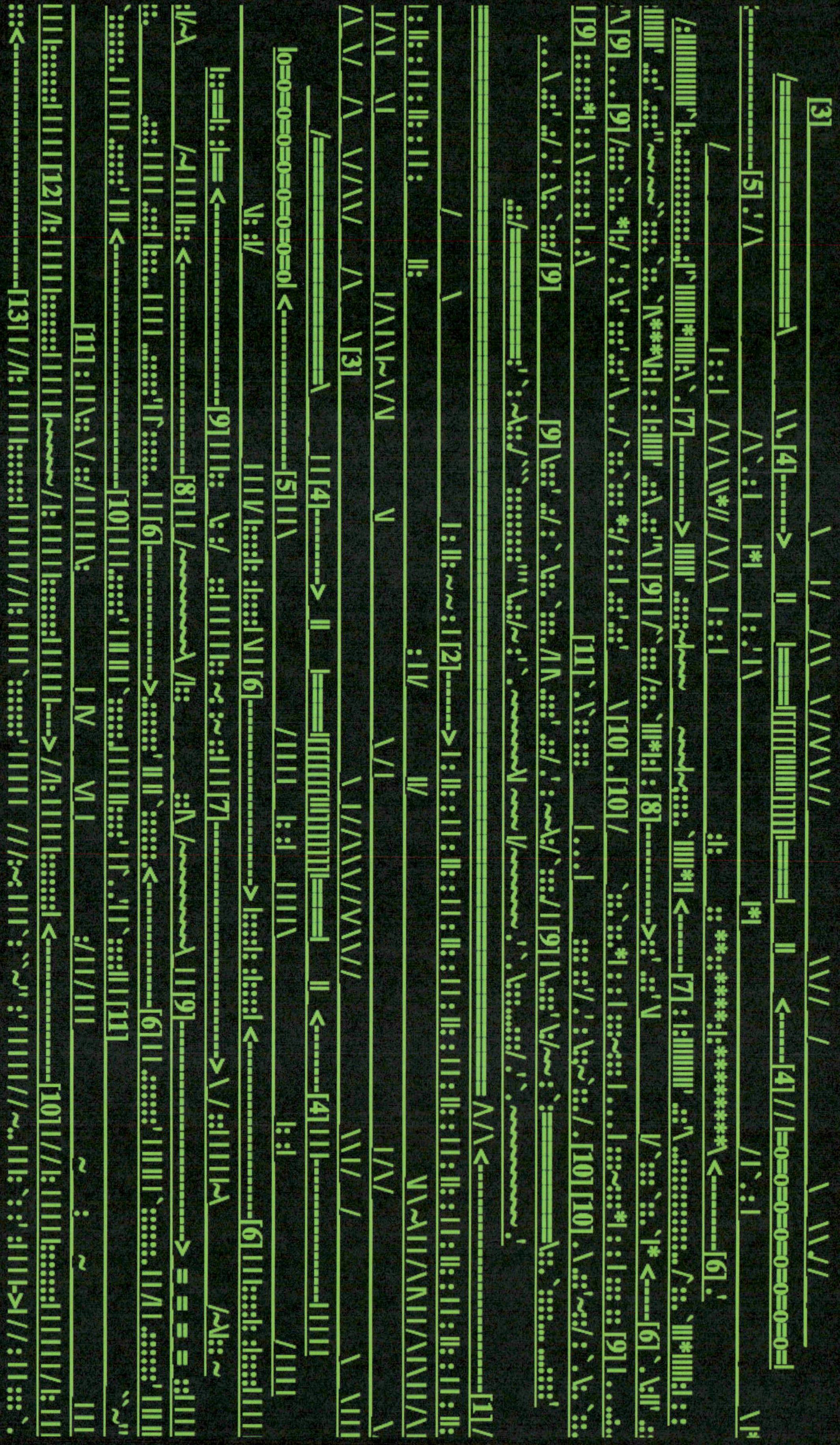

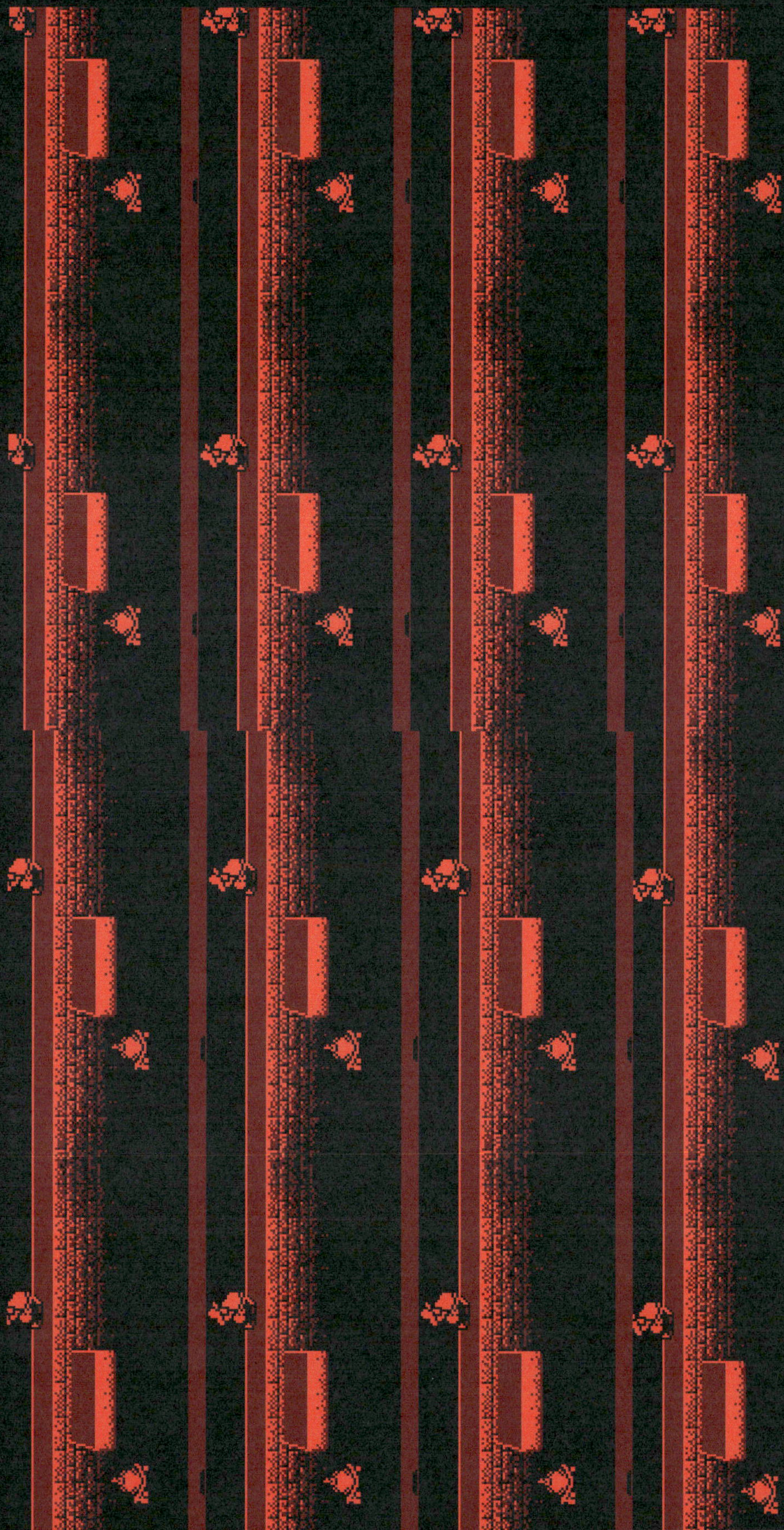

404 (not found)

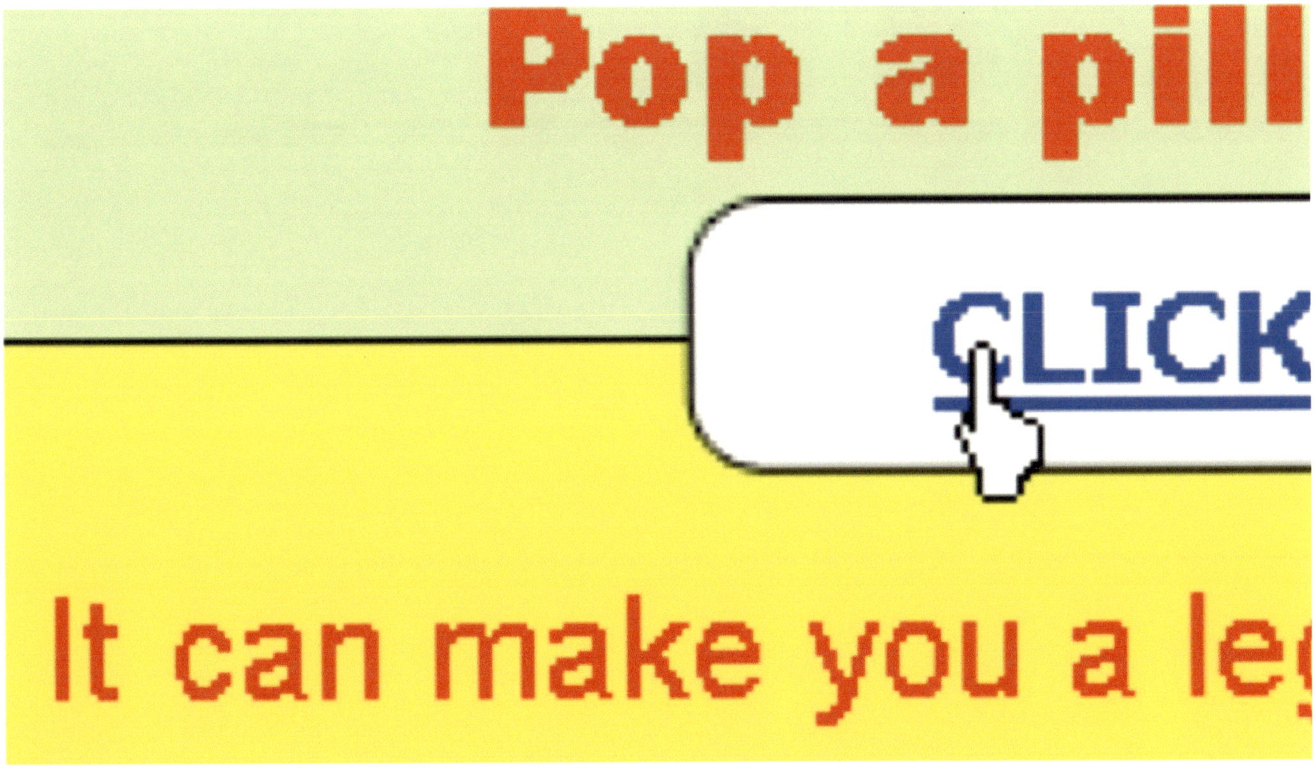
Pop a pill
CLICK
It can make you a le

Click to play

61 plays

Oasis - Sad song

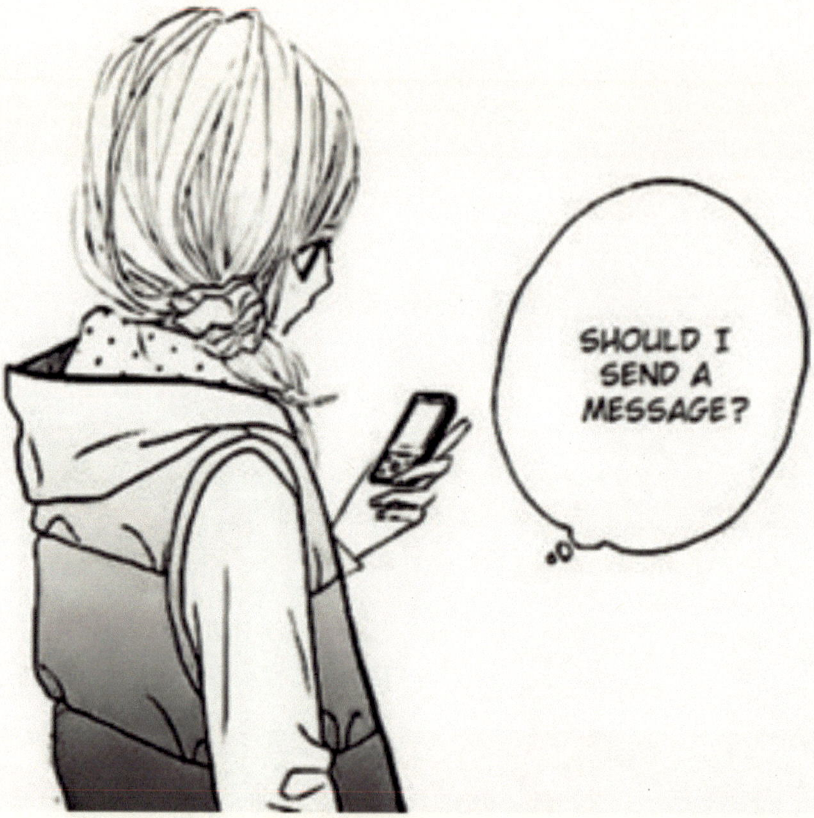

7 hours ago | 2,805 notes
Source: sikeu

✖ ⟲ Reblog

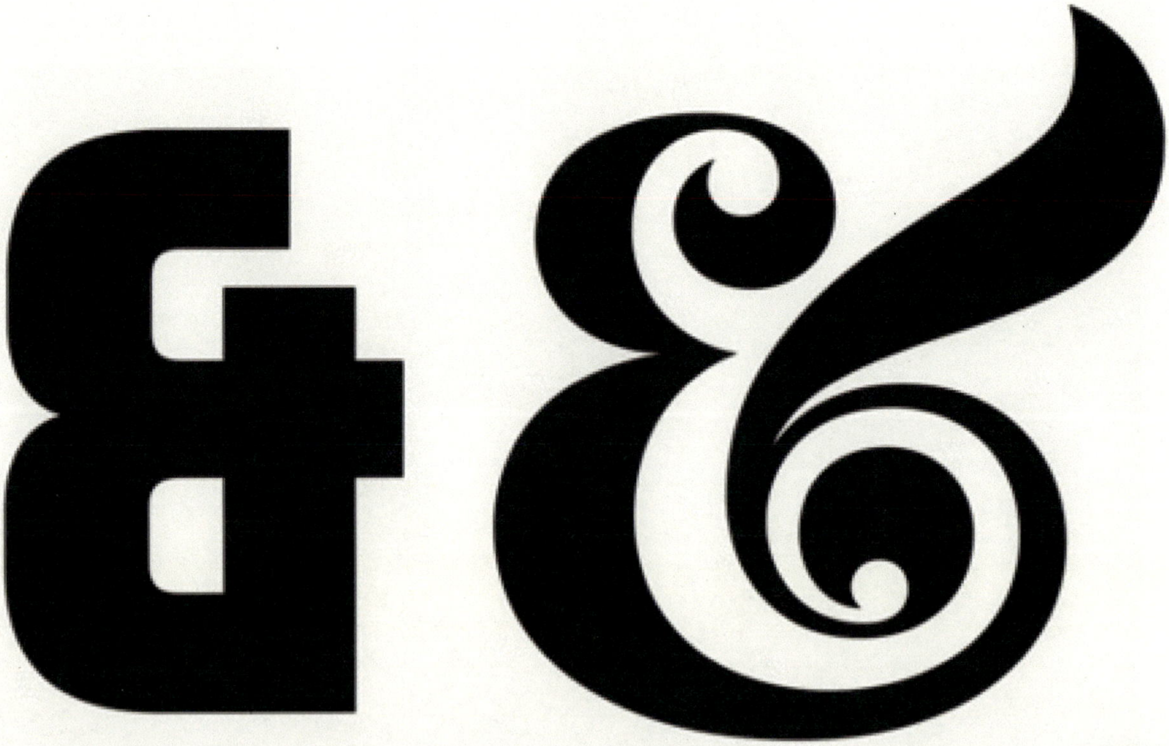

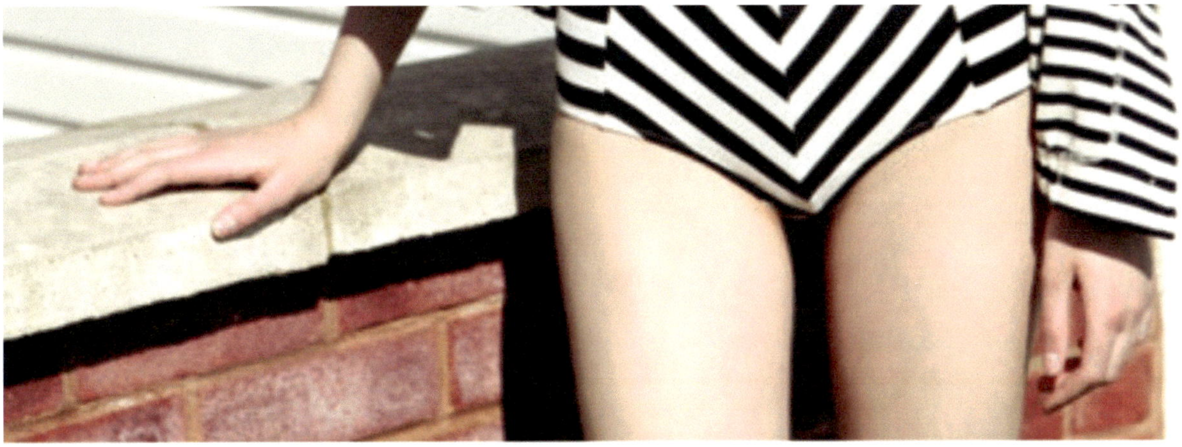

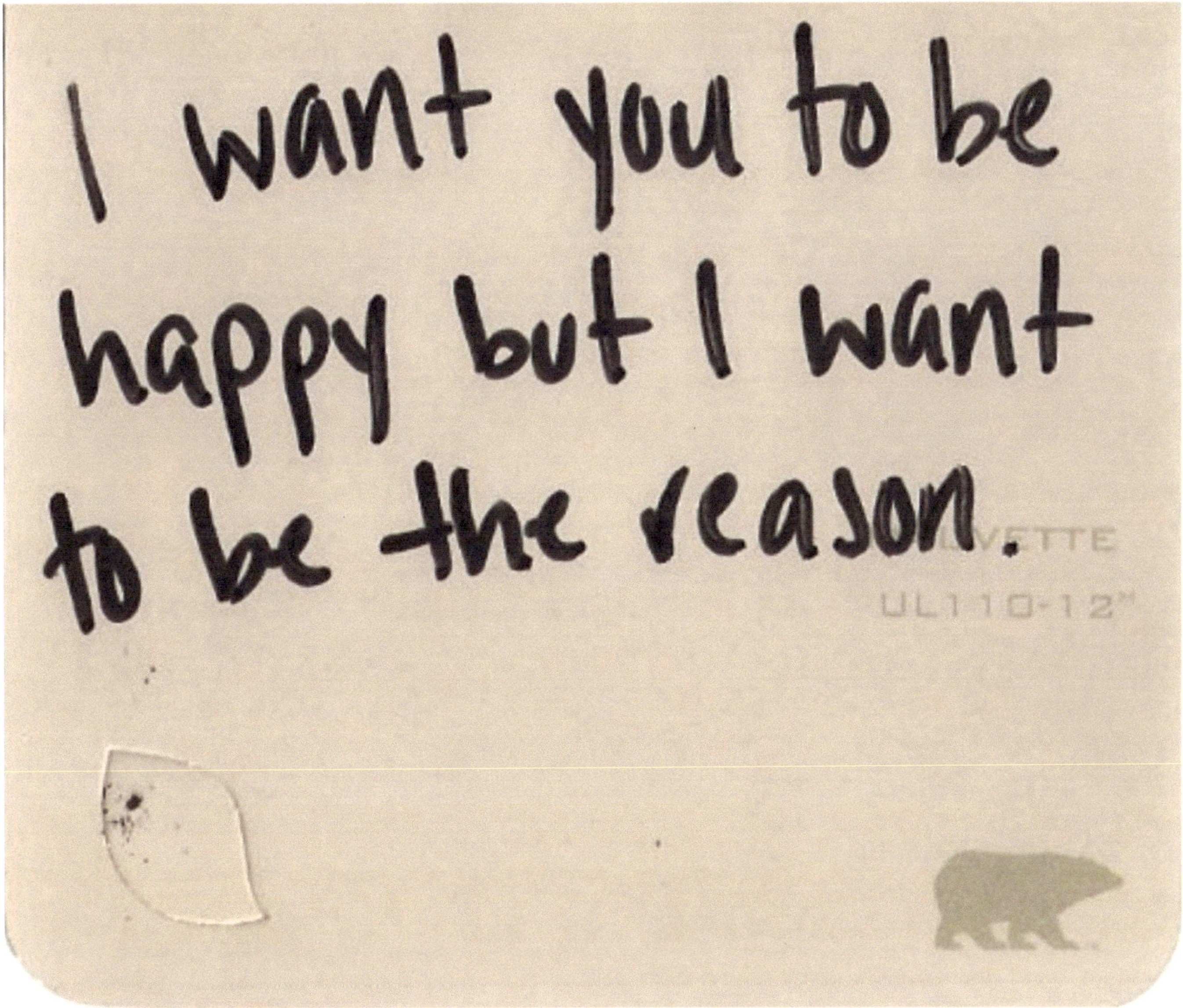

Anybody you miss...?

Anonymous

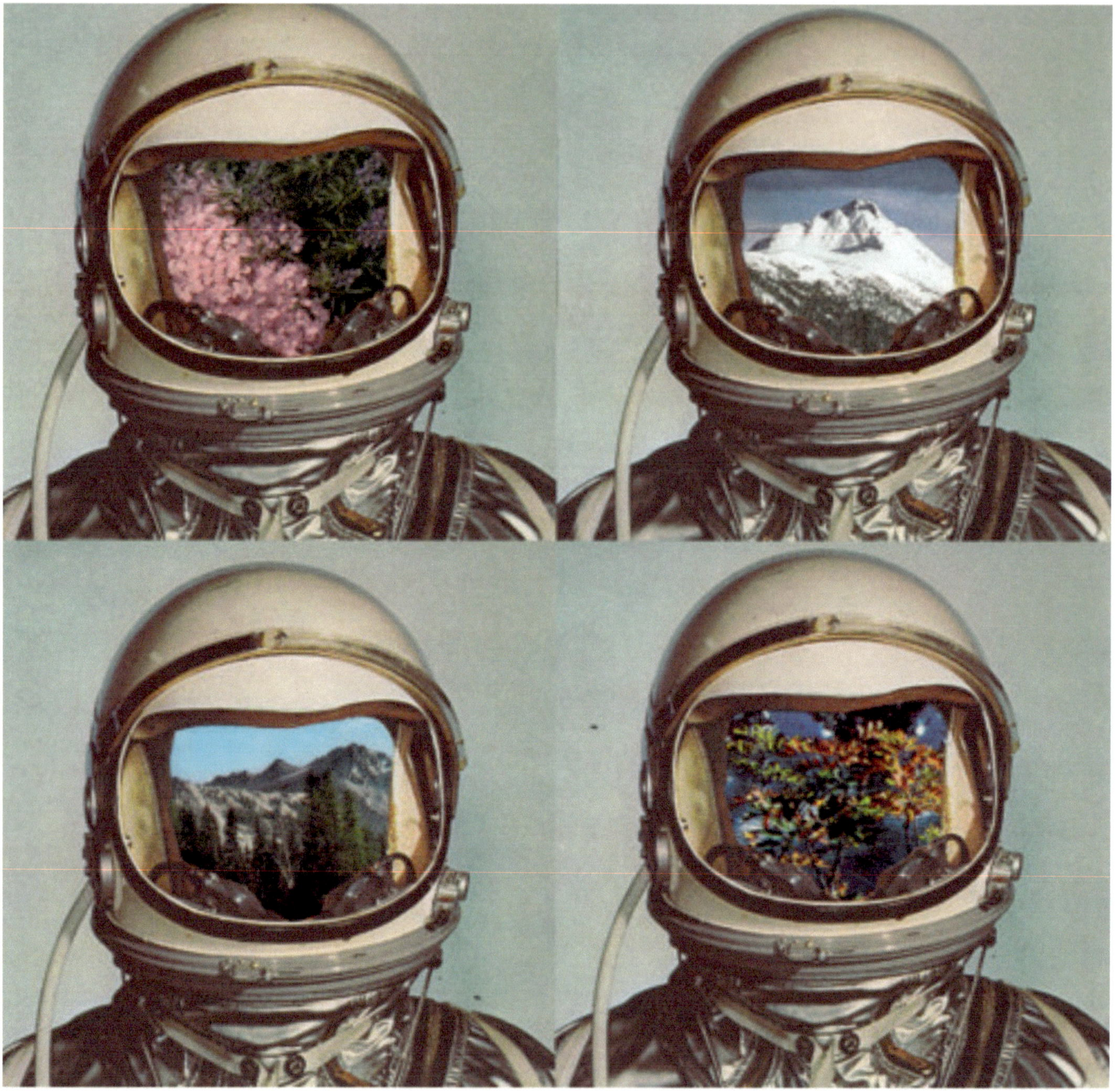

poisoninaprettypill liked this

valelee23 reblogged this from con-sabor-a-vida

siimply-eri reblogged this from rego-the-weirdo

afrochronicshoe reblogged this from rego-the-weirdo

♥ 4585
→ 26 Sep 11 at 5 pm

BAD ✝ KID

196001

links

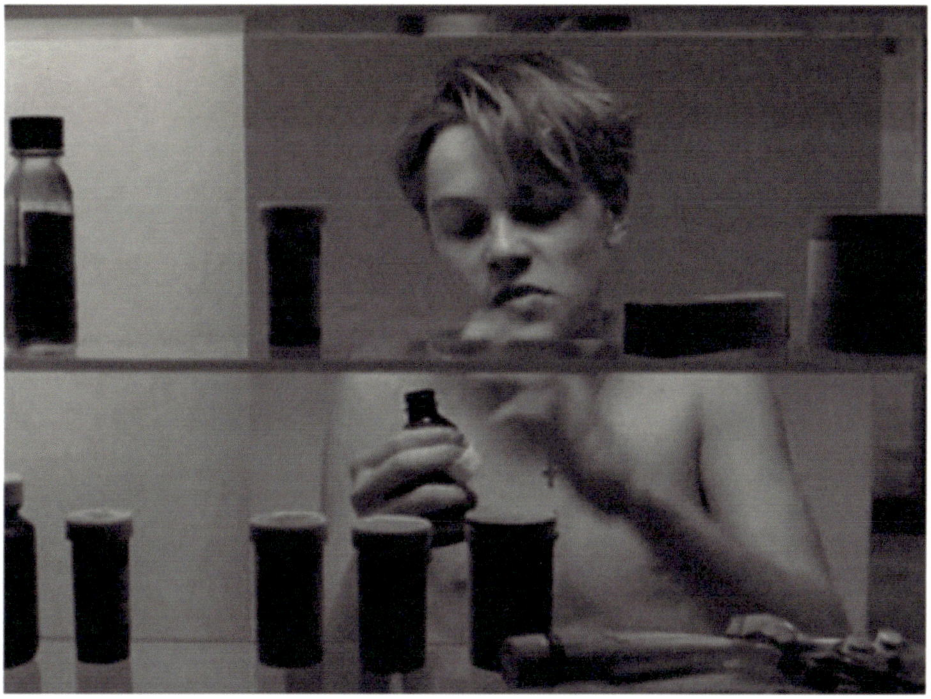

Posted: 3 days ago, with 4688 Notes

paujnk100-1 reblogged this from alldaysyouspentwithme

alwaysundecided liked this

sexonsundayss reblogged this from loudwhisperss

jazzy-b3atz reblogged this from ronniebitchhhh

ronniebitchhhh reblogged this from titohwolf

oibiscooito reblogged this from lesbico

ibarnie reblogged this from itssneverends

ibarnie liked this

kklas reblogged this from medudududuuddusa

6psychopaticmarik6lover6 reblogged this from cccuts

succulentshit reblogged this from amorycondon

madafacka-justsmile reblogged this from bewhoyoureallywannabe

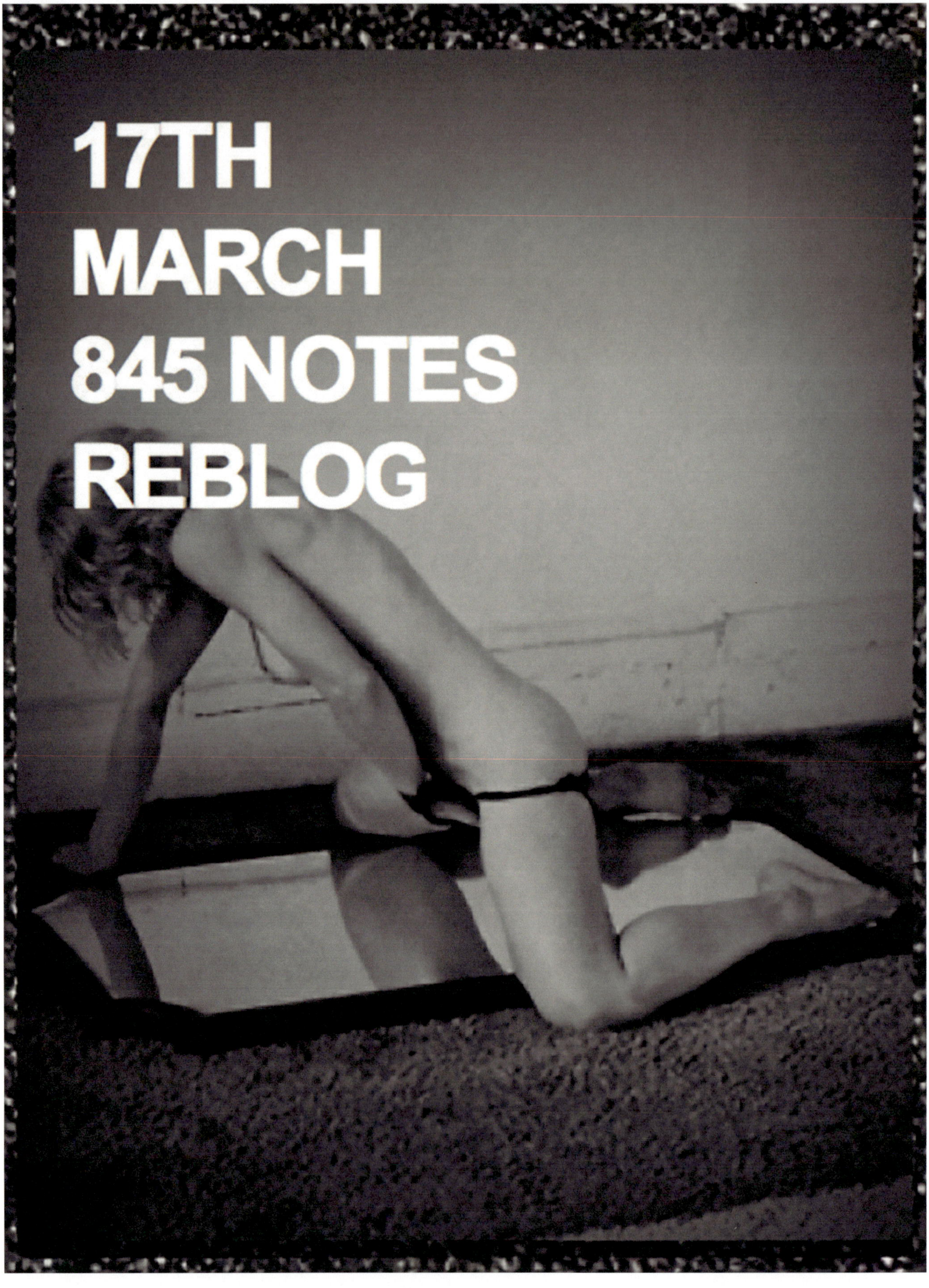
17TH
MARCH
845 NOTES
REBLOG

バブルの吸殻

archive / rss / ask / my face / faq / theme

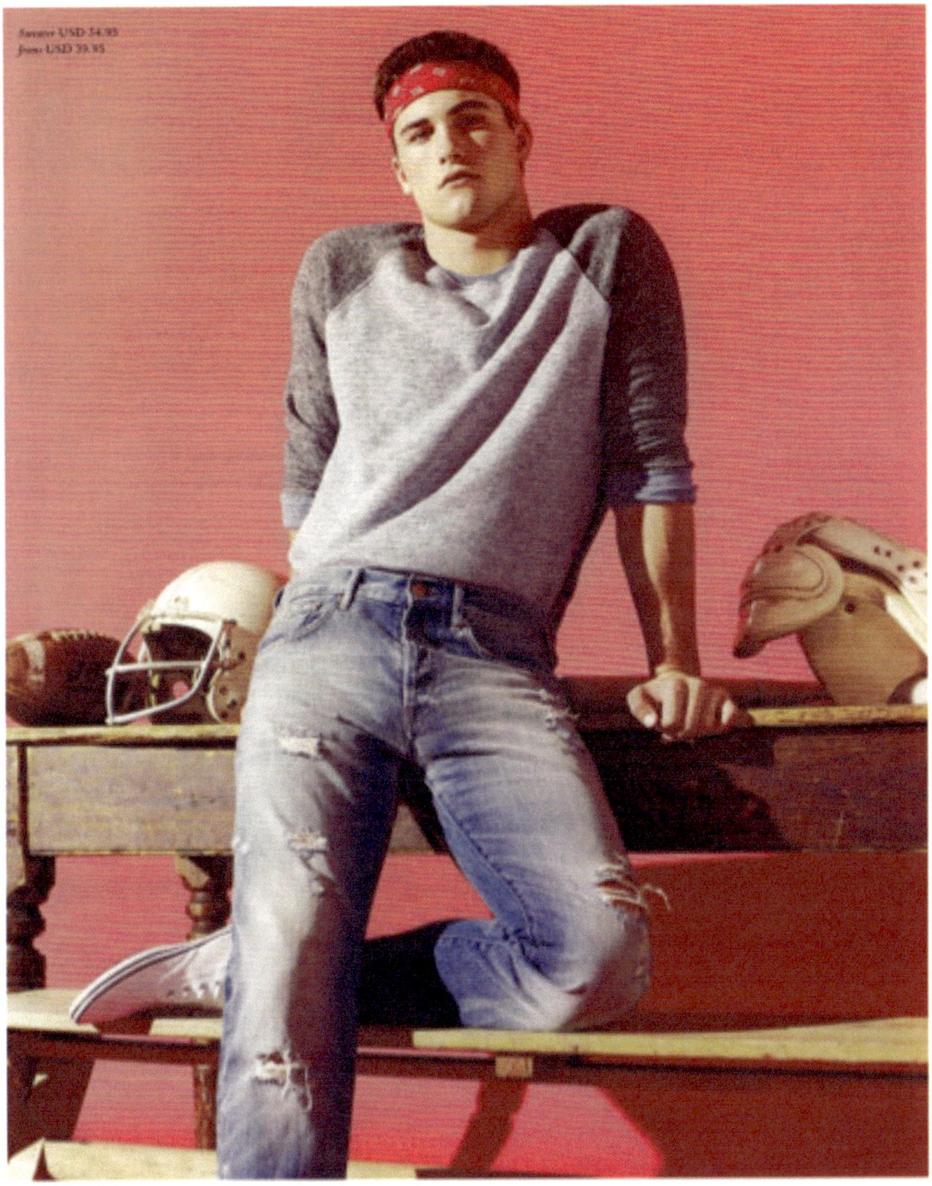

(Source: love-less, via undergroundalex)

2 days ago · 155 notes · March 22nd

1. white-boy-wasted reblogged this from mail-models
2. paper-n-pencil liked this
3. swimaboy reblogged this from undergroundalex
4. zarathusta reblogged this from dayindecember
5. the-beat-of-my-drum liked this
6. totallynick liked this
7. negro-ovejas liked this
8. dayindecember reblogged this from well-prepped
9. methustos reblogged this from undergroundalex
10. byndilaupsteen liked this
11. murderouswaltzing reblogged this from undergroundalex
12. diegokiller reblogged this from h-iv

zoom

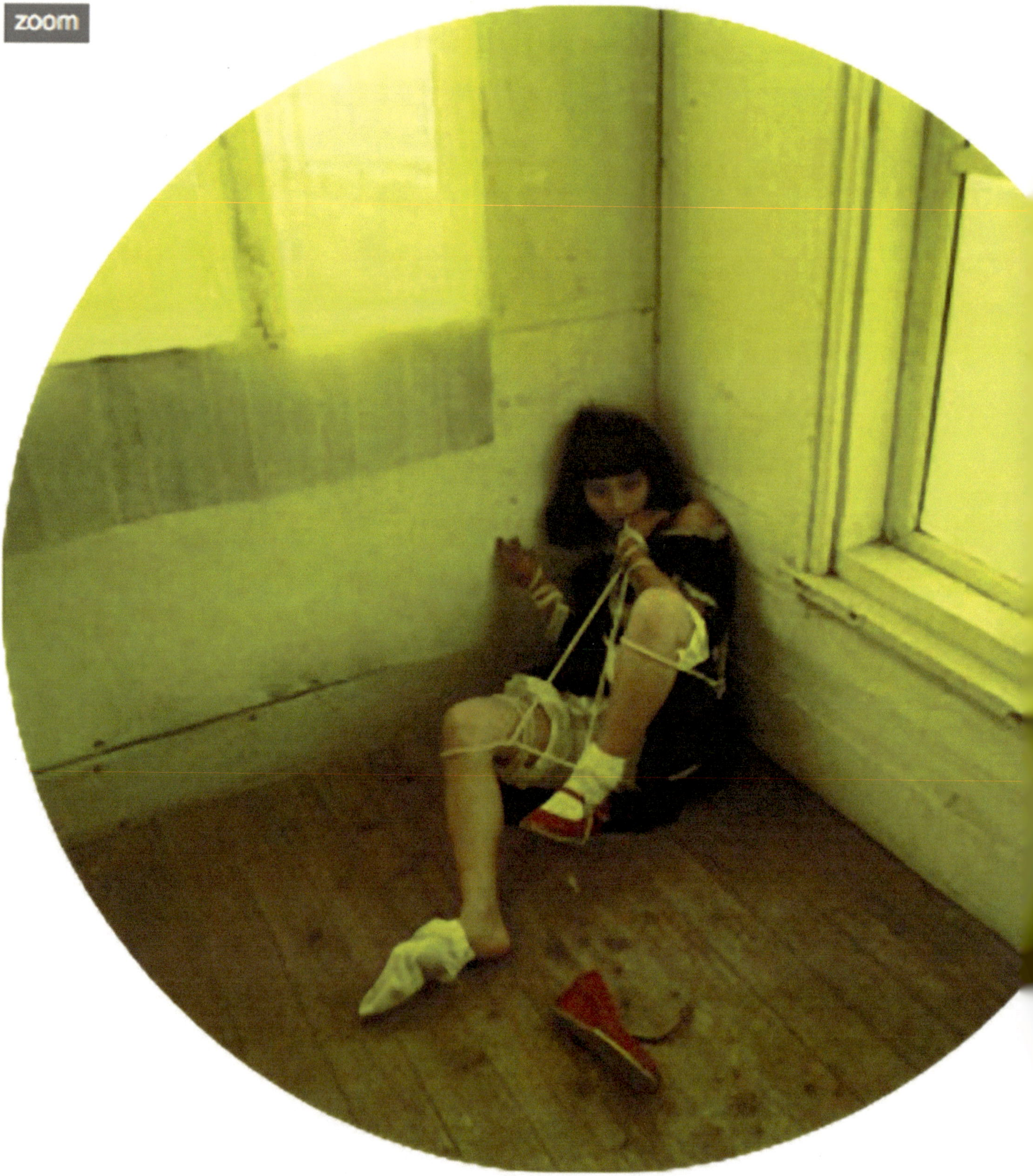

howdoyoufeet:

| "Shuji Terayama"

#shuji terayama #foot #feet #lace #bondage #girl #jappo #oriental #fetish

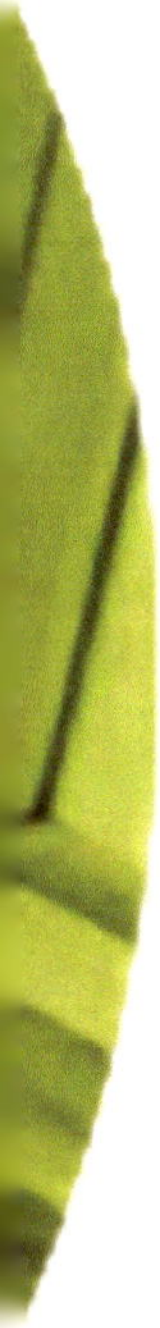

home

message

archive

©

my sanctuary~!

I'm a monster trapped in my own nightmare. Nothing more to it (>°д°)>

links →

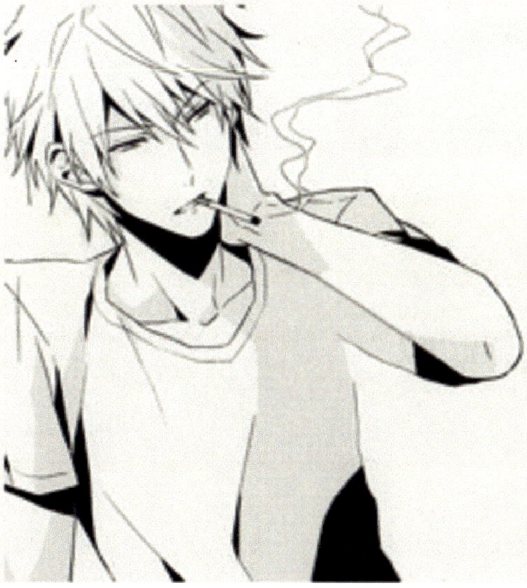

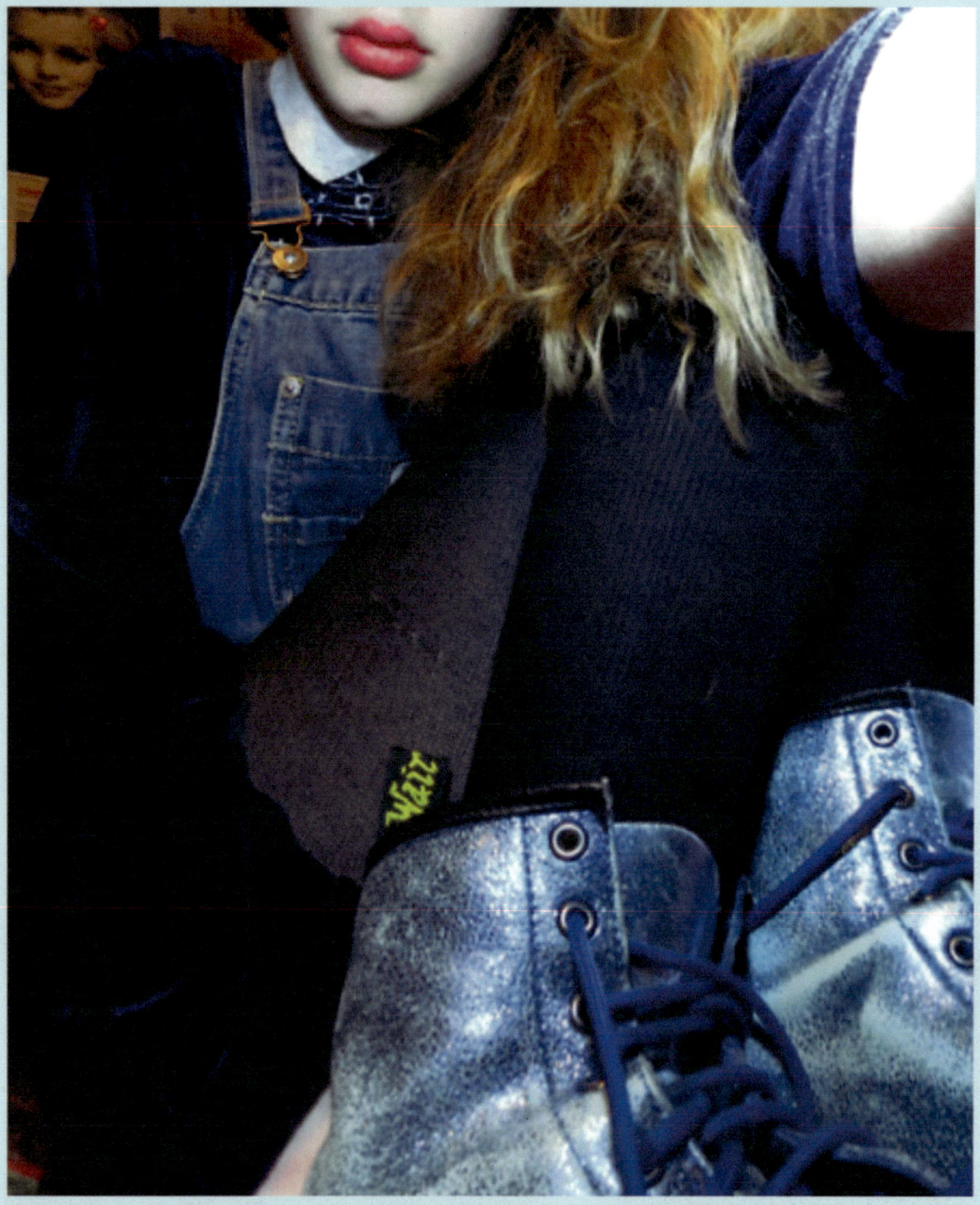

Anon, calm down, here's todays outfit:

- blue glitter docs
- blue dungarees
- blue velvet top
- not blue 2004 triathlon shirt
- blue
- blue
- electric blue

• • 35 notes

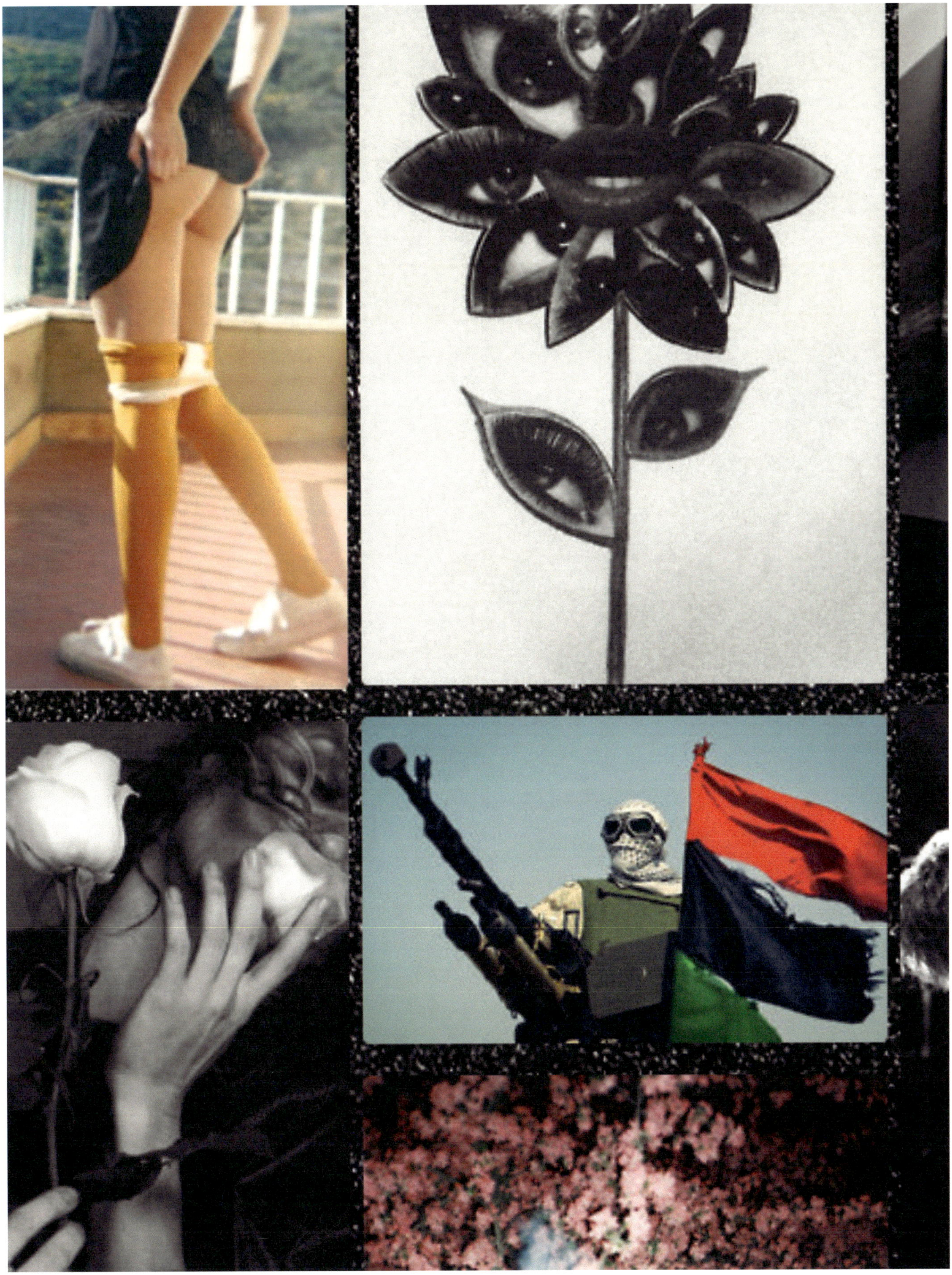

Life is a map untraveled

"there's a piece of me in every single second, of every single day"

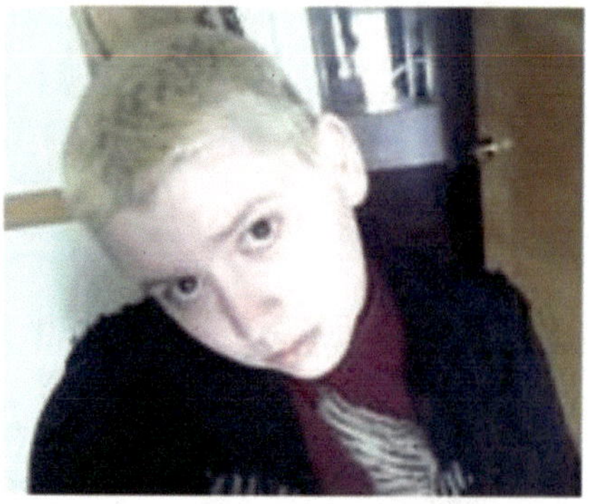

Female
20 years old
PORTLAND, OREGON
United

♥ Brian

"Semi-Homeless teen looking for shelter before fully homeless"

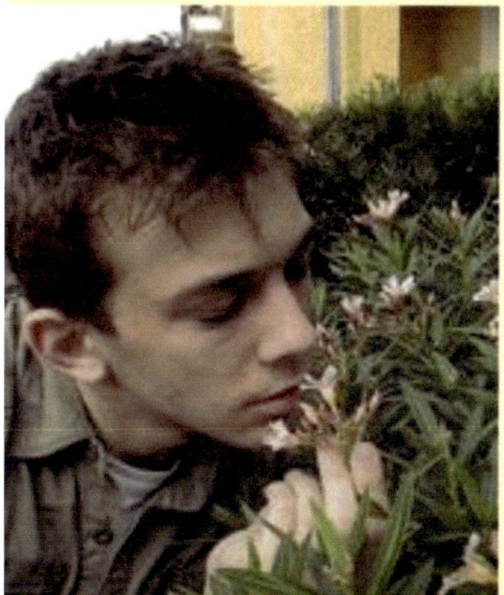

Male
20 years old
Orlando, Florida
United States

♦©♥∓♥©♦

"broken"

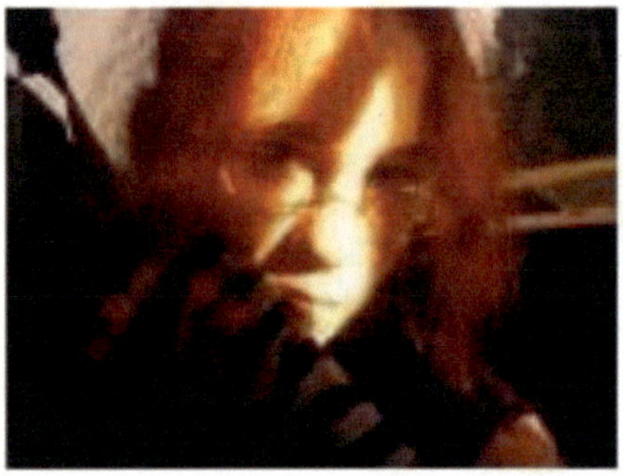

Female
14 years old
Pennsylvania
United
States

Last Login:
6/22/2007

sean loves you

"screw me"

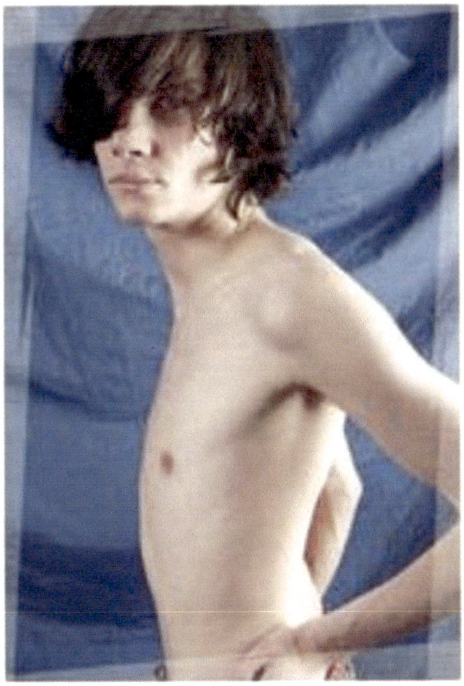

Male
19 years
old
DELAWARE,
Ohio
United
States

Last Login:
6/8/2007

Noé

"Nose to nose, eyes are closed. This is what I said, "We never, ever end.""

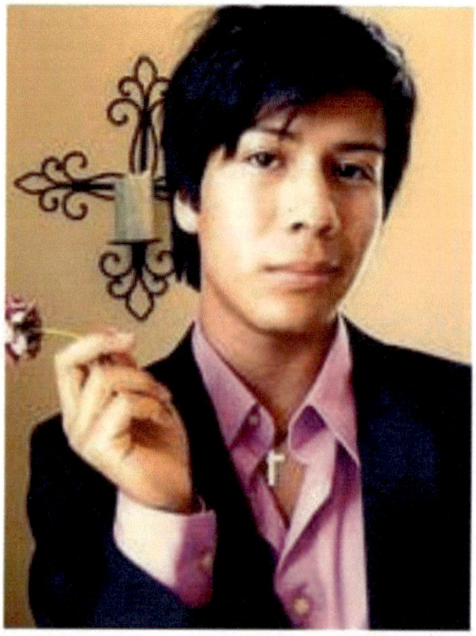

Male
18 years old
Knoxville, Tennessee

Velvet Goldmine X

"As the world fall down... Within you...."

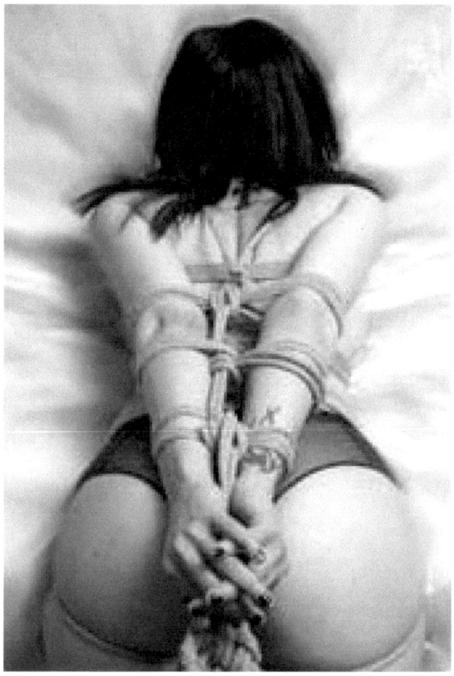

Female
25 years old
Goblin City (valencia), CALIFORNIA
United States

....coco*

"hug me...i'm EMO!! "

Female
15 years old
no where near home,
Illinois
United States

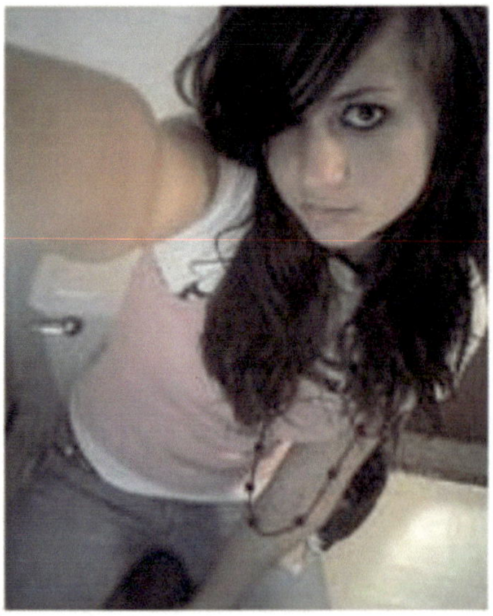

Online Now!

Tim the bisexual toy robot

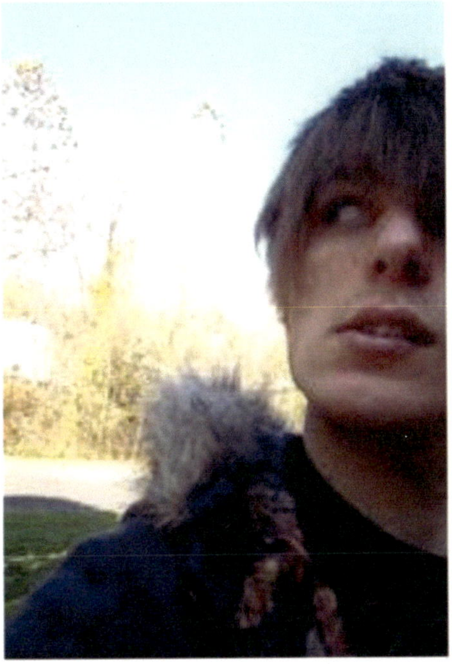

Male
17 years old
New Jersey
United States

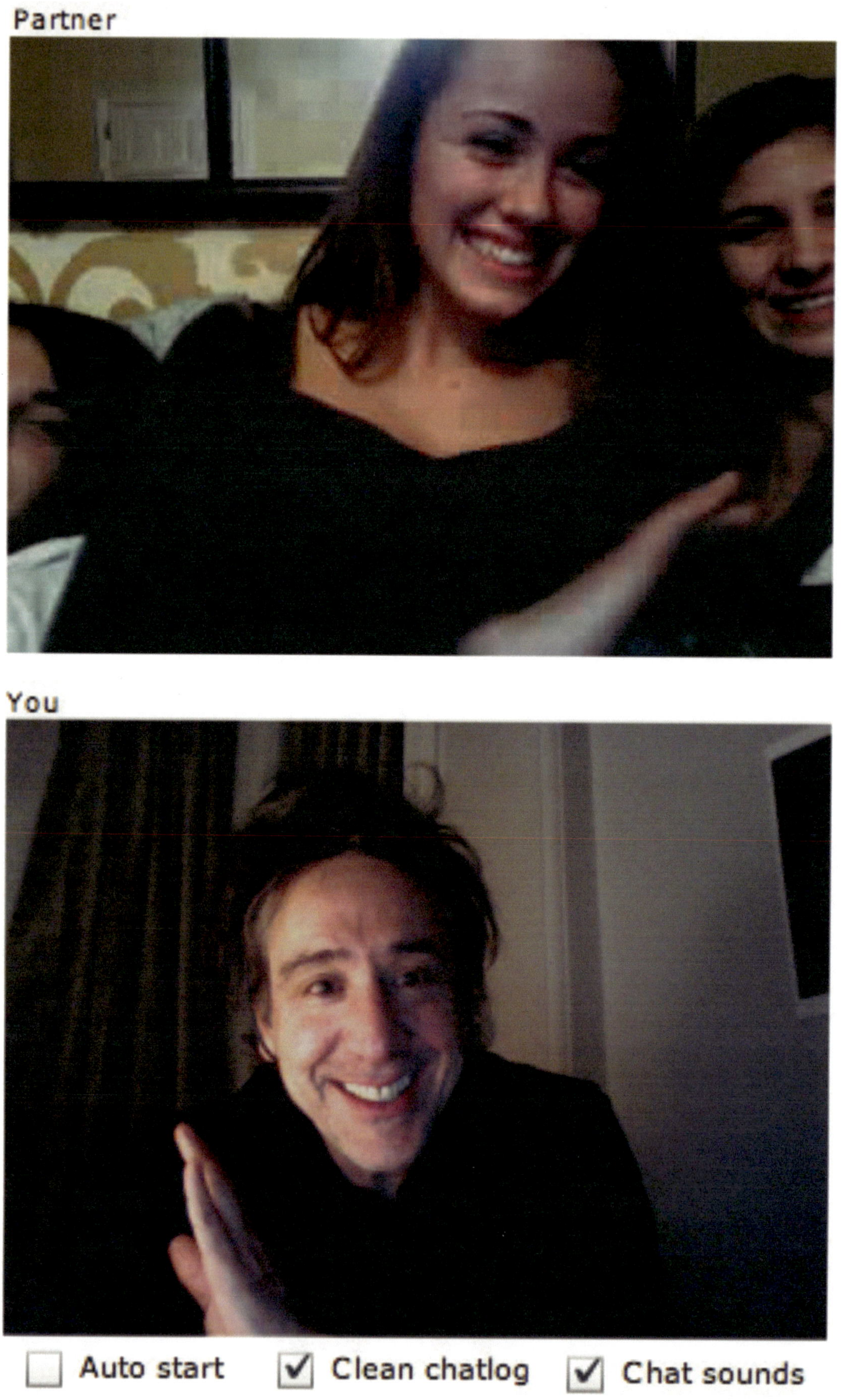
Partner
You
Auto start
Clean chatlog
Chat sounds

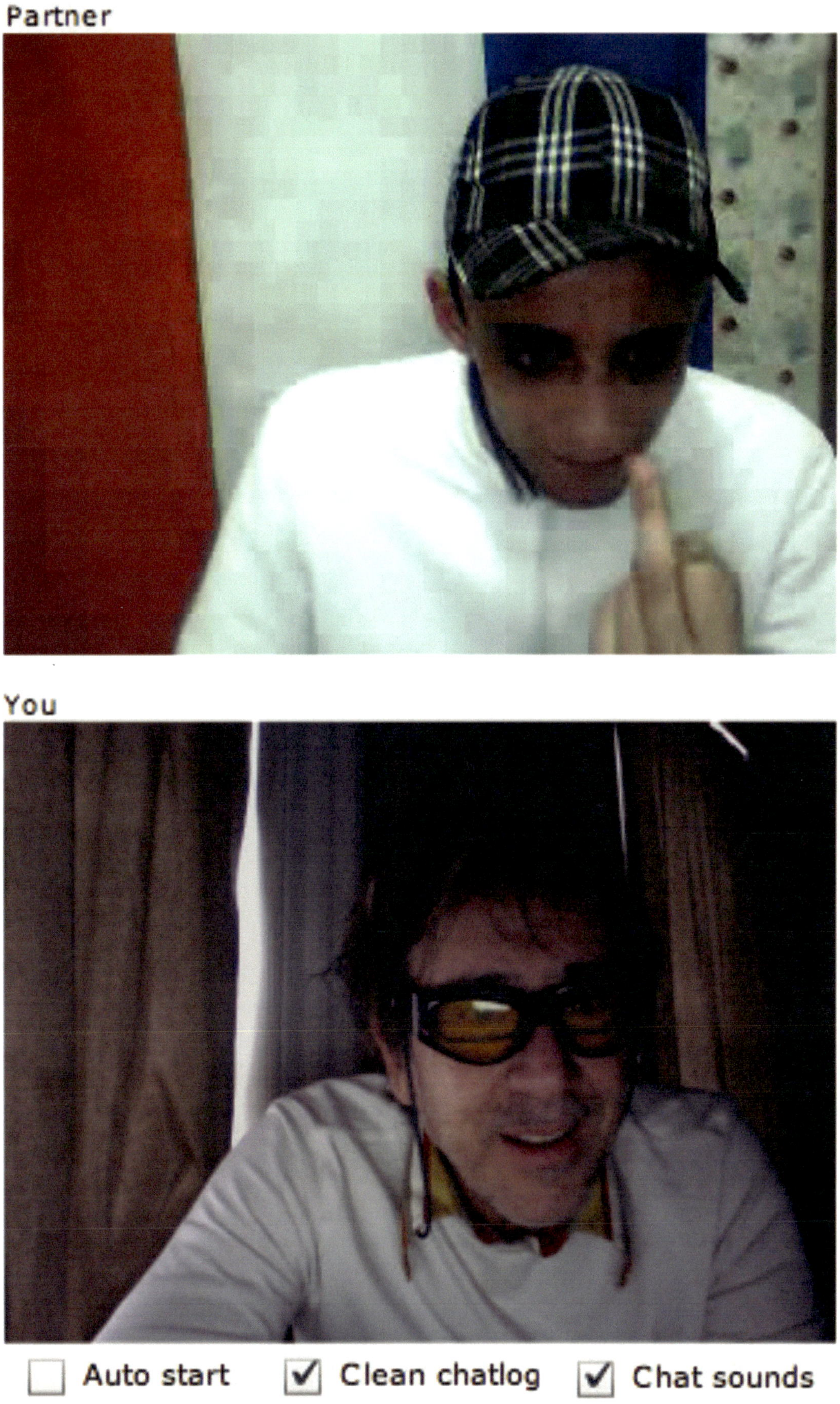
Partner
You
Auto start
Clean chatlog
Chat sounds

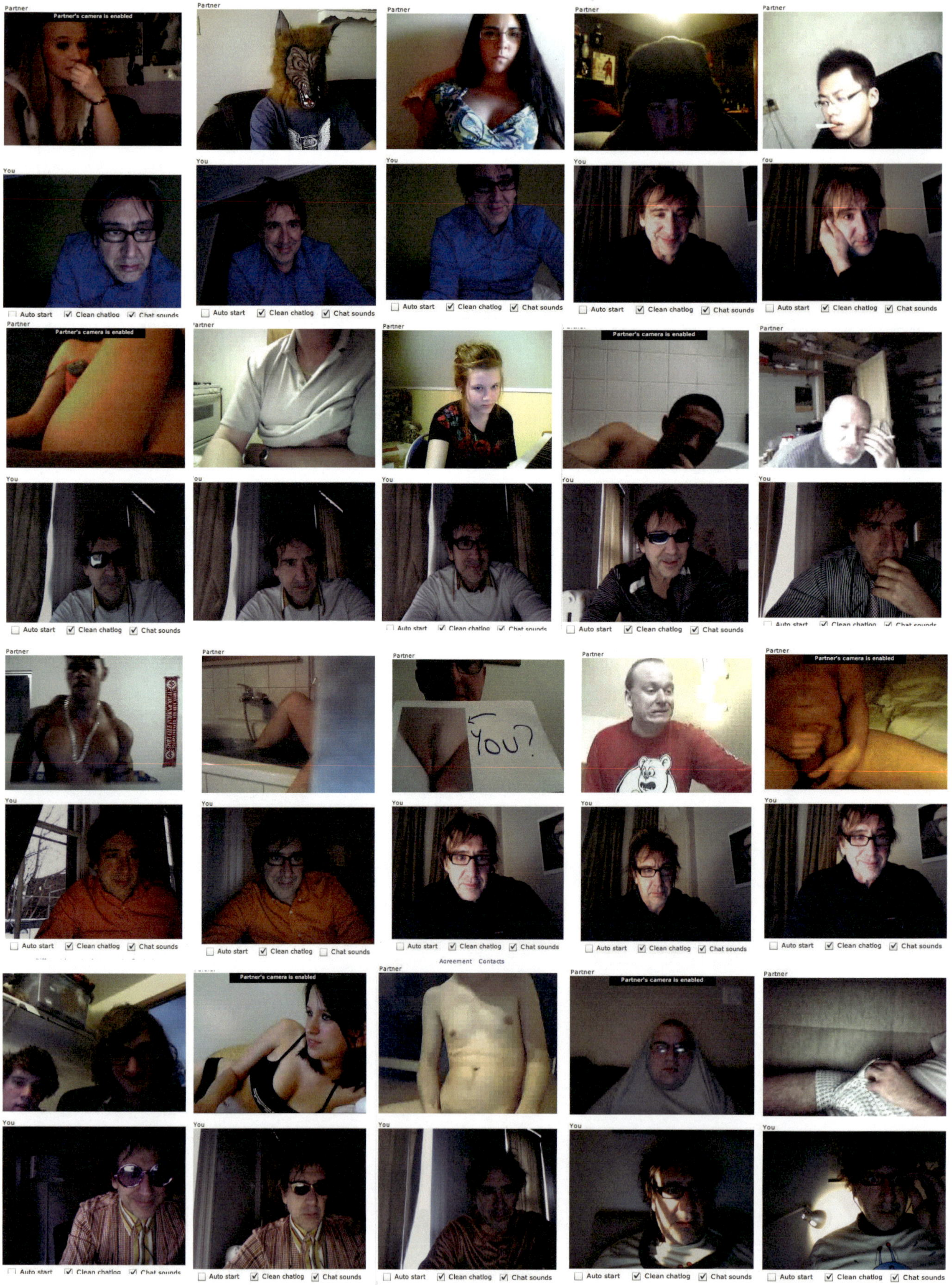
Partner
Partner's camera is enabled
You
Auto start
Clean chatlog
Chat sounds
You?
Agreement Contacts

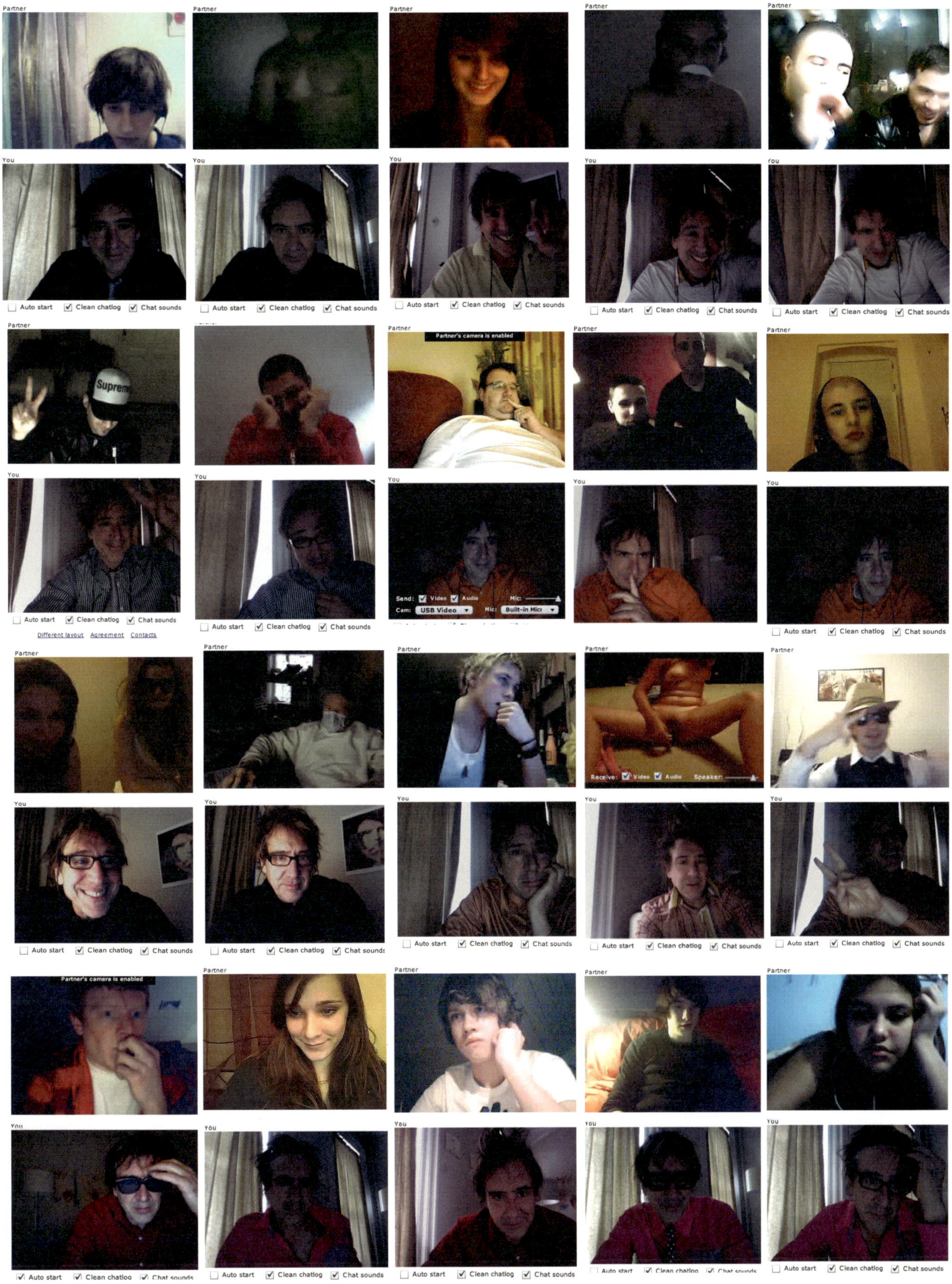
Partner
Partner
Partner
Partner
Partner
You
You
You
You
You
Auto start Clean chatlog Chat sounds
Auto start Clean chatlog Chat sounds
Auto start Clean chatlog Chat sounds
Auto start Clean chatlog Chat sounds
Auto start Clean chatlog Chat sounds
Partner
Supreme
Partner
Partner's camera is enabled
Partner
Partner
You
You
You
You
You
Auto start Clean chatlog Chat sounds
Different layout Agreement Contacts
Auto start Clean chatlog Chat sounds
Send: Video Audio Mic:
Cam: USB Video Mic: Built-in Mic
Auto start Clean chatlog Chat sounds
Partner
Partner
Partner
Partner
Receive: Video Audio Speaker:
Partner
You
You
You
You
You
Auto start Clean chatlog Chat sounds
Auto start Clean chatlog Chat sounds
Auto start Clean chatlog Chat sounds
Auto start Clean chatlog Chat sounds
Auto start Clean chatlog Chat sounds
Partner's camera is enabled
Partner
Partner
Partner
Partner
You
You
You
You
You
Auto start Clean chatlog Chat sounds
Auto start Clean chatlog Chat sounds
Auto start Clean chatlog Chat sounds
Auto start Clean chatlog Chat sounds
Auto start Clean chatlog Chat sounds

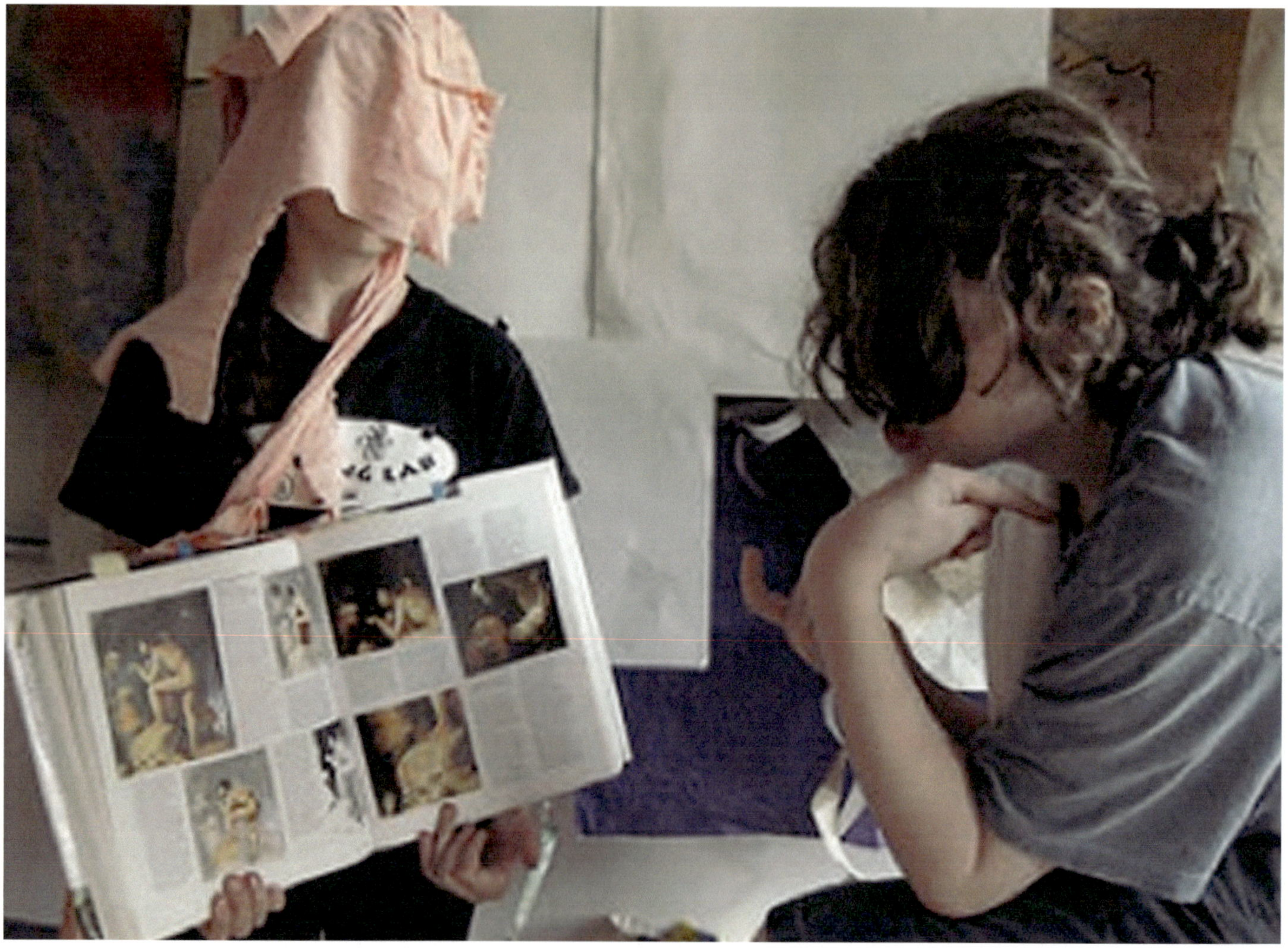

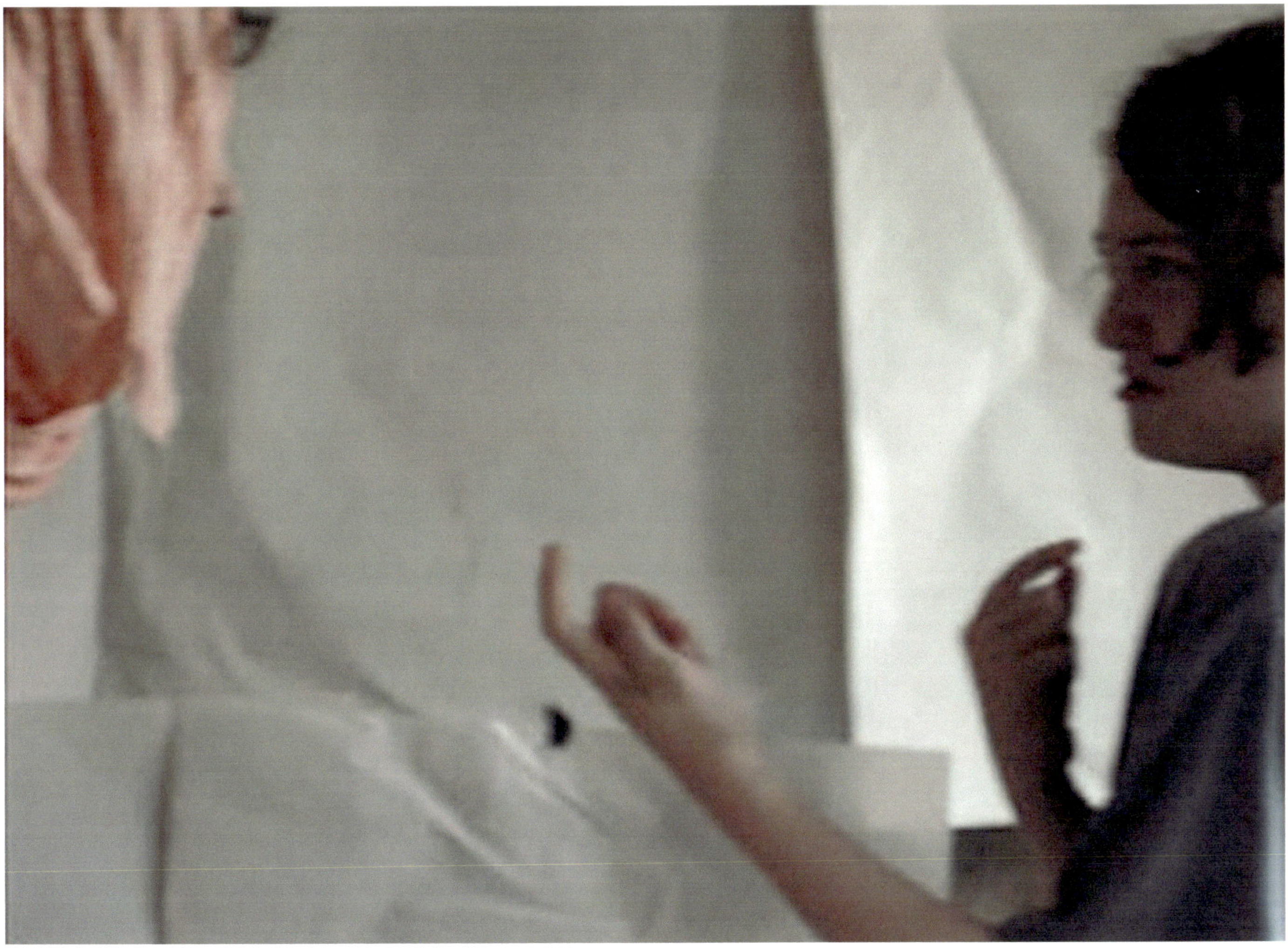

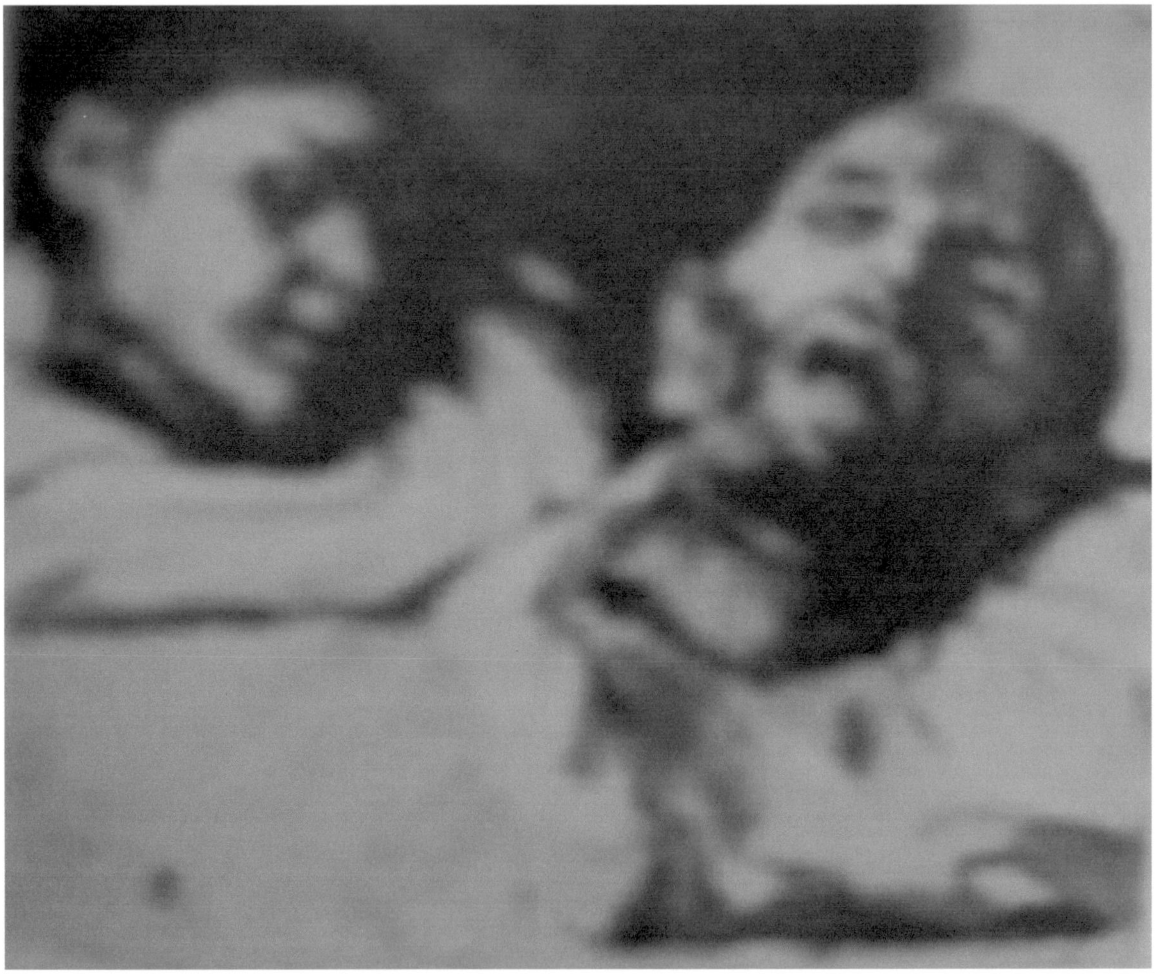

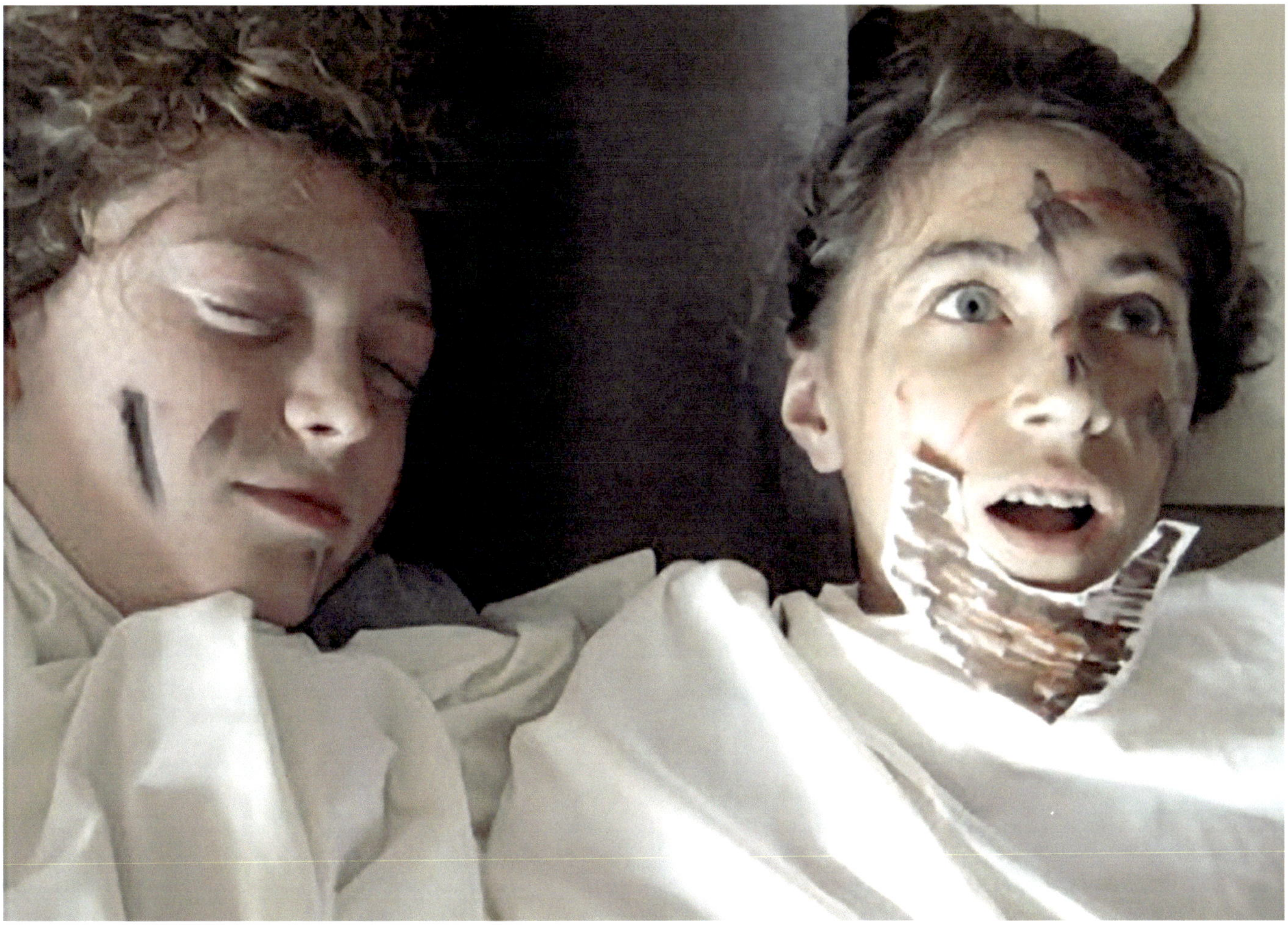

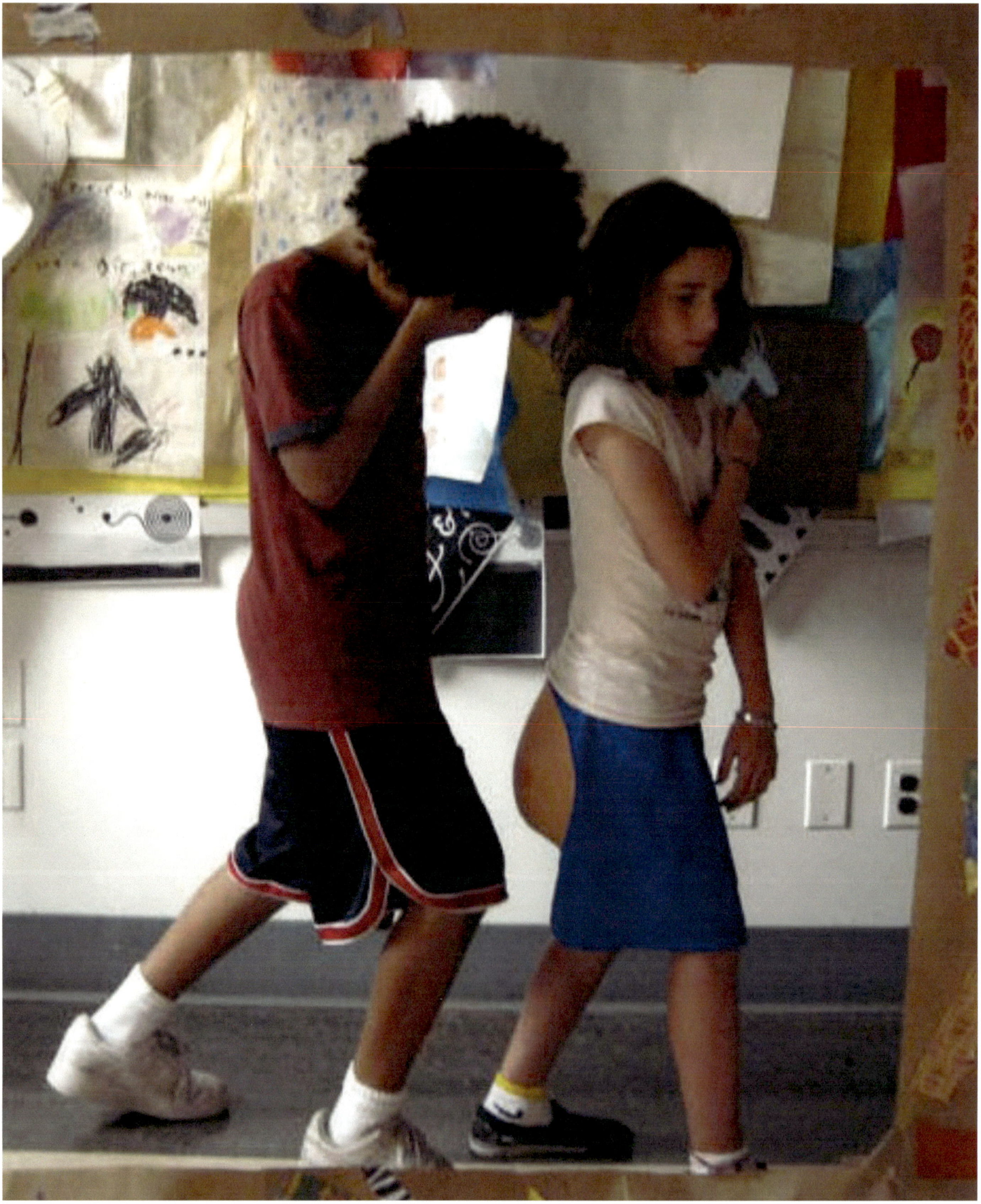

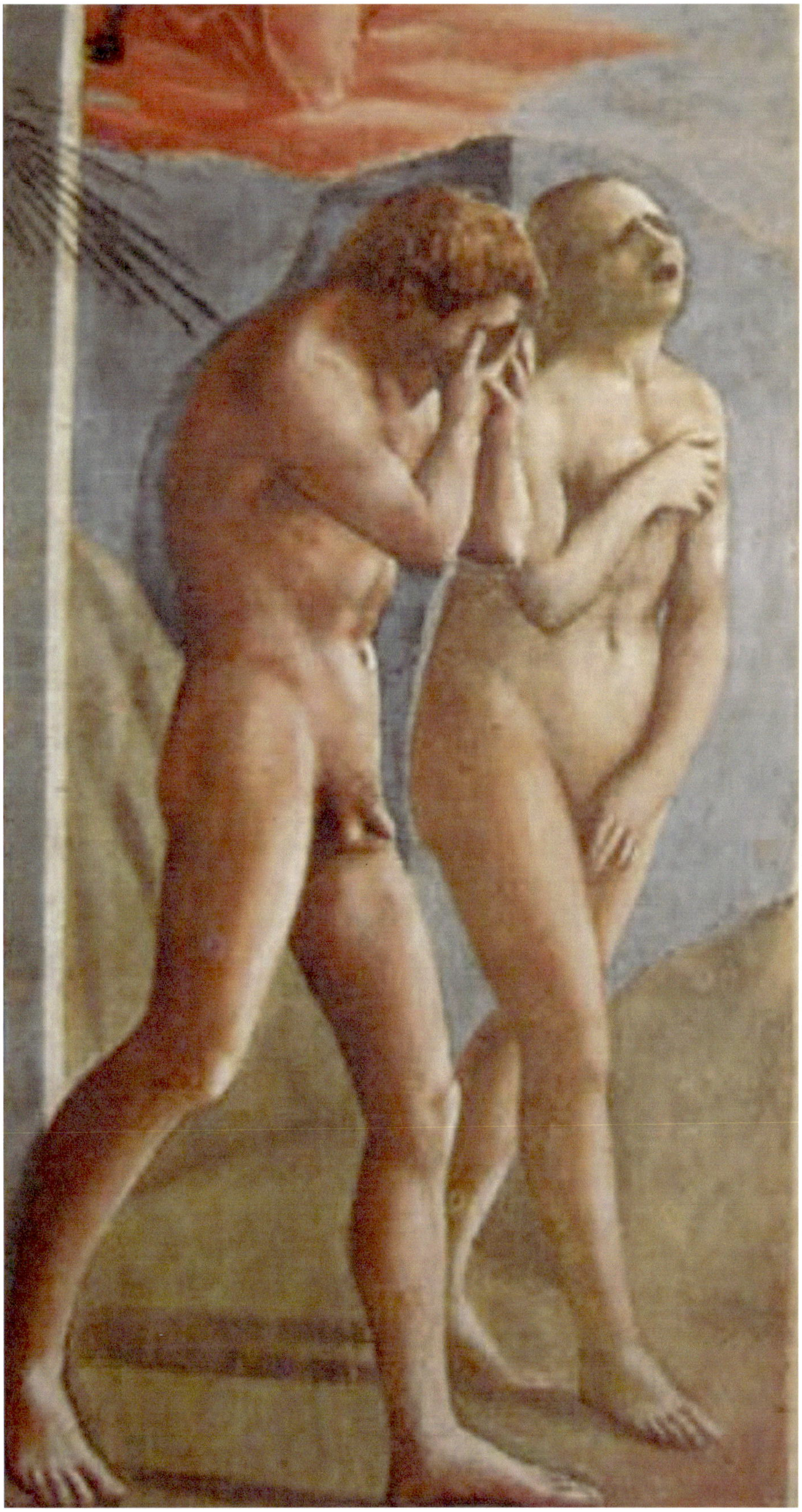

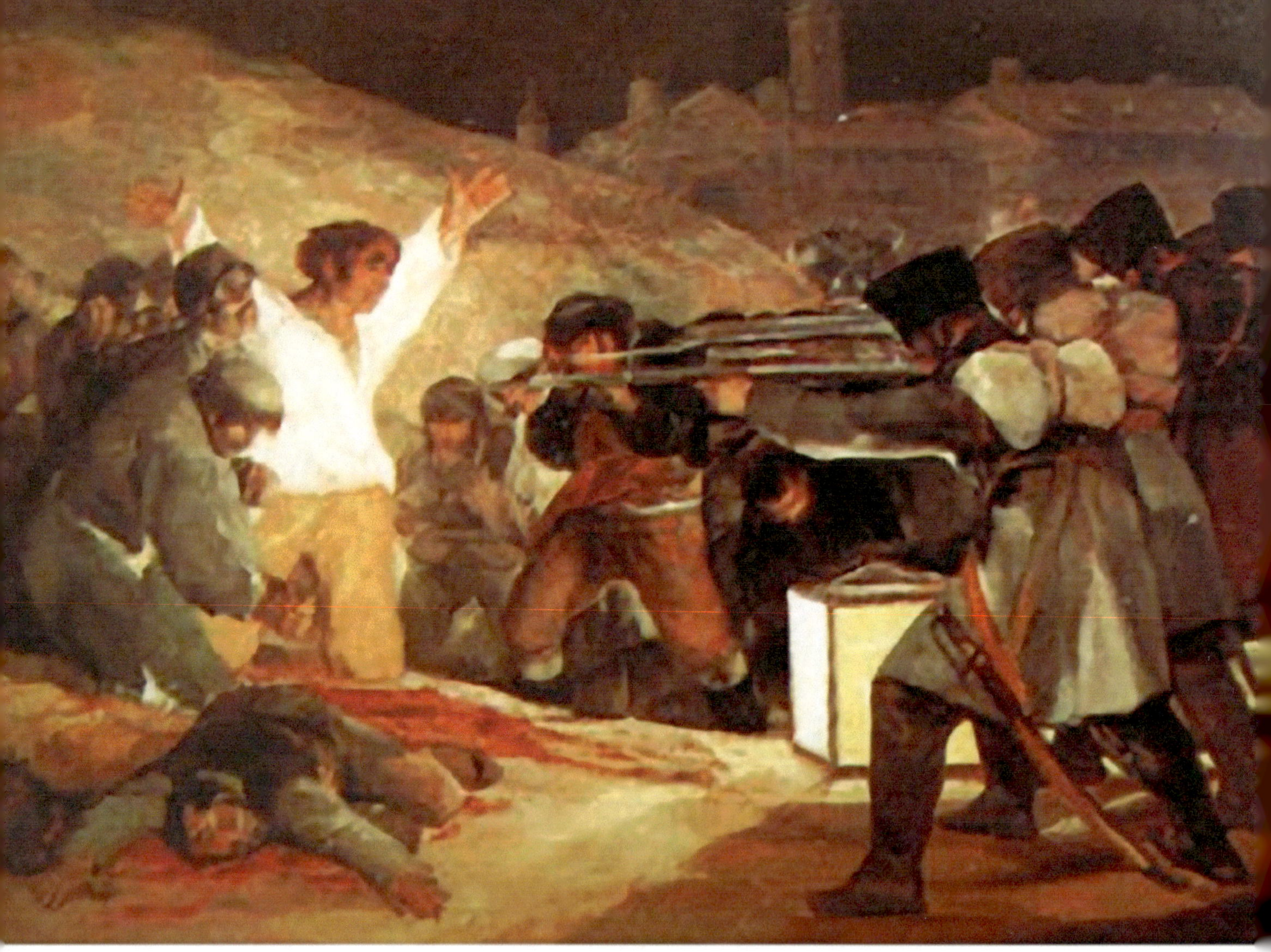

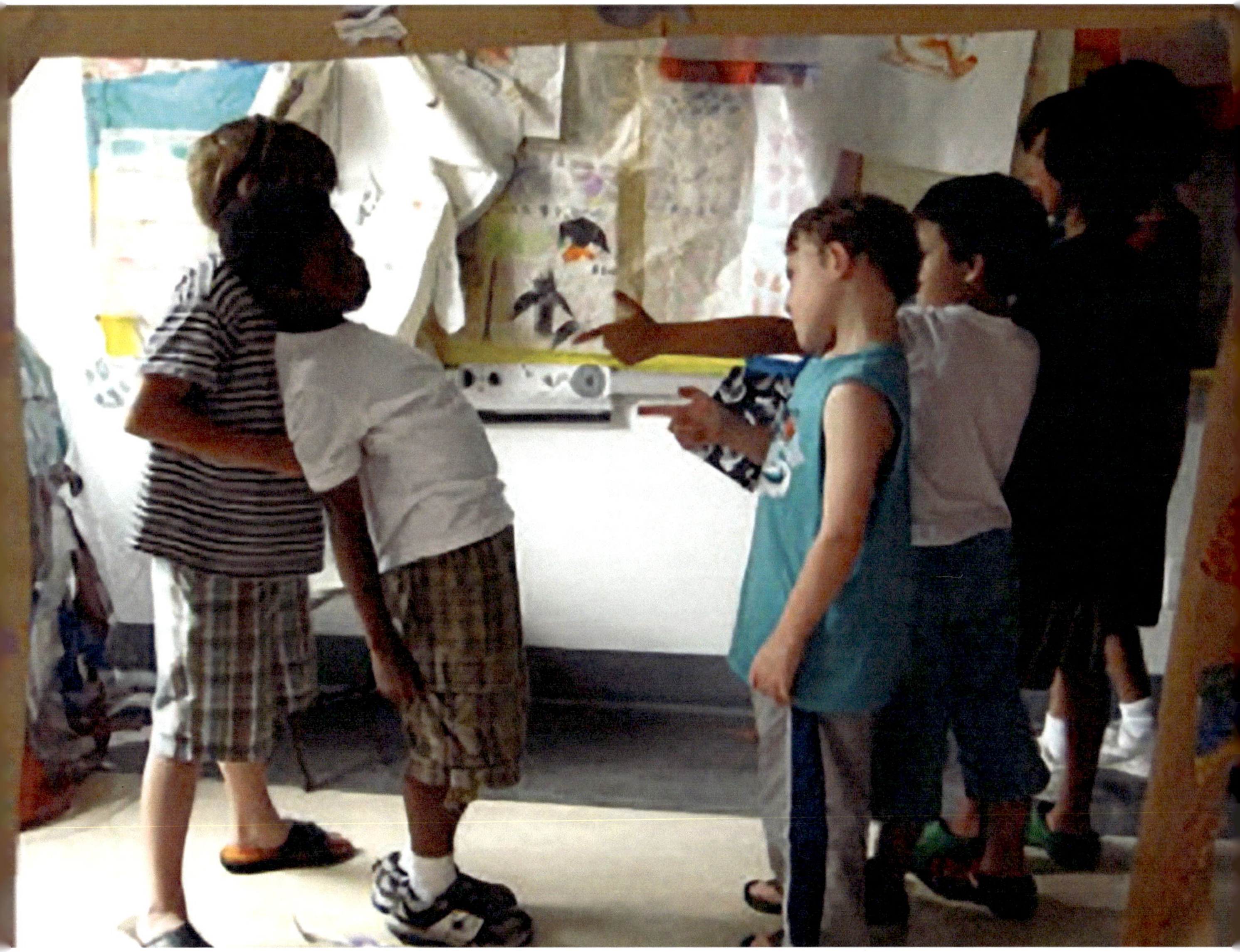

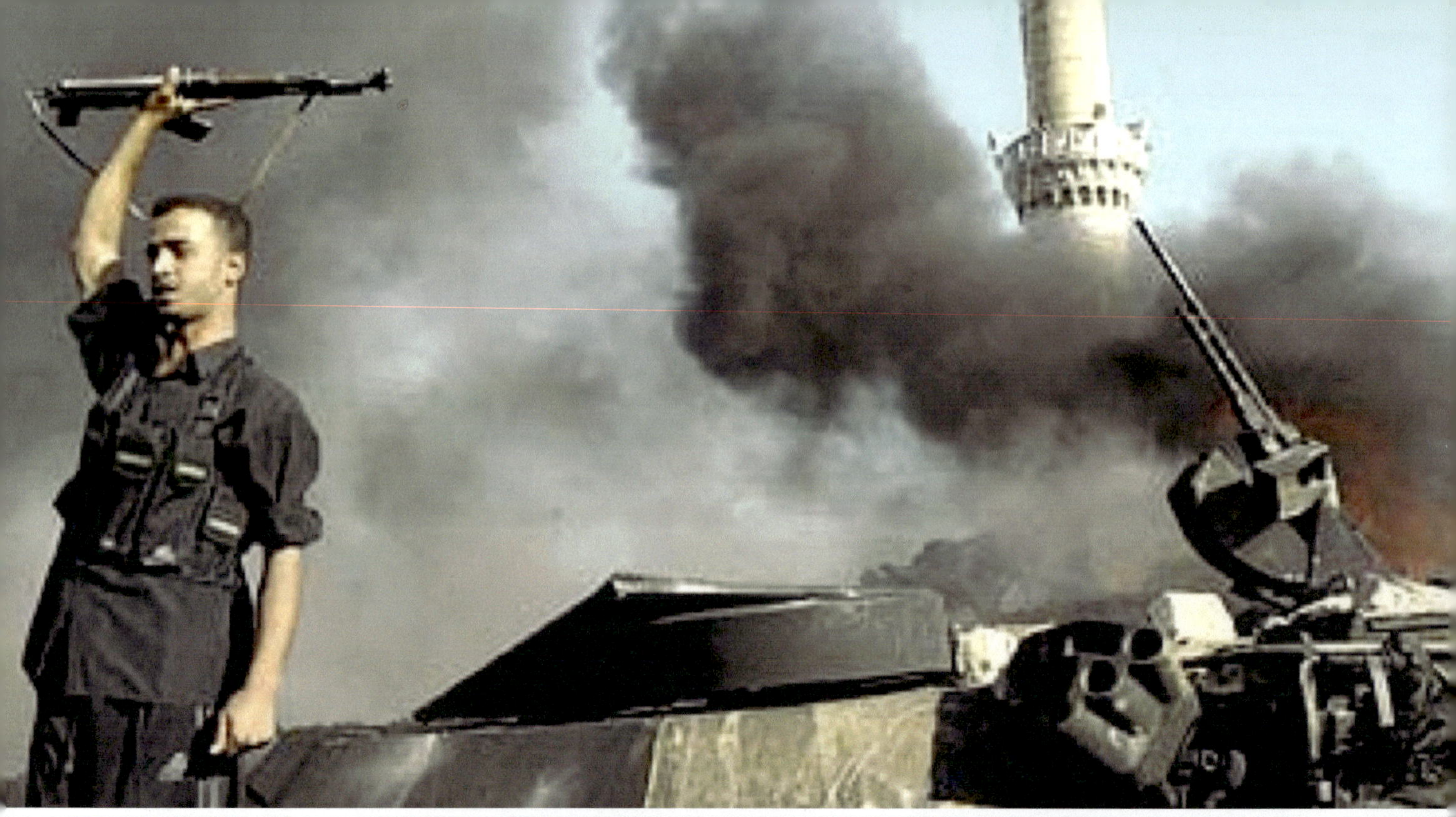
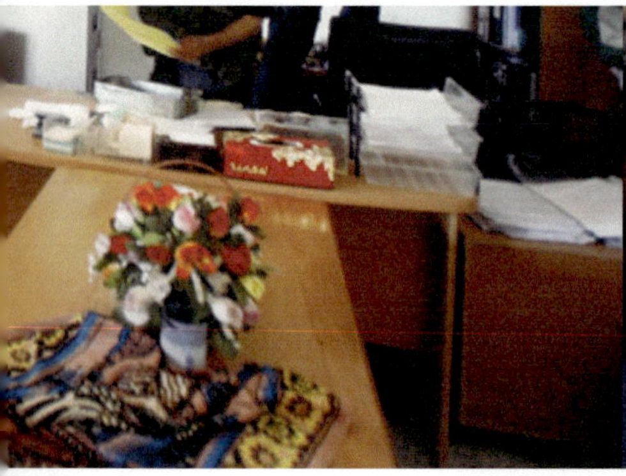
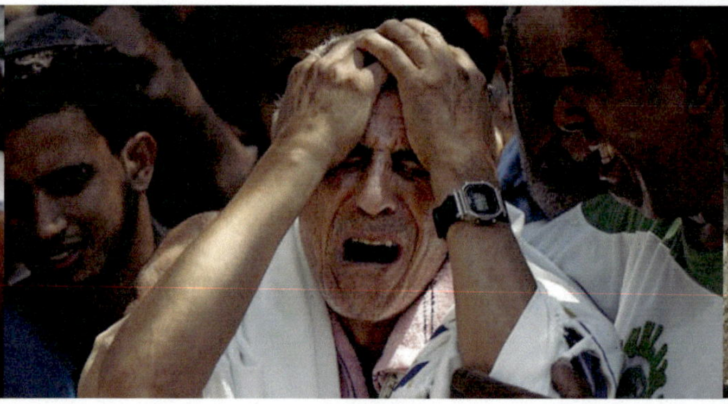
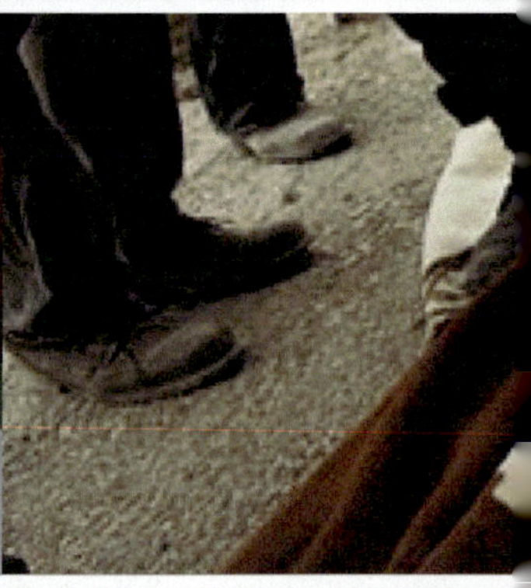
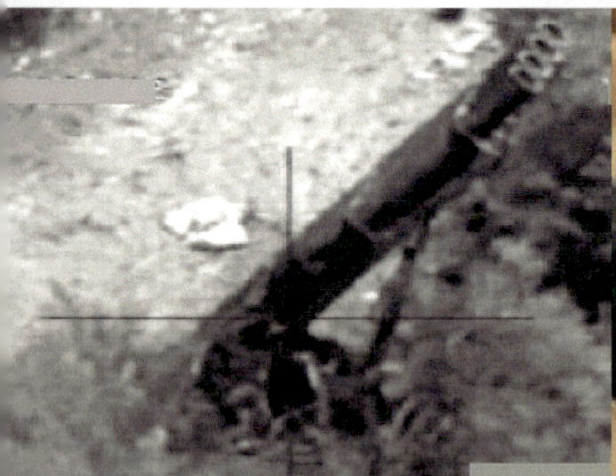
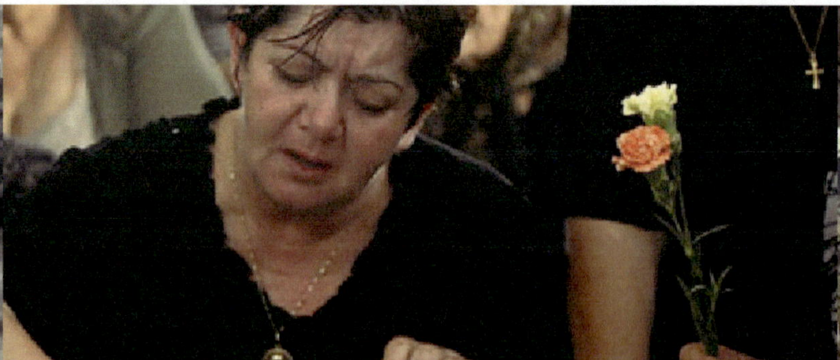
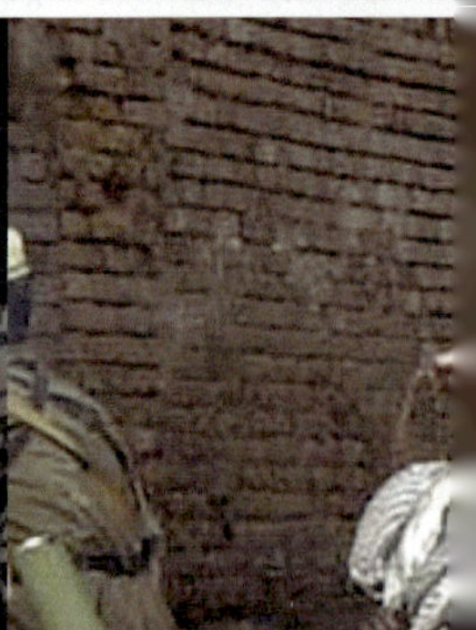
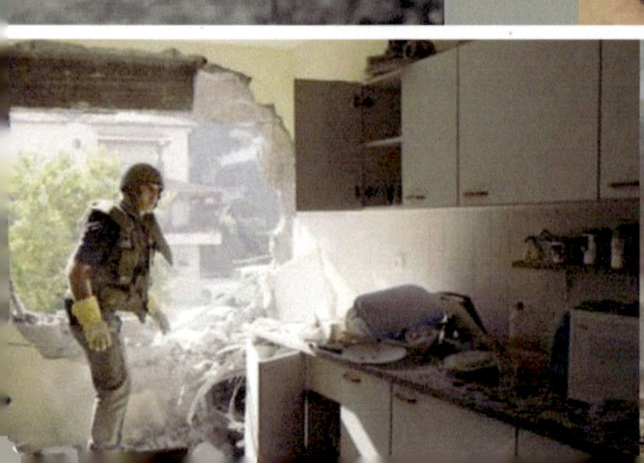
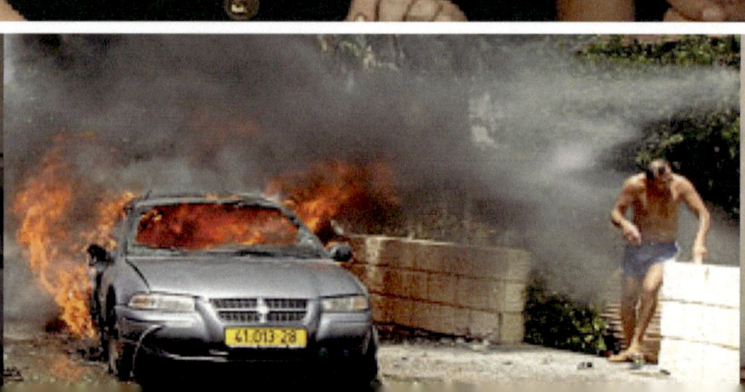
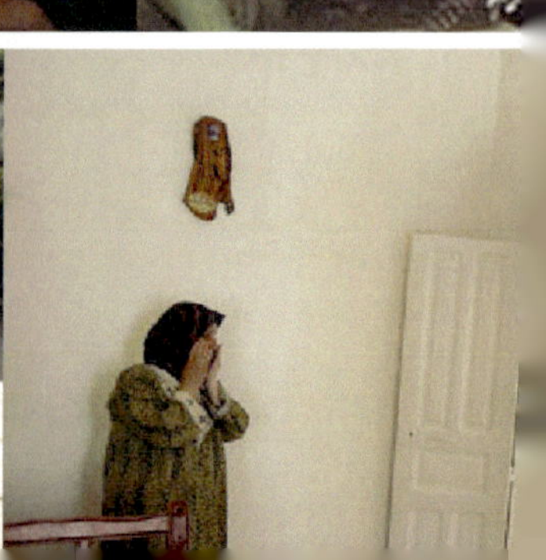

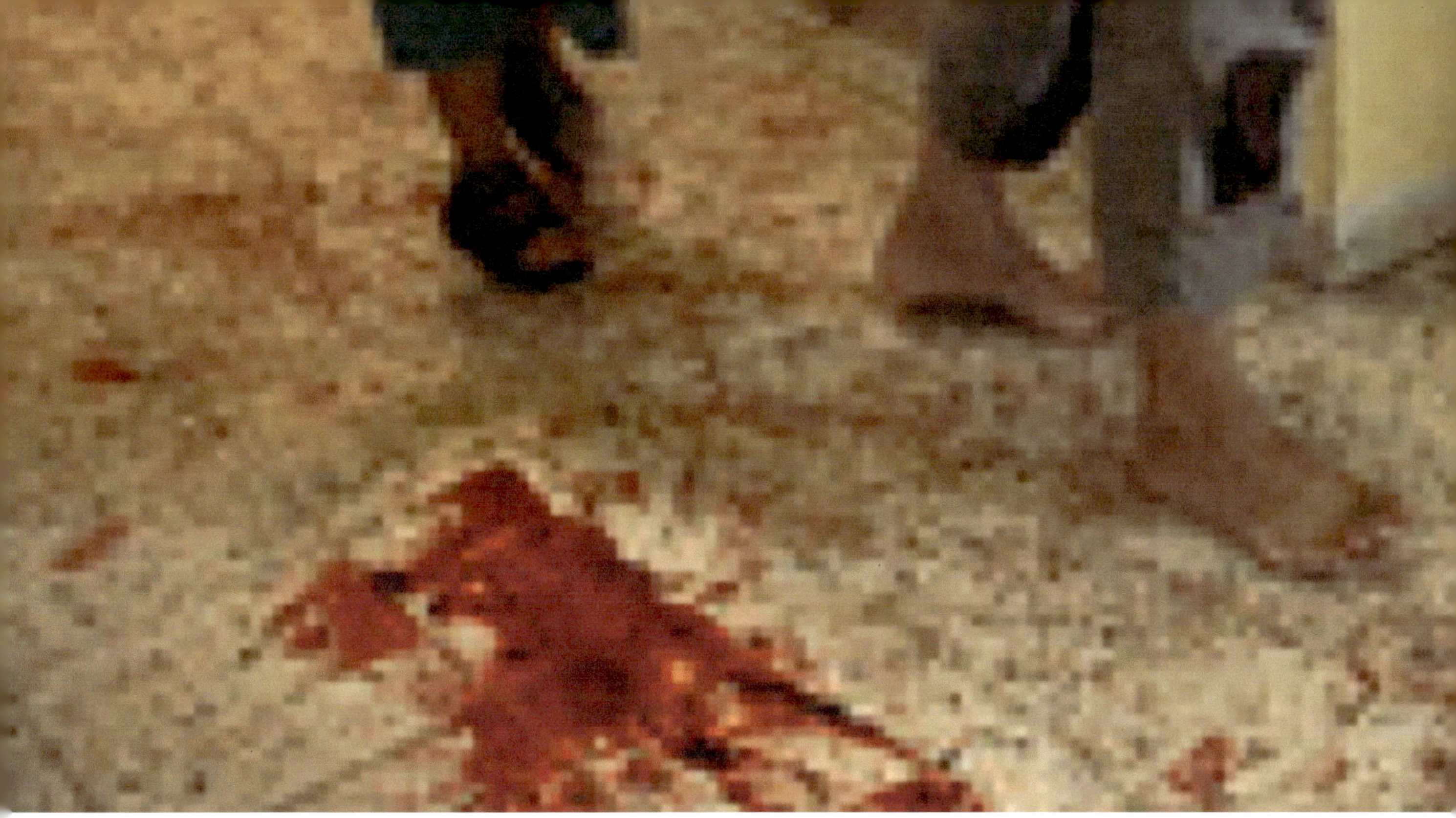

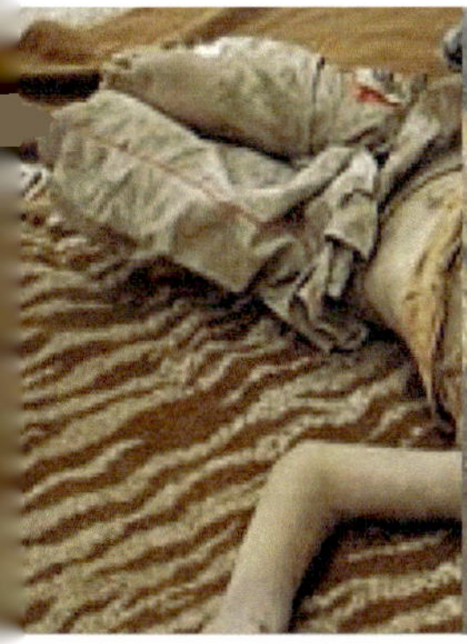

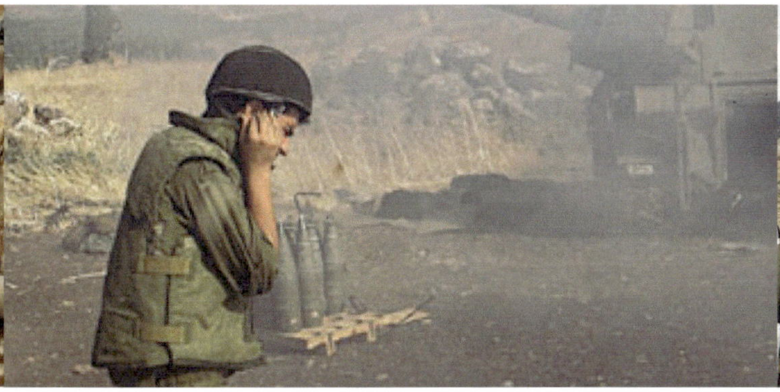

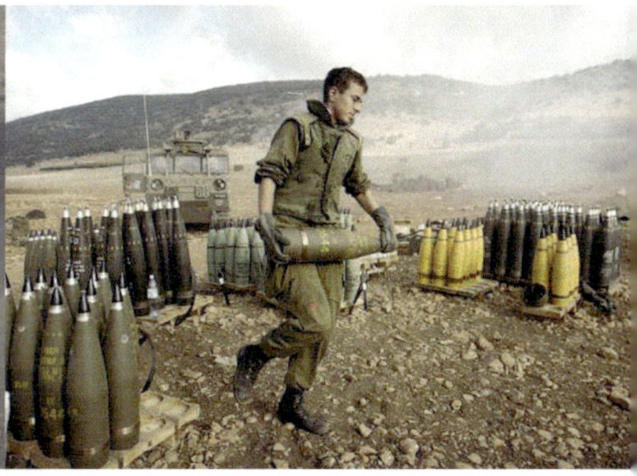

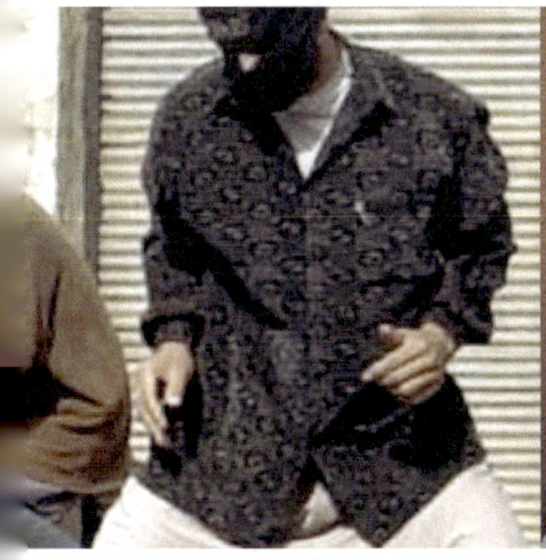

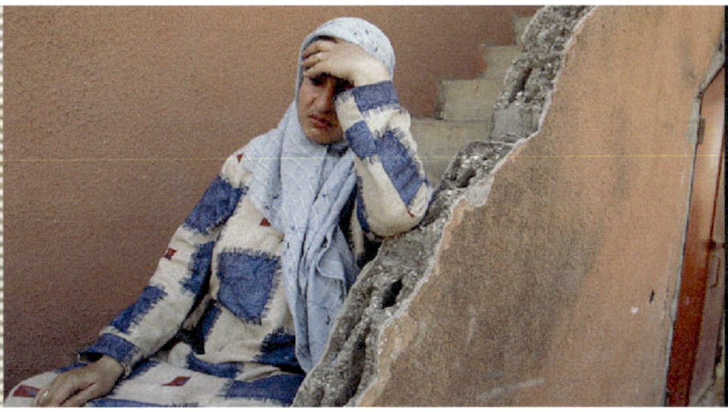

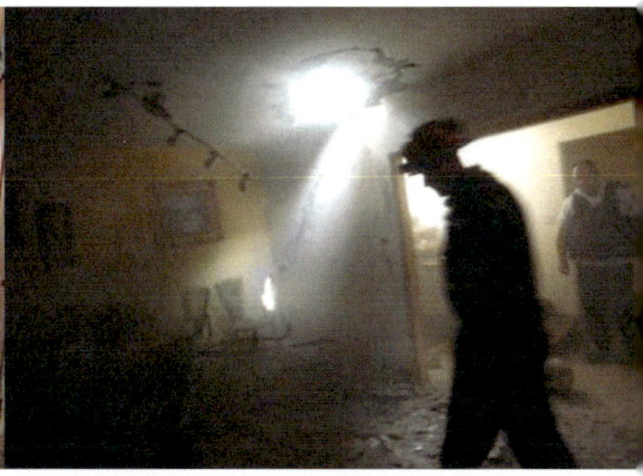

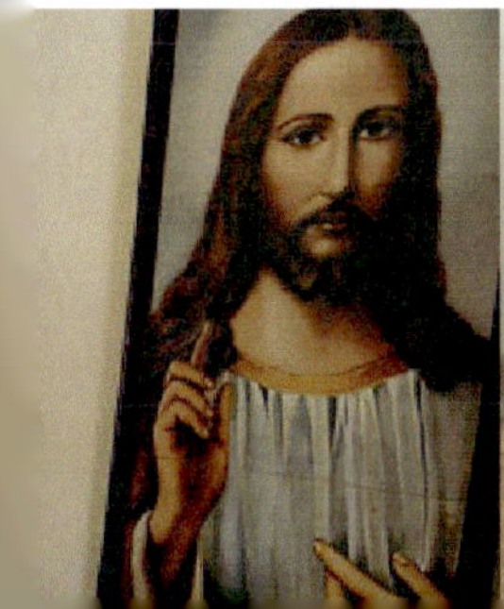

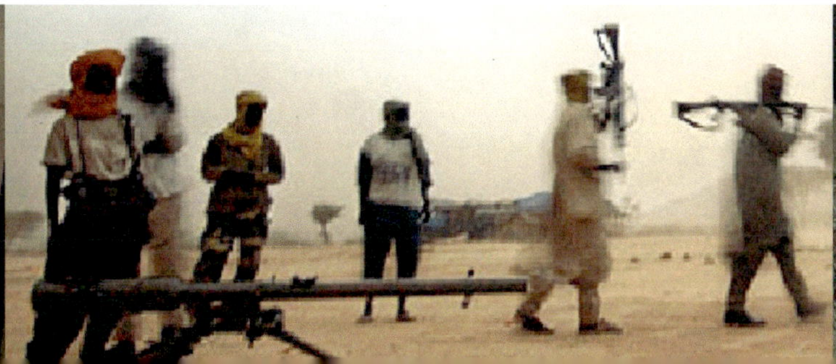

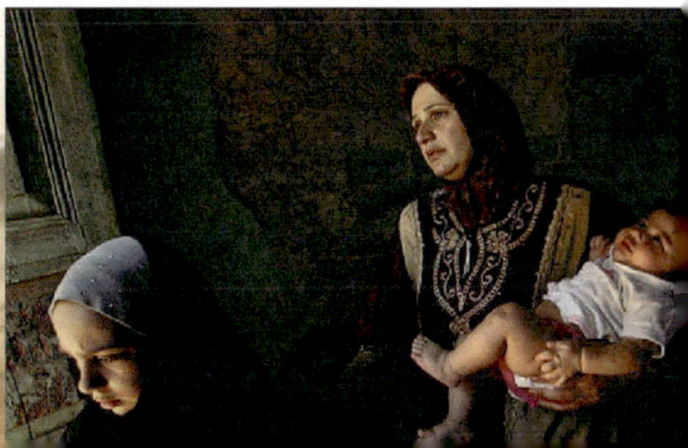

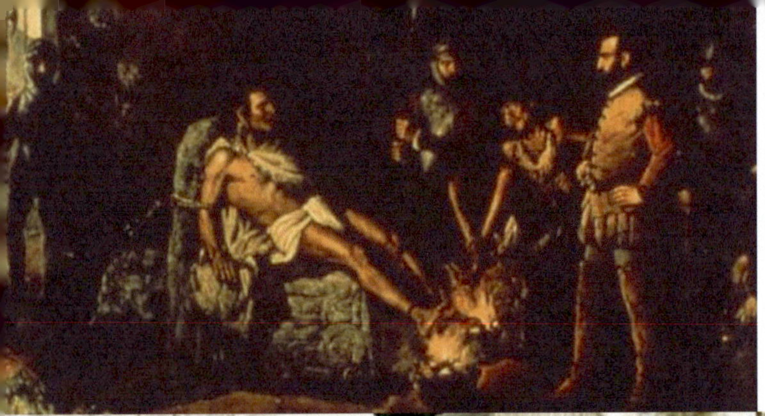

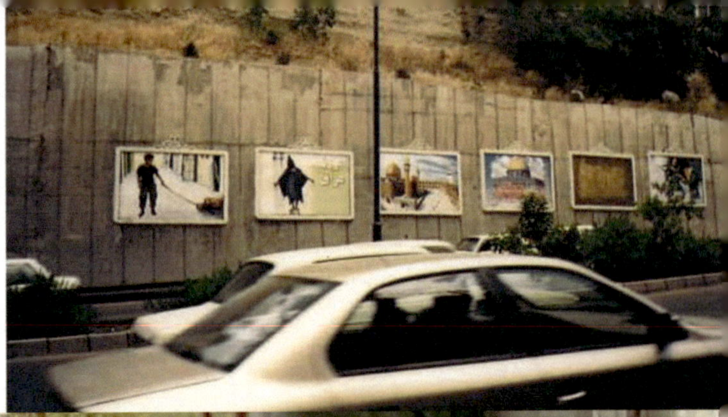

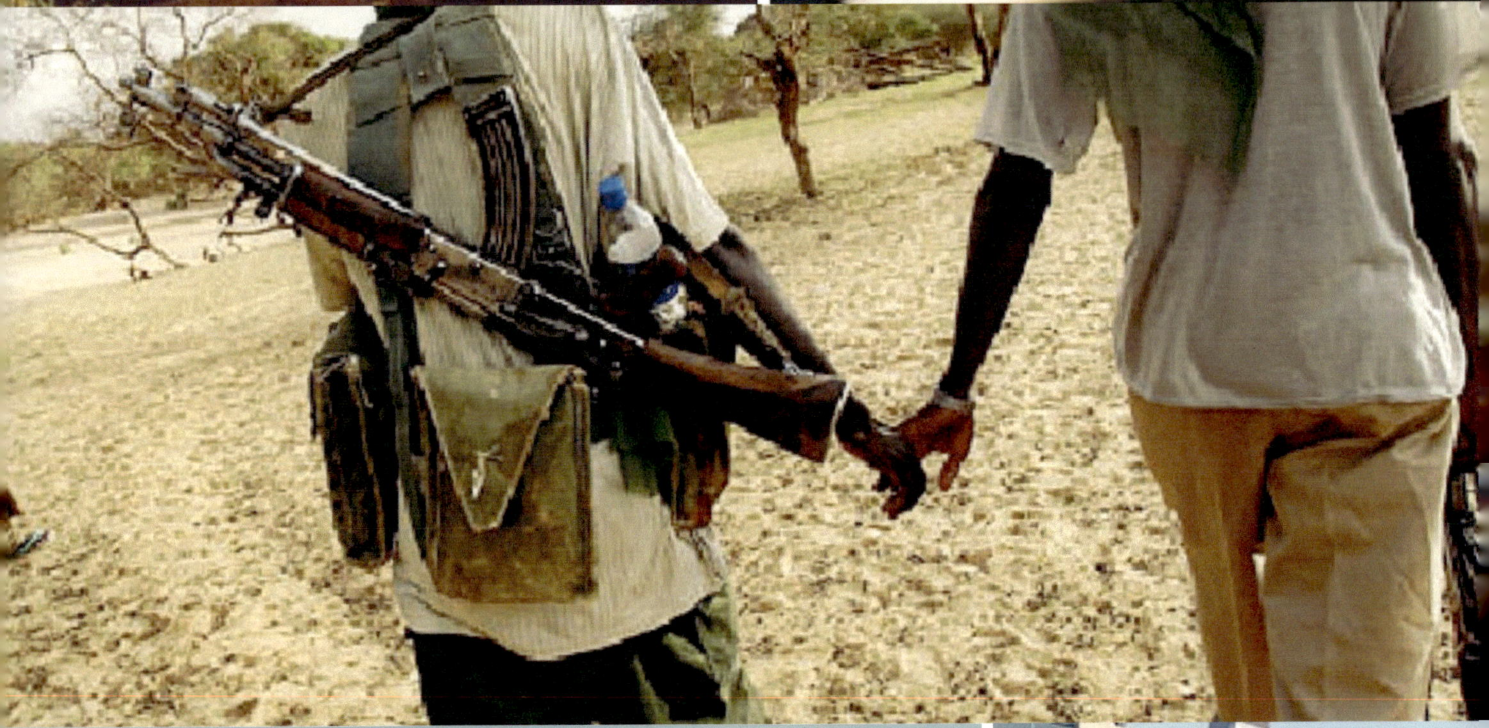

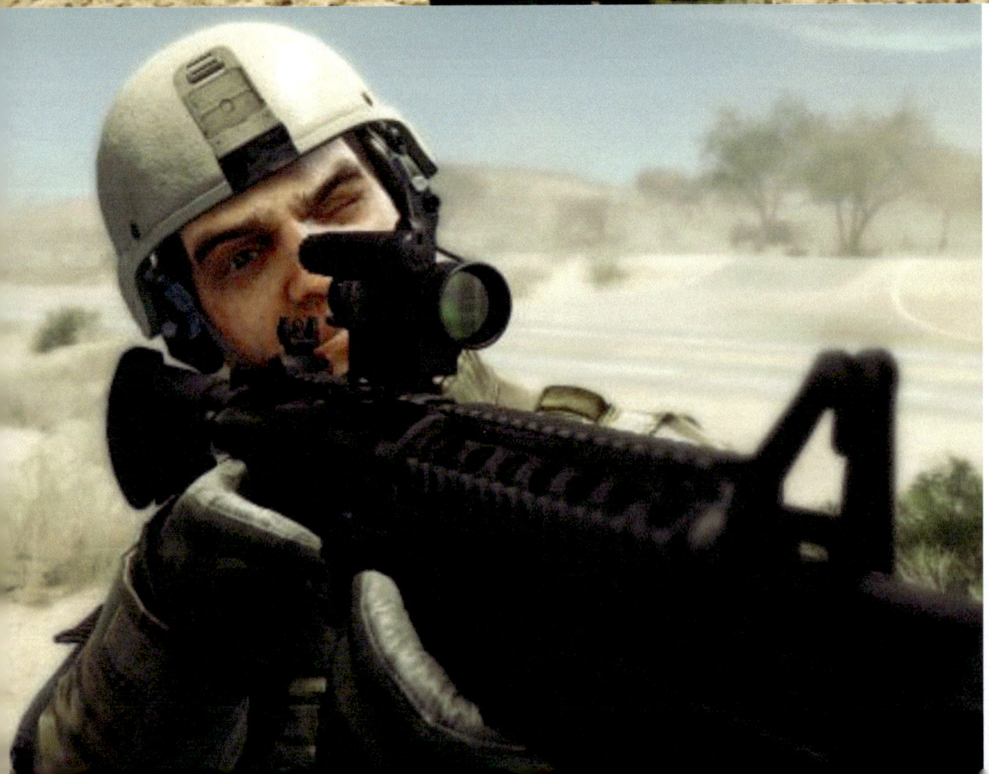

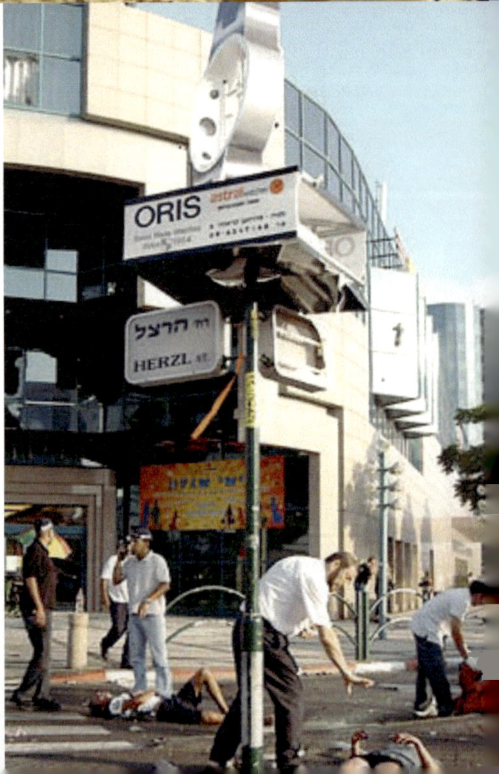
ORIS
הרצל
HERZL

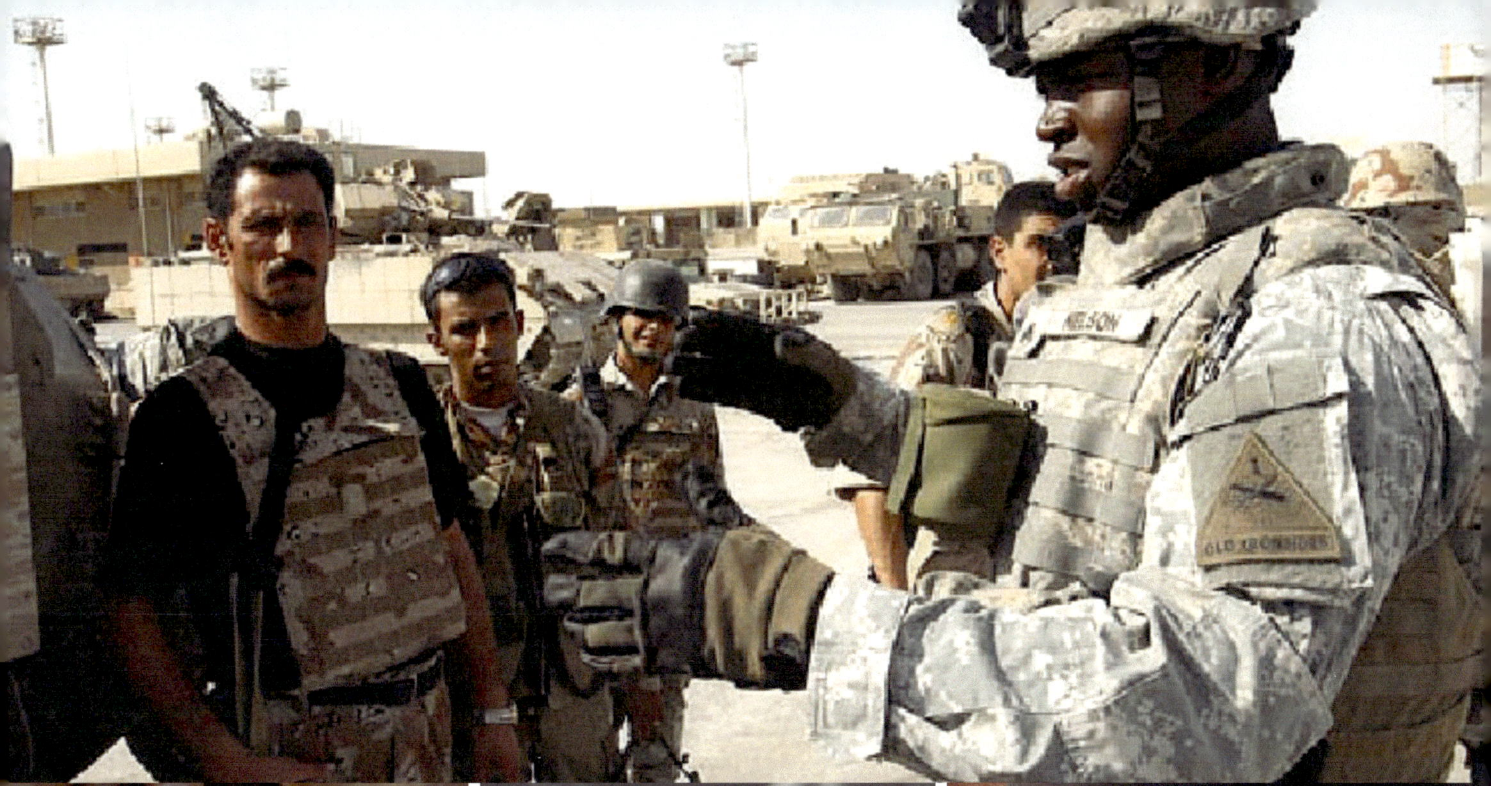

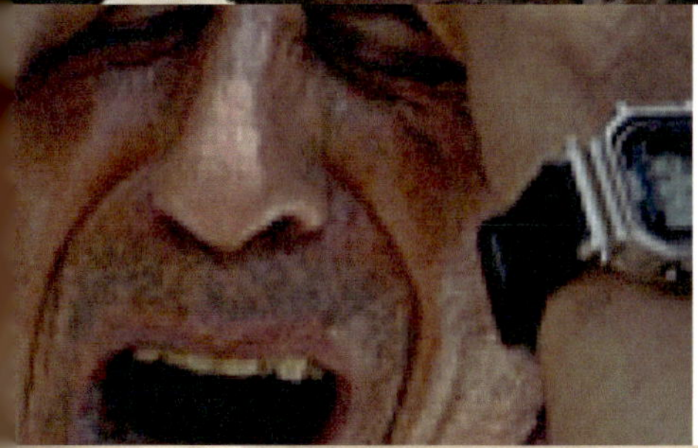

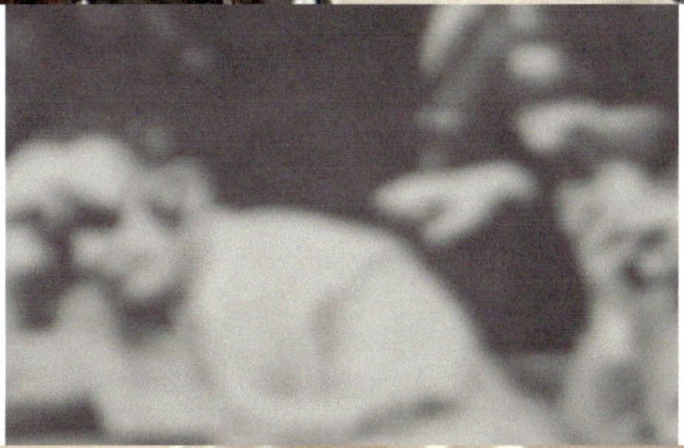

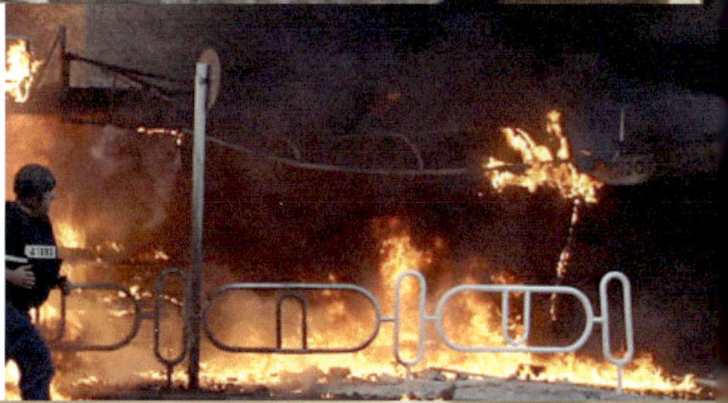

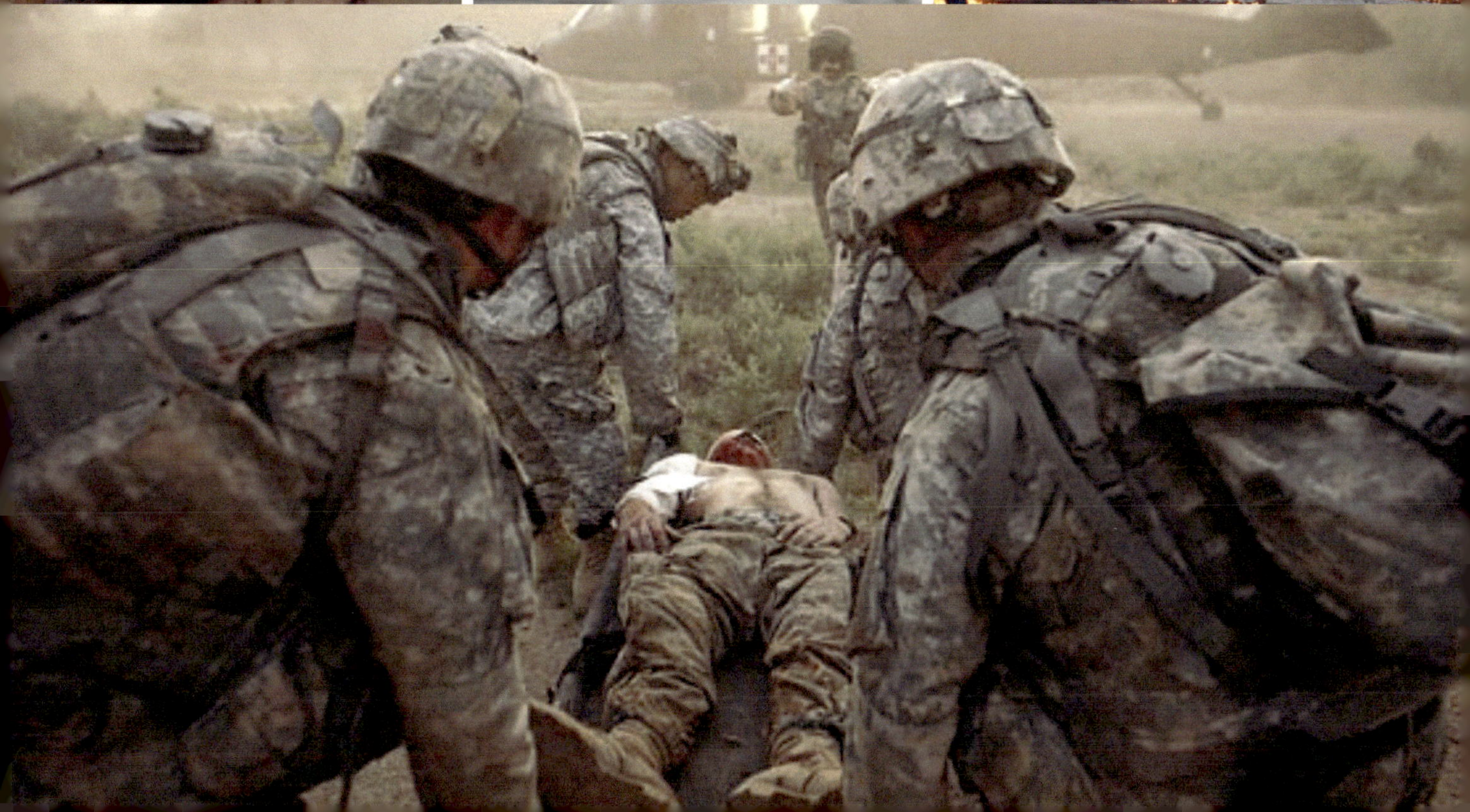

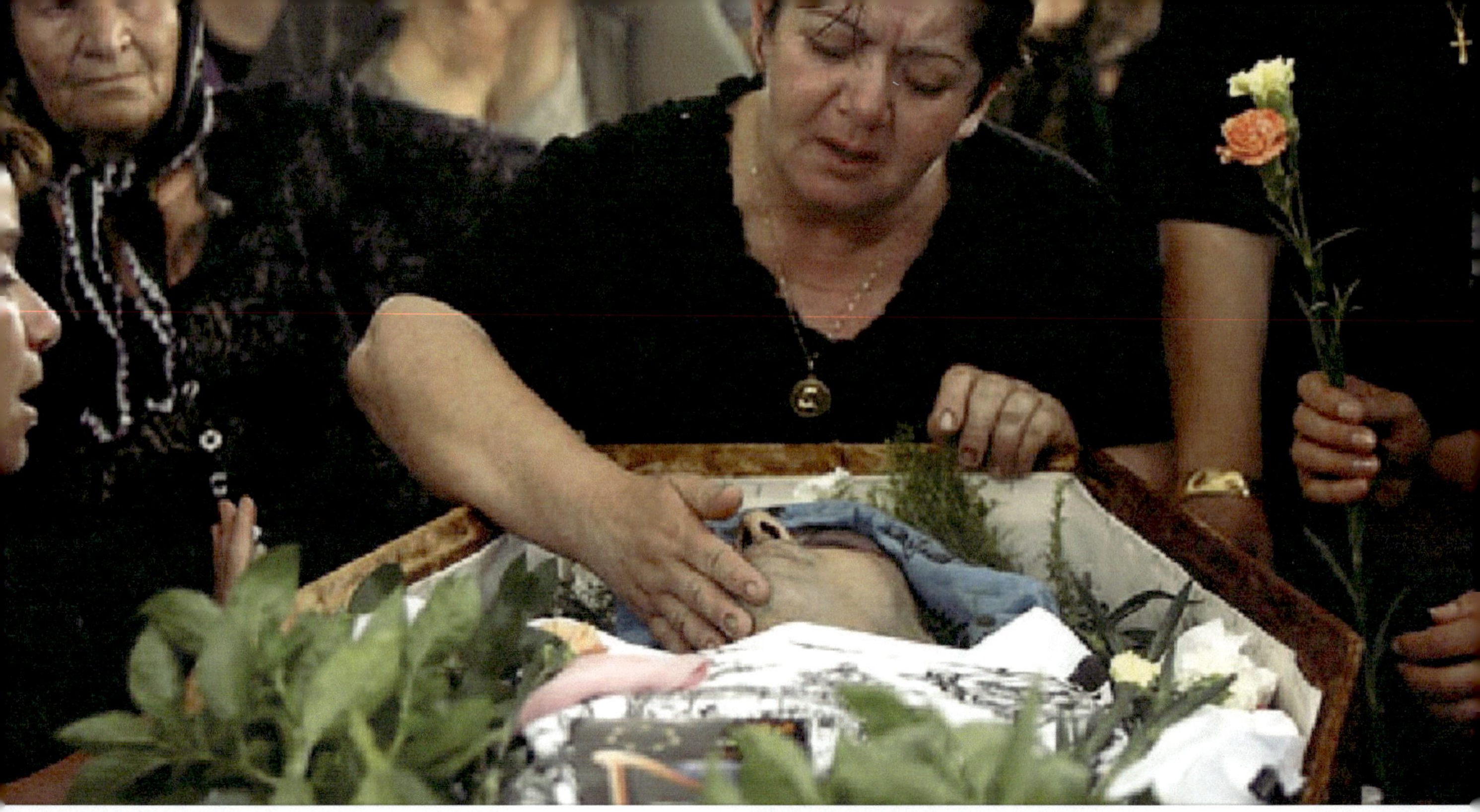
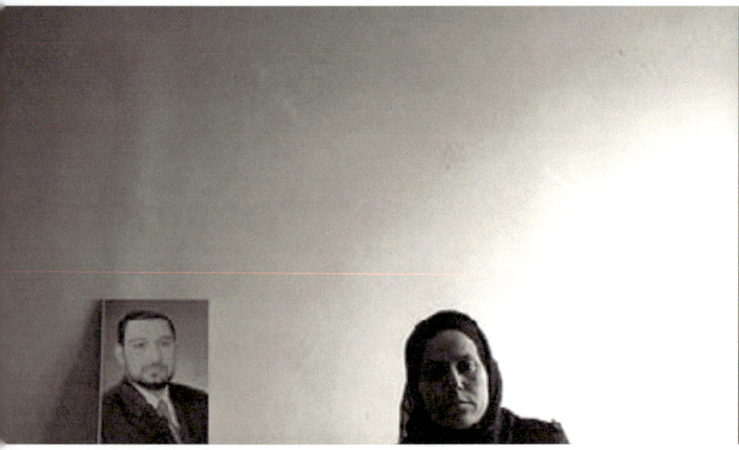
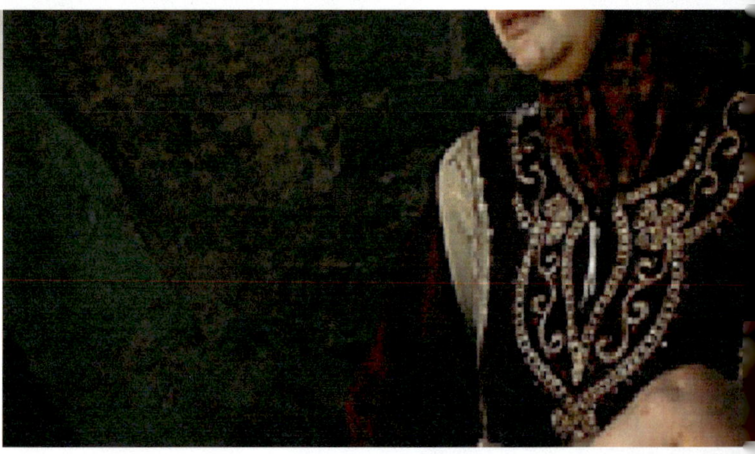
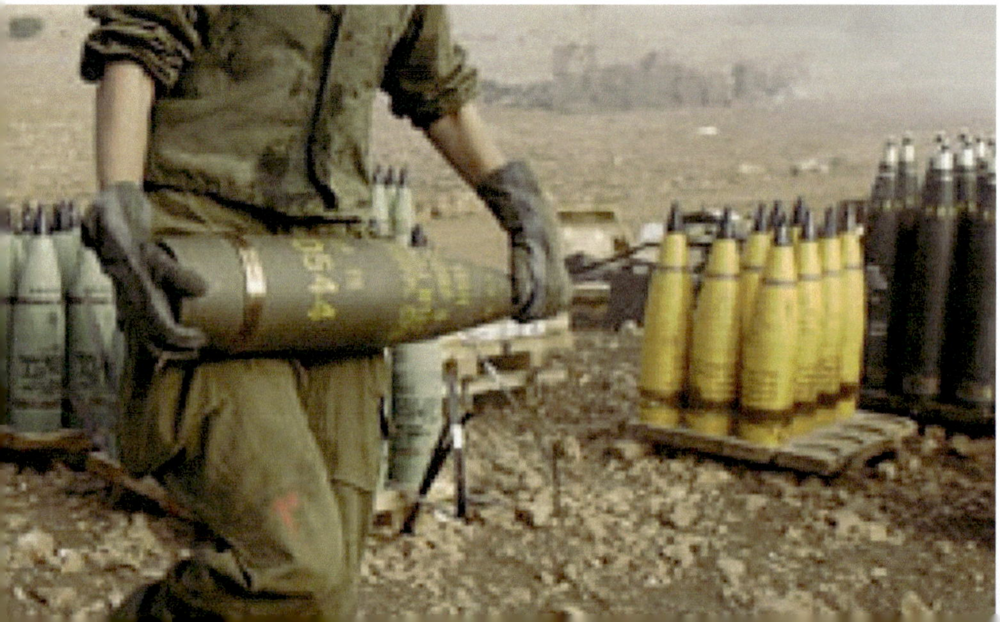
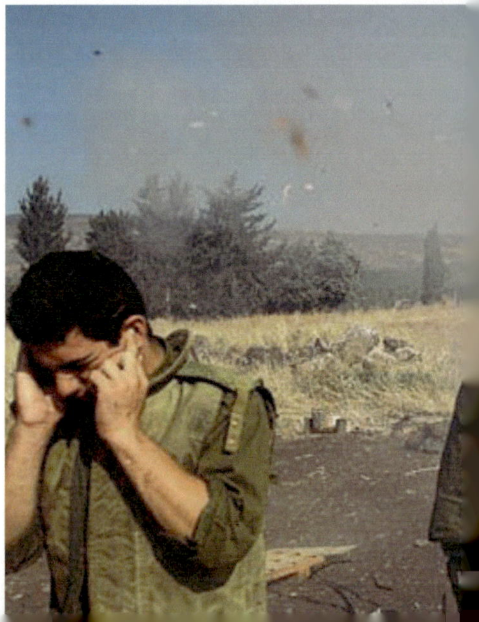

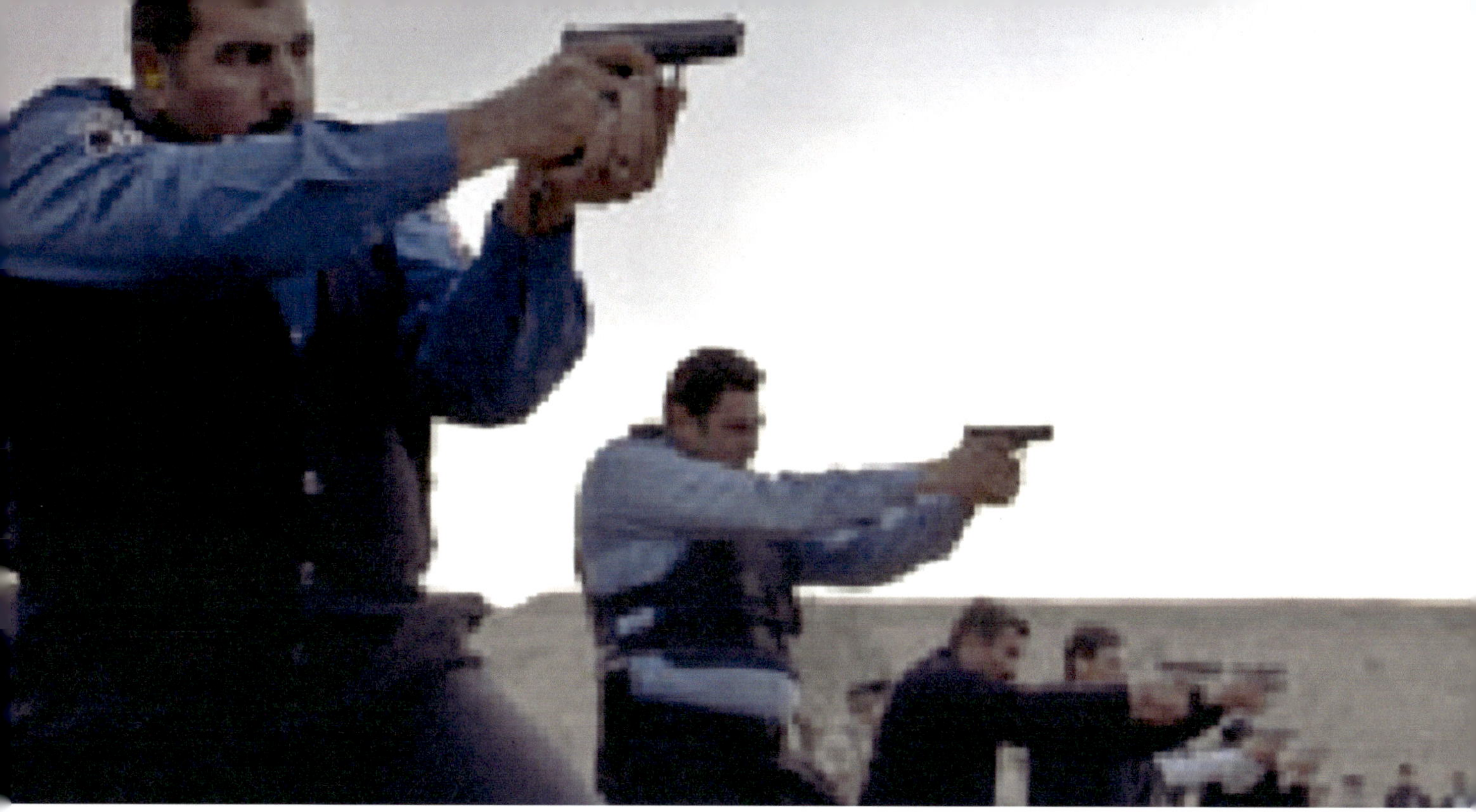
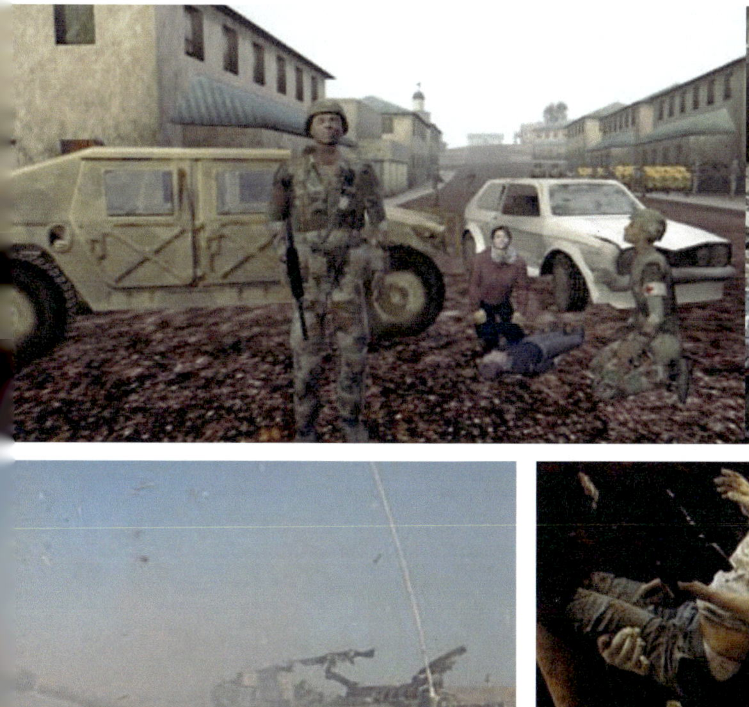
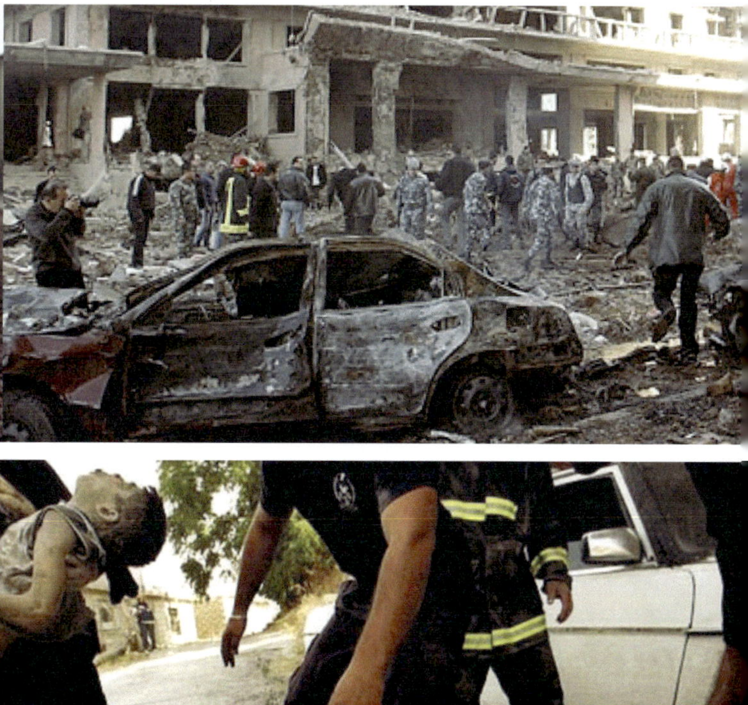
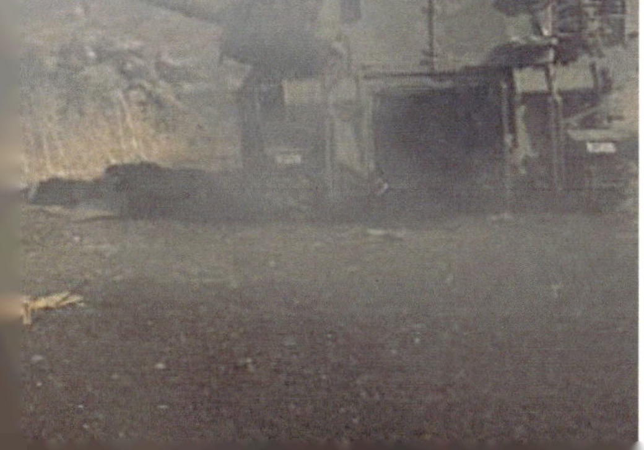
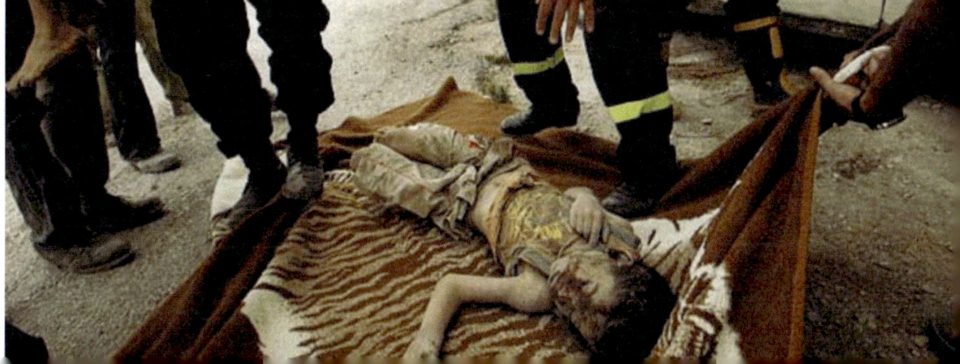

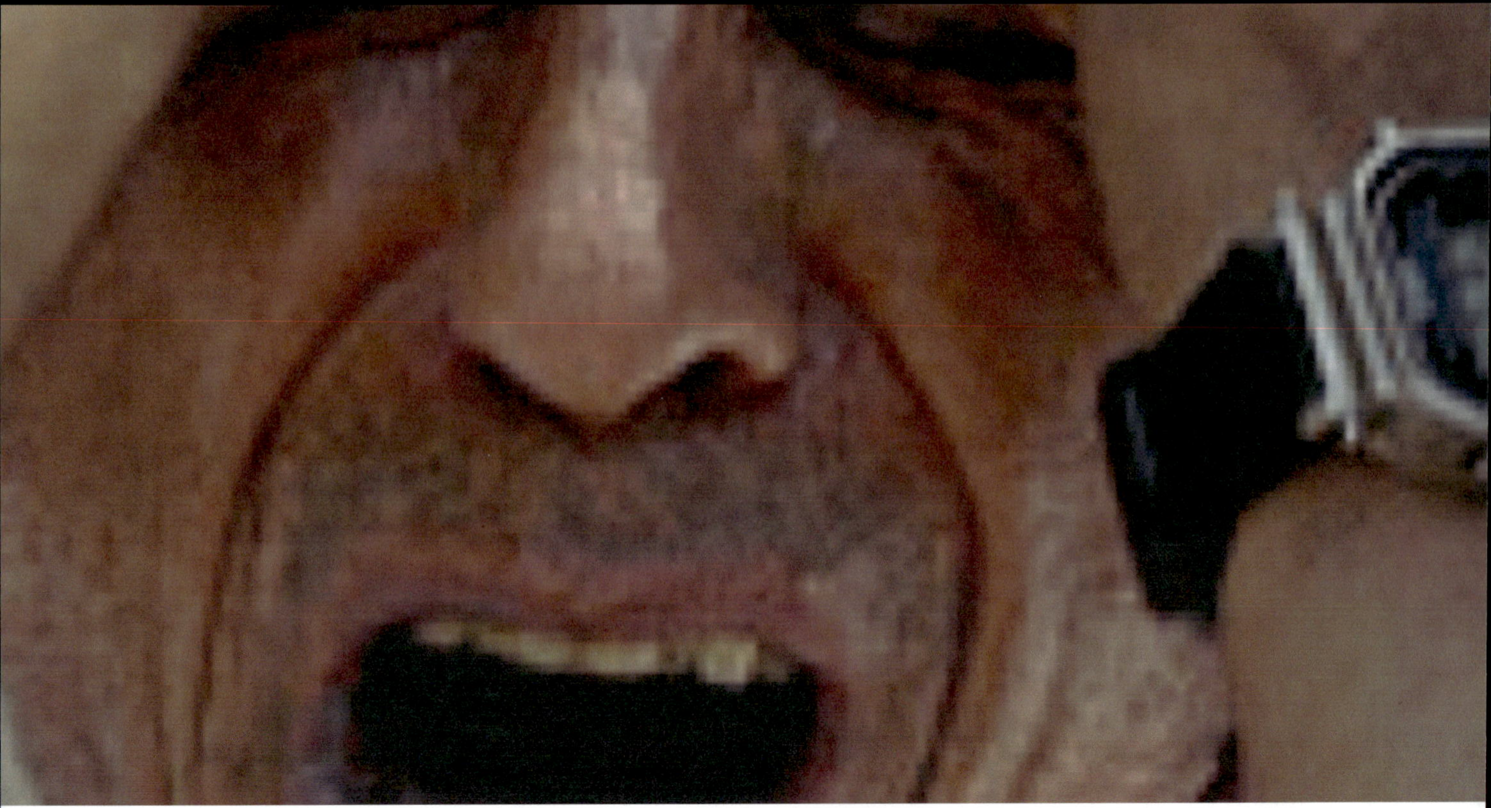

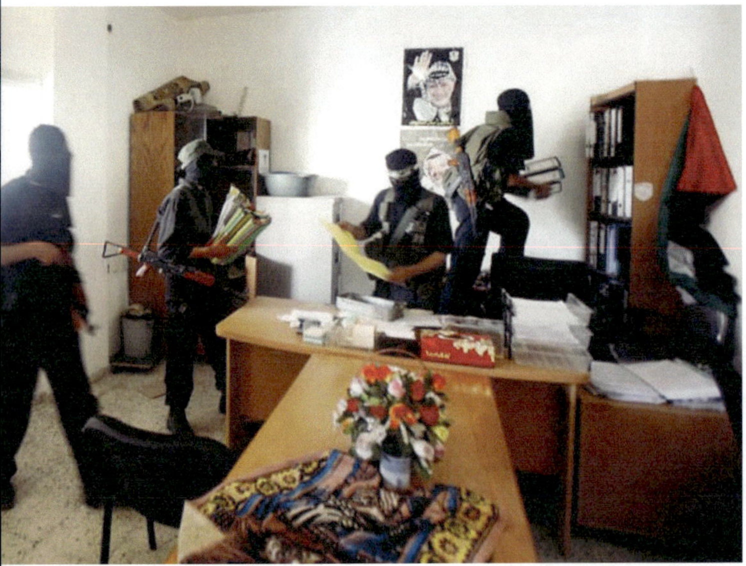

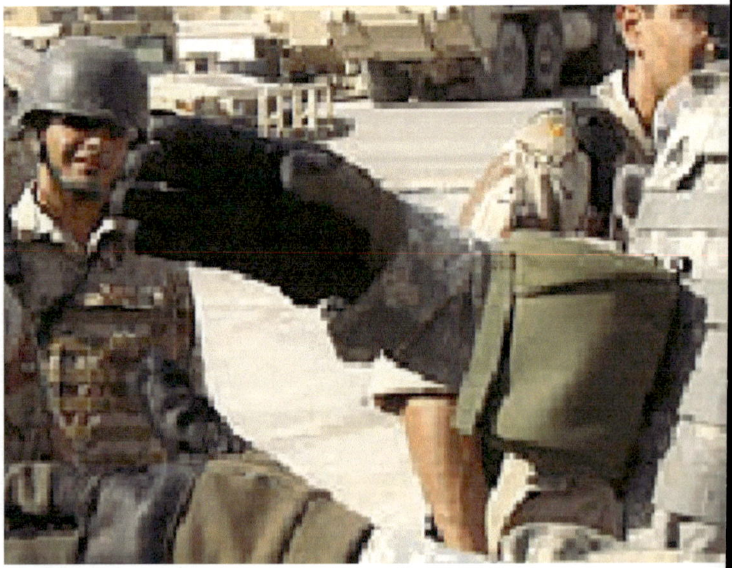

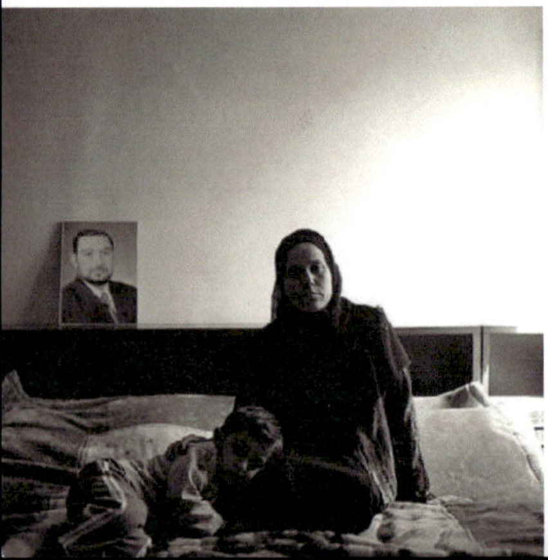

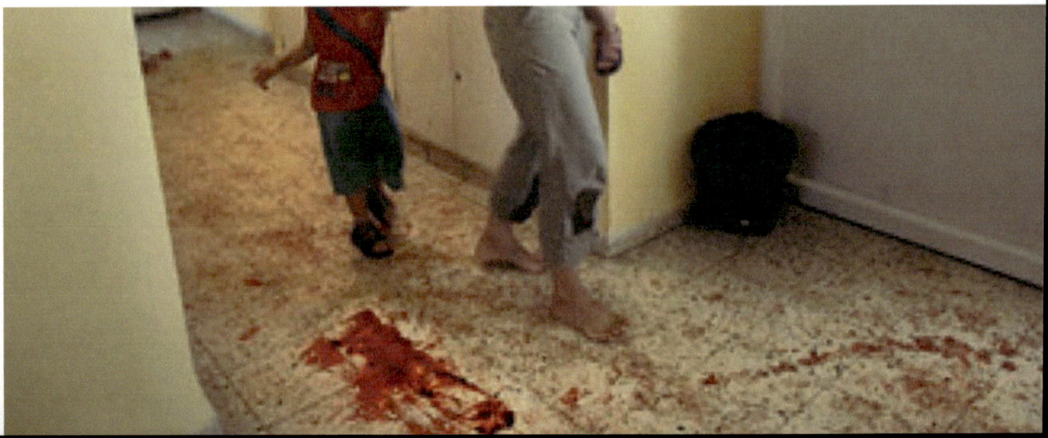

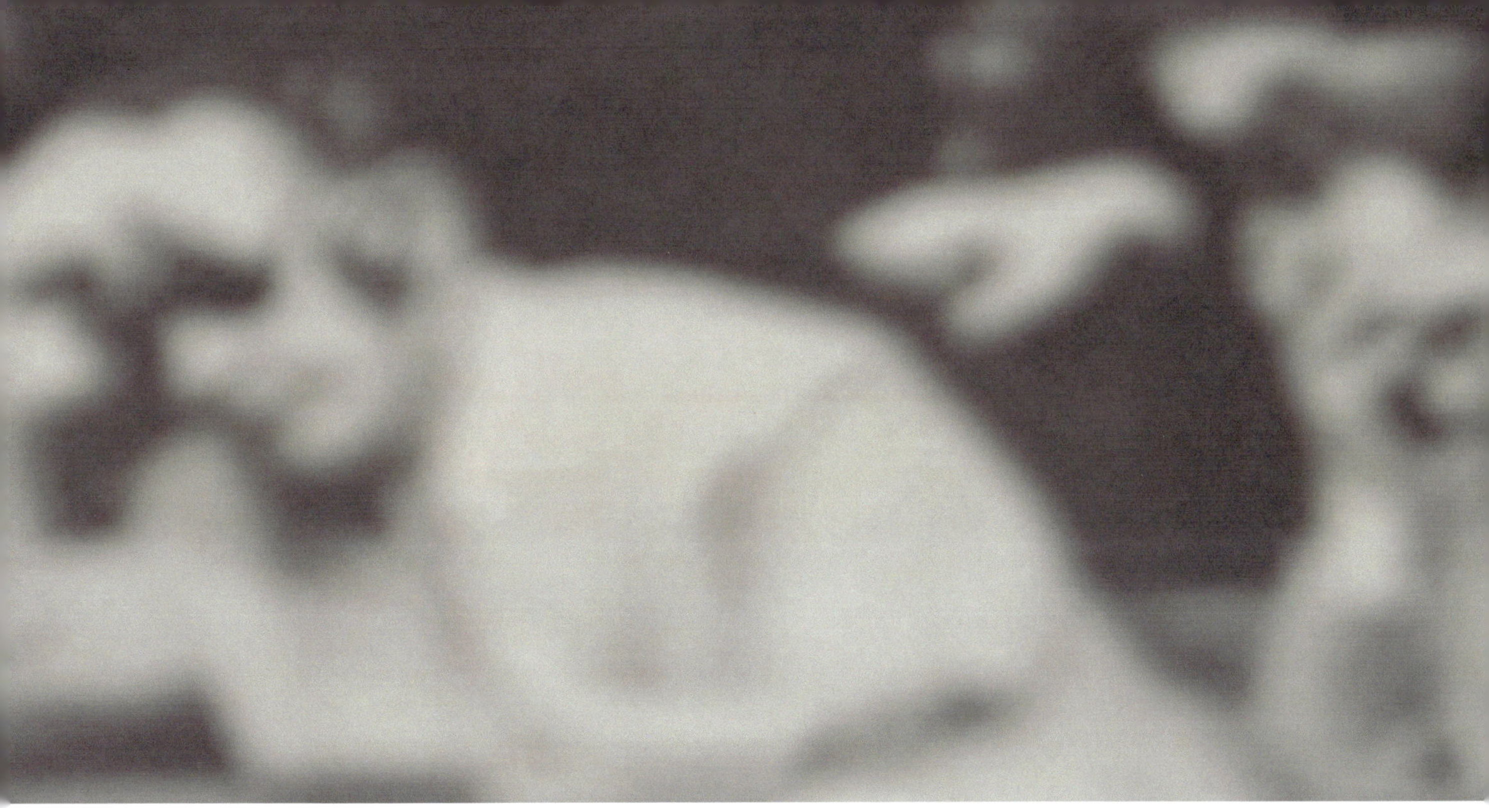

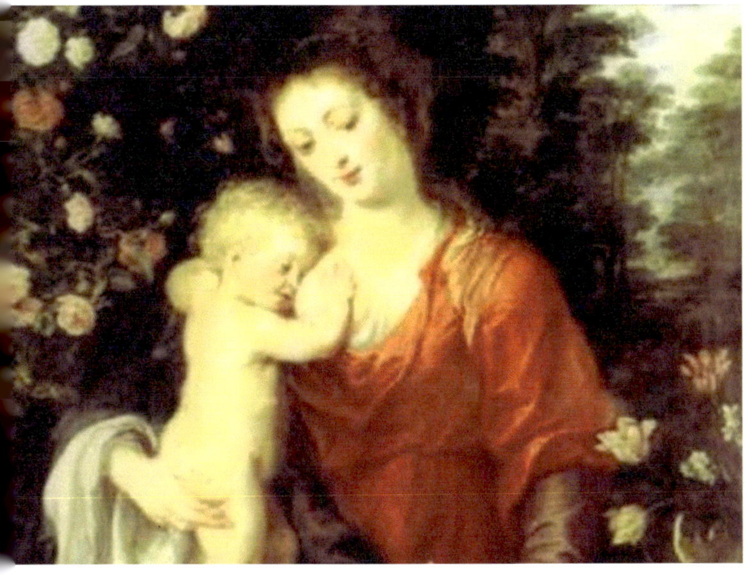

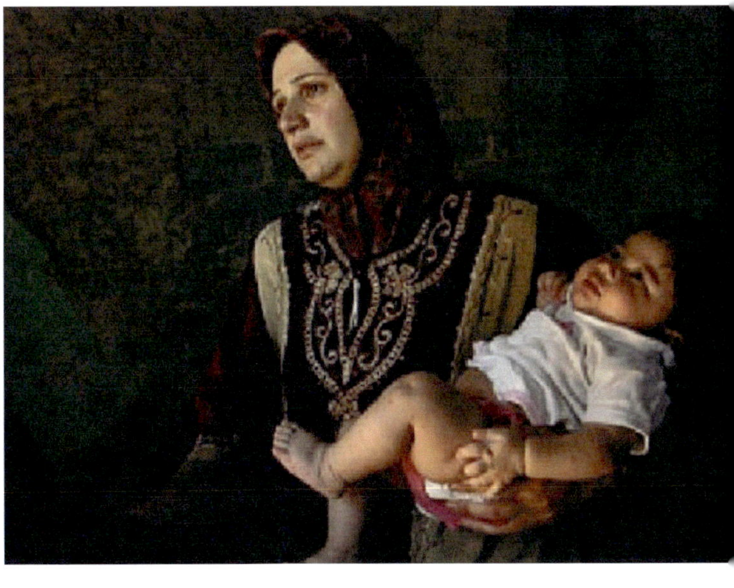

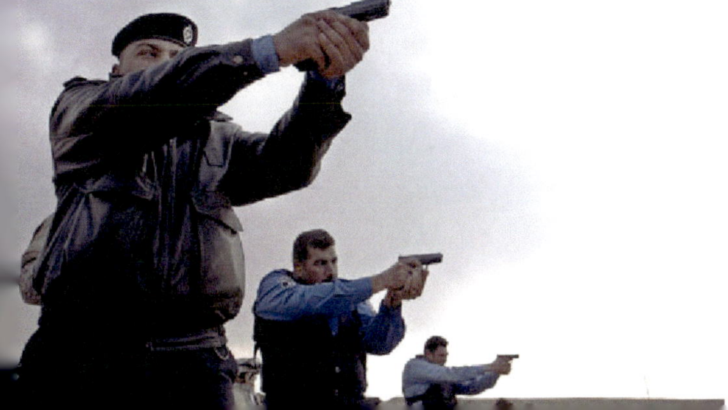

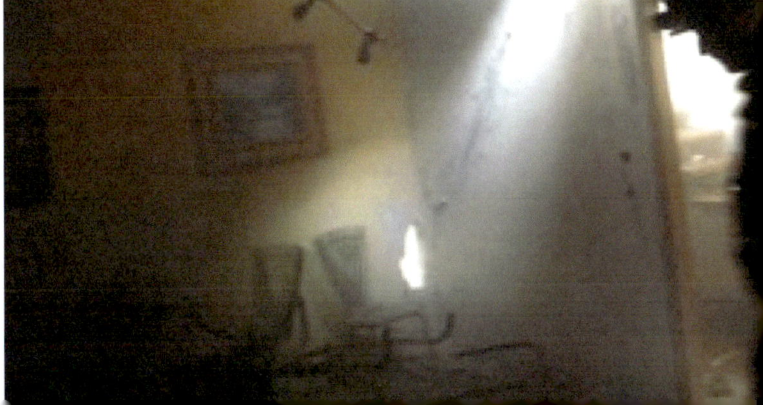

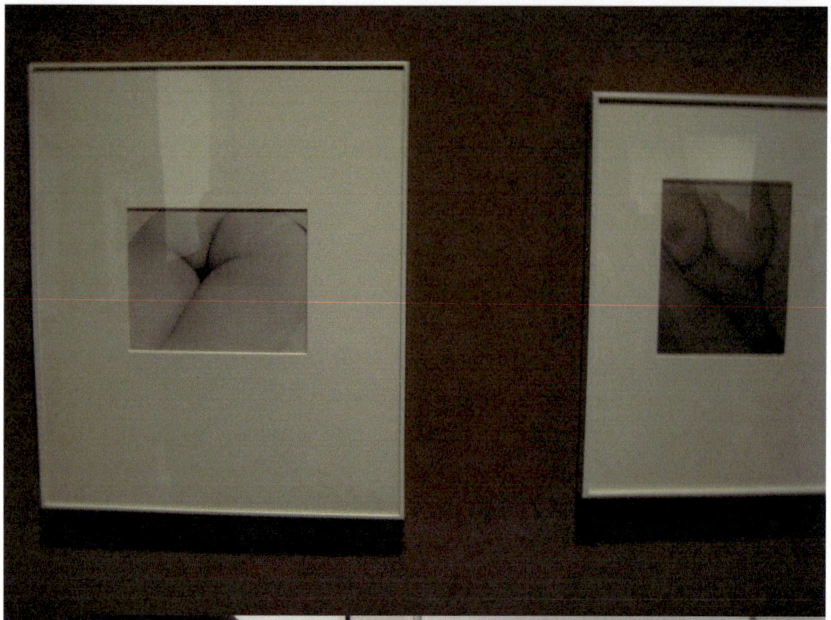
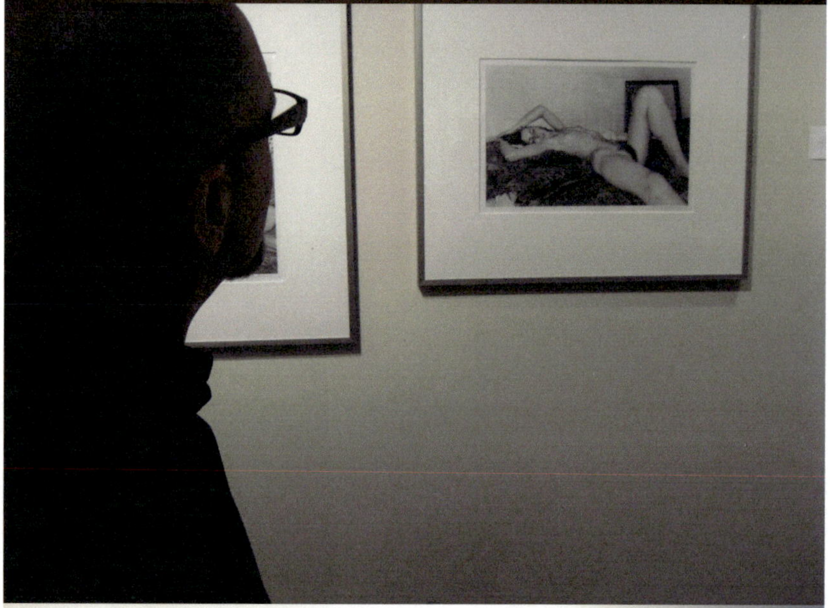
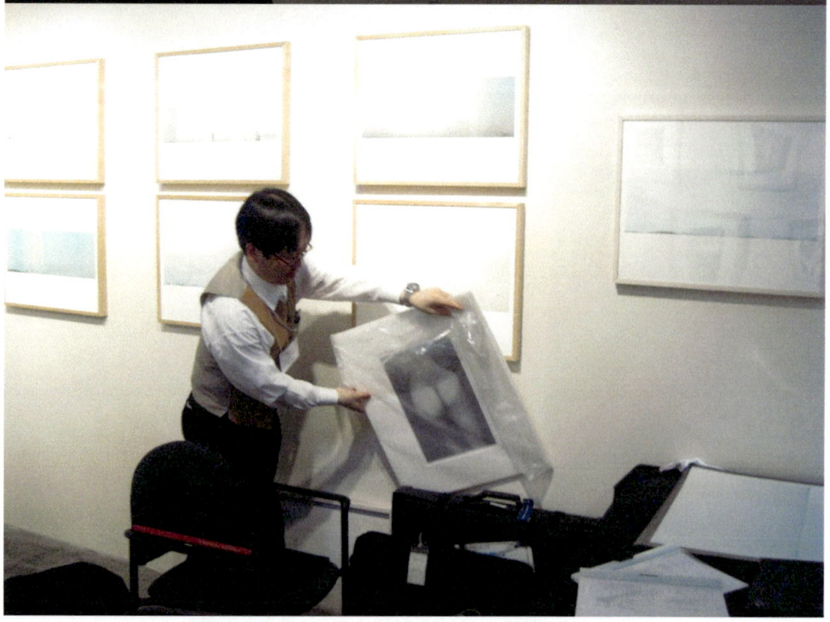

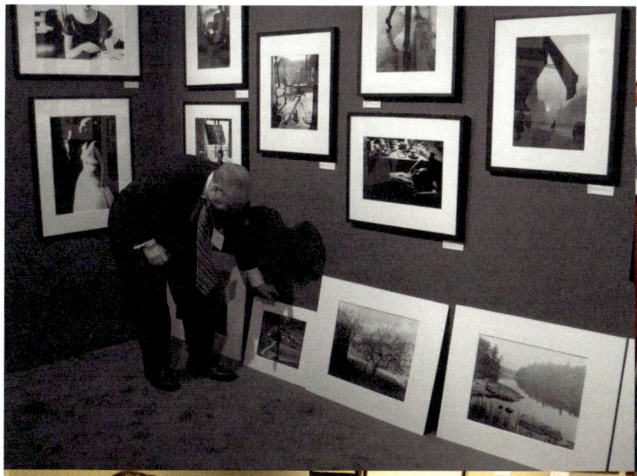
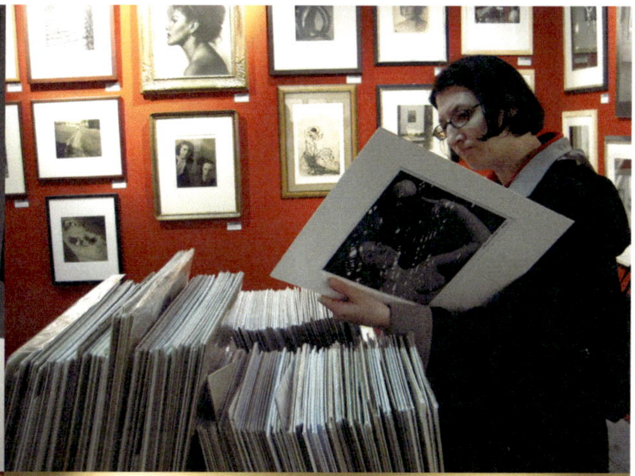
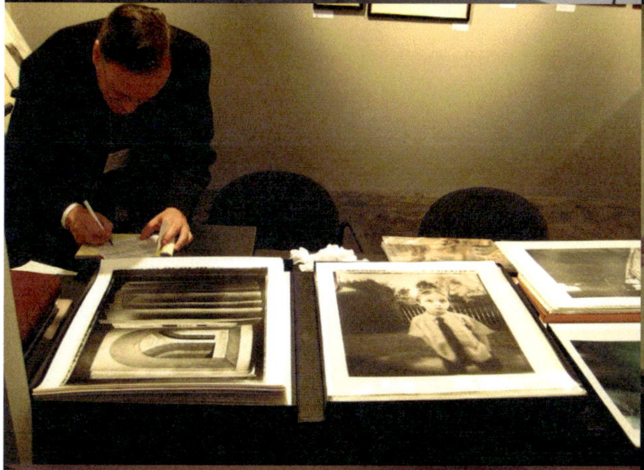
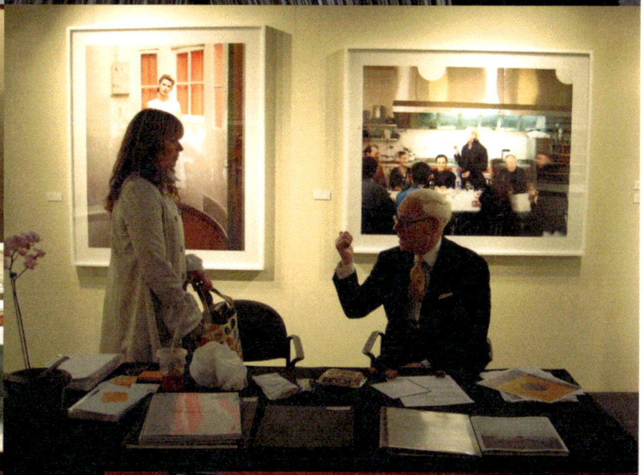
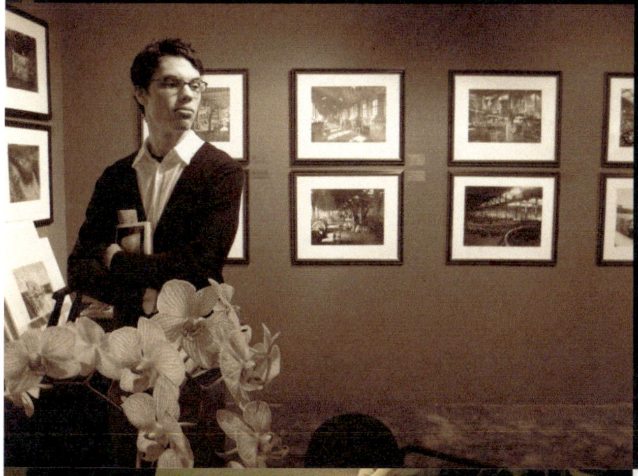
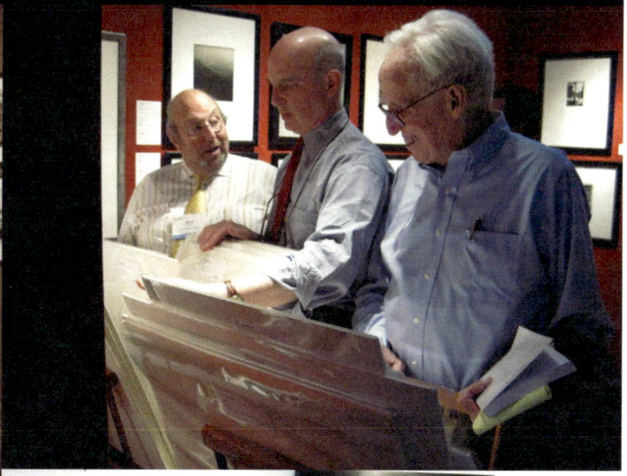
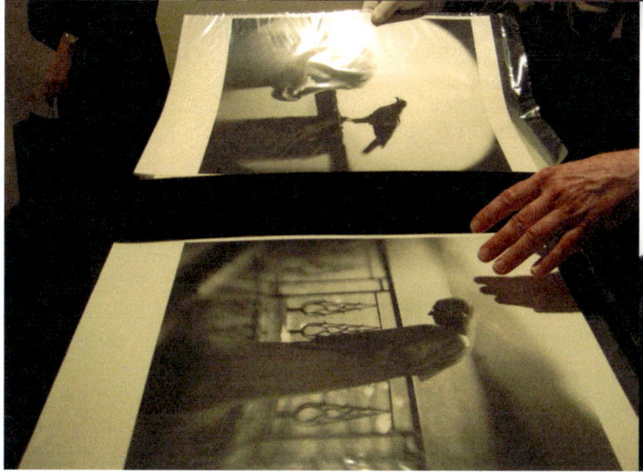
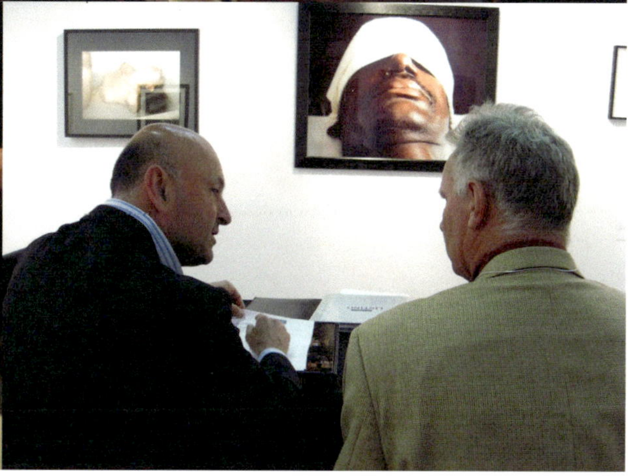

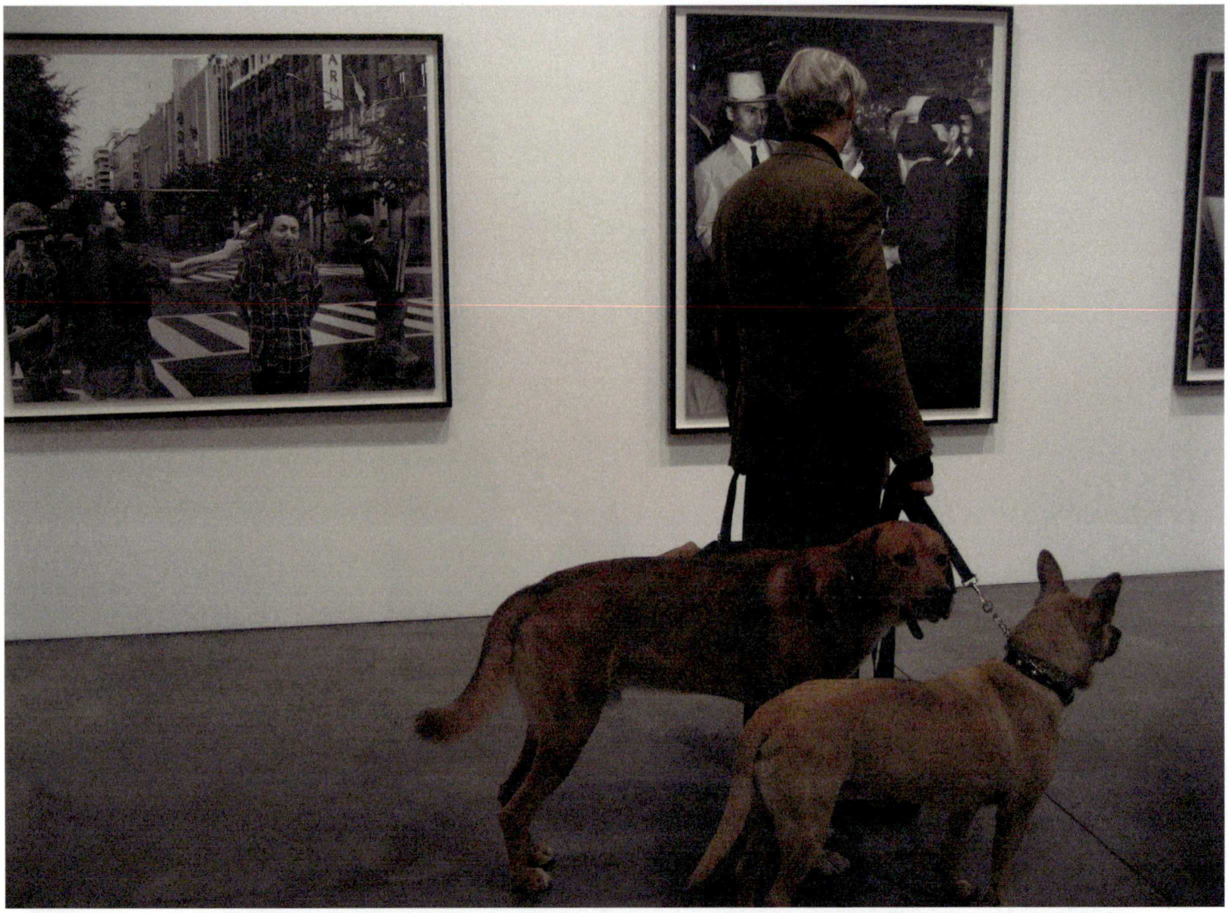

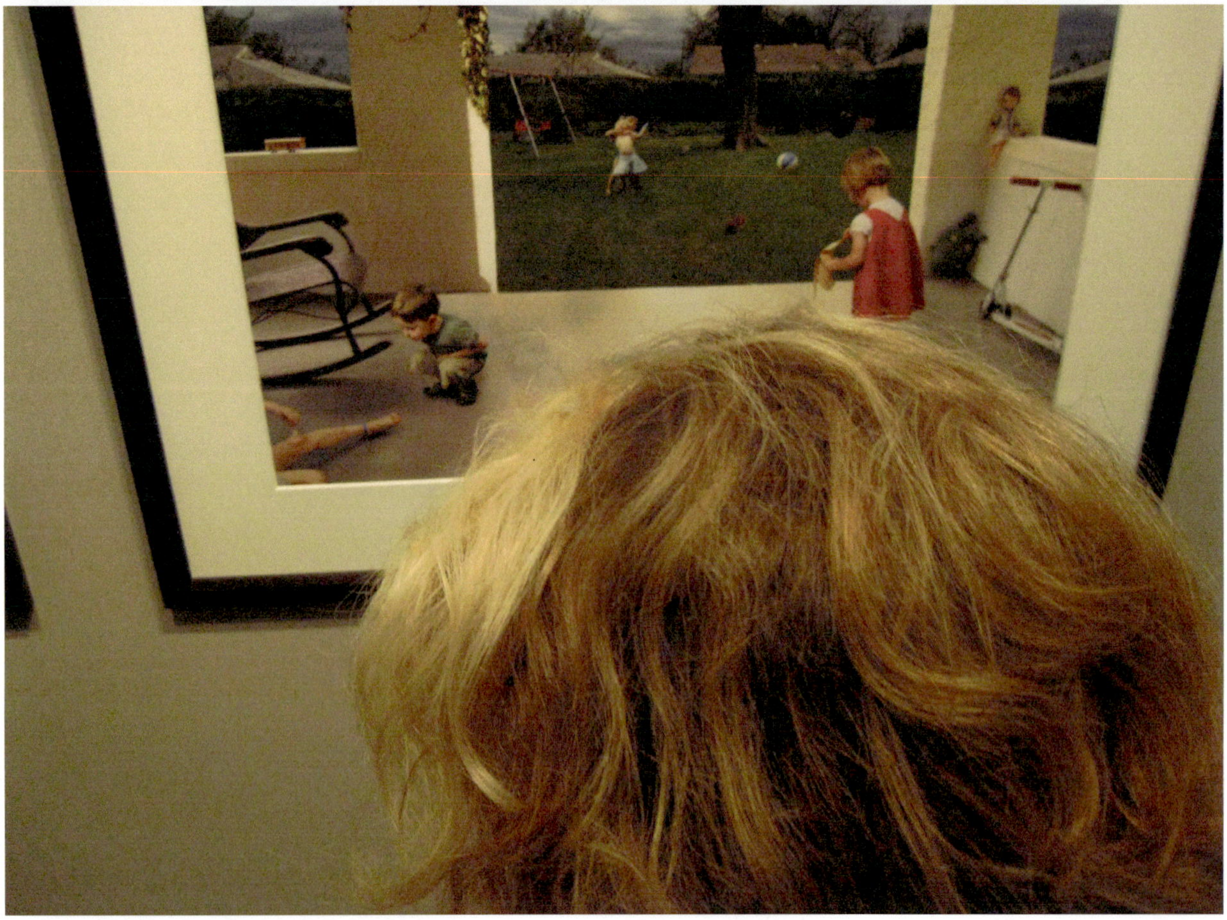

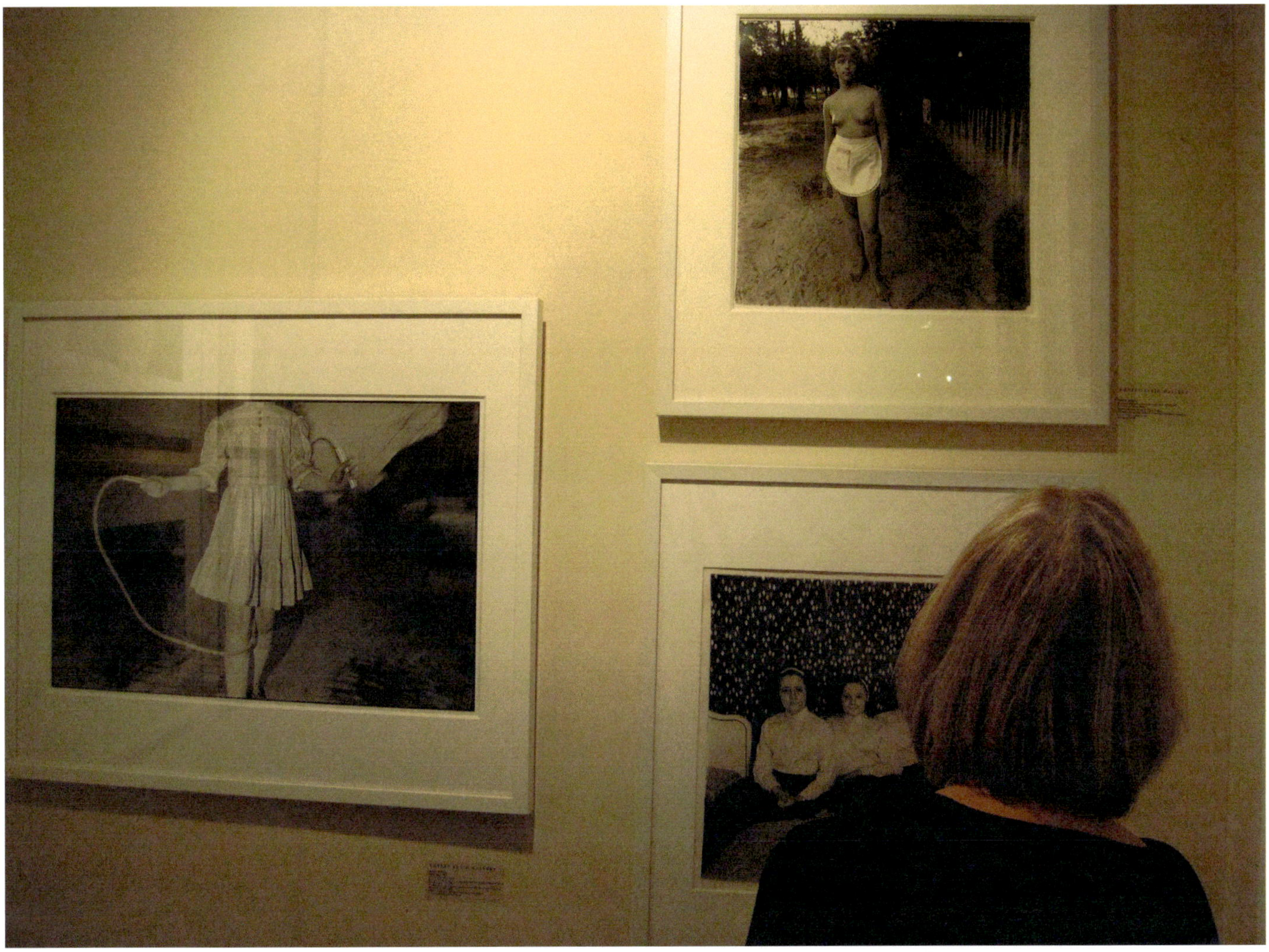

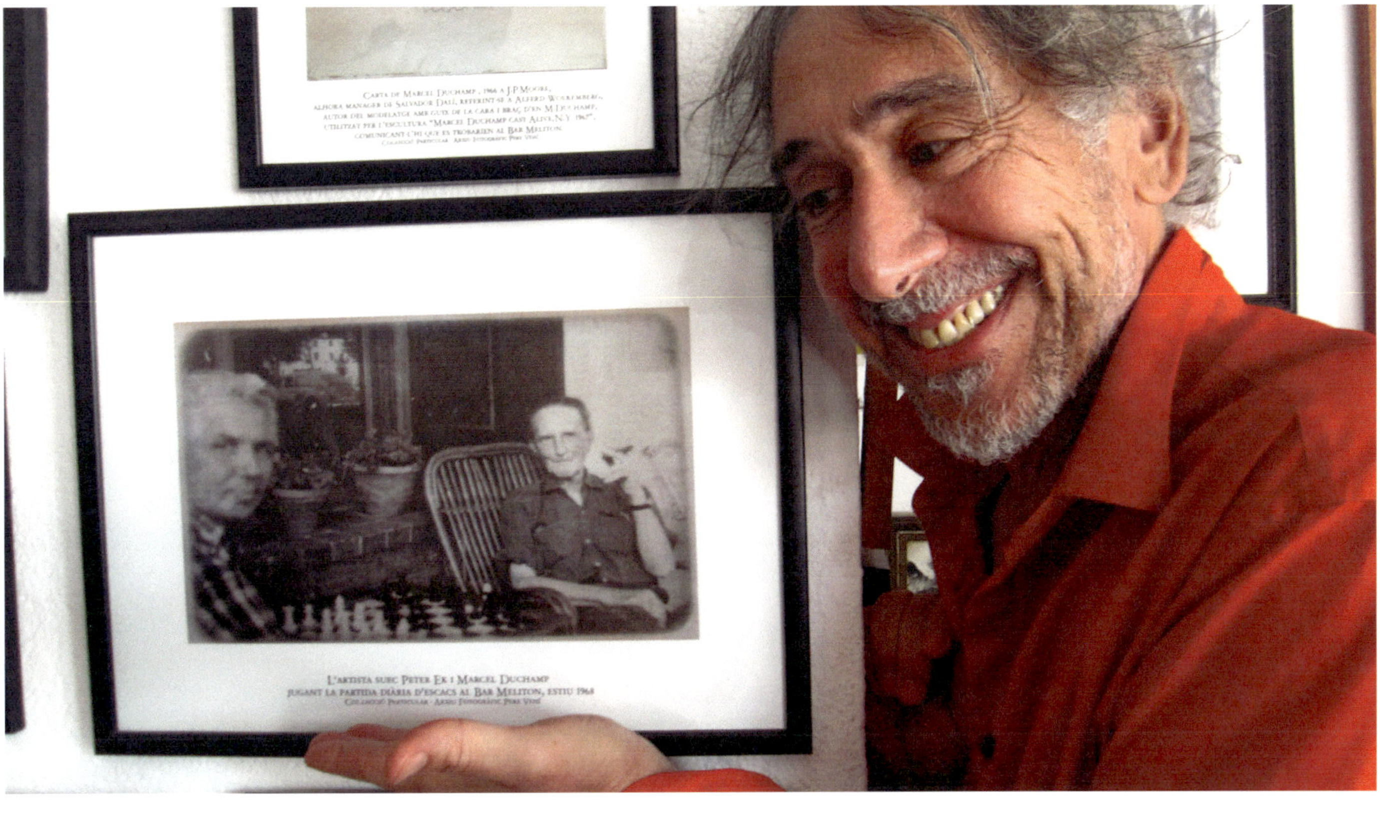
Carta de Marcel Duchamp, 1966 a J.P. Moore,
L'artista suec Peter Ek i Marcel Duchamp
jugant la partida diària d'escacs al Bar Meliton, estiu 1968

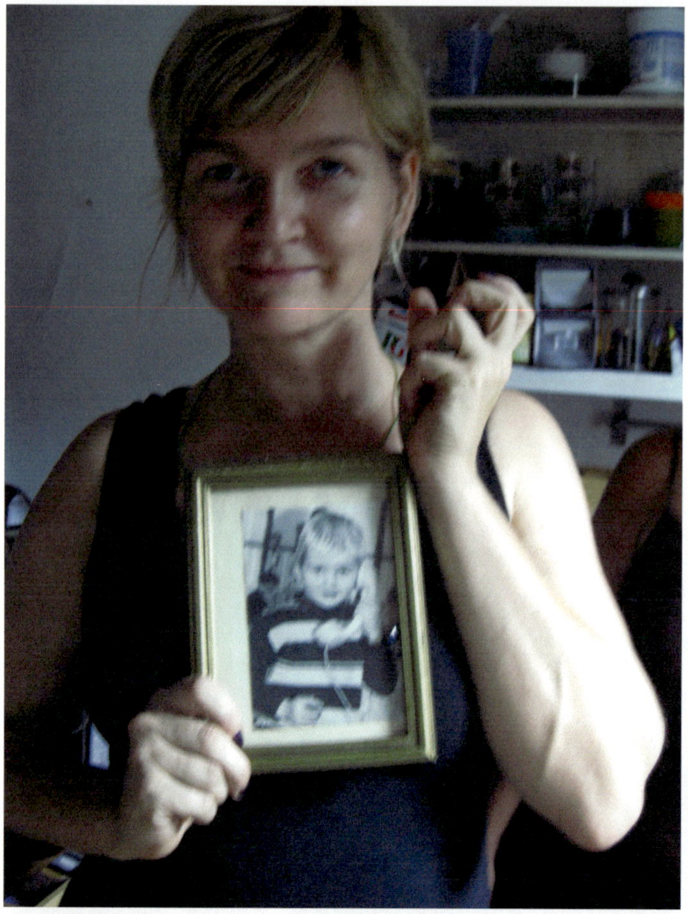

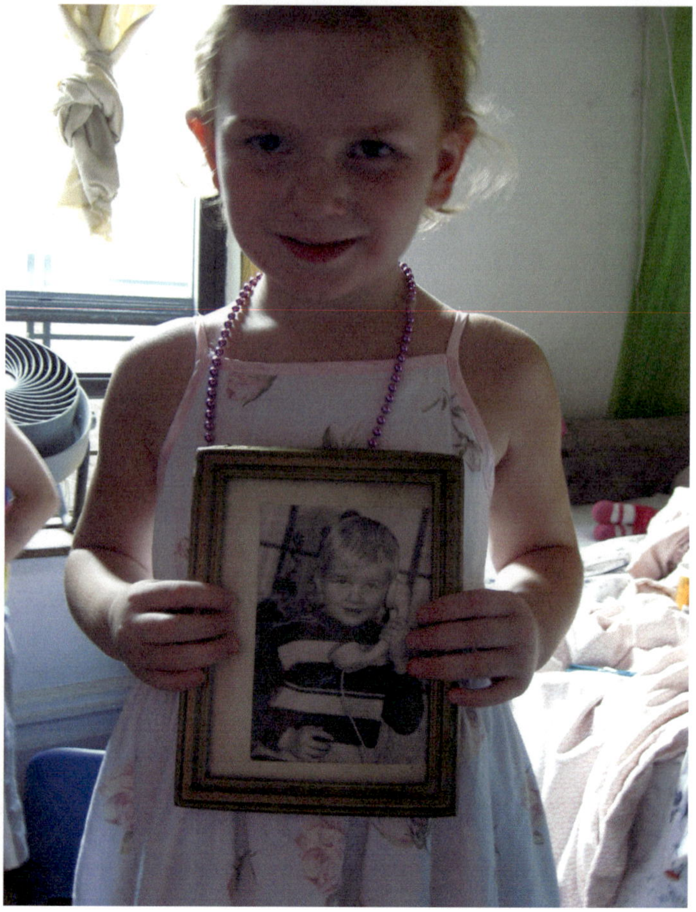

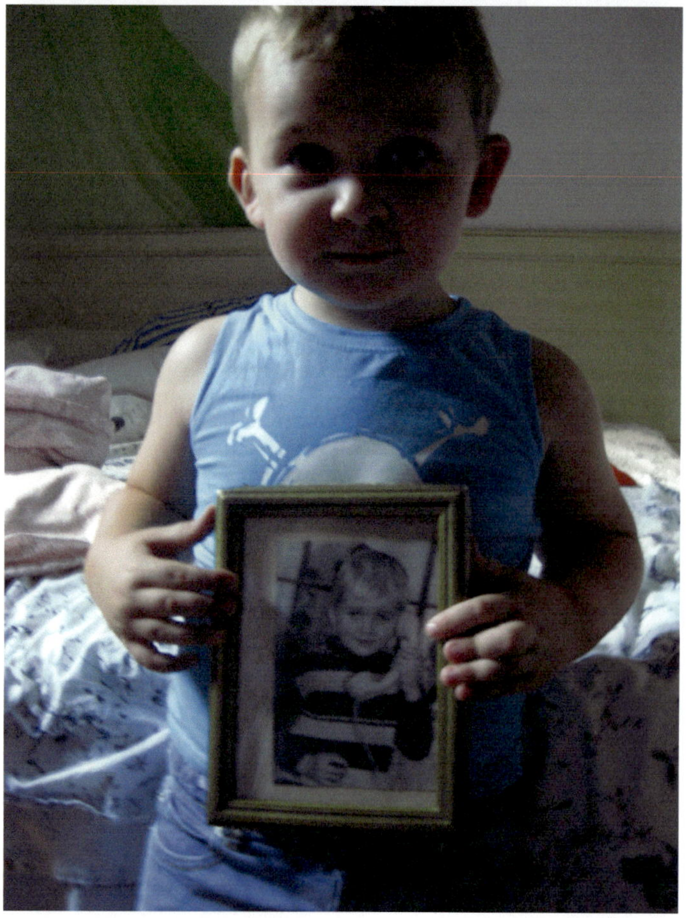

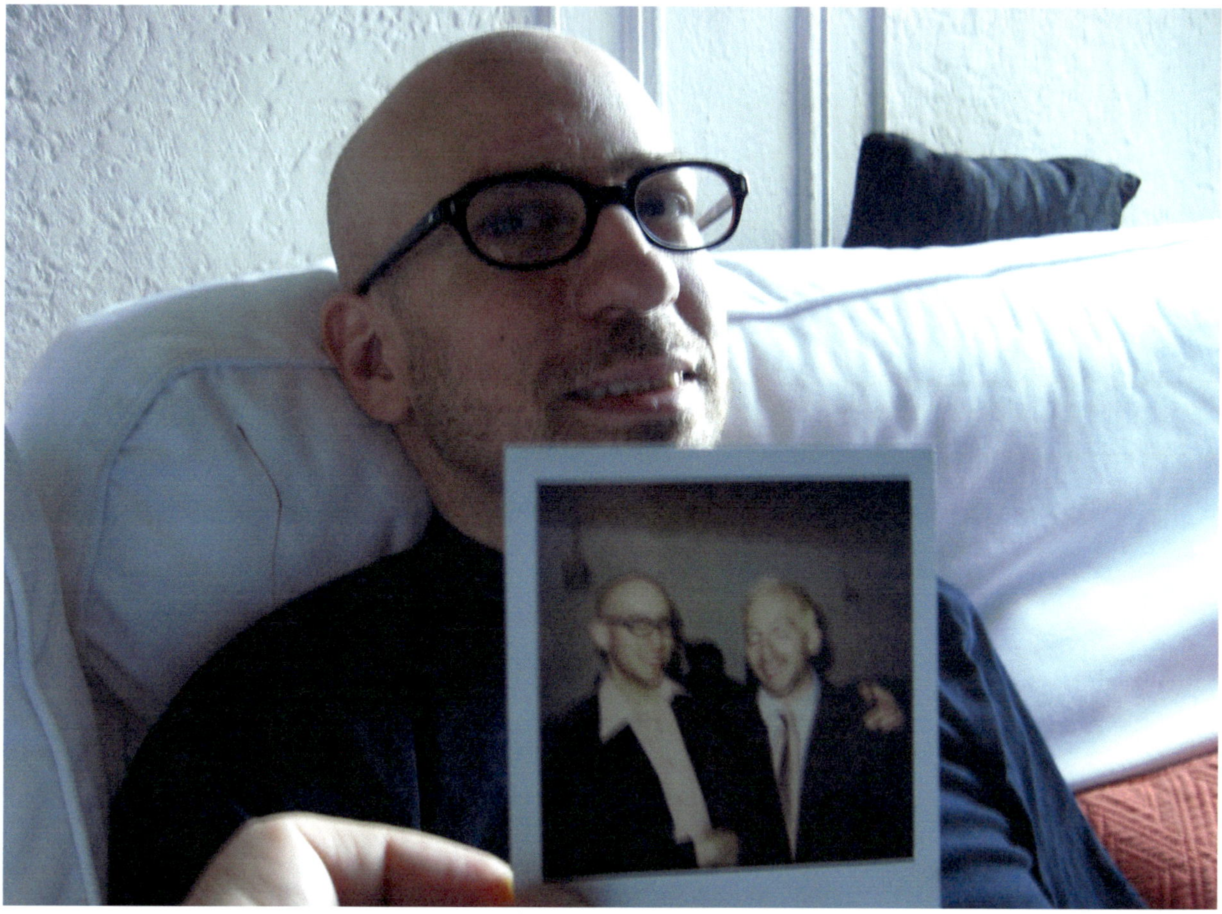

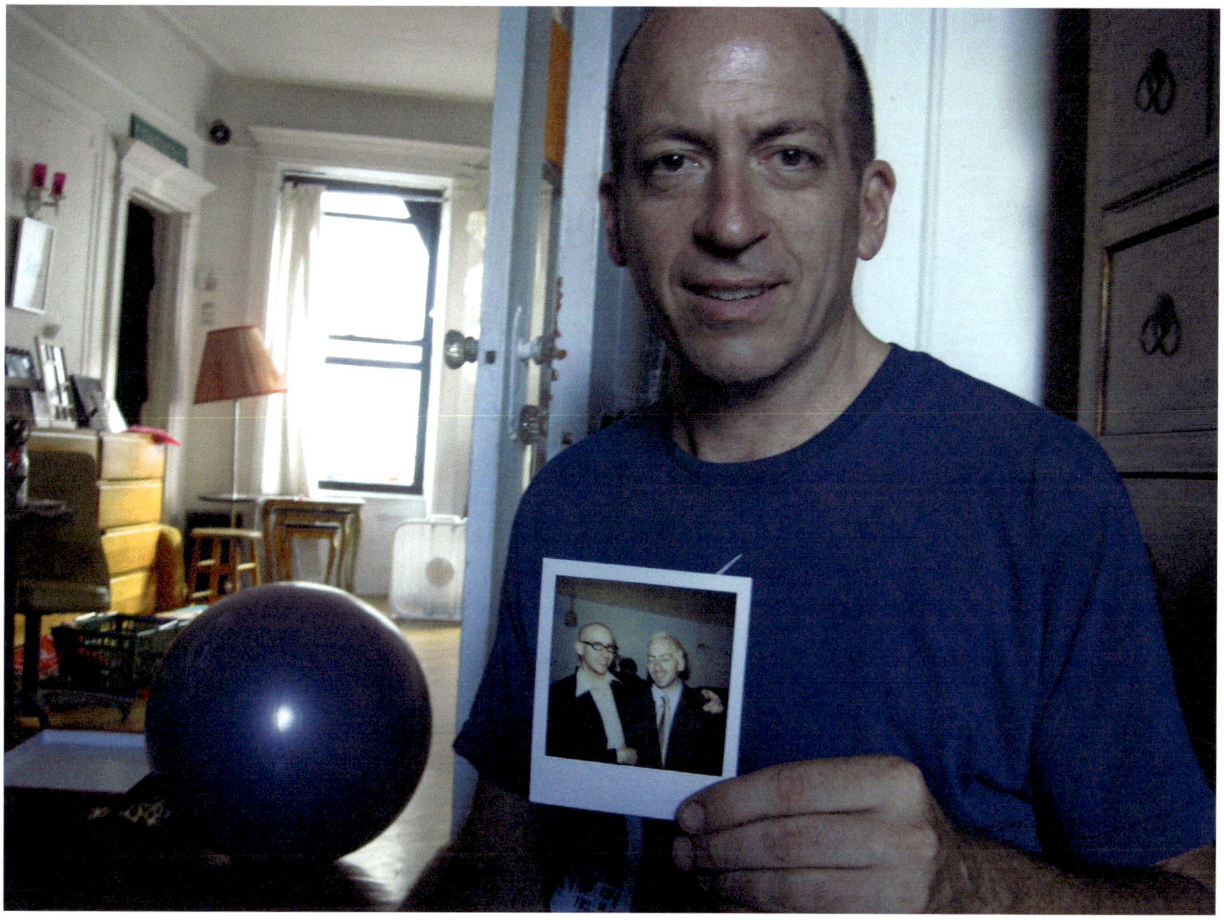

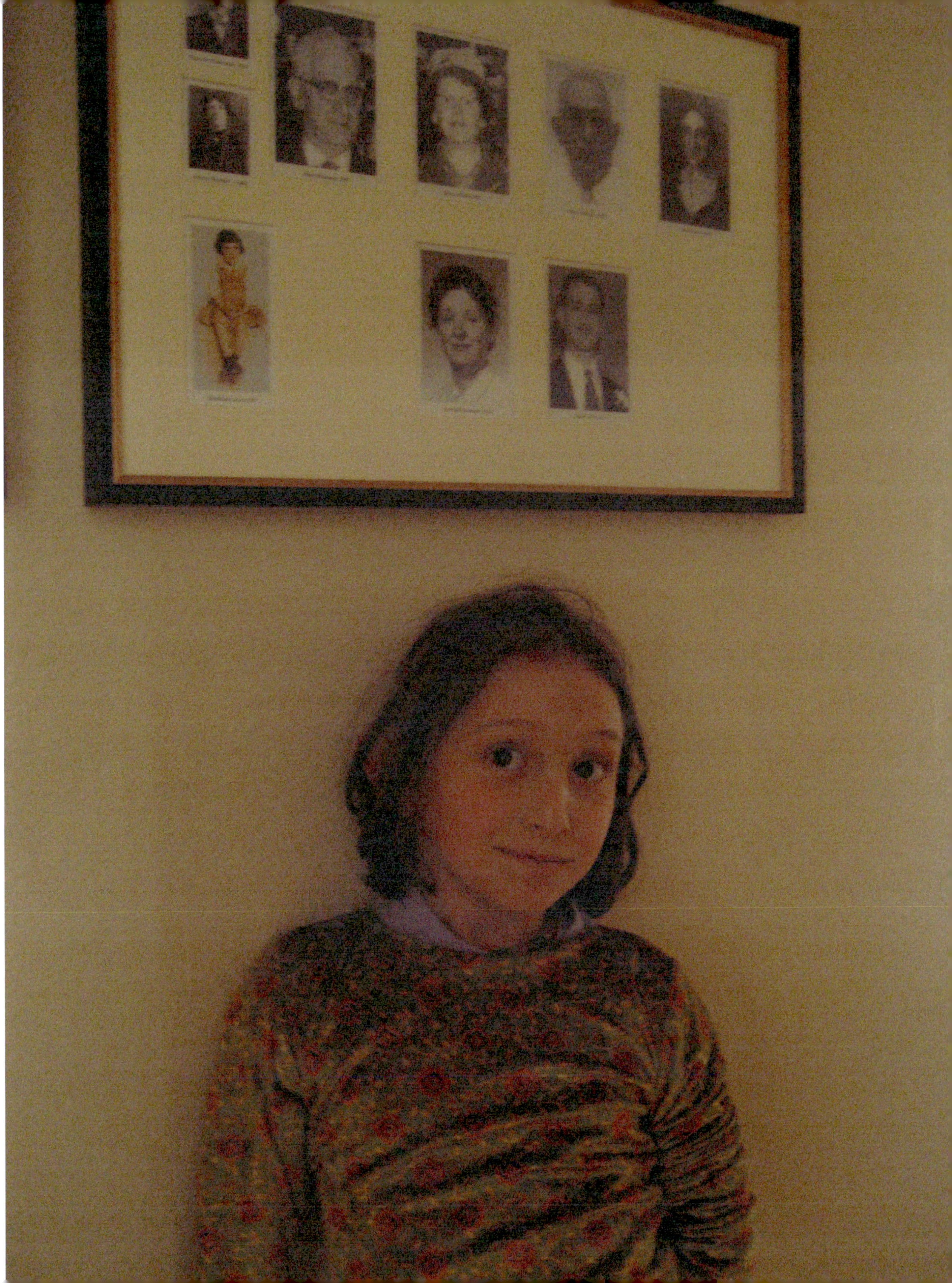

LIST OF PICTURES

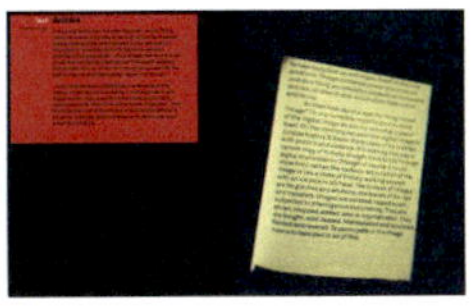

Text Archive

Image Bruised and Crashed

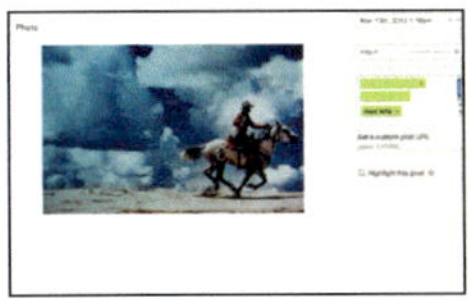

Photo or Photo(tag)raphy

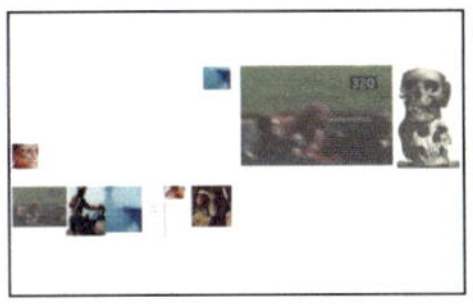

ARCHIVE OF ERASURES

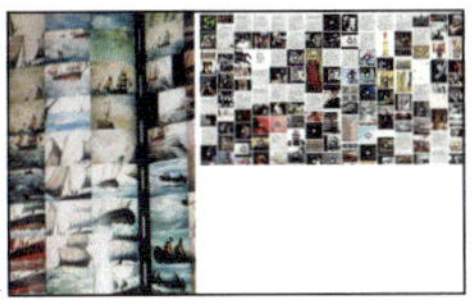

Broodthaers, An Archive at Sea

Tumblr Archive Events of the Multiple

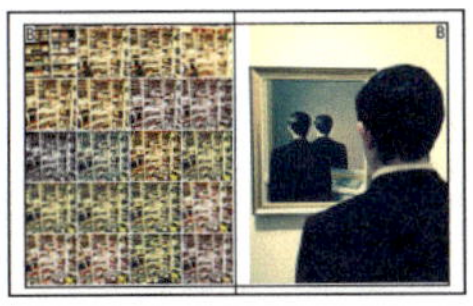

The Colors of My Books

To Be Reproduced and Seen Again

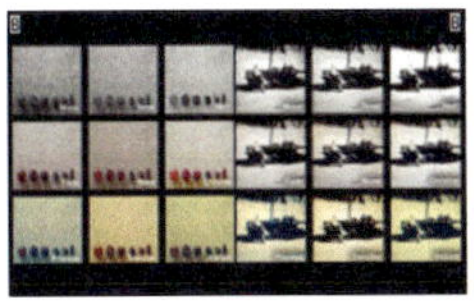

MONO, TONAL, NOIR, FADE, NONE, CHROME, PROCESS, TRANSFER, INSTANT

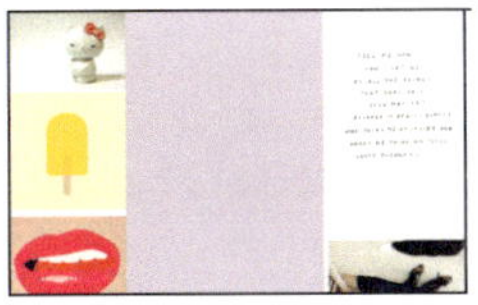

THE TUMBLR ROOM VOL. 2

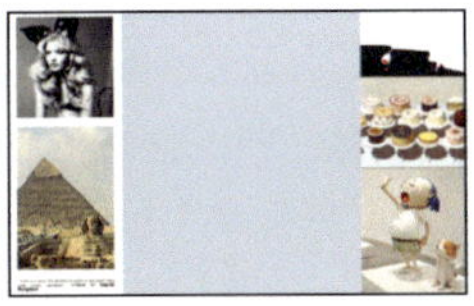

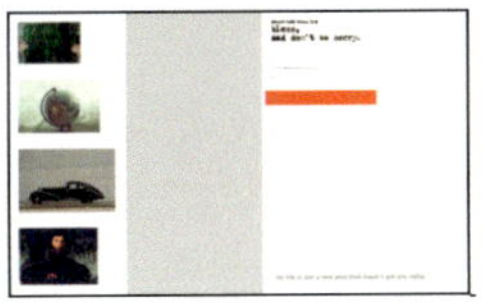

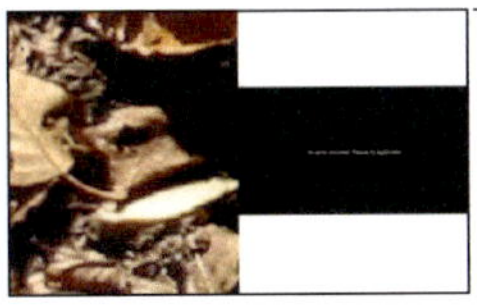

SITES 2

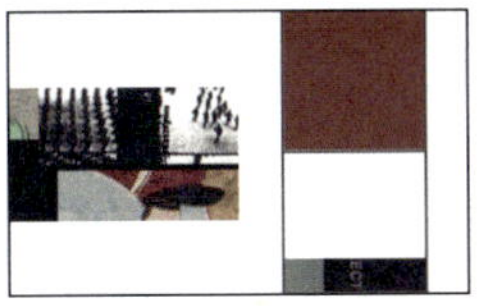

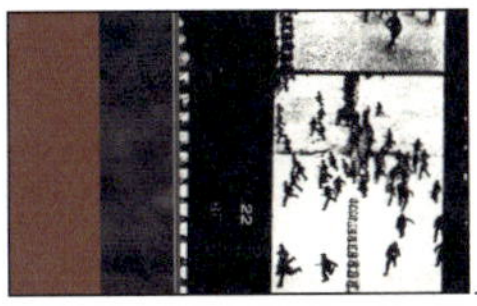

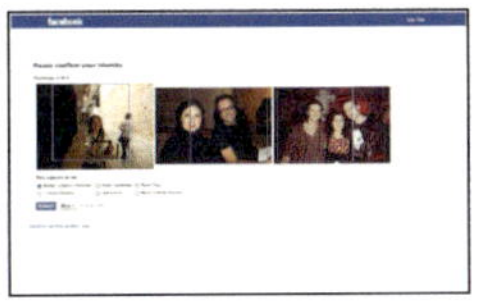

Please Confirm Your Identity

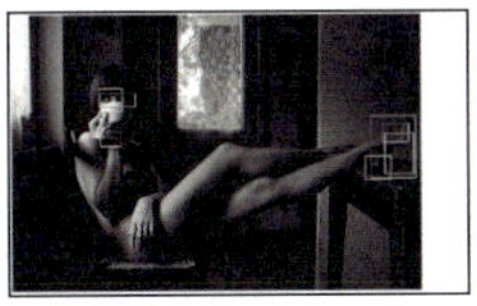

Machine "Seeing"

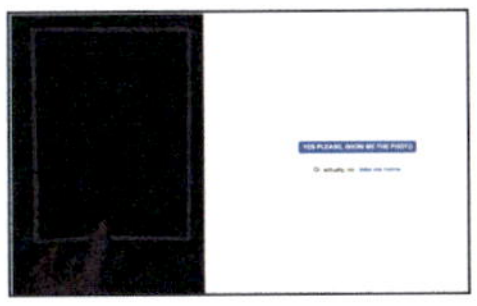

#Image

Yes Please, Show Me The Photo

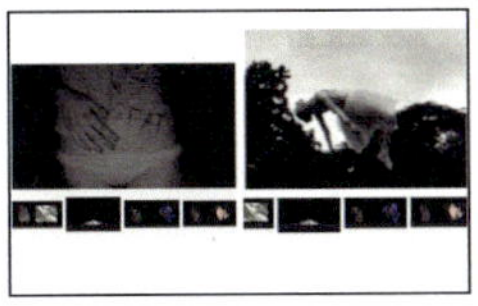

DYSTOPIA AND ITS CONTENT(MENT)S

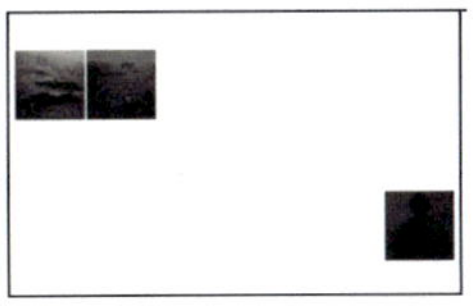

MEMORIES OF PHOTOGRAPHY

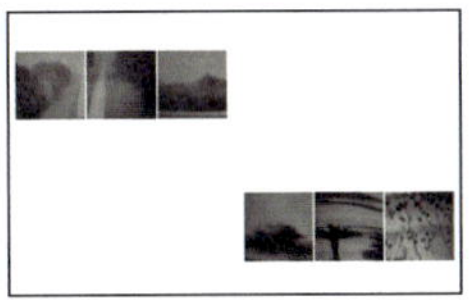

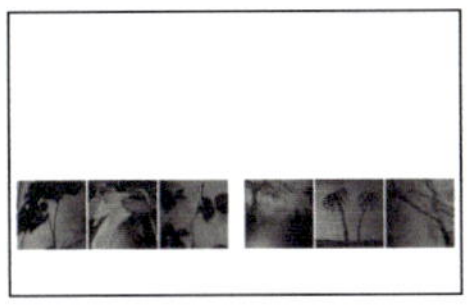

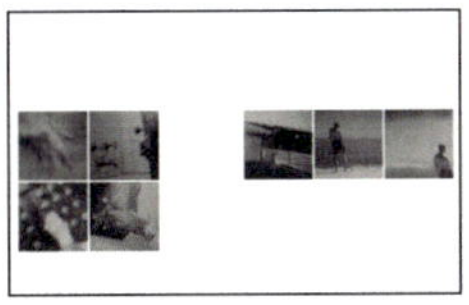

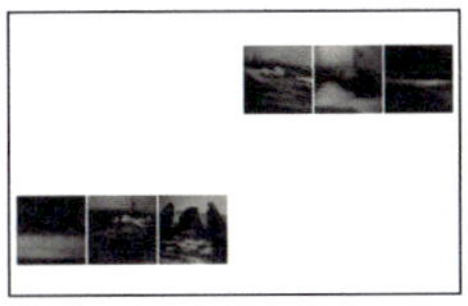

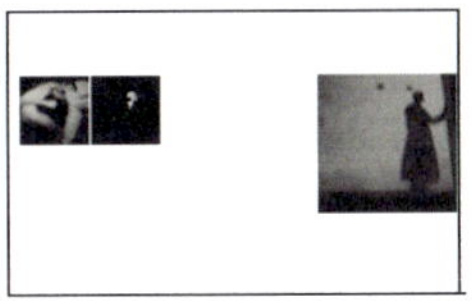

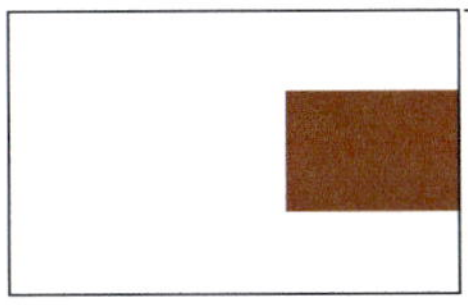

SITES 1

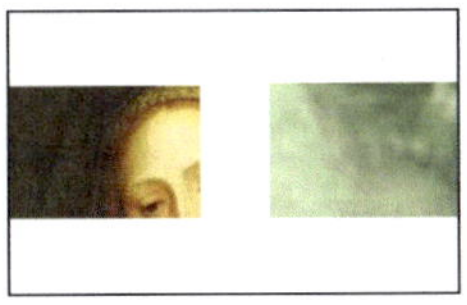

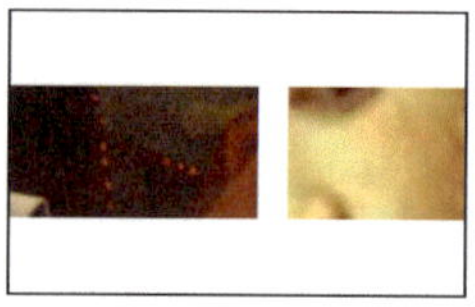

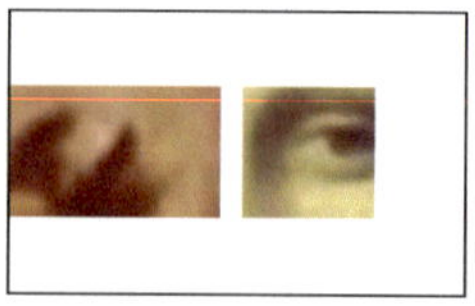

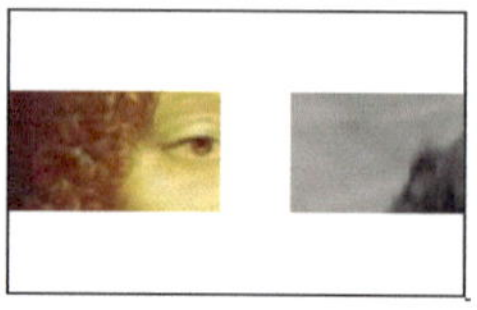

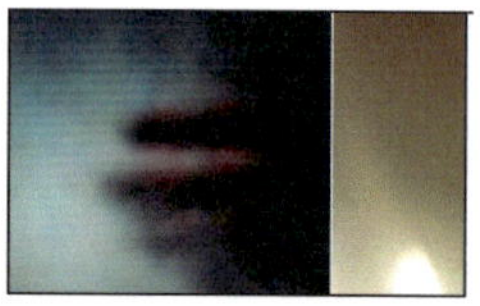

SEEING SEEING

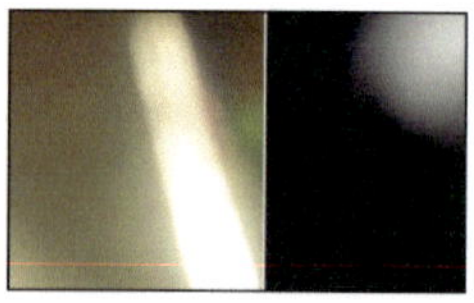

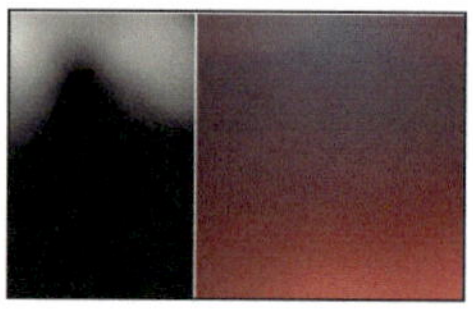

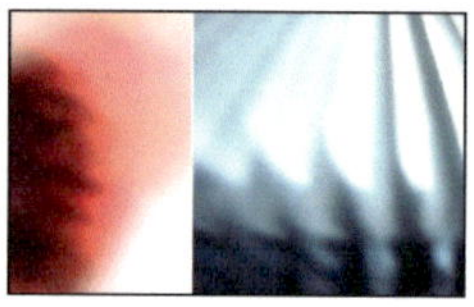

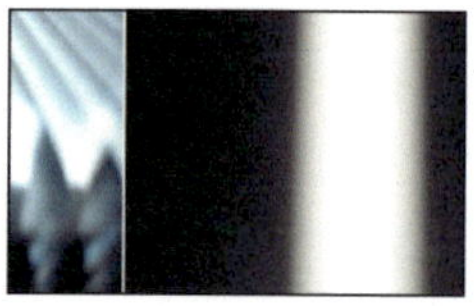

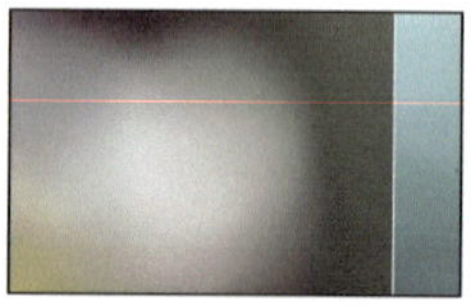

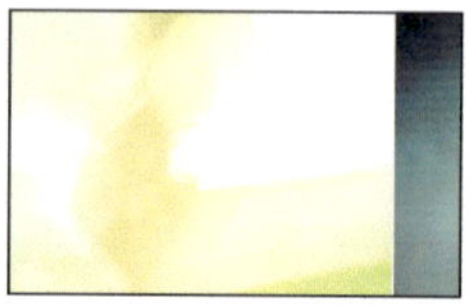

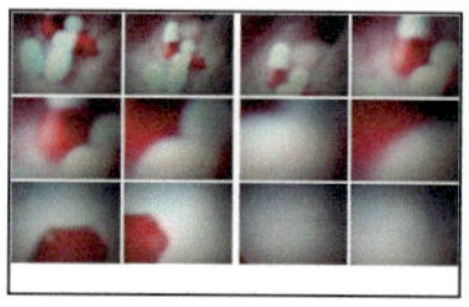

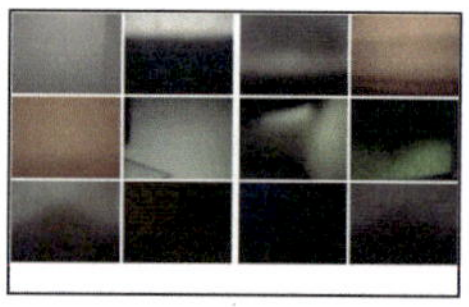

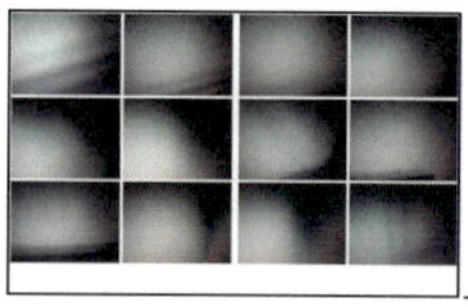

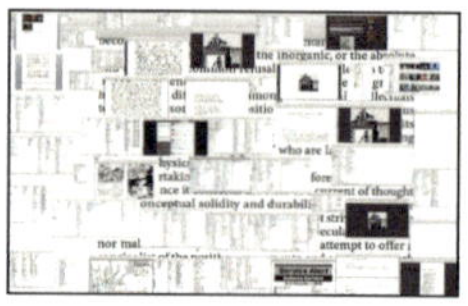

Desktop Viewfinder

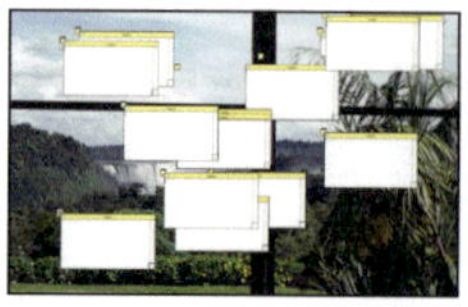

Windows

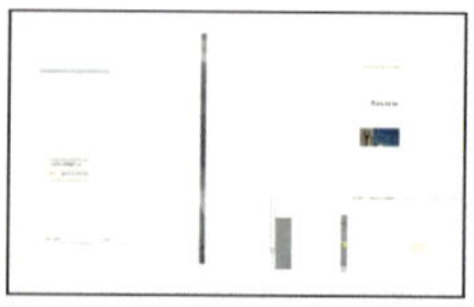

ACCIDENTS

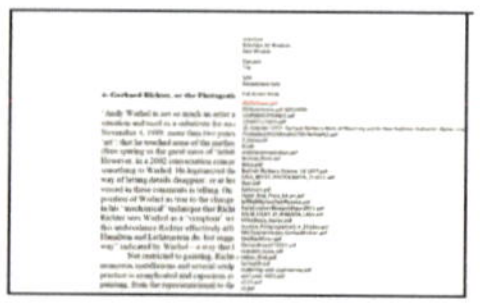

TEXT IMAGE

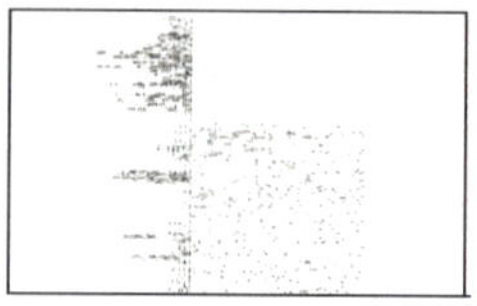

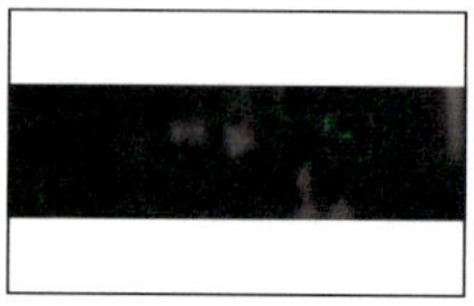

Sight

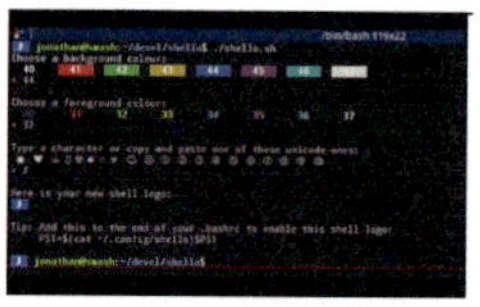

CHOOSE A BACKGROUND COLOR, CHOOSE A FOREGROUND COLOR

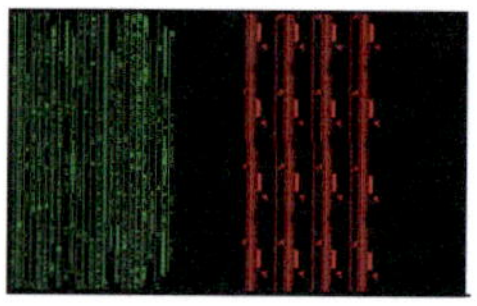

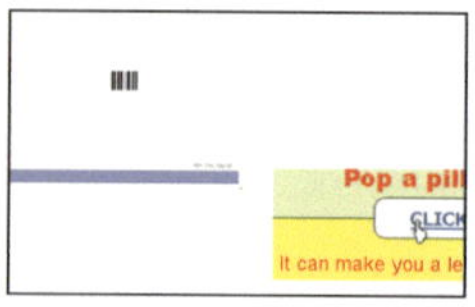

404

Click Pop a Pill

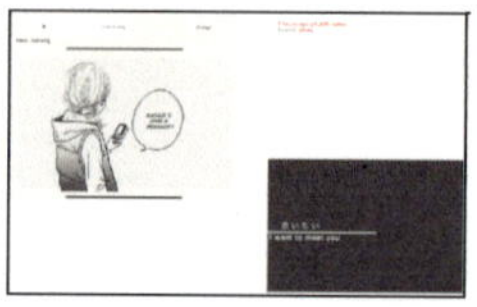

THE TUMBLR ROOM

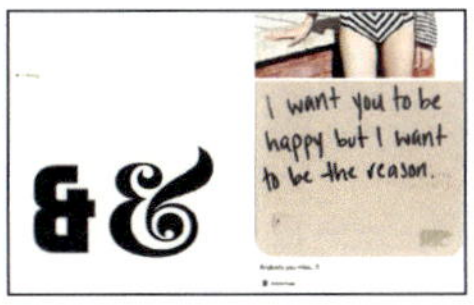

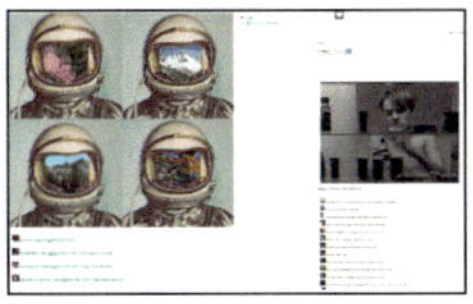

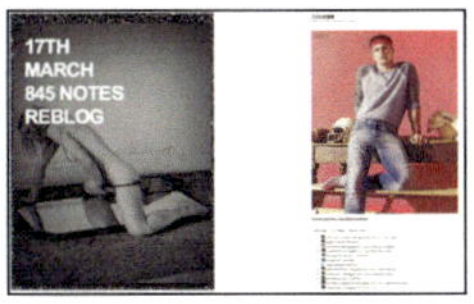

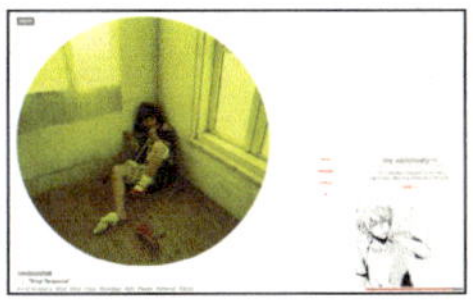

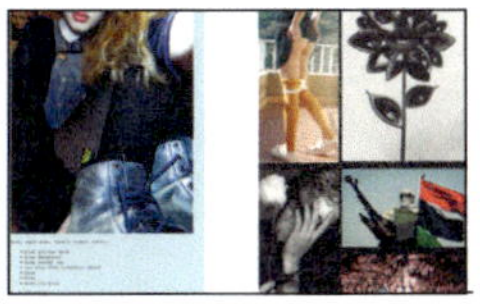

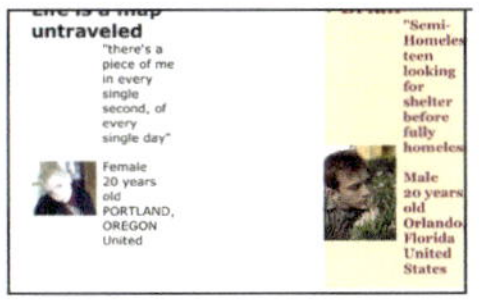

MYSPACE SELF(IE) PORTRAIT

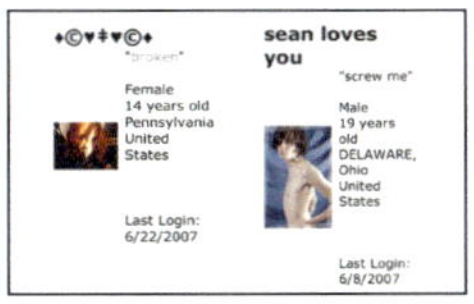

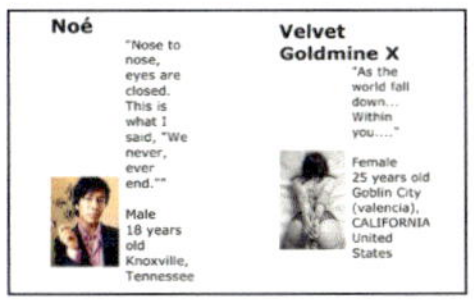

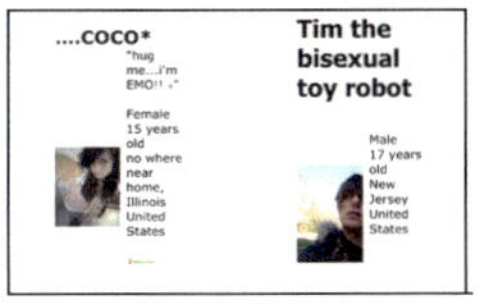

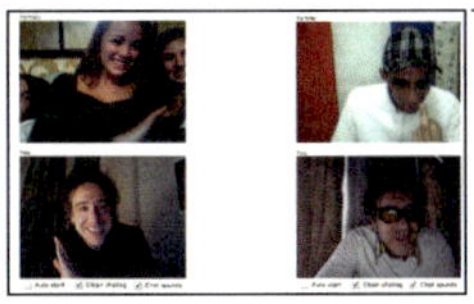

CHATROULETTE

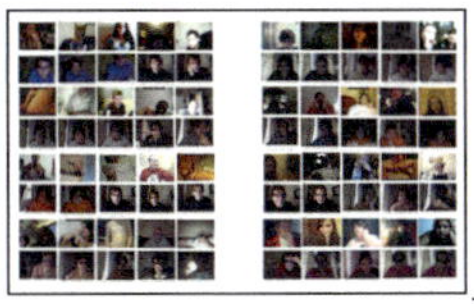

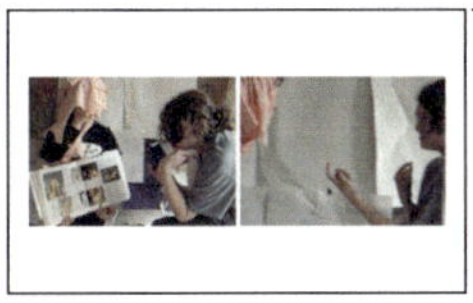

ART AS INVENTION

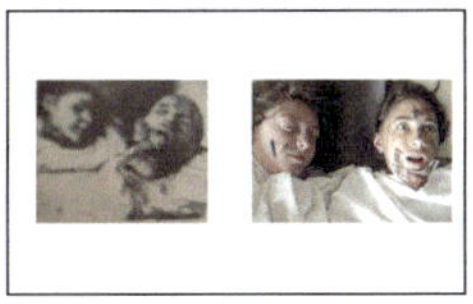

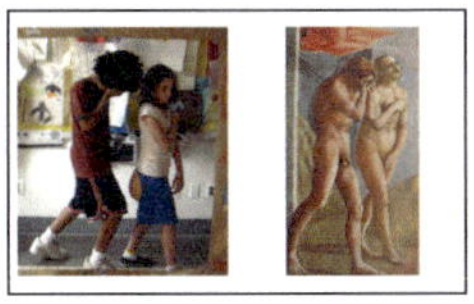

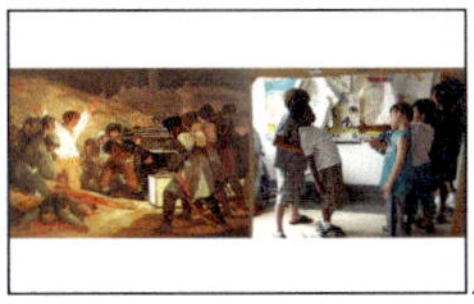

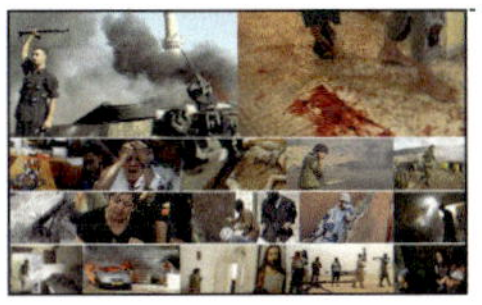

THE IMAGE ALONE
(WHY THE IMAGE IS
NEVER ALONE)

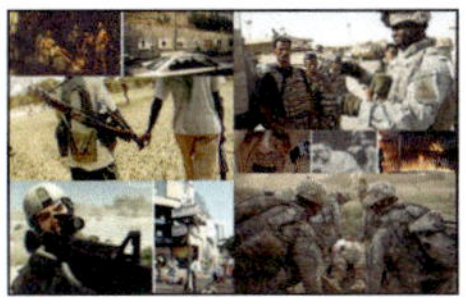

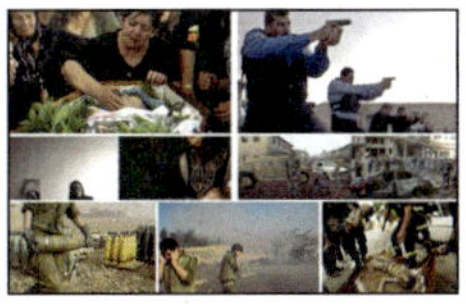

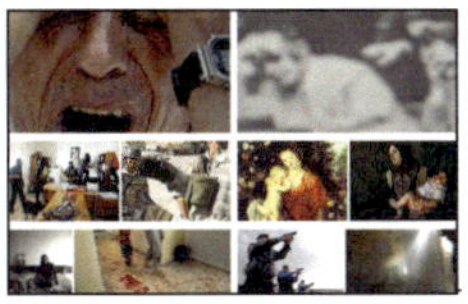

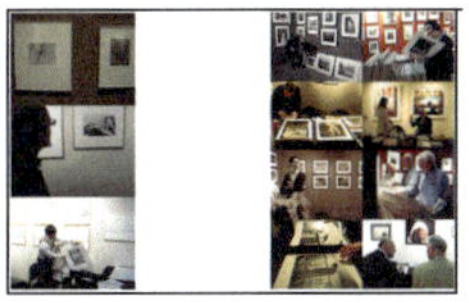

PHOTOGRAPHY:
COLLECTORS,
COLLECTIONS

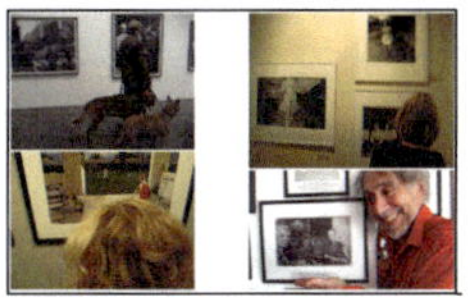

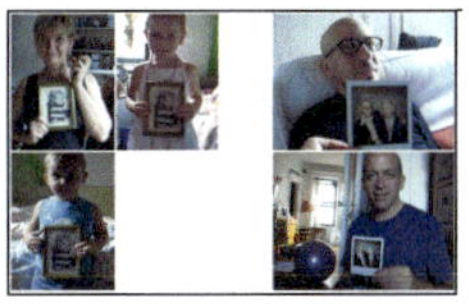

THE INTIMACY
OF AN IMAGE

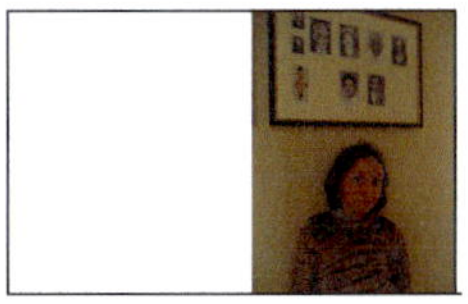

ACKNOWLEDGMENTS

It's never quite clear when one project ends and another begins and oftentimes things are happening simultaneously. But all the while and intermittently I have kept conversations about the image with select friends whom I would like to thank, Daniel Coffeen, Mathieu Borysevicz, and Irena Rogovsky.

Marc Lafia is an artist, filmmaker, and information architect. Trained as a filmmaker with a background in philosophy, art history, and criticism, his work extends across varied disciplines. His installations, photography, feature films, and online and multiscreen computational works have been exhibited and shown at Anthology Film Archives, International Film Festival Rotterdam, the Walker Art Center, the Whitney Museum of American Art, the Tate Online, the ZKM, the Centre Pompidou, and the Minsheng Art Museum in Shanghai. Lafia is the founder and information architect of ArtandCulture.com, for which he has won international design awards from the New York Art Directors Club, *I.D.* magazine, and *Communications Arts*, and best of show at SXSW. He has taught at Stanford University, the San Francisco Art Institute, Art Center College of Design in Pasadena, Pratt Institute, Columbia University, and the Berkeley Carroll School.

IMAGE
PHOTOGRAPH

Book Design by Kiki Bauer

ISBN: 978-0-9882340-7-9

This book published by the CTM Documents Initiative, an imprint of punctum books.

PUNCTUM BOOKS is an independent, open-access publisher dedicated to radically creative modes of intellectual inquiry and writing across a whimsical para-hum-anities assemblage. We solicit and pimp quixotic, sagely mad engagements with textual thought-bodies, and provide shelters for intellectual vagabonds.

THE CENTER FOR TRANSFORMATIVE MEDIA, Parsons The New School for Design is a transdisciplinary media research initiative bridging design and the social sciences, and dedicated to the exploration of the transformative potential of emerging technologies upon the foundational practices of everyday life across a range of settings.

punctum books ✶ brooklyn, ny
http://punctumbooks.com

Made in the USA
Las Vegas, NV
03 November 2026

57422191R00186